Books by William F. Buckley, Jr.

God and Man at Yale
McCarthy and His Enemies (with L. Brent Bozell)
Up from Liberalism
Rumbles Left and Right
The Unmaking of a Mayor
The Jeweler's Eye
The Governor Listeth
Cruising Speed
Inveighing We Will Go
Four Reforms
United Nations Journal: A Delegate's Odyssey
Execution Eve
Saving the Queen
Airborne
Stained Glass
A Hymnal: The Controversial Arts
Who's on First
Marco Polo, If You Can
Atlantic High: A Celebration
Overdrive
The Story of Henri Tod
See You Later Alligator
Right Reason
The Temptation of Wilfred Malachey
High Jinx
Mongoose, R.I.P.
Racing Through Paradise
On the Firing Line: The Public Life
of Our Public Figures
Gratitude: Reflections on What
We Owe to Our Country
Tucker's Last Stand
In Search of Anti-Semitism
WindFall

Editor

The Committee and Its Critics
Odyssey of a Friend: Whittaker Chambers' Letters to
William F. Buckley, Jr.
W.F.B.: An Appreciation
Did You Ever See a Dream Walking?:
American Conservative Thought in the

Happy Days Were Here Again

Reflections of a Libertarian Journalist

Happy Days
Were
Here Again

WILLIAM F.
BUCKLEY, JR.

Reflections of a
Libertarian Journalist

EDITED BY PATRICIA BOZELL

RANDOM HOUSE   NEW YORK

All rights reserved under International and Pan-American Copyright Conventions. Published in the United States by Random House, Inc., New York and simultaneously in Canada by Random House of Canada Limited, Toronto. The essays that appear in this work have been previously published in *Esquire, Family Weekly, 50 Plus* magazine, *National Review, The New York Times, The New York Times Book Review, The New York Times Sunday Magazine, Playboy, Primary Color, Spirit of America, Vanity Fair,* and Mr. Buckley's syndicated column.

Library of Congress Cataloging-in-Publication Data

Buckley, William F. (William Frank), 1925–
  Happy days were here again: reflections of a libertarian journalist/
William F. Buckley, Jr.; edited by Patricia Bozell.
    p. cm.
  Includes index.
  ISBN 0-679-40398-1
  I. Bozell, Patricia B.   II. Title.
PN4874.B796A3   1993b
814′.54—dc20   93-16597

Manufactured in the United States of America
9 8 7 6 5 4 3 2
First Edition
BOOK DESIGN BY NAOMI OSNOS

For Patricia Buckley Bozell
—my editor and my beloved sister

Acknowledgments

I am indebted primarily to Mrs. Bozell, senior editor of Regnery Gateway, who served as the editor of this collection, for her industry, her editorial shrewdness, and for her thoughtful conclusion that her older brother is the best thing to happen to literature since Homer. Samuel Vaughan, who has been my editor ever since happiness came to me as an author, superintended the enterprise. And Chaucy Bennetts briefly retired from retirement to track down my solecisms and set me right in one thousand places. Dorothy McCartney has for many years headed up the research library at *National Review*. I would not give out the date of the Declaration of Independence without first checking with her. I am indebted to Tony Savage for his intelligent typing and collating, to Frances Bronson for her editorial intelligence and for her warm enthusiasm, and to Joe Isola for one more example of his unerring eye as a proofreader. My thanks to Carsten Fries of Random House for his good work as production editor, and to Naomi Osnos, also of Random House, for the attractive design.

Contents

Introduction

BY JOHN LEONARD

I n *Lazarus,* André Malraux told his doctor: "Modern man has been fashioned on the basis of exemplary stereotypes: saint, chevalier, caballero, gentleman, bolshevik, and so on." From this catalogue, the French swashbuckler omitted . . . Buckley.

A Buckley—part Magus, prestidigitating supply side whoopee, and part matador, goring liberal bulls—is in perpetual motion. He edits magazines, proliferates newspaper columns, anchors television programs, skis, sails, and speechifies. In and around these activities, on the keyboard of his Toshiba laptop, from the backseat command module of his customized-in-Texarkana Cadillac limousine, or from the Gstaad chalet, where he oil-paints with Nivens and slide-slips with Galbraiths, or at the helm of his ketch, *Sealestial,* somewhere between the Galapagos and Byzantium, like G. K. Chesterton and Moses Herzog, a Buckley writes letters to the world.

The word *zest* comes to mind, and so does *savor.* Yet all these Buckley motions are accomplished with an oddly sleepy sort of Robert Mitchum look. He was once asked, on *Laugh-In*, "Mr. Buckley I notice that on your own program you're always sitting down. Is this because you can't think on your feet?" He hesitated for a masterly moment; then replied: "It is hard . . . to stand up . . . under the weight . . . of all that I know." But sitting down, he also *lists* . . . leaning away from a Noam Chomsky or an Arthur Schlesinger, Jr., somehow parenthetical, as if in a hurry to write another column. A section of this *Malleus Maleficarum* is devoted to his body English. I am reminded of Richard Weaver's definition of conservatism: "a paradigm of essences toward which the phenomenology of the world is in continuing approximation."

Buckley! Think of another revolutionary pamphleteer, Tom Paine, except that Tom Paine didn't eat Red Wing peanut butter, make jokes, or play the harpsichord. It seems to me that if the culture insists on celebrity ideologues, we are better off with a Buckley performing a Bach concerto for the Phoenix Symphony Orchestra than we are with a Lillian Hellman in Blackgama mink or an Andrew Sullivan in a Gap ad. But I am often wrong, as Buckley has patiently pointed out, for the last thirty-five years, in many letters, to none of which I've ever replied, being shy.

Buckley in 1958: "I don't suppose you are at all conservative?" Me, hedging: "Not very." Buckley: "One hundred dollars a week." Me: "I'll have to consult my fiancée." Buckley: Where is she?" Me: "Radcliffe." Buckley: "Tell her it's *The New Republic.*"

And so, long before he was an exemplary stereotype, I went to work for Buckley as an editorial assistant at *National Review.* I ferried copy to the printer in Connecticut. I monitored the left-wing press. I wrote letters to the *NR* editor criticizing everything in the magazine, to prime a very dry correspondence pump. I was sent to Cuba shortly after Castro's revolution. I went to lunch with Whittaker Chambers, which was like going to lunch with the Brothers Karamazov. I was taught, by Publisher Bill Rusher, how to eat with a fork. I was taught, by Editor Bill Buckley, how to assemble and fly a kite. I was taught, by Managing Editor Priscilla Buckley, how to assemble and fly a paragraph. To this day, the only two important matters I'm certain we agree on are that Bill's sister, Priscilla, and his composer, Bach, are unexcelled in God's creation.

But after a season, I went away: to California, novel-writing, and eventually *The New York Times.* Like so many other young writers he took off the street and published in his pages in the early *NR* days—Garry Wills, Joan Didion, Renata Adler, Arlene Croce—I ended up a liberal. "For a while," Buckley wrote in *Overdrive,* "I thought we were running a finishing school for apostates. . . ." As if to compensate, he finally hired George Will, and I hope he's happy. But what about the rest of us? Why, staring at him on the other side of the barricades, don't we bare our fangs? Where's the Oedipal revolt, so surpassingly expressed in the Cultural Revolution of the Red Guards in China's Guangzi province, when they cannibalized their high school principals?

To be sure, I wrote an article about *National Review* for a satirical magazine in 1963, a parody of Whittaker Chambers's letter to his children in *Witness*. Buckley's response? Four years later, when the *Times* was deciding whether to hire me, he sent them a copy of this article just to prove, as he said, that I wasn't "right-bitten." In *Life* magazine in 1971, in a critique of *Firing Line*, I made fun of his promiscuous analogies, invidious juxtapositions and preemptive obfuscations, in deploying words like "nugatory," "usufruct," "enthymematic," "asymptotic," "propaedeutic," and "endogamous." So he invited me on *Firing Line*. Much later on, reviewing one of his Blackford Oakes novels, I quoted a passage in which the hero ransacks a refrigerator: "There was chicken, ham, cheese, white wine. He put together a plate with slabs of each. . . ." I said this sounded to me like a wet plate. So I was invited, not only to a Christmas party, but to Moscow and Leningrad, with the *NR* staff, where Keith Mano shook his fist at the Winter Palace, reminding me of what Herzen said to Bakunin: "One must open men's eyes, not tear them out."

In *Cruising Speed*, he told us: "I can understand the occasional necessity to execute people, but never to hurt their feelings. . . ." This explains, in part, why he puts up with so many of us—Murray Kempton, Wilfrid Sheed, Allard Lowenstein—who had disappointed him with our disorderly politics and chaotic lives; and why, in turn, we cherish him no matter what he says, and he says plenty here, about John Lennon, Jesse Jackson, Jimmy Breslin, Martin Scorcese, democracy, the Koran, and . . . women, whose "primary responsibility," he says, is "the care of the child," while men are primarily responsible "for the care of the woman."

To speak, however, of the friend is to neglect the exemplar. You may have noticed that even his "apostates" tend to be political, noisy, and trouble-making, as if the world were a wound about which, on our bandages, in our blood, it is necessary constantly to scribble. What is the lesson? To be a serious character in your own life, in your own century. But also to send up ideas like kites, to eat some peanut butter, and to hear some music.

I have paused to quarrel, or to smile, at every other paragraph in these wind-blown pages. There are again the suspect analogies and juxtapositions, and the fancy words—"lucubrations," "eldritch," "fissiparous," "dysgenically," "eristic," "objurgatory," "querencia"—but a lovely essay also defending the writer's *working* vocabulary, the very jazz of composition. If there are predictable enthusiasms (capital punishment, Evelyn Waugh, Chartres cathedral, Star Wars, and the *Titanic*) and predictable *bêtes noires* (abortion, Lowell Weicker, the Democratic Party, drug dealers, Dartmouth College), there are also surprises: That he went to see Mapplethorpe's dirty pictures, although not Scorcese's *Last Temptation.* That he opposes a government bailout of the failed S&Ls, would internationalize Jerusalem, has never gone to a baseball game, nor watched *Oprah*. That he approves of Head Start, and disapproves of the Inquisition.

Most astonishing is what he says about the continuing soap of the Windsors: "There is, to begin with, the absolutely chimerical quality of Princess Diana. If a more beautiful woman ever existed, she was never photographed." Lauren Bacall? Lena Horne? Daw Aung San Suu Kyi? This, perhaps, explains what possessed Blackie in *Saving the Queen.* For remedial reading, may I suggest the Texas newspaper columnist Molly Ivins: "Dan Quayle looks exactly like Princess Di, while Mrs. Quayle looks exactly like Prince Charles. What more could any woman want?"

But this is churlish. What we have here is vintage Buckley on Nathaniel Hawthorne and Malcolm Forbes, Edmund Burke and Dan Rather, free trade and Tiananmen Square, Jack Kemp, Clarence Thomas, Meir Kahane and original sin, not to neglect his favorite composer, on whom he quotes biologist Lewis Thomas, who was asked what we should send up in a rocket to speak on our behalf to whatever alien civilizations there might be in outer space. "I would send the complete works of Johann Sebastian Bach," said Thomas. Pause: "But that would be boasting."

We could do worse than send some Citizen Buckley, too.

ONE

ASSAILING

—Twelve Targets

1

The So-Whatness of Nuclear Winter

APRIL 18, 1985

I wish Home Box Office or one of those cable birdies would undertake to show the viewing public a tape of the testimony, on March 14, of Carl Sagan, who tends increasingly to view himself as The World's Foremost Authority, and Richard Perle, assistant secretary of defense. Carl Sagan was the first witness, Richard Perle the second. Carl Sagan is henceforward qualified to testify on what cruel and unusual punishment feels like.

The forum was a joint meeting between two congressional sub committees with names so cumbersome one begrudges them the space they take up. But, for the record, they were: the Subcommittee on Energy and the Environment of the House Committee on Interior and Insular Affairs, chaired by Representative Morris Udall, D-Ariz.; and the Subcommittee on Natural Resources, Agricultural Research and Environment of the House Committee on Science and Technology, chaired by Representative James Scheuer, D-N.Y.

The question being probed is the policy implications of nuclear winter. Nuclear winter—the thesis that the detonation of XYZ plus one nuclear bomb will freeze all growth for six months, bringing on the probable extermination of all human and vegetable life—is the favorite adopted son of Carl Sagan, among other reasons because it permits him to engage in the kind of eschatological melodrama that brings orgasmic delight to those who want to tell us how awful a nuclear war would be (as if we didn't know). In any event, the congressional committees wanted to know what should we do, now that we know about nuclear winter.

Carl Sagan gave a half hour's performance so arrogant he

might have been confused with, well, me. He graded such reports as he had seen on the subject of how should our policies adapt to nuclear winter as warranting "a grade of D" if submitted to him as a functioning professor. He said that we were going to get nowhere in Geneva because we are sending people over there who don't believe in disarmament. He suggested that Ronald Reagan and his team at the Department of Defense were concealing two reports that were politically embarrassing (the so-called Cadre Report and the Palomar Report). He suggested that Soviet officials and U.S. officials should meet in a single barn and hand over the atomic fission devices that set off hydrogen bombs to an agent who would then send them for detoxification to nuclear energy plants. He brushed off his single critic on the panel, Representative John McCain, R-Ariz., by saying that McCain couldn't point to one disarmament treaty Reagan had favored.

Along came Richard Perle, who delivered about six haymakers, one after the other. He said that for all Sagan's talk about the United States wanting more and more weapons, we had reduced our stockpile during the past fifteen years by 8,000 warheads, while the Soviet Union had increased its stockpile by more than 8,000 warheads. Our megatonnage today, compared to then, is 25 percent less. We have outstanding two proposals for sharp reductions of arms, to which the Soviet Union has not responded. We have suggested the elimination of all intermediate-range missiles. The idea that a Soviet official will turn over triggering devices on a one-for-one basis is one of those academic fantasies that should stay in the academy or go to Disneyland.

But—most important—Richard Perle said that in fact nuclear winter doesn't have any policy implications not already dominant in our strategic policy, because it is the objective of that policy to avoid nuclear war. And if nuclear war is avoided, then the danger of detonating XYZ plus one missiles reduces. Moreover, since it is known that nuclear winter would come more quickly if explosions took place over cities, then isn't it wise to continue research into Star Wars? Our strategic policy, said Perle, is to concentrate on military targets, not cities—and this is so not because of nuclear winter, but because of people. We have no appetite, in our deterrent strategy, to hit people rather than military targets, for reasons unrelated to nuclear winter.

And then, finally, a dazzling challenge: Was Carl Sagan saying that in the event Star Wars proved feasible, we should not deploy it?

The logic of Carl Sagan's position is that we should engage in unilateral nuclear disarmament. He doesn't come out and say this —indeed, he dodges questions on the matter—but that is the subtle hierarchy being insinuated by the unilateralists: namely, that nuclear winter is more to be feared than Soviet hegemony, and therefore we must give up our arsenal. Richard Perle—and Ronald Reagan—tell us we can do better. We can avoid both Soviet hegemony and nuclear winter, as we have done for forty years now.

2

Jesse on My Mind

MAY 25, 1985

For thoughtful people it is a cliché that true equality is exhibited only when you permit yourself to get as mad at a minority member as you would at a fellow fraternity member. On reflection, the clearest sign of the enduring discrimination of white people in America against black people in America is our toleration of Jesse Jackson. If he were a blue-blooded WASP, he would be treated with the contempt appropriately shown for the Reverend William Sloane Coffin, a contempt made possible not because of any lack of recognition of his many talents as an orator and organizer, but the special contempt by which democracies effectively stigmatize those who dwell in cuckooland. They simply disappear from public sight, going off to live more or less permanently in the fever swamps, where they mix with one another as the junkies used to do in Goa. There David Dellinger dwells . . . and Daniel Berrigan . . . and Timothy Leary, Jane Fonda . . .

Oh, but Jesse Jackson is a black leader. It is pointed out that he was the first member of his race to run for President of the United States, which proves what? So did Lyndon LaRouche run for president, and if that man is not nuts, I am Napoleon. Ah, they will say, but Jesse Jackson got 465 votes from the delegates in San Francisco. To which the appropriate response is that all he proved was that a black man will win a lot of black votes, and that he is one hell of an orator, which was true of Gerald L. K. Smith, who was probably an even finer orator, and was a racist mess. Jesse Jackson so intimidated the San Francisco Democrats that they couldn't even muster the resolution to vote a denunciation of anti-

Semitism, for fear of offending Jackson, the anti-Zionist assembly and, one supposes, Jesse's noisy fan Louis Farrakhan.

During the last couple of weeks, Jesse Jackson has appeared before the European Parliament and other audiences there. He denounced Star Wars, which is OK, though he probably knows as much about Star Wars as the European Parliament knows about hominy grits. But he also denounced the Cruise and Pershing missiles in Europe, and these are the spinal column of our NATO alliance. He spoke in those hyperboles for which he is renowned. Thus, "the germ of genocide was not buried at Bitburg; it was transferred to Johannesburg." Catch that, now. The entire Jewish-American world was convulsed when President Reagan said that the young SS buried in Bitburg were "as much the victims" of Hitler as the victims of the Holocaust. That trivialized the Holocaust, they wailed; and they had a point. Along comes someone who says that Buchenwald was no different from life in South Africa—where are the protests? You are getting the point. They don't protest because he's merely a black preacher saying dumb things.

He returns to this country and addresses a rally in New York commemorating the Vietnam War. "Our only joy is that the military occupation of that land is over," he says about a country (Vietnam) more heavily militarized than any other country on earth, from which 650,000 boat people have fled, a figure exceeded only by the number of blacks that have immigrated to South Africa. He goes on to Chicago, where he tells an interviewer that "the same forces that are anti-Semitic in the morning, by three o'clock of that same day manifest their anti-blackness"—one of those runny slurs freighted with meaninglessness.

But why go on? Jesse Jackson is the man who toasted Fidel Castro and the memory of Che Guevara, two totalitarians, one of them a sadist to boot. Jesse Jackson has become what we used to call a fellow traveler. Whatever foreign line Moscow takes, Jesse Jackson is now taking. His toleration of rank anti-Semitism in his entourage is a matter of record. His endorsement of totalitarian trends here and abroad is documented. Why is he always at center stage?

Because he is black. And because, being black, he has a large following, which following backs him as slavishly as white racists once backed Senator Bilbo and "Cotton Ed" Smith. But as long as he moves about with the immunity that now protects him from the kind of ostracism he has so diligently earned, then one can say with meaning: There is true condescension in America for the black, and that condescension is strongest among the elite. Jesse Jackson couldn't be elected squad leader by American hardhats. But the media elite, they patronize him. They figure he's just being a little uppity, and what do you expect?

3

Cuomitis

JANUARY 23, 1986

Mario Cuomo, Governor of New York, seems to be saying that there is so much anti-Italian prejudice in America he has no choice but to contend with it by running for president and getting elected. Oh, yes, and if he runs for president and isn't elected, why, that means he was right the whole time, there's a huge anti-Italian prejudice out there.

It's an odd thing to talk about anti-Italian prejudice in the most influential state of the Union in which the governor is of Italian descent and a Democrat, and one of the two senators is of Italian descent and a Republican. The second senator is of Irish descent.

Ah, Mario would say, but New York is different. To which observation the balance of the country would no doubt say, Thank God. But in fact New York State is two demographic realities: New York City and upstate. And Mr. Cuomo did well in both regions. If he were nominated for president by the Democratic Party, the following is a pretty safe bet, namely that more voters would vote for him merely because he is of Italian descent than would vote against him because he is of Italian descent.

Mario Cuomo's sensitivity is something of a phenomenon. Sensitivity is in many respects an admirable human trait, but it can paralyze one's judgment. A fine example of this is the now famous statement by Mr. Cuomo that there is no such thing as the Mafia. To suggest that there is, is to engage in anti-Italian defamation. Presumably all those people who shoot each other and get electrocuted simply adopted Italian names to confuse us. Mr. Cuomo sometimes seems to be implying that to concede the existence of a

Mafia, membership in which is predominantly Italian-American, is the same thing as suggesting that all Italian-Americans are members of the Mafia.

His hypersensitivity causes the governor to make gross gestures every now and then. Joseph Sobran, the syndicated columnist, last spring stoutly defended President Reagan's decision to go to the cemetery at Bitburg. This defense caused a cartoonist in Albany to depict Sobran as a Gestapo guard at a Nazi concentration camp, a vile act of polemical aggression. Because Governor Cuomo had smelled anti-Italian prejudice in one of Sobran's columns, he picked up the telephone and congratulated the cartoonist. Last week, after Governor Cuomo had courageously recommended clemency for a thoroughly reformed convict who has served eighteen years for a crime he might well not even have committed, the governor ran into protesters, one of whom carried a banner, KILL A COP, GET PAROLED BY THE WOP. One hopes no public official will think to call that protester to congratulate him on his eloquence.

"His is a classic case of St. Mario's paranoia," commented Roger Ailes, the bright Republican media consultant. "I think he's quite a disturbed man. It's beyond being thin-skinned. He always has to invent a moral crusade to justify his out-of-control ambition to be president. We're all heathens and his job on earth is to save us, and that's what he's doing here."

One hopes Mr. Cuomo will not now accuse Mr. Ailes of anti-Italian prejudice. If he does, he will need simultaneously to account for the fact that Mr. Ailes is right now managing the reelection campaign of Senator Alfonse D'Amato, who is not a member of the Mafia, who supported President Reagan's visit to Bitburg but is not pro-Nazi. All these things need to get said nowadays if the mere mention of the Mafia as primarily an Italian-American organization induces the governor to tell you that a) the Mafia doesn't exist, and anyway, b) it isn't primarily Italian-American.

Granted, it is easy to be called a racist. Such black leaders as Benjamin Hooks and Jesse Jackson regularly say it of the President of the United States. At a trial a few weeks ago, a cuckoo lawyer turned to me and asked darkly whether in using the term "a white lie" I had intended anti-black insinuations. One can't deny that there is ethnic prejudice, but it tends, in America, more and more to manifest itself fraternally, rather than inimically. More Italians, as I have suggested, tend to vote for the Italian candidate than Irish or Jewish or Hispanic tend to vote against a candidate because of his Italian ancestry.

If Mr. Cuomo runs for president, I shall pray that he will be defeated, but in doing so I shall conceal from Providence the knowledge that he is an Italian-American. God's anti-Italianism, as we know, has reached such limits that he had to go all the way to Poland to find a pope.

4

Black Thought, Black Talk

JULY 9, 1987

Listen carefully, I beg you, to these two or three sentences written by an English teacher (C. Webster Wheelock) in Manhattan and published as a part of an essay in *The New York Times* on our "Shrinking Language." They teach more than most of the rhetoricians you will hear from now to the end of the year.

"I recently sat through," the teacher begins, "a graduation ceremony in which one of the speakers used the adjective 'incredible' four times and its synonym 'unbelievable' once. Why did he appear to suggest by his choice of language that the accomplishments in question went beyond the laudable to the improbable? And why did all of us listening to him easily and automatically discount the value of the expressions he had selected? The answer lies in the steady erosion of power in an important part of our language over recent decades."

The English teacher is concerned over implausible raves. They are the treacly counterpart of their opposite, which are implausible negatives—except that these do more damage because they are built on bile. What Senator Edward Kennedy said last week about the nomination of Robert Bork as an associate justice of the Supreme Court should drum him out of the councils of civilized men engaged in democratic exchange. It will take more than just one book by Arthur Schlesinger, Jr., to clean up this act.

"Robert Bork's America," said Senator Kennedy, quoted in large type in the issue of *The New York Times* published the day before the lesson from the English teacher, "is a land in which women would be forced into back-alley abortions, blacks would sit at segregated lunch counters, rogue police could break down citizens' doors in midnight raids."

Now either Senator Kennedy was drunk when he uttered these lines, in which case he should not drink before he drives or orates, or else he has proved as irresponsible as any demagogue in the recent history of the United States. It is hard to imagine anyone in this century—Bilbo, Smith, McCarthy, Coughlin—coming up with charges so withered in distortion and malice.

Consider the question of abortion. If Bork voted to reverse *Roe v. Wade,* he would need four other judges whose consciences instructed them that it was a bad constitutional decision. Does it then follow that women would be forced into back-alley abortions? Only if the solid majority of the American people went on to write anti-abortion laws. Kennedy knows as well as Planned Parenthood that that would not happen. To withdraw the license of *Roe v. Wade* is not to illegalize abortion.

And why would blacks sit at segregated lunch counters? Where has Robert Bork defended Jim Crow? He was always opposed to state laws enforcing racial segregation, which is different from upholding the right of the state to proscribe conduct though even on this point, libertarian Bork is at one these days with the overwhelming majority of the voters who would kick out of office anyone suggesting any return to Jim Crow even privately administered in one's own hot dog stand.

What has Bork said that would give to rogue police the right to break down citizens' doors in midnight raids? And while we are at it, when police do break down citizens' doors in midnight raids, what is there inherently to convince us that they are rogue police? Might they be answering a woman's cry against a rapist or a murderer? And what other four Supreme Court justices, and what fifty state legislatures, are going to start a campaign to give license to rogue police?

But this is heady business, this victimology by which some irresponsible men and women prosper. Benjamin Hooks, the head of the National Association for the Advancement of Colored People, who fancies himself engaged in the promotion of toleration in America, proclaims that Bork "would in effect wipe out all of our gains of the past thirty years."

That would be an extraordinary commission. Somebody

should inform Teddy Kennedy and Ben Hooks that Bork is not being nominated dictator of a brand-new country; that not one Supreme Court decision has overthrown a single one of the one hundred decisions Bork has written in his five years as a federal judge; and that if, in their nightmare, he were nominated and approved as dictator, Robert Bork would not wish to transform the face of America in the image of Hieronymus Bosch. The voters should be reminded that such as Kennedy and Hooks are heavily engaged in attempting to transform a land of civil and vigorous discourse into a republic of slander. And that slander, which includes the abdication of reason and conscience, is, as Orwell taught, the road to totalitarianism. Kennedy's vituperation of Bork is in a class with Goebbels's vituperation of the Jews.

5

Excavating the Titanic

S enator Lowell Weicker, I kid you not, has gulled the Senate of the United States into passing a bill the relevant section of which reads: "Notwithstanding any other provision of law, no object from the R.M.S. *Titanic* may be imported into the customs territory of the United States for the purpose of commercial gain after the date of enactment of this act."

The day's news tells us that the French expedition that has been exploring the *Titanic* for several weeks has fingered the ship's strongbox, which it is proceeding to remove. The French fifty-four-day, $2.5 million expedition is underwritten by something called the Ocean Research Organization, a British corporation. There is also backing from an American television company. There is a lot of talk circulating, some of it to the effect that artifacts taken from the *Titanic* are going into a French museum. There is, one gathers, the possibility of a televised opening of the strongbox, much as was done when the safe of the *Andrea Doria* was opened under spectacular auspices, giving the worldwide audience an intimate view of soggy thirty-year-old low-denomination currency.

Now, one of Senator Weicker's points is that U.S. technology discovered the location of the *Titanic,* and that Dr. Robert Ballard, the scientist who led the expedition that discovered the *Titanic* in 1985, recommended that the ship be left undisturbed.

But why?

Eva Hart, an eighty-two-year-old survivor of the *Titanic* disaster, is quoted: "The grave should be left alone. They're simply going to do it as fortune hunters, vultures, pirates." Doing "it" means, we are to suppose, taking from the *Titanic* such oddments as plates, wine bottles, jewelry, strongboxes that would otherwise remain within the vessel's creaky carapace.

One doesn't quite know what to make of it, and it doesn't help at all to read the remarks of Senator Weicker when he introduced his bill. Sometimes, on reading Weicker and trying to understand him, one wishes one had rather been assigned to decipher the Rosetta stone. He told the Senate that "it is only a matter of time before the world is going to have to turn to these oceans for food and fuel." So? So, "When the Earth does turn to the oceans for its food and its fuel, do not forget it has to be a resource that lasts millions of years rather than just a decade or two to satisfy our most immediate desires." Well, if we promise not to forget, then what? I mean, what does that have to do with the case for leaving the _Titanic_ intact under the water?

Senator Weicker assured his colleagues that he spoke with special qualifications on the subject—"As a proud lay member of that community, one who himself has spent days on the bottom of the ocean"—and perhaps forgot to decompress sufficiently on the way up.

Here is what troubles:

1) Who told Congress it has any right to tell an American who wants a plate from the dining room of the _Titanic_, which an independent salvage operation pulls out and is willing to sell, that he/she can't have it? The plate contains no communicable germs. It is not a lethal instrument. It is not a threat to the separation of church and state. So who is Lowell Weicker to tell the American collector that he can't be the willing buyer in dealing with a willing seller?

2) I have several times sailed over the corporal remains of the _Andrea Doria_, and record that there is no difference at all in the quality of the sensation sailing over it with its safe still in place or not in place. The _Titanic_ is two and one-half miles below the surface of the ocean, and any yachtsman passing over it will be aware that he is doing so only by taking micromeasurements on his Geographical Positioning System. It is impossible to understand exactly why he is supposed to feel different about the experience if the _Titanic_ is missing its full inventory of kitchen equipment, which reposes now in the living rooms of collectors.

3) If the Weicker vow were to be universalized, would we need

to return to the Pyramids everything that has been taken from them? Some of the treasures from the Pyramids reside in museums, some are privately owned. Many that are now in museums were once in private hands.

I for one admire the enterprise of the consortium that is spending much of the summer retrieving from utter uselessness artifacts that, for some people, exercise an alluring historical appeal. Wouldn't want one myself, but then I don't collect stamps, and my collection of fatuities by Lowell Weicker is so huge I've run out of room.

6

The Birth of BuckPac

AUGUST 16, 1988

Transcript of a press conference at Sharon, Connecticut, Monday August 15, 1988:

Q: What is the purpose of "Buckleys for Lieberman"?

A: To generate support for the defeat of Lowell Weicker.

Q: So that it is primarily the retirement of Weicker rather than the election of Lieberman that you wish?

A: You can't have the one without the other. As for Joe Lieberman, he is a moderate Democrat, and it is always possible that he will progress in the right direction. There is no such hope for Lowell Weicker.

Q: Why do you call your organization Buckleys for Lieberman?

A: Within my own family there are a good many Buckleys grounded in Connecticut. An informal estimate suggests that there are about eleven thousand Buckleys in the state. Buckleys for Lieberman intends to devote its primary attention to mobilizing their support for Lieberman.

Q: What do you propose to do about Buckleys who advise you they are for Weicker, not for Lieberman?

A: That matter will be referred to the Committee on Genealogy. It is entirely possible that there are, in Connecticut, persons who call themselves "Buckley" whose birth certificates would not bear out any such presumption.

Q: You mean to say you would challenge the legitimacy of a Buckley who announced his intention of voting for Weicker?

A: This is a very serious business. The future of self-government depends on retiring such as Weicker from the Senate. Correction, there is no such thing as "such as Weicker." He is unique.

Q: How do you propose to establish that?

A: That is the responsibility of the Horse's Ass Committee.

Q: The what?

A: The Horse's Ass Committee.

Q: What are its purposes?

A: To document that Lowell Weicker is the Number One Horse's Ass in the Senate. The committee, which is engaged in research, is absolutely confident that it will win any challenge, from anywhere, nominating any other member of Congress: Lowell Weicker will emerge as the winner.

Q: Just how do you define a . . . horse's ass?

A: Oh, you know. The kind of person who says dumb things dully, you know . . .

Q: Well, what kind of research is the . . . committee you speak of engaged in?

A: Researching the speeches and public utterances of Lowell Weicker over the past eighteen years. We have a few specimens ready for release at this time, but many, many more will be made public by the Degasification Committee.

Q: Excuse me?

A: Oh, yes. Well, the Degasification Committee is engaged in attempting to clean up the quality of public thought, and intends to demonstrate that the bombast, murk, and pomposity of Lowell Weicker's public declarations are a threat to democratic ecology. Hence the need for a Degasification Committee.

Q: Does the Buckleys for Lieberman Committee intend to do any active work beyond research?

A: Oh my, yes. We have already formed a political action committee. The BuckPac. Contributions will be solicited from all Buckleys, state by state.

Q: Are you limiting financial contributions to people called Buckley?

A: No. Special membership goes to all Buckleys, whether Buckley is the surname, the maiden name, or the Christian name. There have already been inquiries from out-of-state Buckleys. Some of these will send money to BuckPac. Others actually plan to

immigrate to Connecticut, become residents, and vote for Lieberman.

Q: Well, what happens when you run out of Buckleys?

A: Our Ethnographic Committee is compiling the names of
Connecticut residents that appear most frequently in the telephone directories. We propose to encourage the formation of co-
ordinate committees. You will not be surprised, I am sure, to know
that "Smith," "Jones," "Gomez," "Guttman," and "Rosselli" are
among the top forty in frequency that appear in the Connecticut
phone books. But we do not propose to neglect any citizen of
Connecticut, even those with unusual, not to say unique, names.
Our strategic objective is a committee representing every surname
in any Connecticut phone book, taking the civic lead from
Buckleys for Lieberman, to help in the campaign to liberate Connecticut, and Congress, from Lowell Weicker.

Q: Does the committee have an address?

A: Indeed. It is P.O. Box 1464, Sharon, Connecticut 06069.

Q: And officers?

A: Of course. William F. Buckley, Jr., is president. Christopher
T. Buckley is vice president. Priscilla L. Buckley is secretary-
treasurer. James W. Buckley is chairman of the Horse's Ass
Committee. Mrs. Jane Buckley Smith is head of the Genealogy
Committee. James Buckley Heath is head of the Ethnographic
Committee. And Bruce Buckley Smith is head of the Degasifica-
tion Committee. Other appointments will be announced in due
course. Regular press releases will be issued. Good day.

7

Lenny Explains

Whee!—just like that. On Sunday morning, Leonard Bernstein called out loud in *The New York Times* on Mike Dukakis to stop all this silence about the L-word and come right out with it. "I dreamed I heard Michael S. Dukakis say, 'I am proud to be called a liberal.' " And, hours later, Mr. Dukakis said just that. For the very first time, after more than one year's campaigning. Leonard Bernstein is a happy man today.

Now in the course of stamping his foot in protest against Mr. Dukakis's coyness on the subject of liberalism, Mr. Bernstein informed the readers about what liberalism really is and how close we have come in America to losing it. "George Washington was a revolutionary, as were Jefferson and Franklin. . . . All these forefathers were therefore liberals." Well, as a matter of fact, these gentlemen were not really revolutionaries; they were secessionists. And none of them was a liberal in the sense in which the word is currently used. Jefferson is the man who said that government is good which governs least.

The liberals are mad not only at the failure of Dukakis et al. to use the L-word, they are also mad at the depreciation of the word. " 'Liberal,' " says Mr. Bernstein, "is a word soiled by the greedy, reactionary, backward-looking impulse toward tyranny." Gee whiz. That means Ronald Reagan is all those things, a lot more. But one must render this in the florid language of the same man who does so much with a Mahler symphony. He sees himself with 110 players bending to his inspiration when he writes.

"Tyranny? In our free, beautiful, democratic republic? Yes. It is possible, and even probable, which is why we must constantly guard against it. Tyranny assumes many forms. To tax the factory workers and the outright poor so that the rich can get richer is tyranny. To call for war at the drop of a pipeline . . . to teach jingoistic slogans about armaments and Star Wars," etc. (there is much more ornamentation in the original), "these are all forms of tyranny."

Mr. Bernstein tells us the nearest we ever got to tyranny was in the days of Senator Joe McCarthy. He does not, in his feverish essay, devote one sentence to discussing tyranny under communism or the efforts of those who have labored to contain that tyranny. That's their problem, that lack of focus—the kind of thing that led Jimmy Carter to warn against our "inordinate fear of communism" at about the time genocide was going on in Cambodia.

The most agitated Leonard Bernstein has been throughout his public lifetime was in January 1970. He threw a big cocktail party for the Black Panthers in New York. The Panthers, you will recall, were a group of revolutionaries whose planted axiom was that the United States was racist, unjust, and had to be destroyed. Their leader rejoiced over the assassination of Robert Kennedy, featuring a picture of him lying in a pool of his own blood, his face transformed to the likeness of a pig. At Mr. Bernstein's luxurious apartment his guests were lectured by Black Panther Donald Cox, who began by announcing that if business didn't provide full employment, then the Panthers would simply take over the means of production and put them in the hands of the people, to which prescription Mr. Bernstein's reply was, "I dig absolutely."

You get the sinking feeling that Lenny does not realize that one of the reasons the L-word is discredited is that it was handled by such as Leonard Bernstein over the years with his dislocated perspectives. The liberals were easy prey for the Black Panthers. Tom Wolfe caught it all definitively when he wrote about "mau-mauing the flak catchers":

> There was one genius in the art of confrontation who had mau-mauing down to what you could term a laboratory science. He had it figured out so he didn't even have to bring his boys downtown in person. He would just show up with a crocus sack full of revolvers, ice picks, fish knives, switchblades,

hatchets, blackjacks, gravity knives, straight razors, hand grenades, blow guns, bazookas, Molotov cocktails, tank rippers,
unbelievable stuff, and he'd dump it all out on somebody's
shiny walnut conference table. He'd say, "These are some of
the things I took off my boys last night . . ."

And the nubile liberals would do their little shuffle, digging it
all, as Lenny digs liberalism. But he will go back to music soon, as
Michael Dukakis will go back to the John F. Kennedy school of
government.

8

Eight Down, ? To Go

L iz's eighth was fittingly vulgar. The helicopters buzzed about, one parachutist tried to break in from the heavens above, and the wedding was hosted by Michael Jackson (details courtesy of Liz Smith) "formally attired in a dinner jacket, with a large diamond pin at his throat instead of black tie. He wore another diamond medal on his chest and bright silver boots." The father-of-the-bride who gave Liz away is almost thirty years junior to the bride, who stepped forward to marry the groom, twenty years her junior. He was in turn accompanied by best man, hairdresser José Eber, "wearing his customary trademark straw hat, dyed black to match his tuxedo for the occasion." The chimpanzee that was to have brought in the wedding ring did not turn up. Bad chimpanzee! Did he have no sense of the occasion?

Liz was dressed in a $30,000 yellow floor-length Valentino, giving her one more wedding dress to add to her swelling collection. The guests were kept waiting (a Taylor trademark) and became very nearly mutinous at an odd sign of austerity in the bacchanalia, to wit the word that went quietly: No booze until after the ceremony. I mean, it was now 6:13! Can you imagine, 6:13 and no booze at a Hollywood extravaganza? You'd think Major Barbara had arrived by parachute with a squadron from the Salvation Army. But, finally, the bride and groom were together and the officiator, "non-denominational Minister Marianne Williamson," began the ceremony, with, understandably, carefully selected words:

"Elizabeth is literally God's gift to you for your healing and her healing." One searches for the meaning here, but perhaps the reference is to Elizabeth's having met the construction worker at Betty Ford's clinic where both were in for alcohol-drug treatment. The minister went on, "Elizabeth and Larry and you guests understand that so much of the illusion that is happening here right now has nothing to do with the meaning of this ceremony. We invite the power of God to enter us." I believe in an omnipotent God, and only for that reason therefore believe He was able to penetrate the ceremony (if He were one shade less omnipotent, He would not have made it). Williamson went on, "As you join together, from this point on nothing will be experienced alone." Nothing has ever been experienced alone by Elizabeth. "Through the grace of God we may love more deeply than we have ever loved before."

That is quite a challenge, for those who remember, e.g., Elizabeth's love for Mike Todd and for others here and there in the course of her nuptial parade. There are, to be sure, those who are skeptical about the uniqueness of Larry Fortensky. One guest, Stella Barraza, commented to *The New York Times*'s Seth Mydans: "She is a legend and she's still around after all these years and she's still every bit as beautiful. But I don't really think this one is going to last. He's so much younger. It'll be Number Nine in no time at all, you watch." Mr. Fortensky is indeed only thirty-nine, and one has to conjecture that the love Elizabeth feels for him is biological, which raises the interesting question, Why was marriage necessary? They could have continued to keep house together and saved the expense of the wedding, the innocent will speculate.

But you see, the wedding was a smash economic success. "Earnings from the access has been estimated in the press at millions of dollars," writes Mr. Mydans, referring, one supposes, among other sources of revenue to what *People* mag paid for photo exclusives. How the rest was raised we don't know. One assumes that Nancy Reagan and Gerald Ford weren't charged admission at the gate, but then—how? "Much of that money, the reports say, is to be donated to AIDS research, a cause to which Miss Taylor has devoted considerable effort." Miss Taylor might have done more for AIDS if she had taken greater pains to obscure her life-style. After all, AIDS is communicated primarily by self-indulgence, and Elizabeth hasn't left any fingerprints in the annals of self-denial.

There is something there that repels about using hallowed ceremonies, which weddings are, as a kind of cookie-cutting assembly line for serial marriage. It is one thing when a couple discovers a deep incompatibility, and sets out again, even a third time, in search of a happy life. Elizabeth Taylor has been the model of self-indulgence. Her latest, to someone manifestly incongruous in age and background, is one more log added to the bonfire of cynicism. Perhaps I feel especially on the subject, given that she and I both were first married on the same day, in 1950.

9

Count Me Out

OCTOBER 16, 1990

The widow of John Lennon asked rather more, in the memory of her late husband, than some of us are willing, let alone anxious, to give, however much we regret the tragic circumstances of his passing. John Lennon was a source of inspiration to many people (including my son), and as has wisely been counseled, it is unwise to insert oneself in other people's religious quarrels. But Yoko Ono asked not merely that Lennonites celebrate Lennonism, but that all of us do.

I am reminded of the clerk at the London pub who read and reread, quaffing his curiosity along the way, the personal ad that asked for volunteers for a two-year trip up the Congo River, the payment for the entire period 100 pounds, with the warning that the probability of death or pestilence was very high. After his fifth rereading and fifth beer, he called the telephone number given, carefully spelled his name, gave his address, and announced that he was *not* volunteering to go on the trip.

You see, Yoko wanted the whole world—every radio station, in every country—to sing out, at a given hour, the song "Imagine," nominating it in effect as a kind of international anthem. Now I do not know the melody of "Imagine," but I have the lyrics in front of me, and what it amounts to is a kind of Bible, as written by the sorcerer's apprentice.

> *Imagine there's no heaven*
> *It's easy if you try*
> *No hell below us*
> *Above us only sky*

Imagine all the people
Living for today.

I venture to say that those who imagine in that direction ought to make every effort to restrain themselves. The homilies of John Lennon have a hard time up against those of Christ, who spoke the words "Eye hath not seen, nor ear heard, neither have entered into the heart of man, the things which God hath prepared for them that love him."

It is quite difficult to understand Mr. Lennon's point in wishing that all that life stands for is the present moment, today. And the notion that there is only sky above us suggests a kind of ethereal vapidity that is downright depressing. And what are we to say about the word "heavenly" if heaven doesn't exist?

It is hard to say the song gets worse, because there is hardly anything worse than to think that John Lennon is a mere memory, rather than a companion of the angels. But the second verse asks us—

Imagine there's no countries
It isn't hard to do
Nothing to kill or die for
And no religion too
Imagine all the people
Living life in peace.

Well, we certainly want to imagine a world in which everyone lives in peace, but you see, that is only possible in a world in which people are willing to die for causes. There'd have been peace for heaven knows (assuming heaven existed) how long in the South, except that men were willing to die to free the slaves, and Hitler would have died maybe about the time John Lennon did, at Berchtesgaden, at age ninety-one, happy in a Jewless Europe. There have got to be reasons that even affected John Lennon to prefer one country over against another. I happen to know this to be the case, since a long time ago he asked me to help him get papers permitting him to live in the United States, rather than in Great Britain.

More?

Imagine no possessions
I wonder if you can
No need for greed or hunger
A brotherhood of man
Imagine all the people
Sharing all the world.

No, thanks, I don't want to imagine a world in which Yoko doesn't possess the goods that John left her, with which possessions she is capable of exercising a great deal of charity, though not so profusely as to leave her penniless, and a public charge.

The person who invented heaven passed along a commandment ordaining that one must not covet other people's goods, and most thoughtful social philosophers agree that property is an important basis, indeed probably the most important basis, of human freedom.

So it goes, and the chorus of "Imagine" is—well, it is too subversive to appear in family reading matter.

10

The Perils of Perotocracy

JUNE 12, 1992

W e may soon need a constitutional amendment that reads: "No American citizen, irrespective of race, color, religion, or previous condition of servitude, shall have the right to vote for the office of President of the United States."

I speak of the ongoing campaign of Ross Perot and specifically of his most recent appearance on the *Today* show, from which two specimens.

On the subject of presidential debates: He is for them. But "we're not talking about debates where newscasters ask you a question. We're talking about the old college debate where you stand out there all alone without thirteen handlers and jocks sitting down there signing you, telling you when to talk and when not to talk. The point is we're talking about real debates on real issues. . . . I would not have any interest at all in one of these, you know, blow-dried guys sitting there asking all three of us questions in a pompous way. Now, let's just get in the ring, get it on."

That sounds terrific. Provided you do not pause to analyze what he actually says:

1) In the presidential debates, beginning with Nixon-Kennedy, there have never been any "handlers" sitting there advising their candidate what to answer to a question. The candidates have always appeared on their own.

2) In college debates, and indeed in all debates, strict time limits are imposed, necessarily so.

3) In every presidential debate since 1960, real issues have been dealt with and tough questions have been asked.

4) Going back two presidential races, we have had the follow-

ing moderators and interrogators asking questions of the candidates: Jim Lehrer, Peter Jennings, John Mashek, Bernard Shaw, Ann Compton, Andrea Mitchell, Margaret Warner, Edwin Newman, Georgie Anne Geyer, Marvin Kalb, Morton Kondracke, Henry Trewhitt, Barbara Walters, Diane Sawyer, Fred Barnes, and James Wieghart. I don't know whether any of the above blow-dry their hair, and don't much care. I do know that they didn't ask pompous questions.

One is drawn to the conclusion that a pompous question is a question Ross Perot can't answer, which makes just about every question pompous.

Or consider Mr. Perot on the question of abortion.

"When the dust clears, it's a woman's choice. Each human life is precious. We should not create a human life unless we want to create it. It is absolutely irresponsible for thinking, reasoning human beings to thoughtlessly create a human life they don't want."

Every viewer is supposed to get from the above a little tingly feeling of satisfaction, the pro-choice people because he says it's up to the woman, the pro-life people because he says nice things about fetuses.

But analysis needs to set in. If, referring to a fetus, you use the designation "human life"—moreover, human life that is "precious"—you have laid down a philosophical plank from which there is no retreating. What we do in civilized societies is protect human lives, precisely because they are precious. But if we did that, abortion would be forbidden.

Quite right, we should not create a human life unless we want to create it, but we do. Massively. About 1.7 million last year alone. So if we should not do it, what ought to be the consequences of doing it anyway? Well, none. It is the woman's choice.

"It is absolutely irresponsible for thinking, reasoning human beings to thoughtlessly create a human life they don't want." Ah, but women who conceive a baby they do not want are either a) inattentive to prophylactic detail (she hasn't used the pill, he hasn't used the condom) or b) she got carried away by the passion of the moment and, unlucky in love, created a "precious human life."

What is it proposed we do about unreasoning, thoughtless

women? Well, blow-dry your hair and risk being denounced as pompous when you answer: Nothing.

That is Mr. Perot's stand on abortion: Denounce thoughtlessness and a lack of reason, praise the precious human lives created athwart that thoughtlessness and lack of reason, and get out of the way of anybody who wants to abort for any reason. Under a Perotocracy, nothing will stand in the way of Planned Parenthood via abortion.

As an alumnus of college debating teams, permit me to say on their behalf that the kind of thing Ross Perot is getting away with wouldn't graduate him onto the sophomore team.

11

It's a Wonderful Life

JULY 20, 1992

I t is fortunate for Professor Galbraith that he was born with singular gifts as a writer. It is a pity he hasn't used these skills in other ways than to try year after year to bail out his sinking boats. Granted, one can take satisfaction from his anti-historical exertions—the reader gets subversive pleasure out of his Sisyphean labors, and some wholesome pleasure from his yeomanry as a sump-pumper. Indeed his rhythm and grace recall the skills we remember as having been developed by Ben Hur, the model galley slave whose only request of the quartermaster was that he be allowed every month to move to the other side of the boat, to ensure a parallel development in the musculature of his arms and legs. I for one hope that the next time a nation experimenting with socialism or communism fails, which will happen the next time a nation experiments with socialism or communism, Ken Galbraith will feel the need to explain what happened. It's great fun to read. It helps, of course, to suppress wistful thought about those who endured, or died trying, the passage toward collective living to which Professor Galbraith has beckoned us for over forty years, beguiling the subliterate world, here defined as those whose knowledge of what makes the world work is undeveloped.

His current conceit is that the United States has become a "culture of contentment." His objective is to account for our failure to expand the public sector at a faster rate than we are doing.

His tone of voice, in describing the culture of contentment, is indispensable to the psychiatrist's posture at the bedside of the patient. The reason the United States is . . . stuck with its fixed ways is that we are ruled by a class of contented Americans who like it this way because this way leads to a continuation of their contentment at the expense of the less fortunate. They manage their continuation in power by a series of political and philosophical stratagems apparent only to careful students of the knavish practices of the contented.

Now in defining the culture of contentment, Professor Galbraith has some easy and some not so easy explaining to do. His first problem is that the United States is, after all, a democracy, with a universal franchise; so that if the majority of us were agonizing in a cauldron of discontent, all we'd need to wait for is the next election. Ah! JKG thought of that, and here is the explanation: 1) Enough Americans are living off the larder of contentment to overwhelm the exploited minority. And then, 2) that minority who are discontented have no reason to believe that political action works, and accordingly they don't bother to vote.

Then there are concrete clusters of people, and philosophical lacunae. He deals with these. The farmers, for instance. "Agriculture works well only under a widely accepted and much celebrated form of exploitation, that by the farmer of himself, his family, and his immediate hired hands." The farmers are kept docile by subsidies and by refreshing the working class as required, inasmuch as we all see "the need for the resupply or, less agreeably, for keeping some part of the underclass in continued and deferential subjection." The thing to remember is that they are not in revolt against their revolting work.

And then we have Social Security, which brings a measure of contentment to the aging: thus are they pacified into accepting the status quo.

The manufacturing class is pacified by our longtime program of heavy weaponry, done to satisfy our paranoiac concern over world communism and its alleged appetite to control the world. Billions of dollars were spent and are being spent on useless military armament, the only purpose of which expenditure is to enrich the contented class. How did this come about, given the antimilitary tradition of post–World War I America? Simple: "Weapons expenditure, unlike, for example, spending for the urban poor, rewards a very comfortable constituency . . . Until World War II, the fortunately situated in the United States, the Republican Party in particular, resisted military expenditures, as they then resisted all government spending. In the years since, the presumed worldwide communist menace, as frequently it was designated [Correction. It wasn't designated as a "presumed worldwide menace," but as a "worldwide menace"], brought a major reversal: those with a comfortable concern for their own economic position became the most powerful advocates of the most prodigal of military outlays." In other words, the rich decided it would pay off to have huge military war expenditures. Communism was convenient. It remains unclear why fascism wasn't convenient for the same reasons twenty years earlier.

Mr. Galbraith moves on to absorb phenomenon after phenomenon, his responsibility being rather like that of the Marxist scholar to integrate any event into the grand ideological picture. About the savings and loan fiasco he is at his most indignant. He grooves the scandal into his syllabus by nice little evasions. "The once modest insurance of deposits by the Federal Government was raised to $100,000 on each S&L account. The selective view of the role of the state was never more evident. The foregoing changes were variously enacted or instituted mainly in the early 1980s. They set the stage for what was by far the most feckless and felonious disposition of what, essentially, were public funds in the nation's history." As to the indictment, Mr. Galbraith is correct: the S&L bailout—a government deed—is indefensible. As to the responsibility for it, he is mischievously vague. *The foregoing changes were variously enacted or instituted mainly in the early 1980s.* The relevant changes were the suspension of Regulation Q, which limited the powers of S&Ls to pay interest; and the rise from $50,000 to $100,000 in deposits protected. Both these measures were taken by the Carter Administration in 1980. Unless "the early 1980s" translates to "1980," Mr. Galbraith is guilty of misrepresentation. Few scholars would word such a sentence as, "Pearl Harbor took place in the early 1940s."

And so on. The reason we have a volunteer military is? That the contented find that on the whole it is safer not to join the military than to join it—so why not pay others to do so? (This does not explain the number of otherwise contented young men who apply to go to West Point and Annapolis, but never mind.)

Everything, in a word, is organized around the idea of satisfying the contented class, including such conformity of thought as issues from the modern corporation. Mr. Galbraith has been trying to kill off the big corporation ever since *The New Industrial State,* in which he exaggerated the powers of the "technostructure" in order to establish that big business runs America. This insight America has never discovered, behaving most disobediently by bankrupting hypothetically invincible businesses.

Where Mr. Galbraith gets ugly, and I need to say this with some gravity inasmuch as I write about someone for whom I have respect and affection, is in his handling of social theorists who are inconveniently situated in his Boschean tableau. George Gilder he mentions, though almost in passing, as a bard of the social usefulness of adversity. He cites Gilder's observation that "in order to succeed, the poor need most of all the spur of their poverty." In the author's hands this ceases to be a point of sociological interest, true or false: it becomes only a part of the psaltery of contentment: one more hymn praising the persistence of poverty. Professor Arthur Laffer, who was the idiomatic godfather of supply-side economics, Mr. Galbraith dismisses as though his insights were of zero interest: "It is not clear that anyone of sober mentality took Professor Laffer's curve and conclusions seriously. He must have credit, nonetheless, for showing that justifying contrivance, however transparent, could be of high practical service." In other words, Laffer was propelled only by his ideological anxiety to stroke a ruling class.

Where Mr. Galbraith is inexcusable in his search for disingenuousness is in his handling of Charles Murray, a meticulous scholar of liberal background whose book *Losing Ground* is among the social landmarks of the postwar era. His handling of Murray: "And in the mid-1980s the requisite doctrine [needed by the culture of contentment to justify their policies] became available. Dr. Charles A. Murray provided the nearly perfect prescription. . . . its essence was that the poor are impoverished and are kept in poverty by the public measures, particularly the welfare payments, that are meant to rescue them from their plight." Whatever Murray's modifications, "the basic purpose of his argument would be served. The poor would be off the conscience of the comfortable, and, a point of greater importance, off the federal budget and tax system."

So much for the masterwork of a scholar who has wondered

diligently why the expenditure of $2.6 trillion has not done much to help the poor, and has certainly done much to hurt the poor.

John Kenneth Galbraith can't free himself from his fixations, and it doesn't much matter how overwhelming the evidence: he merely finds a new set of metaphors on which to hang his wardrobe, the current being the "contented" class. Nothing penetrates his comprehensive illusion. He managed, in the seventies, an entire book about China, which he visited while it was in the throes of the Cultural Revolution, in which he could find to criticize only that the Chinese smoked too many cigarettes. Ferdinand Mount, reviewing *Economics and the Public Purpose* in *National Review* in 1973, made the point that Professor Galbraith "is not an economist at all. He is a preacher, and a preacher of the most uncompromising sort. Hence his popularity. Most people have little relish for economic argument but everybody likes a good Hellfire sermon. Better still, Galbraith is irreverent, even raffish. His manner is unbuttoned, almost unfrocked." I suspect this is the reason for his extraordinary popularity in Japan. That is good news for those who worry about Japan's economic preeminence. Prime Minister Pierre Trudeau cited Galbraith as his favorite economist, from which moment on the economic decline of Canada began.

12

I Confess

Two nights before the affair, I had not known it would take place. The woman on my right at dinner, whose husband is professionally engaged in the production of rock music, told me she had not been disposed to go to Philadelphia for "the concert," but now she thought that if she did not go, she might in fact be passing up a historic event. With that prompting, before going out for dinner on Saturday I hooked up my VCR to catch the three-hour abbreviation of the sixteen-hour marathon, and when I got back, sat down with my wife and watched the last twenty minutes, which began with Jack Nicholson introducing Bob Dylan and his two accompanists. Jack Nicholson said that, for the finale, they had saved someone who "transcended history," no less.

Here was an event, philanthropic in design (all proceeds would go to Africans being systematically starved by the implementation of Marxist doctrine in Ethiopia) and impulse. The show-biz aspect of the great Live Aid spectacular was not what engages the attention. It is, rather, a plight one needs to explore. Not a purely private problem. I would not write a column to explore the difficulties I experience in virtue, say, of having a sixth toe. I have become a truth-seeker in the matter of the rock culture, and my problems aren't, I think, unique.

1. More people tuned in on Live Aid, we are told, than tuned in on the Summer Olympics. This datum is absolutely extraordinary, given that sports have been the lingua franca of internationalism through much of recorded history, and that there is an instantly communicable excitement to a sports event (Who's going to win?) that does not attach to a musical event, the excitement of

which comes in through a different sensory apparatus. What is being said for rock music, in effect, is that the entire world is at its feet, that the undisputed international celebrities of the world are the rock stars.

2. If this is so, then why is it that they do not appeal—well, to me? My other appetites are normal. Could it be that there is a dirty little secret no one is prepared publicly to discuss, namely that that kind of thing does not appeal to a whole lot of people who are not willing to confess their alienation from the overwhelming majority of the young?

3. " 'That kind of thing'? Come on now, Buckley, what exactly do you mean?"

Fair enough. Bob Dylan comes on stage, and on either side of him are two famous guitarists from the Rolling Stones. He last shaved, oh, three days before (Why?). He is wearing blue jeans and a scruffy T-shirt arrangement of sorts (Why? Trademark? Change trademarks?). The two guitarists arrive smoking cigarettes, which dangle from their lips for the first minute or so of the first song (Why?). Their arms are entirely bare, and they otherwise wear what looks like a stripped-down dark-colored T-shirt (Why? Heat?). Then intense concentration on Dylan, and neither I nor spouse can pick up a single word he has sung, and we frankly doubt that anyone else could (Why?). The songs were without discernible melody, the voice was whiny, with enough gravel in it to stop Jean-Claude Killy in mid-slope, the guitarists were hard to listen to (Why? Why? Why?). But we were engaged in transcending history.

Of one thing I am absolutely convinced, and that is that there is no doubting the sincerity of the rock-worshipers. I know one or two who are without affectation, and they will, in stretches of solitude, clap on their Walkmans and listen to Bob Dylan before they will listen to Vivaldi, or Verdi, or Strauss, or Cole Porter. Obviously there is a generational imbalance, and that should not surprise, whether one asks about relative young-old enthusiasm for the Rolling Stones, or relative young-old enthusiasm for *Raiders of the Lost Ark.*

But the totality of the mobilization of the young appears to have swept with it the not-young, and one wonders whether the capitulation of the middle-aged suggests a cultural insecurity. If all the world thinks Picasso's double-jawed, cockeyed dames are masterpieces, ought one to defer to universal sentiment? If one does not master rock and roll, is one closing the door on a transformative experience? Is it the equivalent of inviting color blindness? Deafness? Impotence?

Well, I have said it, and in payment for exercising the privilege of skipping the first two and a half hours of tape, I'll make a contribution to Live Aid, reviving the movement of sticking a dime in the nickelodeon to buy five minutes of silence.

—Policy: Confusions Abounding

13

Religion Scorned

MARCH 14, 1989

Religion has been receiving a bad press these days, calling to mind Picasso's famous disparagement of his own work twenty years ago—is God taunting us by putting the spotlight on Jimmy Swaggart, the Ayatollah Khomeini, and John Bird Singer?

The last, for irresponsible nonwatchers of *60 Minutes,* was a Mormon fanatic who got himself excommunicated from his own church, drew his family reclusively to his cabin where he stowed his wives and several thousand rounds of ammunition and more guns than General Custer had—but was killed in an exchange with federal and state troopers. His family lives on, uncorrected by experience.

Is Swaggart's deviant lechery characteristic of evangelical Protestantism? Is Khomeini's genocidal search for schismatics and blasphemers a correct transcription of the word of Allah? Is an excommunicated Mormon paradoxically an example of the practicing Mormon?

On the one hand there are the aberrational representatives of religion who do the damage, but there are also, of course, the nominal Christians, and they do as much damage, however little they are noticed, in part because they have become so humdrum.

A few weeks ago I was seated next to a European figure so august that ladies curtsy when they are presented to him, and he was telling the table at which he sat about the great mischief being done by the missionaries in Venezuela who move in on native tribes and totally break down their cultural order, resulting in deracination and chaos. I cleared my throat and asked which of the

Ten Commandments was responsible for bringing pandemonium to the poor Venezuelan savages.

The speaker hesitated for a moment, and said that, well, he was talking, so to speak, about the techniques used, to which the answer is of course that bad techniques are bad techniques, whether used by teachers, missionaries, lovers, or musicians, but one oughtn't to regret teaching, or evangelizing, or sex, or music because they are here and there sometimes practiced badly. But he seemed to be saying that it is inherent in the cultures of alien people that they should be left alone; to which one can only reply, as one would have done a generation ago when Margaret Mead discovered the unfettered joys of unfettered love in Samoa, that Christianity is the hallmark of civilization, and it is an injunction of Christianity to go out in the world and teach the word of the Lord. Yes, even in the jungles of Venezuela and on the beaches of Samoa and, for that matter, the pastures of Qom.

Granted that the Ten Commandments can convulse not only Venezuelan savages, but Park Avenue socialites. "Thou shalt not bear false witness against thy neighbor"—imagine if that were to become a Zero Toleration law in Washington. One would come away with the impression that a nerve gas had frozen the vocal cords of the entire town. "Thou shalt not covet thy neighbor's wife" . . . Thou shalt not *what*?! People for the American Way would descend upon you and insist that you were violating the First, Fourth, Fifth, and Fourteenth Amendments, the Declaration of Independence, and the Gettysburg Address if you held any such view. "Thou shalt not covet thy neighbor's goods" would put the Democratic Party out of business.

So there is the sense in which Christianity is a continuing revolution against the ways of man, beginning when he fled paradise. But Christianity speaks also about forgiveness, yea, even to the sinner who has sinned seventy times seven times. And that is a great deal more than the ayatollah is inclined to do, and very much more than the Incas or the Aztecs were inclined to do—or, for that matter, the fathers of the Inquisition. But the Christian religion is about how people ought to act, not how they do act, and European aristocrats ought to worry about savages who have been deprived of the knowledge of how they should act, rather than about nonsavages who know how they should act but do not do so.

Christianity has never been tried, the cliché runs. And of course it's true, but so is it true that Christianity has checked the movements of millions of men and women who but for the pull of dogma would know no vital brake upon their behavior. Sometimes the brake is effective, sometimes it is not. But that it should be there outweighs any concern over the excesses of Jimmy Swaggart or the ayatollah or the Mormon extremist or the Venezuelan savage—or the European relativist.

14

Terminological Right of Way

APRIL 7, 1988

When the civil rights bills were passed in the mid-sixties, their principal sponsor, Senator Hubert Humphrey, promised in one melodramatic session that he would "physically eat" the bill he was promoting if ever anyone attempted to use his bill in order to prefer a member of one race at the expense of a member of another race. Senator Humphrey died from other causes than the food poisoning to which he'd have been subjected after the Supreme Court OK'd affirmative action.

A fortnight ago we had the Civil Rights Restoration Act, which now extends to the federal government the right to inquire into the racial or sexual composition of a school's basketball team if its medical school is receiving federal subsidies. And last week, Georgetown University, the oldest Jesuit college in America, capitulated on the lawsuit demanding that it make room within Georgetown for gay and lesbian student federations.

One supposes that Georgetown's administrators would at this point interpose that they did not completely lose the fight. True, Georgetown has not been required by the courts to "recognize" the student homosexual groups. But it is required to give the groups facilities. And, it is conceded, the groups will draw their rations from student funds. So far as one can discern, Georgetown's victory is limited to the asterisk it is permitted to use in its catalogue of student activities after Lesbian Liberation Front: *"not officially recognized by the university." To such farthings are the defendants today reduced, if the juggernaut running over them is labeled "civil rights."

In 1952 the Commission on Financing Higher Education of

the Association of American Universities issued a warning against the dangers of accepting federal funds. "Under federal control, our hundreds of universities and colleges would follow the order of one central institution, and the freedom of higher education would be lost." Among the signers of that document were the presidents of Harvard, Johns Hopkins, Stanford, and Brown. Those learned gentlemen would take from the situation today whatever satisfaction is desired by prophets of doom. But even so, it is hard to imagine that they'd have foreseen a day in which a federal court instructs a religious institution that it is required to countenance, let alone provide quarters for, groups engaged in promoting activity deemed not only wrong but sinful by the moral architects of that institution.

Those who stress (and re-stress) the separation of church·and state are certainly narrowing the area within which the freedom of religious exercise is tolerated. Perhaps in the storm cellar. Here is a scenario: A son sues his father for denying him facilities in the home in which to practice homosexuality with a neighbor's son. The ACLU defends the son's freedom on the grounds that the father's house is a beneficiary of a federally backed mortgage, and therefore the civil rights of all its occupants need to be observed.

Lunatic reasoning? Who, ten years ago, would not have thought it lunatic reasoning that a religious institution dedicated to teaching, among other things, the moral law should be obliged to extend its hospitality to those who seek to flout such laws?

I observed with fascination, only a week or so ago, the plausibility with which Senator George McGovern, as ever on the cutting edge of liberal reasoning, defended the recent civil rights extension. It sounds so reasonable to say that "the taxpayers" do not wish their money to be spent on "any institution" that permits the practice of discrimination. Discrimination against race, ethnic background, sex, and now sexual inclination.

One wonders—I brought this unsuccessfully to the attention of Mr. McGovern—what has happened to the concept of privacy. Just as the idea of civil rights has expanded, one would have expected that the concept of private rights would expand, in an age when the clearest threat is that posed by omnipotent government. But the only private right anybody ever got exercised about in recent times is the right to use birth-control devices. Private clubs are gradually disappearing, under the sanction of civil rights. If I were in Congress I would be tempted, I said to Senator McGovern, even if only on April Fools' Day, to introduce a "Civil Rights Bill for Preemptive War Against the Soviet Union." My only purpose would be to permit me in the campaign ahead to point to all those Democrats who voted against the "Civil Rights Bill of 1988" and thereby stifle a hundred political careers.

Somebody, somewhere, somehow, has got to stop the civil rights thing. It is making a joke out of one after another provision of our Bill of Rights.

15

Sleaze, 18-Karat

JUNE 15, 1989

On the evening of the day George Bush vetoed the minimum wage hike, Senator Edward Kennedy and Senator George Mitchell were briefly interviewed on the evening news. Kennedy put on his I Despair for the Fate of My Country expression, which he can do without notes from his aides, and Mitchell, who is the Democratic majority leader, pronounced: President Bush wants to reduce the capital gains tax, which means: Make the rich richer. For the poor, he has just this message. For you, we'll do nothing.

You know, they talk about the sleaze factor, and by it they mean that you got 3,000 bucks for a speech when you should have gotten maybe 300 bucks; or else you hired your sister-in-law part-time; or else you got a higher royalty on your book than Ernest Hemingway. All of that stuff is vaguely distasteful, and when carried to excess probably should transport the sleazer right to Sing Sing.

But the biggest sleaze factor in Washington has to do not with what legislators do, but with what legislators say. In the classic denunciation, they are when they speak, as they so often speak, poisoning the wells of political discourse. George Mitchell managed in two sentences to utter statements that, in a healthy society, would have got him run out of town with wet towels.

George Bush's recommendation to lower the tax on capital gains can be said to be motivated by a desire to help rich people only by the same reasoning that would permit one to say that Tom Wicker's opposition to censorship issues from his desire to profit newspapermen, or that the campaign for cleaner air is especially motivated by the asthma lobby. Practically any tax reduction, whether of capital gains or of excise taxes on fur coats, is going to help the rich more than the poor viewed in the short run (an inflationary tax is going to hurt the rich less than the poor). But the whole idea in the United States is to make it as easy as possible for people to move in the direction of wealth, and if one reflects that by current standards 90 percent of the American people were poor at the turn of the century, we are not doing badly.

Does Mitchell know (it is possible that he knows it, and also possible that, knowing it, he suppresses the figures) that 70 percent of the ten million tax returns reporting capital gains income in 1987 were filed by taxpayers with gross incomes below $50,000? That one third of them had incomes below $25,000, which is practically the national median income? Does he bother to acknowledge that Bush's capital gains bill specifies a reduction to 15 percent (from the present 28 percent) in capital gains tax *except* for people who earn less than $20,000, who would receive a 100 percent exemption?

And be careful before sniffing that people who earn less than $20,000 never have a capital gain. One million, four hundred thousand Americans with incomes of less than $10,000 reported a capital gain in 1987. Why shouldn't a great big adult senator admit that the probable purpose of reducing the capital gains tax is to improve the general economy?

And then, of course, there is the whole business of picking on the poor by vetoing the minimum wage hike.

The minimum wage is about as discredited as the Flat Earth Society, in which Senators Kennedy and Mitchell have honorary membership. The one absolutely predictable effect of a meaningful hike in the minimum wage is damage done to the poorest workers: An increase in the minimum wage is not going to affect the overwhelming majority of Americans who earn more than the minimum wage. More than half of those who work for the minimum wage are under twenty-five, and many of them are beginning work, learning a new trade, moonlighting, or working part-time. The one predictable result of an increase in the minimum wage would be an increase in unemployment and in inflation, whose impartial levy is on all Americans, but whose ravages are especially devastating to poor Americans.

The minimum wage is an accretion of the New Deal that is not publicly defended by any serious economist. To the extent that the minimum wage is meaningless—i.e., if virtually everyone commands a higher wage than the minimum wage—it is harmless. To the extent that it has meaning—if the wage is set higher than people are prepared to pay—then it is harmful.

Though probably not more harmful than the heavy contributions to illiteracy made by such as Senator Mitchell. Why worry about the sleaze factor involving dollars and cents, when the big-time sleaze mocks the ideals of self-government?

16

Legal Legerdemain

MAY 18, 1990

nthony Lewis of *The New York Times* picks up a sentence from *The Economist* and strokes it for a full column. What *The Economist* wrote was that "one of the most striking differences between the United States and other industrial countries is America's enthusiasm for execution."

Well now—just to begin with—if America has that great an enthusiasm for execution, America must be most fearfully frustrated. We have had 124 executions since the *Gregg v. Georgia* decision in 1976 authorized a return to capital punishment. That's an average of fewer than ten executions per year. During the fourteen years since *Gregg,* we have had about 265,000 murders. If you want the ratio, that makes for about 2,137 murders per execution. And, finally, there are 2,200 men and women on Death Row. If our enthusiasm were so great to execute them, one would think there'd be 200 of them alive today, and none left tomorrow: America has no shortage of electricity.

But our enthusiasm to execute has generated the longest juridical foreplay in history. Inevitably (as with Mr. Lewis) opponents of capital punishment single out for attention such as Dalton Prejean, executed yesterday in Louisiana: ". . . the idea that only especially evil criminals are selected for execution is a joke. The ones who lose are poor, mentally impaired, black—and had lawyers who did not take the case seriously." Well, somebody took the case of Mr. Prejean seriously, given that he killed the cop in 1977 and was alive up until May 17, 1990. Who and what kept him alive all that length of time, against the cosmic drive of U.S. enthusiasm to execute and the scarcity of legal talent?

What is going on in America is that the abolitionists are hoist by their own petard. They struggled for years, and continue to do so, to make effective justice impossible. Along comes William H. Rehnquist, Chief Justice of the Supreme Court, who petitions the legal community to cut down on the number of applications a condemned prisoner, pleading habeas corpus, can make to the federal courts. These are unlimited, and have the effect of keeping high the population of the death houses.

Mr. Rehnquist has been saying for years in effect: Look, if the legislatures want capital punishment for certain kinds of crimes for which the Supreme Court has authorized capital punishment, let them get on with capital punishment. If they don't want it, let them repeal those laws. But don't try at one and the same time to live according to the law and to frustrate the law. All that happens when you do that is a waste of judicial time and the frustration of the democratic process.

Has it occurred to *The Economist* why the United States has reversed itself on capital punishment? Twenty-four years ago, more than 50 percent of the U.S. population opposed capital punishment. Now, 80 percent approve of capital punishment. How come? Have we as a nation drifted toward necrophilia? There is another explanation, namely that societies tend to mobilize their resources as provoked. If there are great scandals on Wall Street, fresh laws and regulations (as Ivan Boesky knows) get passed. If the United States manages nine times as many murders per capita as the United Kingdom, we incline in the direction of the chair at the same time that Great Britain inclines away from the noose. *The Economist* might consult one of its futurists and ask the question: If there were a 1,000 percent increase in capital crime in Great Britain, would Parliament bring back the hangman? Interesting question.

The latest drive to exterminate capital punishment by introducing phony objections issues, not unexpectedly, from Senator Ted Kennedy. His new civil-rights-justice, I'm-going-to-an-integrated-heaven-when-I-die bill says this: Unless the number of people sentenced to death exactly represents their ethnic percentage of the population: No executions. That means (if the bill is passed): No executions.

Forget the blacks, who kill at about eight times the rate of whites (and, mostly, kill other blacks). Consider Japanese-Americans. They kill practically nobody. Don't ask us why; that is another inquiry—they just plain don't. That means that if (to use round figures) there are 1 million Japanese, 20 million blacks, and (not including other minorities) 200 million whites, then unless on execution date you have one Japanese convicted to death, 20 blacks, and 200 whites, you can't execute anybody. Proponents of capital punishment are going to end up having to bribe Japanese to please kill more people, to say nothing of whites.

Liberalism lives on, alas. Liberal reasoning does too, if you can call it that.

17

The Professor Doesn't Understand

AUGUST 24, 1990

T he professor writes to *The New York Times* Op-Ed page to complain. The immediate cause of this open letter to George Bush is the departure of the professor's son, age twenty-one, for Saudi Arabia. The professor bitterly resents this event, and it occurs to the reader to wonder, just to begin with, what the professor told his son when his son signed up for the Marines. If you want to avoid any chance of military combat, it is not a good idea to join the Marines. So why did he do that?

"They [the professor's son and his fellow soldiers] joined the Marines as a way of earning enough money to go to college."

It would strike most Americans that the young Marine had made a bargain, the terms of which are roughly as follows: If you, the taxpayers, via the U.S. Government, will pay the bill for my going to college, I will submit to two years in the Marines during which I will lead a most unpleasant life in various U.S. camps, rising with the dawn, marching much of the day, and submitting to military discipline. Moreover, I run the risk of being sent to a trouble spot, and even the risk of being shot at.

There doesn't seem to be much point in having a Marine Corps (or a Navy, or an Air Force, or an Army) if such forces aren't there to be used when an emergency arises.

These considerations do not affect the professor's reasoning in any apparent way. He writes: "While visiting my son I had a chance to see him pack his chemical weapons suit and try on his body armor. I don't know if you've ever had this experience, Mr. President. I hope you never will." One wonders where the professor has been. No, it isn't likely that Mr. Bush's family will need to stand by while he dons a chemical suit since, at age sixty-six, he is unlikely to be called for active duty. As for body armor, we don't know whether he wears it or not but, proportionately, as many presidents of the United States have been shot at as Marines.

And then the professor wonders whether George Bush has ever had "this experience." And again one wonders. Is the professor the only man left in the United States who is unaware that Mr. Bush was shot down in a fighter plane, having volunteered for military duty before he was drafted? And before there was a G.I. Bill? And that he flew fifty-eight missions off an aircraft carrier?

Then the professor turns to Big Think, as befits a professor. "If American diplomacy hadn't been on vacation for the better part of a decade, we wouldn't be in the spot we are in today. Where were you, Mr. President, when Iraq was killing its own people with poison gas? Why, until the recent crisis, was it business as usual with Saddam Hussein, the man you now call a Hitler?"

Doesn't it sound as though the professor is upbraiding President Bush for his record in dealing with Iraq? But Vietnam taught us, among other things, that the United States can deplore the suppression of human rights (the Reagan administration deplored the atrocities against the Kurds) without sending in the Marines.

The diplomacy under the Carter administration led to the hostage crisis that was one of the causes for ejecting Jimmy Carter from office. What is the professor trying to say, that the Marines should have been dispatched after Saddam Hussein earlier? And against the Ethiopians? And the Cambodians? And the Sudanese? And the Burmese? And the Central African Republic? And Liberia? Nigeria? Hell, China? Russia?

The professor has a hard time thinking. "You diluted gas mileage requirements for cars and dismantled federal energy policy. And now you have ordered my son to the Middle East. For what? Cheap gas?" A quietus was imposed on the crazy energy policies of President Carter because they had resulted in a) a huge increase in the price of fuel, with sacrifices amounting to hundreds of billions of dollars, including high increases in the cost of going to college; plus b) episodic scarcities of fuel that almost certainly saw the professor spending a lot of time on gas lines. To say that the president's policy toward the Mideast is designed to ensure cheap oil is on the order of saying that the American Civil Liberties Union's policies are designed to ensure cheap paper.

The professor caps his piece by quoting a young Marine, a companion of his son. "As we parted he wished us well and said, 'May God forgive us for what we are about to do.' " Sorry, professor, but this sentence, allegedly coming from a young Marine, belongs only in that department of *The New Yorker* headed "Words We Doubt Ever Got Uttered."

The professor teaches education at the University of Wisconsin in Milwaukee. When our Marines have done their duty in the Persian Gulf, I'm for sending them to Milwaukee, where, to judge from this professor, we have at least as much to worry about as from Saddam Hussein.

18

Understanding "Fairness"

JANUARY 31, 1992

The probability is high that one week after Mr. Bush's speech on the State of the Union not one voter in fifty will remember the salient parts, if it can be said that there were salient parts. It will all dissolve in partisan bifurcations, the Democrats talking about fairness, the Republicans about the need to get moving. Mr. Bush has said that if by March 20 his agenda is not enacted, he will declare war on Congress, presumably without congressional approval. If he pursues his threat, this time without the aid of 550,000 troops headed by General Schwarzkopf, there are those who would be grateful if he undertook to make certain clarifications.

On the whole matter of fairness, surely republicans and democrats (note the lower case) ought to insinuate into the public discussion the primary postulate of free economics, which is that what you earn is supposed to be yours, and that therefore what the government takes from you is an exaction. Democrats (upper case) have managed the rhetorical staging to the extent of suggesting that anything that is left to Joe Blow by the government is in the nature of a public gift, and Joe ought to be ashamed, if he is wealthy, of the money he is being given by the government.

It is increasingly difficult to hang on to capital in America, and it pays to remind ourselves that 25 percent of those who are classified as rich fall from affluence every year. It is as simple as this: The dollar earned, if it is a dividend, is first taxed to the corporation, reducing it to about 60 cents. Then it is taxed to the individual, reducing it to about 42 cents. It then reduces in value every year by the amount of that year's inflation, on average about 5 percent, reducing it to 39 cents. Then, when you die, state and federal taxes will move in to the extent of about 65 percent, reducing it to 25 cents, less the cumulative inflation.

Lord Percy of Newcastle in his famous essay declared that it is the purpose of socialist policy to render property forever insecure. He might as well have been talking about Democratic Congresses.

Now on the matter of fairness we have a wonderful illustration before us of the duplicity of Democratic thought. It is everywhere conceded that the luxury tax on boats is going to be repealed. *What!!* Repeal the tax on the item most clearly associated with conspicuous consumption, luxury boats? Why, that luxury tax is a mere 10 percent of the sum over $100,000, so that, for instance, the luxury boat that costs $300,000 under the new law is taxed a mere $20,000. Big deal.

Ah, but it transpires that the boat-buying public has dug in its heels. Buyers have canceled boat orders, citing the burden of the tax. Others have closed the door on the visiting broker or salesman. And who are up in arms in the state of Maine? Why, boat builders. They are more numerous there, per capita, than in any other state. And they, most of them unemployed, want that tax repealed and don't want any arguments on the subject. And guess who is going along on the repeal of that tax? None other than Mr. Fairness himself, George Mitchell. He is even willing to interrupt his filibuster against a reduction in the capital gains tax for just long enough to come out in favor of a repeal of the luxury tax.

But of course the reasoning of President Bush and of most economists (and of the legislatures of Japan, Germany, France, Canada, Sweden) reflects exactly what the boat builders of Maine have concluded—in the case of capital gains, extra inducements are needed in order to persuade Americans to risk their savings on entrepreneurial activity. In 1986, 600,000 companies were capitalized by Americans willing to take risks. During that decade twenty million new jobs were created.

Are we talking about fairness? Mr. Bush and his supporters should emphasize the two points, the first that governments should begin by being apologetic about the money it takes from those who have earned that money, and that it is an affront to the principle of equal treatment under the law to penalize Mary more heavily than John just because she earns more money. And second, the Republicans should stress that experience tells us every day the same thing the boat builders of Maine have learned—learning that has reached even the theretofore impenetrable mind of their senior senator—that marginal impositions act as drags on economic speed as surely as accretions on the hull of a racing boat guarantee to slow it down.

19

It Is Too Much!

MAY 12, 1992

L adies! Gentlemen! . . . Come *on* now. Come. *Please.* P-l-e-a-s-e! *Cut it out!* If we read one more article, see one more graph, hear one more sermon, view one more documentary about the Meaning of Los Angeles, we will a) resign; b) commit suicide; c) call back the Founding Fathers and tell them just try it all over again.

One feels sorry for everybody in Los Angeles—with the possible exception of the police. But one feels sorriest for the speech-writers for presidents and presidential candidates.

Over the weekend, one major newspaper presented us with a graph to indicate that the polarization between white and black income continues. I remember a very brilliant professor who once said to me, "No proposition is so simple that it can't be rendered unintelligible to me by putting it on a graph." The idea of this one was: The plight of black Americans was bad enough in 1967, when their income was first recorded separately. But look how bad it is now! One then views two lines separated by about half an inch (1967), which jiggle on up in the direction of northeast, where they are separated by about two inches (1990).

But if you stare long enough at that graph, what you discover is that in 1967, the median white earned half again as much as the median black ($8,000 over against $5,000). Now, the situation having gravely worsened, we discover that the median white income is $36,000, the median black $21,000. In other words, in 1990 the white American was earning just over half again as much as the black. Call the situation unimproved. But do not call it worsened.

The problem Bush et al. have is pretty obvious. It is that there isn't anything striking that a president can do about it, let alone a presidential candidate.

It is worth repeating the figure used with some effect by Carroll Campbell, the governor of South Carolina. Since 1965, we have spent $2.6 trillion on welfare. That's two thousand, six hundred billion dollars. Things are here and there a little better, and things are here and there a little worse.

Head Start is a good idea that, however, doesn't really need federal funding, because where it is most relevant is in states whose own resources are at parity level. Parity level is here defined as the money a state receives from Washington for special projects being about equal to the money the state sends to Washington.

California and New York and Massachusetts and Texas and Florida can't expect to get "free" money from Washington. Anything Washington spends it has to raise in taxes or else borrow. The incidence of taxation is roughly equal to the per capita income of a state. If Los Angeles needs more money for more Head Start programs, it is simply loony to suppose that President Clinton or President Bush or even President Perot is going to extrude that money.

It should be the basic axiom of American economics: In every situation except a very few (Mississippi, West Virginia), money coming in from Washington is the same money you just finished sending to Washington.

There is only one question to ask a presidential candidate that makes any sense. It is: What do you propose to do about the rate of illegitimate births? But ask that question and you are most unlikely to get any answer worth remembering. Even the most resolute Democrats are going to find it hard to campaign against Reagan and Bush on the grounds that they have greatly contributed to the rate of American bastardy.

But that rate has been booming in the past twenty years. It is the single greatest cause of a) poverty, b) illiteracy, c) crime, d) drugs, and e) unemployment. Illegitimacy among whites has risen substantially in the past twenty years, from 6 percent to 17 percent. But among blacks it has risen from 38 percent to 62 percent. Produce one illegitimate child and you contribute to all of the above: poverty, illiteracy, crime, drugs, and unemployment.

I do not have the resources, but perhaps you know some statistician who does. Ask this question: If you subtract all single-parent households from the data, how then do we fare in America? How many teenage boys brought up by married parents are unemployed? In prison? Living below the poverty line? Illiterate? On drugs?

Some, sure. But the figures would, I warrant, suggest we were living in the nearest thing to paradise on earth.

There is a law against promiscuous sex that we are not permitted to cite in the public schools because it was pronounced in the Bible, and we mustn't frighten the American Civil Liberties Union into thinking we are headed for a theocracy. We must be guided not by the Mosaic Code, but by the *Playboy* philosophy.

But to make the moral point is a bore these days. You must confine yourself to empirical points. Too many young girls are engaged in unsafe sex. There: You can say that and get away with it. Or you can say: Not enough young unmarried pregnant girls get abortions. You can say that. But presidential candidates can't say these things. Which is why they just drone on, and nobody listens.

20

His Supreme Preppiness

FEBRUARY 14, 1992

G ranted that when presidential primary season sets in, the least abnormality, or the most sensationalizable normality, becomes the focus of the procrustean imperative. But surely the treatment given to George Bush because he was surprised by something called a "bar code scanner" takes the cake.

I have specifically in mind the book critic of *The Washington Post*'s *Book World,* who wrote a column reprinted in the *International Herald Tribune* under the headline, HIS SUPREME PREPPINESS STOOPS TO DO GROCERIES. It will win any prize for the year's most fatuous venture in snobbish anti-snobbery.

To begin with, Jonathan Yardley takes off on Mr. Bush's full name (which is George Herbert Walker Bush). He is so taken by this exercise that he does it twice, calling him at one point, "George Algernon Fortesque Leffingwell Bush" and, a little later, "George Taliaferro Belmont Cabot Bush."

There are two problems with this. The first is that George Bush did not name himself, his parents did. Moreover, I see no reason for assuming that a person whose parents elected to give him/her three given names is putting on airs. Much more likely they are seeking to please multiple aunts, uncles, and in-laws. I have a sister whose first names are Mary Margaret Priscilla Langford. So? So what?

I don't know whether Mr. Yardley has more names than he customarily uses. I do know that George Bush is known as George Bush, or, when he signs documents, as George H. Bush. To read snobbery into the long form of his name suggests kindergarten training in class resentments.

Speaking of which, there is the "His Supreme Preppiness." Are we really disposed to designate all graduates of Andover as Supreme Preppies? My eyes and ears are moderately well trained and I couldn't tell a graduate of Andover from a graduate of Scarsdale High School, though as a matter of fact that isn't the case with Groton, which seems to implant in its students an accent that is pretty distinctive: Would Mr. Yardley refer to Franklin Delano Roosevelt as an obvious preppie?

But what choked up Mr. Yardley—or rather, unhappily, did not choke him up—was The Episode. George Bush went to a convention of the National Grocers Association along the campaign trail and saw, evidently for the first time, the means by which a can of tomatoes gets priced at the counter, which is by flashing its electronic fingerprint below a beam of light that relays the information to the cash register and to a computer that tallies the diminished supply of cans of tomatoes.

George Herbert Walker Bush expressed a quite elated surprise over this technological accomplishment. Mr. Jonathan Can-it-be-true? Strike-me-dead-if-it-is! Yardley is so indignant he cannot, verily, stand it.

"The man who runs the United States of America confessed, however indirectly, that he's so out of touch with the daily lives of his constituents, he doesn't even know how they go about buying the food they put on their tables." George Bush "comes from and is utterly a part of a world in which the supermarket is where the servants go."

That is the statement of a true populist snob. Just to begin with, does anyone suspect that FDR did his own shopping? Or Averell Harriman? Or Nelson Rockefeller? Or Andrew Carnegie? Or, for that matter, John Fitzgerald Kennedy, who never even bothered to keep money in his pocket, because there was always someone there to pay for it; besides which, he most often got it free? Yet these gentlemen are securely situated in history as true advocates of the people. If there was a populist breeze in the air, Nelson Rockefeller would rustle.

What is the point in putting on airs, pretending to do what in fact one doesn't (for whatever reason) incline to do? Herbert Hoover, that austere intellectual, used to play Canasta four hours every Sunday. So? So he liked to play Canasta four hours every

Sunday. I have never seen a professional baseball game, an episode of *Dallas,* or of *Roseanne,* or of *Geraldo,* or of the black lady who is alternately fat and thin, I forget her name.

So? So I waste my time and take my pleasures in other ways. Does that make me ignorant of human anxieties, problems, vexations? Such a person as George Bush "should not be relied upon to have an especially acute sense of what life is like for someone squirreling away $50 a month under the illusion that this will pay for his child's college education or his family's protection against catastrophic illness." What c-r-a-p.

The biggest bleeding heart in Great Britain is the Prince of Wales, and if he ever entered a grocery store, it was given to him under a Christmas tree. By the criteria of Mr. Yardley, Edward Gibbon shouldn't have written about Rome, so removed was he from Roman life. After all, he was born 1,300 years after Rome fell.

TWO

ANALYZING

1 THE GREAT GORBACHEV YEARS

—1985: GORBACHEV COMES IN
JANUARY 12, 1985

They say about the typical corporation's annual report that it is to be compared with a girl's bikini in that it reveals enough to maintain interest, while concealing all the vital details. The chestnut applied to the initial joint declaration of Shultz-Gromyko in Geneva, Switzerland, in January, just before the ascendancy of Gorbachev.

There was in it only one item of special interest—special interest to those who fight a losing war against the suffocating coils of modern clichés. In this case, it was the indiscriminate use of the term "arms race."

The first psychological objective of the Soviet government is to brand our strategic defense initiative as aggressive in intent. Mind you, it is exactly that in Bolshevik dialectic. A counterrevolutionary, Lenin taught, is an aggressor against forces that will ultimately prove to be ineluctable, but whose consummation is indeed hampered by obstructionists.

By such reasoning, a high frontier against atomic missiles is an act of aggression. Indeed, by such reasoning a shield is an act of aggression against an arrow, and a roof is an act of aggression against rain and cold.

It isn't difficult to understand Soviet terminology, even as a psychiatrist can without great exertion familiarize himself with the systematic perversions of a patient convinced that grasshoppers roost all over him, or that the world is flat, or that only Democrats are compassionate. But what does disturb is the willingness of normal people to incorporate into their own vocabulary the distorted terminology of the Soviet Union.

George Shultz could, without giving offense, quite simply insist in his dealings with the new Gorbachev regime that "arms race" be limited to a discussion of weapons designed to kill people, as distinguished from weapons designed to keep people from being killed. That really is not too complicated to manage. Or, put another way: If that is too complicated to manage, then we have little reason to be hopeful about the complications that attend the only kind of arms reduction treaty to which we should be willing to conform.

Secretary Shultz, if spot reporting is accurate, sought to evade the subject by reminding the Soviet bargainers that, after all, in respect of Star Wars we are at this point engaged only in research. To this one doesn't know exactly what Gromyko responded, but in all probability he insisted on distinguishing between research and testing. And, in a way, he has logic on his side. Do you call it research or do you call it testing when last year we succeeded in having Missile A, launched from one position, accost Missile B, launched from another position, and knock Missile B to smithereens? Research without testing really leaves you only with scientific problematics. Alamogordo was necessary, before we could know we actually had an atomic bomb.

The basis of President Reagan's strategic defense initiative is the assumption that if we succeed in the technology we seek, one anti-missile missile can cope with or neutralize more than one missile. If that is the case, then unless the Soviet Union were to increase its missile arsenal by a factor many times greater than the shield we succeeded in building, the United States would, little by little, become progressively safer.

Now efforts along those lines are simply not properly termed an "arms" race. Add to the point that the United States has indicated that on arrival at a certain point of efficacy we would be willing to share with the Soviet Union the fruits of our research, and the Soviet argument that we are engaged in an "arms race" pretty well evaporates. True, in order to develop the technology required to knock out an incoming strategic missile, we necessarily pass by way stations that threaten what the Soviet Union calls its defensive capability. We would be able to knock out the satellites they use to observe what is going on in Montana and Wyoming.

But the pursuit of anti-satellite technology is something the Soviet Union is engaged in at this very moment, and unless the

Soviet Union suddenly renounced its traditional opposition to on-site inspection, we would appear to have no alternative than to pursue the technological objective of being able to knock down anything in the space above that might conceivably threaten the lives of Americans.

So let us get on with it: No more reference to arms races if the reference is to detoxify the space above us. As well, call the search for a cancer killer a killer search.

—1988: So Long, Evil Empire?
June 2, 1988

At twenty-seven, he was an agricultural economist with Moscow's Institute of Economics and a university lecturer. But Josef Stalin looked kindly on him during the Great Purge, and instead of shooting or exiling him, trained him as chief of the U.S. division of the People's Commissariat of Foreign Affairs. From there he went as counselor to the Soviet Embassy in Washington, becoming ambassador in 1943. In 1946 he went to the United Nations Security Council and established the Soviet tradition of vetoing any moves designed to promote peace with freedom. In 1946 he became deputy foreign minister. And Stalin's approval of him made him a candidate for the Central Committee of the Communist Party. He became first deputy foreign minister in 1949 and foreign minister in 1957. He was directly involved in the diplomatic and military action against the students in Budapest, serving under Nikita Khrushchev. Under Leonid Brezhnev, he presided over the great purge of the Prague Spring in Czechoslovakia in 1968.

Andrei Andreyevich Gromyko is now the president of the Soviet Union, and was the first person to greet President Ronald Reagan as he descended from Air Force One at Vnukovo Airport on Sunday.

The itinerary of Mr. Reagan might have been conceived by the Brothers Grimm. No fairy tale could have made the trip more regally satisfying. The rich decor was courtesy of dead czars, the last one executed by someone in honor of whom a Russian city is named. The grand paintings and decorations were done by European and Russian masters of the eighteenth and nineteenth centuries. The children were trained to sing American folk songs in English. And beginning with Gorbachev himself, the Russian court was choreographed to sing, if every now and then with a touch of diffidence, the praises of peace and coexistence. Ronald Reagan lectured to the intellectuals about an obscure episode in an obscure Russian novel and received a standing ovation. It was a dream, it was nirvana, it was—mind-blowing.

There was that one terribly sour note, sounded day after day. Every time Mr. Reagan looked especially pleased, especially satisfied, especially carried away by the *Gemütlichkeit* of it all, you would hear a voice. Not a Russian's voice, but a good, twangy American voice, and always that voice would ask the same question:

"Is this what you called the evil empire, Mr. President?"

"What was that about the evil empire, Mr. President?"

"Tell us about the evil empire, Mr. President."

Finally, worn down by this hectoring over his melodramatic excess of years gone by, Mr. Reagan said, "I was talking about another empire."

We sinners believe because we were taught to believe, and do give internal assent to, the mandate to forgive seventy times seven times. But Mr. Reagan is engaged now not in forgiveness, but in what George Orwell called vaporization. Big Brother decides to change a historical or a present fact, and evidence inconveniencing to the new thesis is simply made to—disappear.

Run the fingers lightly over the globe, pausing to stop at outposts of the Soviet empire. In Nicaragua, using Soviet arms, they are promoting war and aggression and drafting seventeen-year-olds while suffering a 60 percent cut in their standard of living.

In Cuba, where people continue to die in the effort to flee from it, there is dire poverty and the most aggressive conventional armed force in the Western Hemisphere, paid for by the Soviet Union.

In Bulgaria, the dictator Todor Zhivkov reigns. Several years ago he sent a secret agent to inject poison into the veins of a Bulgarian refugee poet as he was promenading over Waterloo Bridge in London.

In Poland, General Wojciech Jaruzelski, proconsul for Gorbachev, hacks down those who fight for a free labor union movement.

In Ethiopia, starvation is imminent for two million people at the hands of a dictator shored up by the Soviet Union.

In Southeast Asia, dire poverty and huge supplies of weapons keep the North Vietnamese in charge of the human misery brought on by Soviet-backed aggression.

Mr. Reagan does well to encourage changes in the Soviet system. Something wildly exciting is indeed going on in the Soviet system. But to greet it as if it were no longer evil is on the order of changing our entire position toward Adolf Hitler on receiving the news that he had abolished one extermination camp. The Soviet Union has a very long way to go before it brings reasonable freedom to those who live under it. But we sow only confusion when we retract the statement that it is evil to support the systematic suppression of human rights everywhere your empire reaches. Gorbachev may be the spokesman for what is being attempted within the Soviet empire, but Gromyko continues as president of what continues to be an evil empire.

—1989: EXITING AFGHANISTAN

FEBRUARY 9, 1989

Everyone who has reached the second week in a semester on political philosophy is introduced to Machiavelli's maxim that one must not cut off the enemy's line of retreat, and these days we need to repeat that maxim to ourselves at least ten times per hour, because if we do so only nine times, some of us would be greatly tempted to wish the mujahideen all the luck in the world in doing exactly that, cutting off the line of retreat and capturing or otherwise disposing of the friendly Russian army that during the past nine years has presided over the murder of 1.2 million Afghans.

Comparable figures are illuminating. The (prewar) population of Afghanistan being about 16 million, the death of 1.2 million is the equivalent of about 18 million Americans dead. If an army were retreating from the United States having spent nine years attempting to conquer the country and killing 18 million people in the effort, one shouldn't be surprised if in its retreat the enemy army experienced signs of American displeasure. But such has been the pictorial focus on what is happening that the headlines and color stories tend to feature the retreating Soviet soldiers as noblemen going home, and the mujahideen as wild men bent on barbaric atrocities.

This has reached the point where we are supposed to read, if not contentedly, then philosophically, about Soviet bombing of escape routes and land mines placed in the way of potential harassment. And this morning's news informs us that General Boris Gromov, the commander of the last Soviet battalion scheduled to leave Afghanistan, has determined to be the very last man to step foot on Soviet soil. The Associated Press reports that General Gromov will step onto the "friendship bridge" leading to the Soviet border post of Termez at 10 A.M. local time on the last day. And from a Soviet newspaper: "He will cross, without looking back. Then he will stand and make a speech—just for himself. It will last one minute, seven seconds. The speech will neither be written, nor will it be heard."

We should all be in favor of short speeches. But if we're going to set up Attican theatrical backgrounds to commemorate the moment of the Soviet departure from Afghanistan, why doesn't General Gromov use up his one minute and seven seconds to fire a bullet into his head? That, or sky-dive into the nearest monastery to devote his life to repentance.

The diplomatic world is surcharged with complexities even to the point of shielding us from the knowledge of what the enemy is up to. Messrs. Evans and Novak recently reported most plausibly that the plane that brought down in flames Pakistan leader Zia was sabotaged by—sophisticated Soviet chemical explosives. But any effort to pursue an investigation of that question was blocked. By the Soviets? No no no, you don't understand. By the United States. Why expose Soviet perfidy when détente is at an exhilarating boil?

Several years ago the evidence was overwhelming that a Bulgarian-sponsored terrorist under the supervision of the KGB was commissioned to go to Rome to kill the pope. Suddenly the story . . . well, sort of evaporated. It became the consensus of our leaders that not much was to be gained from flatly pinning on the

Kremlin the responsibility for trying to kill the Vicar of Christ on earth. There are still some Christians on earth who might, well, resent that. In 1963, as soon as it became known that Lee Harvey Oswald was a sure-enough communist who had spent over a year in the Soviet Union, the connection between him and the Kremlin became, well, progressively attenuated. And it wasn't until much later that it leaked out that he had been spotted visiting the Cuban Embassy in Mexico a couple of weeks before the assassination. If the American people had been told that Oswald killed their hero Mr. Kennedy on orders from Castro, they might have demanded war on Castro.

Machiavelli's line of retreat, in the broad scene, means the retreat of the whole communist enterprise from its pristine mandate to go out and conquer the world. Accordingly, we stuff our vision with great bales of diplomatic perspective, and now we have just about reached the point where we are all expected to celebrate the nobility of the Soviet Union in pulling out of Afghanistan.

But the mujahideen are not going to cooperate with us, any more than the Russians cooperated with Napoleon when he decided to retreat from Moscow in 1812. General Kutuzov was not going to let the French off quite so easily. He had a wonderfully cold winter working for him, and about as many snipers as there are dead Afghan freedom fighters. The myth of Napoleon suffered mortal wounds. It required three more years to put him away permanently, but the resolve to do so was annealed. This time, they'll probably award Gorbachev not a lifetime on St. Helena, but a Nobel Peace Prize. Machiavelli can be taken too far.

—1989: GORBACHEV MEETS THE POPE

DECEMBER 5, 1989

The big event last weekend took place in Rome, when Mikhail Gorbachev met with the pope. What happened at Malta nobody really seems to know; indeed it's possible that nothing happened at Malta. Most dispatches spoke of the happy "chemistry" between their leader and our leader, which was a relief from discussing chemical weapons—the heavy inventories of which were a subject the president raised, apparently to no effect. His point is that we would be willing to destroy all of our chemical weapons except for 2 percent of our existing stock if the Soviet Union would take comparable measures. So far as we can gather, this elicited from Mr. Gorbachev only a vague nod of the head.

That was an improvement over what we got from him on the subject of Central America. The Sandinistas' Daniel Ortega has the worst timing in the history of totalitarianism. He visited Moscow at just the wrong time. He visited North Korea at just the wrong time. And now he dispatches the most modern anti-aircraft weapons ever manufactured by Russia, ships them to El Salvador to the rebels, and the damned plane comes crashing down. All the television cameras view the anti-aircraft weapons, exposed like the Rockettes—to end once and for all the argument over whether Nicaragua is helping the neighboring rebels in El Salvador. Answer, yes.

But whose weapons were they? Well, Nicaragua is having a hard time manufacturing tamales these days, let alone anti-aircraft worth more than Picassos; so everybody knows the stuff came in from Moscow, possibly through Cuba. But there is Gorbachev, the wholesome man in the gray flannel suit, looking George Bush in the eyes and saying the stuff did not come from the Soviet Union.

Now on the whole, I think it prudent to humor Gorbachev for a while. After all, it was only two years ago, commemorating the seventieth anniversary of the Bolshevik Revolution, that he declaimed: "In October 1917, we parted with the old world, rejecting it once and for all. We are moving toward a new world, the world of communism. We shall never turn off that road." Ho-ho-ho.

But of course Bush must not taunt him. And when Gorbachev says that just as he is going to try to stop exporting his way of life, we should stop trying to export *our* way of life, which includes everything from the Bill of Rights to Disneyland, Bush would be wrong to look up, smile, and say, "Are you sure you don't want a little of our way of life? Like maybe some soap and some toilet paper?" No no, let him have his pride. It could be worth billions to us, if it works out down the road. After all, if it had worked out the first year Gorbachev was in office instead of the fourth year, 600,000 dead Afghans would be alive, so don't provoke him.

On the other hand, one can't be completely idle when his lieutenants get out of hand. On *60 Minutes* last Sunday, Mike Wallace had a taped interview with Gennadi Gerasimov, the chief press spokesman for the Soviets. Mr. Wallace asked how might the communists explain the drastic reversal in communist policy betokened by the visit to the pope. We got from Gerasimov (Ready? Sit down; maybe a glass of water): Well, said G., it's true that communism is evolving. "But so is Christianity. After all, there are very few differences between communism and the early church." Very few differences, just the Ten Commandments.

The Gerasimovs should be beheaded in any public exchange, all those lying blackguards who served so willingly the kind of regime favored by the Stalins and Hitlers of our time. But let Gorbachev be, even as we let the emperor of Japan slide by without asking him any searching questions such as, Where were you on Pearl Harbor Day? The chief of state must be our instrument, and to make that possible, his dignity must be preserved—for as long as he makes this possible.

On this, Gorbachev has yet to deliver. There is no Bill of Rights in the Soviet Union, and his destructive arsenal is pretty well intact. But he has made major, irreversible concessions, foremost among them his statement to the pope that from now on the Soviet Union will honor the freedom of conscience. This is being said about a country that forbade the publication of the Bible.

In 1970, visiting Zagorsk, the central Russian Orthodox seminary and surveying the tatterdemalion remnants of the old Russian priesthood, I commented that to hope that the hundred-odd priests permitted to survive could save the Soviet Union for Christianity was like eyedropping holy water into hell. And now we learn that a full 50 percent of those who have lived behind the Iron Curtain profess themselves as Christians. Indeed, the gates of hell have not prevailed against us.

—1989: HALLELUJAH!

NOVEMBER 10, 1989

When the news came in, President Bush sat quietly in his large chair in the Oval Office and said in grave tones that we must not overreact. He is absolutely right about this. *Jingle bells! Jingle bells! Jingle all the wayyyy!* It is proper to deem it a historical development, but its significance must not affect our judgment. *Oh what a beautiful morn-ing! Oh what a beau-ti-ful day!!!* After all, there is tomorrow to think about in Germany. *Germany?!?! What do you mean, 'Germany'? You mean West Germany or you mean East Germany?* and the score allows for many variations. Calmness is in order.

I remember the day in 1973 when as a delegate to the General Assembly of the United Nations, occupying the chair, I had to sit there and listen to the ambassador from the German Democratic Republic lecturing to the Third Committee (Human Rights Committee) on the differences between life in his own country, where the pastures of the people were evergreen and life pleasant, and just, and equable, in contrast to life "elsewhere" in Europe, dominated by strife and competition and all the vexations of bourgeois life. I interrupted the speaker to make some reference or other to the Wall that obscured the view of the communists' green pastures, but all the professional diplomats of course knew all about the Wall and about communist rhetoric—I learned early during my brief service in the United Nations that the thing to remember is that nobody pays any attention whatever to anything anybody says in the United Nations, which is one up for sanity. But the insolence of the East German diplomat stayed with me, as a freshman diplomat, who never graduated.

And so I wrote a book about the United Nations that fall, and made reference to the special hypocrisies of totalitarian states which, instead of isolating in such secrecy as is possible what goes on there, actually go about the world boasting about their civil depravity. But the Wall and what it represented stuck in the mind, as it did with so many people—the antipodes of the Statue of Liberty; the great symbol of gulag life—and a few years later I wrote a novel based on a young idealist's determination in 1952 to attempt to reunite Germany, a political effort finally frustrated by an assassination of the young, upward-bound idealist. By the GPU? No, by my hero, Blackford Oakes, under orders from Washington, because Stalin had said the alternative was a Third World War. I dramatized that novel (*Stained Glass*) and in March of this year, on Good Friday, it was splendidly produced by the Actors Theater in Louisville, Kentucky.

Still the ugliness of divided Germany hadn't left me, and in 1978 I went to Berlin actually to look. It is hard to describe the impacted loathsomeness of it. Every season, the communists added one more obstacle to stand in the way of the occasional Houdini who got through. That was the winter they added the dogs. It had begun with a concrete wall. Then barbed wire. Then watchtowers with machine gunners. Then huge spotlights. Then land mines. Then mountains of sharded glass. It is a comment on the limited resources of the communist imagination that they forgot to plant poison ivy alongside the Wall.

And so I wrote a novel based on another young German idealist, determined to prevent the construction of the Wall when on August 13, 1961, all of a sudden it began to materialize. My young German, who as a Jewish child had been spirited to England for safety, leaving his parents to die in a Nazi camp, had his contact in East Berlin, a secretary to the monster Ulbricht, predecessor to Honecker. And the word was that if three NATO tanks charged through the Wall that first day during its flimsy stage, the East Germans, backed by the Russians, would make a great show of opposition, but actually they would yield, as Khrushchev did not want a showdown with the West—not in August 1961, a full year before the missile crisis in Cuba. But the U.S. military, under orders, seized the little column of tanks that had been secretly pulled out from the U.S. armory by young, trained resistance Germans—and so we never knew what would have happened if we had asserted our rights to co-governing East Berlin. My young German hero, Henri Tod, did not live to see the sun set on the growing wall.

It was a great day, November 9, 1989, and one day must be nominated for international celebration. *Joshua fit the battle of Jericho, Jericho, Jericho! Joshua fit the battle of Jericho! And the wall came tumblin' down!*

—1992: THE SOVIET UNION IS DEAD

JANUARY 9, 1992

Mikhail Gorbachev took the time—on the day he resigned his office and, so to speak, officially declared the U.S.S.R. dead—to write a personal letter to Ronald Reagan. It is worth paying special attention to the words he used.

To begin with, the whole exchange has a certain piquancy. Consider: Ronald Reagan was the leader of the antagonistic world into which Gorbachev was born, and of which he took charge in 1985. Reagan is the man who ordered tactical nuclear missiles to be deployed in Europe, stripping the Soviet military of any possibility of nuclear blackmail. It was Reagan who by calling for a Star Wars defense augured the end of any possibility of a successful first strike. And, not least, it was Reagan who designated the world over which Gorbachev was called to preside as "the evil empire."

To write a friendly letter to the man whose policies enhanced the forces of dissolution at work within the Soviet Union is extraordinary to begin with. To do so on the day that all Gorbachev's remaining dreams were extinguished—the survival of the Union of Soviet Socialist Republics, however reformed, and the universal rejection of that socialism to which Gorbachev continues to cling —is on the order of exhibiting a Stockholm syndrome, writing pleasantly to one's captor. But now listen to what he said:

"These days I keep thinking of what has been accomplished over the past years. They have been filled with a stream of events, some no small achievements, and tough trials. All has not worked out as one would have wanted. And yet I hope that the historical process will put everything into proper perspective."

We have here a burst of fatalism, but also ("the historical process will put everything into proper perspective") a touch of the determinist to the end. Perhaps Lenin was wrong only in suggesting that the iron laws of history would bring communism in the twentieth century—perhaps it will need to be a dream, fulfilled sometime (this is not clear) in the future.

"It fell on you and I to make the first and perhaps the most difficult steps on this path [to unity]," Gorbachev wrote.

The Kremlin had obviously removed from Gorbachev knowledgeable English translators. But here the historical determinist steps into human shoes, and says that the path toward the end of the Cold War was pioneered by himself—and by Ronald Reagan. He seems to be saying that there were qualities unique in both of them that made it possible to synchronize their efforts.

"I recall our meetings in Geneva, Reykjavik, Moscow, California. I remember the emergence, first of mutual understanding, and then of friendly feelings, and I remember how the ice of mistrust in the relations between our countries was broken. . . . In my future activities I intend to be instrumental in ensuring that what you and I started together is not lost, but has a worthy continuation. Raisa Maximovna and I are sending our warmest greetings and sincere wishes of all the best to Nancy. Chances are we will meet again in the future. We would be very pleased if that were to happen."

Here Mikhail Gorbachev lapses almost totally into the idiom of Amy Vanderbilt etiquette, but note the continued insistence here on the personalities that effected the important changes. In America, enemies of Ronald Reagan were busy saying that he uniquely could never understand the Soviet Union because he was too inflexible in his habits. That criticism of Reagan was left-ideological.

And Gorbachev does not give time to his own critics, who point out that he wasted three precious years by attempting to maintain socialism in the Soviet Union, and also imperial control over the republics. He is saying, simply: You and I were primarily responsible. He is exactly correct.

Reagan's reply was characteristically generous and warm: "You have our greatest respect and admiration for the dignity and grace you have demonstrated during these obviously trying times." And the invitation to come over and visit was characteristically Californian, concluding, "and, if your schedule permits, we would enjoy the opportunity to take you to the Reagan Presidential Library which chronicles many of the historic steps we walked together."

On the role of Gorbachev, Peter Rodman, senior editor at *National Review,* is most eloquent:

"Mikhail Gorbachev will go down in history as the man who

destroyed the Soviet system, by mistake. He refrained from systematic resort to brutality of the past. On this point he stood his moral ground, and for that in a perverse way he may even have deserved the Nobel Peace Prize he has received. Only in a Soviet leader, however, can it be considered an exemplary act to refrain from murdering one's own people."

Still, he did not, and he emerged a personal friend of Ronald Reagan.

2 THE ACADEMIC SCENE

—HANOVER BLUES

FEBRUARY 27, 1986

I t is nothing short of astonishing that events at Dartmouth College continue to crowd the news: ABC, CBS, NBC, three syndicated columnists, countless editorials. One junior wrote elegantly to the student daily: "Having left the Hanover plain for the sunny beaches of Florida last August, I returned in 1986 with a heightened sense of perspective. You see, it was my first term off in over a year, and when one has been here that long, one tends to nonchalantly accept the various campus events and debates as—if you'll excuse my use of a much abused word—normal. It took four months on the 'outside' and countless conversations with interested Floridians (who had the benefit of a disinterested and somewhat cosmopolitan view) for me to discover that Dartmouth is the repository of a unique perspective."

Hooray for whoever taught that student how to write English, but the current furor makes the study of English seem, somehow, effete—no, that is a bad word, because, as with their Indian mascot, Dartmouth will come up with a lobby, in this case the gay lobby, to denounce you as a homophobe. The president of Dartmouth, Mr. David T. McLaughlin, reintroduced ROTC, which was one of the totemic victims of the student madness of the Vietnam years, and finds for his pains he is all but asked, by faculty resolution, to resign.

The college president leaves town on January 20, and lo, he returns to find his office occupied by protesting students, many of them black. They want to know what in the hell the president was doing off campus on Martin Luther King's birthday. Most people don't remember where they were on Easter Sunday, let alone Martin Luther King's birthday, but the poor president had to plead that he was talking in Florida about Dr. King. Not enough. The students wanted, and got, a school holiday so that everyone could chin about race relations and the accomplishments of Dr. King.

Now McLaughlin faces the most severe challenge to his moral authority. A lynch mob, which calls itself the Committee on Standing, met to try twelve students who, after weeks of frustration over an exhibitionistic protest against apartheid—the protesters had created on the campus green, and maintained there, several shanties designed to promote the cause of divestment—organized one night to tear the damned things down. This was done without anybody's being threatened, let alone hurt, never mind the caterwauling of two girls sleeping in the shanties who chose under no provocation to act hysterically. Among the judges of the students was a former editor of the college newspaper that had called for the students' expulsion. Another "judge," a faculty member, had publicly referred to the twelve as evil. An assistant dean had referred to the defendants as "heartless, chicken-shit people." The *New York Post* editorial writer recalls the disequilibrium of the Dartmouth faculty. "After the 1980 presidential election, the same faculty voted overwhelmingly to condemn Ronald Reagan's landslide victory. It reminded the historians among them of the election of Adolf Hitler."

Four of the students were, in effect, expelled; eight were suspended.

I have forever and beyond believed that schools should make and execute their own rules. But if those students are dismissed, notwithstanding that no action was taken against the illegal shanty construction team, none against the students who had occupied the president's office—the record of Dartmouth's permissiveness in dealing with left-oriented protests is massive—then Dartmouth's president forever loses, and should lose, the respect of the millions of non-Hanoverians who have somehow got engaged in what is going on there.

What's going on at Dartmouth is a kind of solipsistic crystallization of ideological interest groups whose cause militant, a few years ago, was the elimination of the Indian, which for generations was Dartmouth College's symbol, implying ethnic prejudice against Indians only to the extent that Yale graduates could be accused of a contempt for bulldogs. Their causes proliferated—gay rights, apartheid, peacenikery, you name it—and there arose —a sign of health—a student newspaper that, although now and again more hot-blooded than the kind of thing you'd have expected from the Founding Fathers meeting in Philadelphia, has nevertheless been a robust and bright attempt to restore balance. The students who tore down the shanties were mostly associated with that paper, the clearly intended victim of the vindictive petulance of the Committee on Standing. The president is on the spot. He should try amnesty, and a fresh start for Dartmouth College.

—THE GREAT PURGE
MARCH 15, 1988

A group that actually calls itself the Committee on Standing has recommended that one senior and one junior at Dartmouth (John Sutter and Christopher Baldwin) be suspended from college for a year and a half. Two other students were given lesser penalties. There is (as always) an avenue for appeal. But the judge who decides the question whether to hear an appeal is a pronounced partisan, a hostile critic of *The Dartmouth Review,* of which Baldwin and Sutter are the principal figures.

To grant an appeal, let alone a diminution of the sentence, would require Dean of Students Edward Shanahan to exhibit qualities he has not so far shown in the explosive disruption at Dartmouth involving Professor William Cole. And it seems absolutely clear that the new president of Dartmouth, Mr. James Freedman, wishes above all things in life to appease the college's Afro-American Society, which has engaged in the kind of activity against Sutter and Baldwin that reflects the manners of the Ku Klux Klan, from which the students' forebears may well have suffered.

The Dartmouth Review's editors were charged with disorderly conduct, harassment, and violation of privacy at the expense of Mr. Cole, a professor of music. The background of the incident was the publication in *The Dartmouth Review* of an astonishing transcript of the kind of thing that evidently passes for music education at Dartmouth. Professor Cole, the tape recorder revealed, sounded as though he were strung out on dope, reciting a disjointed soliloquy on the subject of poverty, racism, and the kitchen stove, peppered by the language of the streets, as one would most charitably call it. The *Dartmouth Review*'s publication of this specimen of Dartmouth education would be hailed as robust investigative journalism in most circumstances. But Professor Cole is black.

The *Dartmouth Review* editors reported the furor caused by their publication to the newspaper's lawyer in Washington, who counseled them to go to Professor Cole and to advise him that the *Review* would publish any comments Cole had to make about the exposé. It was the meeting between the four editors and Cole that brought on the formal charges. That meeting lasted just under four minutes. A transcript of what was said exists. It took place in the classroom of Professor Cole just after he had dismissed his students, a dozen of whom, on their way out, saw and overheard the exchange. Baldwin and Sutter a) attempted to press upon Cole a letter communicating the *Review*'s willingness to publish Cole's comments; and b) asked Cole to apologize for references to *The Dartmouth Review* as racist in language that would have embarrassed the late Lenny Bruce.

Cole a) declined to read the letter, b) ordered the editors out of the classroom, c) lunged at and broke the flashbulb attachment to the camera of the student photographer, and d) protested violently the machine that recorded the exchange.

A few days later, the Afro-American Society mobilized a rally. This was done by exhibiting a huge poster on which was written: "WE'VE GOT TO GET RID OF ALL YOU INCOMPETENT NIGGERS"— JOHN SUTTER, EXECUTIVE EDITOR, DARTMOUTH REVIEW. Sutter denies ever having mouthed (or thought) those words. One black girl student testified that the words were spoken, and a second black girl tentatively affirmed this. But if the statement had been made when and where it was allegedly made, a dozen people would have heard it, and none of them testified to having done so.

The rally having been organized, it was addressed by President Freedman, who, although he made a pass at neutrality pending the investigation by the Committee on Standing, clearly identified himself with the protesters and helped to whip up a kind of Jacobinical rage against the editors that, a week later, flowered in the extraordinary penalties levied. To tell a college senior to go away for a year and a half is to tell him to interrupt and conceivably even to abort his career.

What is going on at Dartmouth is in embryo what we saw happening at the early stages of the great debauches of the sixties. And the most direct cause of it is the disorderly fixation of faculty and administration on the notion that if a teacher or student is black, he can do pretty well anything he likes. At the student rally, a demand was even made that Professor Cole be supported. President Freedman proceeded to do everything short of anointing him. There may be obscure aspects of the controversy, but there cannot be two sides to the question of Professor Cole's behavior. His deportment, whether judged academically or socially, was indefensible. To appease Cole by suspending the students who exposed him is a perversion that will do to Dartmouth what that bloodstain did to Lady Macbeth.

Passion Among Intergroons

March 26, 1987

If one were to ask, What are the young people who run the *Yale Daily News* majoring in? the answer would surely be, Toleration. So engrossed are they in the subject that probably they would not answer the question, What subject is your minor? because the word "minor" comes too close to the word "minority," and those who major in Toleration can't run any risk of suggesting that there is anything minor about minorities.

The purpose of the endless drive toward equality ought to be a relaxed sense of security. But the seizure of equalitarianism has exactly the opposite effect, guaranteeing perpetual insecurity. One thinks of women at Yale University, for example, as pretty secure provided they do not insist on using men's urinals, but they are being so frequently reminded of their insecurity that they become convinced of it.

A recent communication from the editor in chief of the *Yale Daily News* (H. Andrew Romanoff signs himself "Andrew," as his imperial Russian ancestors might have done) is addressed to former editors of the *Yale Daily News,* in which he details "several projects" in which his board is engaged. He comes to the board's major:

"At the same time, though, we recognize certain problems the *News* has had. Foremost among them is the threat of prejudice. To eliminate any discrimination in our paper or in our staff, we created a special panel, initiated discussions and scheduled meetings with the leaders of different campus cultural groups—The Asian American Student Association, The Black Student Alliance at Yale, Despierta Boricua [a Puerto Rican group] and the Movimiento Estudiantil Chicano de Aztlan [a Mexican-American group]. We plan to meet soon with the Gay/Lesbian Co-op. I was glad to see that through frank dialogue we were able to address some of the concerns. We will maintain an unswerving dedication to fairness, and will do everything in my power to insure that these efforts continue."

Thirty years ago Randall Jarrell published a novel, *Pictures from an Institution,* designed to make people laugh. Here is a sentence from the narrator about Benton College, whose trendy egalitarianism of 1954 is the meaty orthodoxy of the *Yale Daily News* in 1987.

"And there were what I [the narrator] used to call to myself token students: black students, brown students, yellow students, students who were believers of the major creeds of Earth—one or two of each. If there is in Tierra del Fuego a family of fire-worshippers with a daughter of marriageable age, and a couple of thousand dollars a year to spare, they can educate her at Benton."

One would think that a single sentence published every now and then in the *Yale Daily News* would suffice. It would say: "Membership in the editorial or business boards of the *Yale Daily News* is achieved by merit in competitions in which gender or race plays no role." What is it that the editor of the *News* talks about when visiting members of the Movimiento Estudiantil Chicano de Aztlan? A pledge that the *News* will come out in favor of bilingual education? What is there to say to the gays—that no competitor will be subjected to a Rorschach test? What is there to say to the women's groups?

Ah, plenty. Andrew and his ministers have drawn up imperial decrees on the matter, field trips in toleration.

"We are committed to eliminating sexism. Through a process of discussion and investigation, we are trying to examine sexual discrimination and end it. Last month, the editorial board voted to change its policy on gender differentiation: we now refer to female first-year students as 'freshwomen' and to mixed-sex groups and individuals of unknown sex as 'freshpeople' (singular, 'freshperson')."

Ah, what the late Randall Jarrell would have done with that. The president of Benton College was oh so tolerant that he "yearned for men to be discovered on the moon, so that he could prove that he was not prejudiced against moon-men." Andrew Romanoff would go Jarrell one better, by insisting that he was not prejudiced against moon-persons.

It is disappointing that in a college that attracts major talent, the ideology of egalitarianism should, even among aspirant writers, have such a deadening effect on the ear. I predict the revolt will one day come (as surely it must come) not from the cloddish ideologues of the male sex, but from the women. "Don't you call me a freshwoman to my face," a freshwoman will freshly say to a tone-deaf freshperson, and the bells will ring, and personkind will cheer.

—The Indian at Dartmouth

October 18, 1988

It must be hell at Dartmouth College if you are a member of the faculty or the administration—or, for that matter, a student—and your inclinations are just, well, normal. You might be a political Democrat while questioning, along with the late Hubert Humphrey, the use of civil rights bills in order to discriminate against qualified white students seeking admission. You might be a graduate who is perfectly capable of looking at a facsimile of an Indian warrior without saying to himself, teeth gritted, "The only good Injun is a dead Injun!" The only tolerable conclusion the outsider can reach about Dartmouth these days is that it is being run by ideological loonies.

The big case last winter involved the four students who were given the American equivalent of ten years in gulag for ventilating their resentment of a professor of music who spends most of his time in scatological ruminations deploring racism in general (he is black). The four students published a verbatim transcript of the professor's lucubrations, requested that he reply, and before they knew it, two of them were suspended for eighteen months on grounds of "vexatious oral exchange." President James Freedman of Dartmouth launched the one-hundredth attack on the student conservative newspaper, which sits there in Hanover like Fort Douaumont in the First World War, apparently impregnable and a symbol of the viability of the resistance. The people of *60 Minutes* have been at Hanover, N.H., recently, and in the next month viewers will see an account of the nine lives of *The Dartmouth Review* up against the massive forces of the administration and faculty.

But given this background, what happened in the first week in October is breath-catching in its stupidity. It is as if in the middle of a televised debate, George Bush were to turn to Michael Dukakis and say, "You know why I can't stand you, Mike? It's because you're a dirty little Greek immigrant." If that were to happen, Mike Dukakis would become the next President of the United States with the votes of every non-Turk in America, including this columnist.

What Dartmouth did was to celebrate the fifteenth anniversary of coeducation. And the principal speaker was: Mother Bloor? Krupskaya? Mrs. Stalin? . . . No—Angela Davis, the best-known female communist in the United States. She was, during the turbulent seventies, among the Ten Most Wanted fugitives on the FBI list. She was apprehended and tried for complicity in murder, and a mouthpiece got her off. She went from trial to the Soviet Union to a triumphal tour, in which she denounced the United States and all its institutions. She was given the Lenin Medal. And in the last two elections she ran for office: for Vice President of the United States on the Communist ticket.

She was introduced at the august ceremony in Dartmouth by a dean, Mr. Dwight Lahr. The press was not permitted to record her speech, and only an edited videotape will be released (obviously, somebody in the office of Dartmouth's President Freedman decided that the celebration inaugurated by Angela Davis should be less than absolutely prime time). But a facile editor of *The Dart-*

mouth Review took notes on that introduction, which included the following: "Angela Davis's life is an example of how one committed black woman activist has chosen to make a difference." We must be grateful that Angela Davis's example is not more widely imitated, else there would be a progressive shortage of white males.

The dean went on to name her accomplishments, including the award of the Lenin Peace Prize, which, said in that way, seems indistinguishable from the Nobel Peace Prize. And he ended by saying, "It gives me great pleasure to introduce Angela Davis, who will address us on the topic, 'Women, Race, and Class.'"

What Ms. Davis went on to say need not contaminate a whole lot of newsprint. A sample sentence was: "The Bush campaign is literally saturated with right-wingers, racists, fascists, and Nazis." When Ms. Davis expressed herself more categorically, she announced that the "socioeconomic system of capitalism has to be abolished if we are serious about eradicating the evils of racism." And she confused some listeners by saying that the feminist movement was made up of "women, some women, some white women."

Asked if these "white" feminists adopted the cause of racism, Ms. Davis answered in the affirmative, explaining that "they are incorporating structures of racism themselves."

She received a standing ovation.

There are those who are prepared to say, the hell with it. Give the whole college over to the Indians.

—THE PROTESTERS AT WESLEYAN

MAY 14, 1985

Spring is the silly season for students, but some springs are sillier than others. A bunch of students a fortnight ago closed down, or did so in effect, a building in Columbia University, in protest against something or another, probably South Africa, or Nicaragua, or Chile, or not enough federal aid. They didn't quite reach the heights of their predecessors twenty years ago, who succeeded in wounding Columbia so deeply—turning it into a university in which one could not think or talk or write without risking goon treatment—that it took ten years (in the estimate of many who know and love the place) fully to recover. But they tried.

A few days ago a student at Brown concocted a Byzantine complaint against CIA recruiters, and proceeded to attempt a citizen's arrest. So it goes, mostly with impunity, since nobody gets around to prosecuting mere students for interfering with the civil rights of others. But occasionally they get their due. They certainly got it at Wesleyan University, because there to survey their behavior was William Manchester.

He addressed his letter to the student newspaper. In a story in the same paper, a student had been quoted as declaring, "The Marines are basically an instrument of American expansionism." That, he said, was the reason he protested the Marines' presence on campus (they were there recruiting). Indeed such presence was "insulting us by having soldiers in our library." The student classified the Marine credo, thoughtfully, as "crap." A second student tore up recruitment pamphlets in the presence of a Marine captain and his sergeant, telling them, "I feel sorry for the trees that were killed to make these." Eloquent, that. And then a third student rushed into print to boast of his resourcefulness. Having failed to engage the serious attention of the Marines, he wrote, "I asked whether they laughed at their dying buddies." To this, evidently, the Marines answered calmly that they had seen protests before, so our student went on with some wit: "I asked whether it became easier to see people dying after a while."

William Manchester, biographer of John Kennedy, Douglas MacArthur, Winston Churchill, and autobiographer of his own career in World War II, and a member of the community of Wesleyan, addressed a letter to the student newspaper in which he remarked that protests were not unusual, that indeed most American students had been isolationists, even pacifists, before the war. But then—his memory took him back . . .

"After the Japanese attack on Pearl Harbor, I left college, hitchhiked from Amherst to Springfield, and joined the Marine Corps. It is for me a source of pride that before being discharged in late October 1945, crippled by wounds, I had been twice decorated. But it is a source of profound sorrow, deeper than pride, deeper even than tears, that so many of my fellow Marines—

students who had left college campuses as I had—perished in scenes of indescribable horror. It would be unwise to ask me whether we laughed as they lay dying."

Manchester calmly disposed of the notion of the Marines as an "expansionist" force, pointing out that "only Saipan—whose inhabitants voted overwhelmingly to become an American commonwealth"—is now a U.S. possession. Guadalcanal . . . Tarawa . . . the Gilbert Islands . . . are republics. Okinawa was returned to Japan. Iwo Jima is used by both Japanese and American meteorologists. The Philippines got their independence on schedule. And it was of course the same in Europe.

Manchester went on. He noted the newspaper report that in their demonstration, students lay on the floor and "began to moan in the symbolic act of dying."

And commented: "Clearly they knew nothing of how fighting men die. I witnessed over a hundred deaths. Those with the strength to give voice rarely moaned. They shrieked. Bearing witness after that is more difficult. The death rattle is frequent. At the instant of death the cadaver, in a single spastic convulsion, emptied its bowels and bladder. If you are fastidious you may be offended by such matters, but I didn't start this. It gets worse. The dark effluvium of the slain follows—in the tropics it follows quickly. The corpse swells, then bloats, then bursts out of its uniform. The face turns from yellow to red, to purple, to green, to slimy black. I mention these details because the students who demonstrated may contemplate an encore. If they are going to do it, they ought to do it right."

Or be greeted by the contempt that is their due, concluded William Manchester, author, intellectual, patriot.

—Commencement Time!

May 14, 1991

Have you noticed the anomaly? If there is a dumb thing to be done or said, it will almost always be done or said in a college or university.

This is a quite inflexible law, occasionally spotted by novelists (e.g., Randall Jarrell, Mary McCarthy), but not widely disseminated. Most recent campus talk has been about current pathologies in trendy curriculums, which are mostly one more variation on the nihilism that is so irresistibly tempting to dead souls.

But the weekend reminded us that the greatest student harvest of this looniness happens at commencement ceremonies, as witness events last Sunday at Vassar and at Columbia.

Now Vassar has had a difficult time ever since it became coeducational, and on one occasion I was myself required by student silliness to turn down an invitation to give the commencement address. But this time, Vassar's 127th commencement became two commencements, the second one organized by black students who, in the account of *New York Times* writer Lisa Foderaro, "are hoping to establish their own traditions." To which end they imported the Reverend Jesse Jackson as keynote speaker, and up against the traditional sophomore daisy chain, in which lovely young sophomores (of all races) perform a little dance around the maypole, the separate commencement committee sponsored a daisy chain made up of "African violets."

Now if you think this is because there is granitic resistance within Vassar to students of non-white background, how do we account for it that the presidents-elect of the senior class and the student government are black, and the junior class president-elect is Asian-American, and the president-elect of the sophomore class is Hispanic? Hardly sounds like KKK time at Vassar.

But if Vassar seems bizarre, you should note commencement this year at Columbia. There, reports the *Times,* "they prayed in Arabic, pondered in Chinese, and sang Hebrew, Latin, and Southern Baptist strains. The multilingual congregation was dressed in the uniform blue gowns of Columbia University graduates," but the "proud diversity was apparent in the dress of graduates and their families. One graduate wore a piece of African kente cloth on her graduation gown. Several students wore yarmulkes, another a hijab, the head covering of pious Muslim women."

This commencement was organized by a rabbi, who evidently had a few theatrical reservations about his rainbow coalition ceremony because he began his invocation by saying: "We have never sat together before. We are not practiced in this liturgy." I should think not. How many of us can make Koranic calls in good, fluent Arabic?

It is odd that the general call to ecumenical understanding is resulting on some college campuses in the most obdurate denominational ethno- and religious centrism since the sixteenth century. Now if this is going to happen, presumably it is going to happen. What is not easy to understand is the general acquiescence in this phenomenon.

Why is it necessary, at commencement, to stress one's background, if it happens to be different from that of the founders of the college? I never disguised my Catholic background at school or college, but didn't feel it necessary to sprinkle my classmates with holy water at public ceremonies. Is a foreigner supposed to sing out his national anthem when our people do "The Star-Spangled Banner"?

How greatly one misses Randall Jarrell. Everything now happening is simply another manifestation of what he caught, writing forty years ago:

> If Benton [Benton College was his fictitious college in *Pictures from an Institution*] had had an administration building with pillars, it could have carved over the pillars, "Ye shall know the truth, and the truth shall make you feel guilty." Just as ordinary animal awareness has been replaced in many by consciousness, so consciousness had been replaced, in most of the teachers of Benton, by social consciousness. They were successful in teaching most of their students to say in contrition about anything whatsoever: It was I, Lord, it was I; but they were not too successful in teaching them to consider this consciousness of guilt a *summum bonum*, one's final claim upon existence. Many a Benton girl went back to her nice home, married her rich husband—and carried a fox in her bosom for the rest of her life—and short of becoming a social worker, founding a Neo-Socialist party, and then killing herself and leaving her insurance to the United Nations, I do not know how she could have got rid of it.

And these are our *educated* elite! My father once said, in exasperation to his ten children: "Either you go to college or you get educated."

—On Learning from Other Cultures
April 12, 1991

The prime minister of Pakistan has announced to the legislature over which he rules that it is his intention to make the Koran the supreme law of the land, subjecting all aspects of life, from social behavior to civil liberties, to Islamic tenets. If any of the gang at Stanford University who a year ago marched down the campus with Jesse Jackson shouting, "Hey, hey, ho, ho / Western culture's got to go," want to pull up roots and move to an Eastern culture, I herewith undertake to raise the plane fare.

Dinesh D'Souza, the talented young critic whose book *Illiberal Education* is causing campus-watchers to stop, look, and listen, has written an illuminating essay for *Policy Review,* the quarterly of the Heritage Foundation. It is called "Multiculturalism 101," and its purpose is to try to help the multiculture hounds out a little bit in their anxiety to reach beyond Western culture for true learning.

He concludes his essay, by the way, by recommending a dozen non-Western texts that are faithful to indigenous foreign cultures and helpful to Westerners who are anxious to cosmopolitanize their knowledge.

Take, for instance, the Koran, which is proposed to be elevated to Pakistan's equivalent of our Constitution. The Koran stipulates that "men have authority over women, because Allah has made the one superior to the other." Do the boys and girls at Stanford—and at Michigan, and Brown, and Yale—really wish that the Koran be studied while, oh, British common law be slighted?

D'Souza quotes a renowned Islamic scholar, Ibn Taymiyya, who advises, "When a husband beats his wife for misbehavior, he should not exceed ten lashes." Ten lashes is about what some of us had in mind as appropriate for those at Stanford who succeeded in abolishing the theretofore compulsory courses in Western culture that are deemed too "Eurocentric." It has yielded to a required course called Cultures, Ideas, and Values.

Having dealt with Islamic codes on women, the pilgrims in search of better ideas than those of our own culture can study the attitudes of others toward homosexuality, since "homophobia" is one of the central targets of the multicentrists.

It would not be wise to study the cultural role of homosexuality in Marxist Cuba, where practitioners are jailed and sometimes executed; in Mao's China, the problem of homosexuality is summarily dealt with—by a firing squad.

What the protesters against Western values really have in mind, D'Souza confirms, is to induce a dislike for our own culture. To this end, different cultures are more or less assumed to be superior, but it is very hard to use the term "superior" unless one has a scale of values. For instance, if socialist practice is "superior" to liberalism, then it becomes safe to adduce Marxism as a superior means of social organization.

D'Souza (himself an Indian-American) explains: "Multicultural curricula at Stanford and elsewhere generally reflect little interest in the most enduring, influential or aesthetically powerful products of non-Western cultures. 'The protesters here weren't interested in building up the anthropology department or immersing themselves in foreign languages,' comments Stanford philosophy instructor Walter Lammi. Alejandro Sweet-Cordero, spokesman for a Chicano group on campus, told the *Chronicle of Higher Education,* 'We're not saying we need to study Tibetan philosophy. We're arguing that we need to understand what made our society what it is.' Black activist William King says, 'Forget Confucius. We are trying to prepare ourselves for the multicultural challenge we will face in the future. I don't want to study China. I want to study myself.' " William King 101.

A broadly used textbook by the hate-Western ideas folk is called *Multicultural Literacy*—a book that "devotes virtually no space to the philosophical, religious and literary classics of China, Japan, Indonesia, India, Persia, the Arab world, Africa or Latin America. . . . Instead the book includes thirteen protest essays, including Michele Wallace's autobiographical 'Invisibility Blues' and Paula Gunn Allen's 'Who Is Your Mother?: The Red Roots of White Feminism.' "

It is a pity, the whole messy thing, among other reasons because we could all learn from reading classics of other cultures of which D'Souza mentions a few, beginning with the Upanishads, written in Sanskrit, which include the Bhagavad-Gītā, the Katha,

Chāndogya and Svetāsvatara, the burden of which is that God must not be sought as a being separate from us, but rather as a sublime force within us, enabling us to rise above our moral limitations.

There are many such works in the arcana of multiculturalism, but unless they condemn everything from I.Q. tests to Reaganomics, they will not satisfy those whose principal aim is to rage, rage against the longevity of the West.

3 Morals, Religion, and Censorship

—*PLAYBOY* NEEDS YOUR HELP

JULY 13, 1985

I have here a form letter ("Dear Bill") from the editorial director of *Playboy* magazine, Arthur Kretchmer ("Art"), asking me to authorize the use of my name in an advertising campaign aimed against groups who, protesting those features of *Playboy* that made it famous, have urged boycotts here and there against stores that sell the magazine.

The letter is wonderfully complacent in tone, and, in its choice of words, rather more vulnerable than it might have been. Its tone is that of the fraternity president addressing his brothers. "You may not be aware of it, but there are some people out there who don't like *Playboy*." Well, if you are not aware of this, it may be you are not aware that Washington was our first president, and that Congress is a bicameral legislature. The letter goes on, "I'm not talking about those Effete Literary Snobs that you're occasionally forced to drink with in the Hamptons" (the allusion is to *New York Review of Books* types who feel that you don't really need to run a brothel in order to lure people into good reading). "I'm talking about right-wing groups and—because zealotry makes strange bedfellows—some left-wing groups as well." That the editorial director of *Playboy* should cavil at any two people meeting in bed (indeed, in *Playboy,* as often as not the stranger they are to each other, the better), is newsworthy, though not newsworthy enough to make it into the next issue of *Playboy*.

But the letter goes on to complain against "a kind of moral terrorism" via boycotts, and "on-site harassment." Mr. Kretchmer reminds us that last year his magazine won an annual fiction prize and says that "the best writers in the world publish in *Playboy*." This is quite true, though it begs the point, which is that the protesters aren't protesting the best writers in the world, they are protesting, to say it again exactly, those parts of *Playboy* that made it famous. Another way to put it is that if one were to take the whole of the serious content over the last ten years of *Playboy,* segregate it, and stick it between the covers of, oh, *The Atlantic Monthly,* or *Harper's,* these publications would not be enjoying a circulation of 5 million. More like 200,000, 300,000. About what they have without the sex.

What Mr. Kretchmer et al. don't like to face up to is that *Playboy* is also a cultural statement. And not a cultural statement obliquely presented. The first decade or two of *Playboy* contained a protracted monthly essay by its founder, Hugh Hefner, in which he tirelessly deplored, assailed, and mocked traditional moral views involving licit and illicit sex. The proposed *Playboy* ad for which signatures are being solicited begins, "The American Experiment, after more than 200 years, is working out just fine. Americans are still free to speak, to write, to think and act as they choose. That's what the American Experiment is all about."

But you see, the American Experiment is not working out just peachy-keen. The current issue of *Newsweek* magazine announces that by the end of the decade as many as one half of the children of America will be raised by single parents. Between 1970 and 1980, illegitimate births in the white community rose from 6 percent to 11 percent, and in the black community, from 38 percent to 55 percent.

Because they all read *Playboy*? Of course not. But it is unquestionably the case that self-indulgence ("The Me Decade") has a great deal to do with the fragility of personal relations. Wanton sex, like wanton booze or wanton idleness or wanton thought, breeds undesirable things, among them bastards, but also broken homes. And broken homes breed things like violence, neglected children, and drug addiction—the stigmata of modern America. Most emphatically not what the American Experiment is all about.

It is hardly *Playboy's* exclusive responsibility that this should be so. But we have traveled a long distance from Nathaniel Hawthorne, who awarded a scarlet letter to adulterers, to Hugh Hefner, who thinks adultery is good plain American wholesome fun and takes pride in his magazine as the principal architect of the sexual revolution.

I add this, that I have frequently written for *Playboy*, as I would write for any journal that addressed five million readers. And I gave a straightforward answer to the question why I did this, feeling as I do, in a *Playboy* interview published fifteen years ago. I write for *Playboy*, I said, because it is the fastest way to communicate with my seventeen-year-old son.

—SEX AND PARADOX

APRIL 10, 1986

Last Sunday night the CBS program *60 Minutes* devoted attention to the problem of teenage pregnancies. The narrator, Ed Bradley, stressed that although the program featured black promiscuity, the rise in white teenage pregnancies was very nearly as startling as that among blacks. The protagonist of the documentary was a bright and articulate woman in her thirties who looked a little like Lena Horne. She and a black doctor had a well-developed thesis. It was as follows: a) Promiscuous teenage sexual activity is no greater in the United States than in Europe. b) We have many more teenage pregnancies than does Europe, however, because we are a "prudish" society. c) Evidence of our prudishness is the difficulty local school boards have in instituting sex education programs, which are opposed by many parents. d) These programs are absolutely necessary because of the failure of parents to undertake such teaching at home.

It all sounds very neat, notwithstanding that the camera goes on to show children who a) have taken the sex courses, but nevertheless b) have borne, and continue to bear, children. But what strikes the viewer most is the sudden switch in the orthodox line of liberal argumentation.

Whenever the subject of religion comes up, whether we are talking about a common prayer recited in the schools or the discussion and treatment of religion more seriously than merely as an opening ceremony, the First Amendment rampart-watchers rise to declaim that religion is a matter for the home. It is never asked whether, in fact, children are receiving religious instruction at home. But with respect to sex, the moment you get pregnancies or venereal disease, it is quickly inferred that desirable sexual habits are not taught at home, and therefore it is the responsibility of the public schools to teach sex.

If you ask: Why does it not follow, then, that it becomes the function of the public schools to teach religion?

Ah, the rejoinder is anticipated, because, don't you see, public problems are the result of casual sex habits: Last year it cost the public $17 billion to look after illegitimate children.

But there is of course an appropriate counterrejoinder. It is that instruction in religion diminishes promiscuous sexual activity. If a child is taught to believe that premarital sex is "wrong," and if the conscience is cultivated and trained, among other things by invocations of divine sanction, illicit sexual activity is by no means eliminated, but it is reasonable to suppose that it diminishes. If a conscience is to develop among young people, then they will ask themselves not merely utilitarian questions (Is sex fun? Answer: Yes), but also corollary questions (Is sex without regard to other factors OK? Answer: No). It is impossible to deny, however secular the spirit of the age, that the activation of the conscience by religion is an important factor in the development of character. Why should a society concerned with the sexual explosion not be asking itself these questions, and exploring the absence of religious training in the schools and its possible relationship to abandoned moral sanctions?

It is difficult to take seriously the notion that the problem focused on is the result of the "prudishness" of our society. In the first place, it is hard to think of a society as "prudish" in which _Penthouse_ and _Hustler_ and _Screw_ are available at the local newsstand, in which the local movie theater specializes in R-rated films and the local kiosk rents out X-rated films for a dollar a night, and rock 'n' roll lyrics urge instant capitulation to the libido.

But then, also, what is it that has caused a rise in illegitimate children by a factor of 600 percent during the past twenty years? Our slide toward prudishness? The opposite, of course, is clear as the nose on the face of Pinocchio. During the past twenty years, we have had a) diminished religious training in the schools, thanks to the Supreme Court; b) a sharp increase in federal care for dependent children, thanks to Congress; and c) a sharp rise in the availability of sex-oriented material, in song, in movies, in television, in books and magazines, thanks to our entrepreneurs. The notion that a thirteen-year-old girl wise in street wisdom can't learn that the ingestion of a pill suffices to prevent pregnancy, or that a boy can't master the intricacies of a condom without elaborate instruction at school, is as laughable as the proposition that you need classroom instruction in order to teach children how to smoke cigarettes or drink beer.

Our thought leaders have got a lot of paradoxes to face. To avoid doing so, they have developed near-perfect prophylactics.

THE STRANGE USES OF TOLERANCE
JANUARY 26, 1985

Do you agree that opponents of abortion ought not to threaten the lives of men and women who operate abortion clinics, or their property? The answer is presumably that yes, you agree. The overwhelming majority of Americans believe in the rule of law, and that means that you take your protests not in hand, but to your legislature or court. But all morally dynamic societies are accustomed to externalized forms of indignation, and these are often ugly, though their motivation isn't always ugly.

Nathaniel Hawthorne wrote an American classic about how women were treated when caught in adultery. *The Scarlet Letter* [as already noted] was a visible stigma, designed to draw perpetual attention to one woman's breach of matrimonial faith. It was society, speaking at that time, finding its own voice, declaring its solidarity behind monogamy. The branding of an adulteress strikes us now as infamous and cruel, but it was better than what was routine a few hundred years earlier and still is in some societies, namely the execution, often by torture, of the adulteress.

Defenders of white supremacy during a long and ignoble period of American history adopted a variety of means by which to signify their displeasure at ruptured social conventions. These included flogging, tarring and feathering, and occasional lynching. The idea of racial integrity was very big in America, and the law recognized it as integral to the social structure, forbidding, as was done in many states, interracial marriage.

John Brown's body lies a-moldering in the grave because he decided to take into his own hands his battle against slavery, and this he did by itinerant attacks and killings of targeted slaveholders and their spokesmen. Nat Turner, like John Brown, was also hanged because he led a rebellion against slavery that resulted in considerable carnage.

But have you noticed? John Brown and even Nat Turner are slowly making their way back into the kinder passages of history books. At worst they are called zealots. It is not held in any question that their cause was just. It is only specified that they should have turned their energies not to different causes, but to different means of achieving their ends.

And so we see that societies tend, eventually, to judge the exertions of prophets on the basis of current attitudes toward right and wrong. Adultery is no longer an offense people get excited about. Racism, on the other hand, is, and from any cosmopolitan gathering of civic-minded citizens one could put together enough volunteers to crew a man-of-war to set out against Capetown, armed with letters of marque and reprisal from the Black Caucus of Congress.

"How do societies resolve conflicts between two opposing moralities?" _The New York Times_ editorial asks, confessing its disappointment with President Reagan's handling of the abortion rally in Washington. What did Reagan do wrong? He did ask for "a complete rejection of violence as a means of settling this issue," to be sure. But the president reiterated his commitment to "ending the terrible national tragedy of abortion." That is what upset the _Times,_ because it views the abortion decision of the Supreme Court as one that "gives practical, even brilliant voice not to abortion and not to its foes but to tolerance."

But what does that mean? Would the appropriate answer to the opponent of slavery have been that he should be tolerant toward those slaveowners who disagreed? What defenders of tolerance appear incapable of understanding is that there is a school of thought that makes it not a mark of moral jingoism to assert responsibility for protecting the lives of the unborn, but a mark of fraternal obligation. If it is true that an infant is on Day Minus One for all intents and purposes as human as an infant on Day Plus One, then it is something other than mere passage through the womb that confers on that child the protections we grant under the Fifth and Fourteenth Amendments to the Constitution, which derive from the Fifth Commandment of the decalogue that specifies that thou shalt not kill.

—ARE YOU "RESPONSIBLE"?

APRIL 10, 1990

At a public encounter the other day at Lynchburg College in Virginia, a student asked former Senator George McGovern what was his position on abortion. He replied that in his judgment American women could be counted on to behave responsibly on the question whether to have an abortion, "so let's leave it up to them." This brought uproarious applause from most of the crowd, and the air was thick with the incense that hovers over a Solomonic statement, hallowing the moment.

The trouble with Mr. McGovern's statement is that it is palpably wrong, misleading.

The current argument is on the question whether a woman should be permitted to abort a fetal pregnancy. Now whether your answer to that is yes, or whether your answer is no, clearly we are talking about an unwanted child. But if the child is unwanted, why did it materialize? We all know the answer to this, do we not? The woman who became pregnant either a) was ignorant of the paraphernalia by which unwanted pregnancies are avoided; or else b) she was not ignorant, but recklessly failed to take the proper precautions; or else c) she was carried away by passion, perhaps in an inebriated state, and simply hoped she would not become pregnant; or else d) she was raped.

Now with the exception of the last category, which accounts for one half of 1 percent of the pregnancies that are terminated by abortionists, is it correct to say that the woman in question was behaving "responsibly"? Presumably not: If you don't want a child and have the option not to have one, then it is not behaving responsibly to become pregnant. And if one behaves irresponsibly in the matter of conceiving, why should George McGovern assume that responsibility sets in between the moment of conception and the moment of abortion?

Most people don't think it entirely responsible to bear illegitimate children, right? This is so notwithstanding that many moralists would admire more the woman who bore the child she mistakenly conceived than the woman who aborted it. But illegitimate birth is nevertheless, viewed on the whole, an act of irresponsibility. Children are supposed to have legal fathers and mothers. If they do not, their parents can be said to be behaving irresponsibly.

Well, in 1970, 10.7 percent of all births in America were illegitimate. In 1986, that figure had more than doubled, to 23.4. That adds up to a lot of irresponsibility. Broken down by race, white illegitimacy in 1970 was at 5.7 percent. By 1986 it had tripled, to 15.7 percent. Comparable figures among blacks were 37.6, rising to 61.2 percent. That would seem to be irresponsibility on a massive scale.

The point, then, is that women who go to an abortionist, or who procreate illegitimate births, are not the best judges of right and wrong, even if society agreed that they should in their own situation be the executors of the critical decision, whether to give birth or to abort.

Theology teaches that the conscience is supreme. This means only that you cannot commit a moral wrong unless you know it to be wrong or believe it to be wrong. It does not mean—anarchy would be the result—that all the decisions an individual arrives at are morally correct because he fails to recognize that they are morally wrong.

And this is the nature of the quarrel between those who believe in the woman's "right" to abort and those who do not. If abortion is objectively wrong, a society may nevertheless wish to abide by the woman's right to pursue her own conscience and proceed to abort. But latitudinarian activity by the society does not sanctify the uses to which such activity might be put. If society licenses the sale of liquor, it does not derivatively license drunkenness. And of course the great divide between the two camps has to do with such questions as do not affect the drunkard, who for the most part damages only himself and his own reputation—if while drunk he attacks someone else, he gets hauled up on assault charges.

Leaving us, then, with the obvious question, the source of the intellectual and moral difficulty: Is a mortal assault on a fetus something on the order of assault and battery? Or is it no different from stuffing a tomato in a blender?

These perplexities may continue to confound us. But really, one shouldn't designate the class of people who have this problem as the class of especially responsible people.

—See No God?

September 3, 1992

The business about co-opting God as a Republican brings a smile —or it should. Especially when the rebuke that attracts the most attention comes in from the National Council of Churches.

It isn't all that surprising, come to think of it, that the council should be shocked by the reference to God. Some observers of its declarations over the years would be shocked to hear "God" mentioned by the council, whose concerns are overwhelmingly secular. Its position reduces to: If the National Council of Churches doesn't mention God, candidates for the presidency have no right to mention God.

And then the council's letter takes one or two strange positions. "We believe it is blasphemy to invoke the infinite and holy God to assert the moral superiority of one people over another, or one political party over another."

What? God's bodkin! We are not talking about whether God is on the side of a higher or a lower minimum wage. Was it indeed blasphemous for the abolitionist parties to claim God's sanction for their cause against slavery? If the Soviet empire was evil, as Ronald Reagan finally persuaded Mikhail Gorbachev et al. to agree, by what standards was that evil judged to be so, if not God's? Professor B. F. Skinner's?

"As our Pledge of Allegiance affirms," the council went on, "we are 'one nation, under God.' Not 'over' God or in any other way owning God." Surely nobody at the convention in Houston superordinated the GOP over God? If so, the networks weren't watching, nor the press.

"Any partisan use of God's name tends to breed intolerance and to divide." This condemnation is as sloppily thought out as it is sloppily worded. It is the business of politics to cultivate intolerance—of those ideas deemed hurtful to the republic. Was it wrong for the speaker to ask for intolerance to those who are indifferent to the epidemic of AIDS? Or of poverty? Or of discrimination? If the Republican and the Democratic parties are not engaged in trying to divide the American people, they are not doing their duty.

The specific offense, one gathers, that brought all of this on was the line by President Bush in which he called attention to the word missing from the whole of the Democratic platform, namely: God. Practically all thought on the matter is stillborn because of our superstitious adherence to the notion that separation of church and state requires us to ignore God in the formulation of policy.

But 85 percent of the American people believe in God, and if so, we naturally wonder in what direction God would move us, when dealing with public questions that have a moral dimension. On the question of abortion, for instance, what is "right" is of major concern—to those who believe that a belief in God is also a commitment to explore divine postulates.

A century ago the fight against slavery became (finally) a palpably Christian mandate. And in our own century, we most confidently asserted that God could not consider as equal a government whose primary philosophical commitment was the rejection of God and, in his non-name, the rejection of any notion that we are created in his image, and are therefore equal and born to be free.

On the matter of political agenda, it is plain that the Democratic Party more or less officially endorses that construction of the First Amendment that tells us that it is unconstitutional not only to permit common prayer in the public schools, but—witness the most recent decision of the Supreme Court—also to permit a rabbi to pronounce a blessing at a commencement ceremony of a state school.

Those who believe that public education oughtn't to be hampered by a dogmatic see-no-God, hear-no-God secularism have every right to denounce the reasoning of the Supreme Court that treats the Founding Fathers' thought like Silly Putty and, in doing so, to call attention to the acquiescence of the other political party to this distortion.

Republicans can't, with piety, plead that God is among their constituents. But they can argue that it is not idle to raise the question of the compatibility of certain public policies with what we know of God's will.

—THE SURRENDER OF THE CORCORAN GALLERY
SEPTEMBER 21, 1989

The critics of those who (along with Senator Jesse Helms) protested the use of public money to finance the "art" of Robert Mapplethorpe and Andres Serrano did a hell of a job of caterwauling over the provincialism of the booboisie who protested the exhibitions. And now we have the final gesture of abject surrender: an official apology by the Corcoran Gallery in Washington. An apology for having elected to feature a display of homoerotic, sadomasochistic photographic art? No no. The Corcoran's director, Ms. Christina Orr-Cahall, apologized to the public for canceling the exhibit. Here was a modern auto-da-fé: not for countenancing heresy, but for denouncing it. I swear, the critics are going to end up convincing the trendy of this world that a crucifix immersed in human urine is an expression of spiritual joy, an insight of artistic penetration, the new stupor mundi of the artistic soul.

Listen carefully, because we need to distinguish as a very first step two phenomena. The first is the historically redundant failure of the literati of the world to recognize genius. Examples abound. Van Gogh sold one canvas during his lifetime. Bach's "St. Matthew Passion" was used as wallpaper. Joyce's *Ulysses* was not admitted into the United States until 1933. Those who wish to add to this list can do so at telephone-book length.

Which tells us what? Tells us that every other day the work of a great artist is being neglected. The problem in the current case is that that is all that is being told us. What is not being told us is that when every other day the work of an artist is neglected, this neglect may be well earned.

Mapplethorpe can be said to be an accomplished photographer, but this does not mean that everything he chose to photograph became great art. Picasso commanded perhaps the greatest technique of the century, but this does not mean that every use to which he chose to devote that technique resulted in great art. This would be so only in the collectors' sense, which would attach considerable value to a "mediocre" building sketch drawn by Adolf Hitler, because Adolf Hitler was a considerable historical character. Mapplethorpe is not yet in the Picasso league. And assuming that he were, the sponsors of a collection of his work in which objects protruding from a male rectum were a feature might be presented as examples of conceptual and perverse failures by great artists.

That an artist should dominate the language, or the paint brush, or clay, does not mean that he will use that skill for aesthetic, let alone exalted, purpose. Artists can profitably use their skills to demonstrate the despicable side of life, which is often tied to the poignant side of life. *The New York Times* asks rhetorically whether Lautrec's depictions of prostitutes are "obscene," to which the answer isn't necessarily the spastic of-course-not. Much depends on what the artist intended. A painting of a detail of the Holocaust is one thing executed by an artist who seeks to convey the horror of it all, something quite different executed by an artist whose intention is to celebrate a historic attempt at genocide.

The whole quarrel over art has in recent weeks tended to overlook the utterly important negative critical function, which is the right of the critic to say, No: this isn't something to which I wish to devote the half-acre's space in my gallery during the month of May. There is competing work by other artists which is of wholesome interest, by which is meant not photographs of Little Orphan Annie, but photographs and statuary by artists who do not seek to outrage convention, in the case of Mapplethorpe by celebrating the kind of activity that caused him to die of AIDS; in the case of Serrano, the kind of infantile antinomianism that thinks it amusing to paint swastikas on the walls of synagogues.

Enter, now, the political dimension. We seem to be hearing

the critics say: No guidance of any sort is tolerable in the course of conveying public money to the support of the arts. Let the dispensers of that money proceed immune from official public scrutiny. To which the answer is, surely: Why? It requires artistic nescience to take the position that anything presented by the Corcoran Gallery with public money ought to be absolutely immune from scrutiny by the public agency that conveys that money. Why should the art critics, themselves the historical practitioners of artistic neglect and misjudgment, alone be responsible for passing judgment?

Senator Helms erred, in my opinion, in failing to qualify his suggested criteria by exempting any art work over fifty years old, since that passage of time can season the judgment sufficiently to distinguish between pornography, for instance, and eroticism—the work of Rodin is an example. But a failure by Senator Helms to react against the excesses of Mapplethorpe and Serrano would have represented a far greater indifference to artistic sensibilities than is being shown by his critics.

UNDERSTANDING MAPPLETHORPE

I was in Cincinnati the other day with a couple of hours to spare, so I went to the Contemporary Arts Center to see the provocative photographs of Robert Mapplethorpe, about which so much has been written. It was these photographs, alongside a work by Andres Serrano ("Piss Christ"), that stirred up first Senator Jesse Helms, who introduced a bill to bar the National Endowment for the Arts from giving money to exhibits that include blasphemous or obscene art/creations, and prompted the sheriff of Hamilton County, in which Cincinnati sits, to indict the director of the gallery that is displaying the Mapplethorpe photographs.

The curator of the Center spotted me and offered to give me and my companion a professional tour of the exhibit. Mr. John Sawyer, we soon discovered, knows more about Mapplethorpe than Boswell knew about Johnson. And he does not disguise his enthusiasm for the photographer's work. He points out details in the photographs we might otherwise have missed, speaking about them with the voice of a coroner dictating his findings to a stenographer, whether he is talking about the irradiations of subtle light, or about the foreskin of the subject's penis. I think it is fair to say about Mr. Sawyer that he is no more "shocked" by what Mapplethorpe photographs than a laboratory technician would be shocked by a microbe he spotted. As far as he is concerned it is work that is done by an artist, and that is all that matters. The flyer you get with your ticket might very well have been written by the curator. Under the heading of "Still Lifes," one comes across the line, "The convergence of both sexes in the flower is emphasized by Mapplethorpe's careful positioning of lens and light to reveal the powdery stamens and the translucent orifice created by the petals." Fuss around with that just a little bit and you could be reading Henry Miller or Frank Harris.

The Center proudly points out that fifty thousand people have come to see the exhibit in the first month. One restrains oneself from commenting that fifty thousand people went to see _Deep Throat_ every day. Unfair, perhaps, but the most wayward photographs of Mapplethorpe were in fact bunched together at one end of the room, and that was the only corner of the exhibit where a line formed. To see anal sex, you have to stand in line.

The utter sincerity of John Sawyer is not ineffective. You could liken exposure to him to START talks dealing with the goal of total disarmament. He speaks—again, like a pathologist reporting on body tissue—about Mapplethorpe's models. Mostly he liked the black male. . . . "There had been practically no photographic studies of the black male until Mapplethorpe" . . . "About one half of his models shown here died of AIDS" . . . "That model over there didn't permit his face to be shown, and later he thought the picture showed his member distractingly large" . . . "The little boy (filmed nude at age six) was embarrassed by the photograph when he reached his teens. But now he is in college and likes it. His mother always liked it" . . . "You say she's 'dykeish'? I see what you mean, but come over here and see the picture of her coming up from a swim in the sea. There. She looks totally feminine" . . . "You notice the total evenness of the color?" (a male fist is inserted into a rectum) . . . "The colors are really quite extraordinary" . . . "Some people find that picture [of a flower] the sexiest in the exhibition."

The mind keeps returning to the world of science, which is like the world of art in that the professional prescinds from the surrounding world the object he is assessing even as the scientist would do. The curator looks at a picture and sees in it only the skill of the artist; the effect of the picture on ambient values, conventions, feelings is simply extrinsic to his concern, rather like asking the doctor doing a biopsy whether the patient has provided adequately for his forthcoming widow—hardly the scientist's concern. The John Sawyers of this world, gazing at some of the pictures of Robert Mapplethorpe, see colors and form and conformation, and are truly astonished that other people are seeing: kink.

It is very difficult for the two worlds to understand each other. There are 150 pictures in the Mapplethorpe exhibit, and by retiring twenty-five of them the public would be left to see the extraordinary work of an extraordinary artist without being asked to suspend the operation of conventional sensibilities. But to withhold these, in the eyes of the Sawyers of this world, would be to perform an act of bowdlerization. They should realize that just as non-artists do and say things that do not merit publication, so artists produce work that may include some best left for study and worship in artists' laboratories.

The ongoing quarrel over the role of the National Endowment for the Arts suffers, as so many quarrels do, from a lack of focus. This is sometimes the doing of the ignorant, sometimes the doing of polemical opportunists. These last would have us believe that those Americans who have been alarmed by a few excesses of the NEA in the recent past are crypto-fascists who favor a general censorship.

Mr. Anthony Lewis of *The New York Times* is not ignorant, and therefore must be set down as behaving opportunistically. The technique is hoary: one associates the opposing argument with unseemly people. As in, "The other side, which one might call the fascist side, favors . . ." Consider, for instance, the matter of the photographs by Mr. Andres Serrano. You will remember the crucifix immersed in the urine of the artist, photographed with the caption "Piss Christ"?

Now I think it entirely candid to say that there is a community of people in America, among whom Mr. Lewis is comfortable, who are quite simply unoffended by such a photograph. For one thing, they think of Christ, if ever they do, as a distracting historical superstition responsible for all sorts of human misbehavior including wars and persecutions; and if some artist wants to express his feeling about Christ—and about Christianity, derivatively—by urinating on a crucifix and calling it art, who are we to object?

Thus Mr. Lewis begins his column—entitled "Fight the Philistines"—"A small band of religious zealots and right-wing political opportunists is trying to show the world that America is an intolerant Puritan country, contemptuous of artists."

How is that for target-bombing those who believe that something is functionally wrong with an agency that begets Piss Christs, and circulates photographs by Robert Mapplethorpe that celebrate (the exact word) homoeroticism and sadomasochism?

The technique, then, is to denounce those who state their objections and to associate them with a great historical pageant of all things horrible. Thus the Protestant minister Donald Wildmon who has objected to some of the work of the NEA "would no doubt prefer to live in the Spain of Torquemada, the Massachusetts of Cotton Mather, or the Soviet Union of Stalin."

Sometimes it is painful to be made to think, but at the risk of inflicting cruel and unusual punishment on Mr. Lewis, one needs to lead him, calmly, through a child's garden of syllogisms.

• Censorship, of a generic kind, is exercised every day by myriad authorities. *The New York Times,* which is the most authoritative newspaper in the country, exercises a benevolent censorship by, for instance, declining to publish pictures of the Mapplethorpe photos under discussion. In declining to do this, it can be denounced for exercising narrow censorship; or it can be praised for exercising good judgment.

• If the word "censorship" is appropriately used to describe a refusal to back a particular exhibit, then it is also appropriately used to describe the very act of selection. For instance: last October the NEA first pulled back from, and then reinstated, its funding of something called, Witnesses: Against Our Vanishing (an exhibition of AIDS-related paintings and photographs). When the agency decided to reverse itself and renew its backing, it did so with one qualification: it declined to supply the money to pay for the accompanying catalogue that was designed to go with the AIDS exhibit. The catalogue was an explosion of anti-Christian odium (the Catholic Church is a "house of walking swastikas"). That catalogue was "censored" by the NEA, we are free then to say.

    • But in that case, censorship goes on at a feverish pace, given the discrepancy between the number of applications for NEA money and the money available. For every dollar of the $170 million spent by the NEA, one assumes that an application for two or three dollars was turned down.

On what grounds? Well, maybe the peer committee didn't think that other photographer was as "good" as Mapplethorpe.

Using what criteria?

Well, er . . . the composition wasn't as good, nor the lighting, nor the . . . subject matter as interesting?

Writes Mr. Lewis: "The critics of the NEA, when they want to sound reasonable, say that after all it is only a question of making sure that Government money does not go for objectionable art. But that argument begs the real question: Who decides?"

But that isn't the most interesting question. The real question: Whoever does decide, and somebody must, is what issues from that decision something that critics can call censorship? Censorship, used in this way, goes on every day, in every way, in a free society—and should.

Recently the columnists Evans and Novak published that an application for a grant from the NEA had been tentatively approved. The idea was to encourage a "solo theater piece." This kind of thing is known generically as "cutting-edge" art, by which is designated what used to be merely the avant-garde with the difference that new forms are currently sought out, the idea being that music, canvas, photography, dance, and sculpture do not exhaust the artistic dimensions of the mind's eye. Anyway, this cutting-edge solo theater piece was designed to feature Karen Finley, an "actress" moved on to cutting-edge art in which she appears nude on stage, having smeared with chocolate "those" parts of her body, after which she engages in acts that are designed to "trigger emotional and taboo events."

Some guardian angel blew a little whistle into the ear of Chairman John Frohnmayer just in time, and Miss Finley was shown the door, and will now need to get backing for her show from, oh, the Rockefeller Foundation. But the episode brought great administrative turmoil to the office of the NEA. A reason for this tension is given in the wonderful calm of Samuel Lipman, the publisher of the *New Criterion,* writing in *Commentary* ("Backward & Downward with the Arts").

Essentially, the difficulty lies (writes Mr. Lipman—who is by the way a professional musician, and music critic) in that the United States doesn't have a culture policy. "In 1981, a chairman, Frank Hodsoll, was chosen for the NEA who lacked a background in art or the arts; the battle for his replacement in 1989 was marked by unseemly competition among various old-boy networks, with the final section of John Frohnmayer being made on the basis of pure political patronage. From the beginning, during Hodsoll's regime from 1982 to 1989, a series of wise and far-reaching administrative reforms—all, now, under Frohnmayer, a thing of the past—were unfortunately wedded to a refusal to make distinctions between programs and grants, between transience and permanence, between high art and entertainment. As was true in the first fifteen years of the NEA, it was felt in the 80's that public support could only be achieved by yoking the agency to the wagons of the glamorous, the famous, and the successful. The White House has abetted this tendency by sponsoring on its premises a mixture of glitz and gloss, Michael Jackson, and now country music."

Lacking a central vision, the NEA has been easily distracted, and has been hospitable to grants that lead to the kind of notoriety brought on by the exhibitions of Mapplethorpe and Serrano. These were for a long time defended on the grounds that the NEA subjected applications to "peer panel review" and that therefore the NEA was not itself responsible for its grants. "This response was so weak, and ultimately so lacking in philosophical weight, that even seasoned arts administrators—including leading voices at the NEA itself—were soon panicked into claiming that in making provocative grants the NEA was only fulfilling its proper function, since art itself was in its essence provocative. This line of argument, so far from improving matters, merely had the effect of reducing not only the NEA but art itself to being the handmaiden of anger, violence, and social upheaval."

Mr. Lipman shrewdly ties it together. Artists like Mapplethorpe and Serrano aren't, in their seizures, engaged in making art, but in making polemics. "That being so, it was inevitable that cutting-edge grants would come to be defended by the arts establishment not in terms of artistic achievement but in terms of free speech."

4 THE NOMINATION OF CLARENCE THOMAS

—THE RESISTANCE OF BLACK LEADERS

JULY 4, 1991

The twenty-four hours after the nomination of Clarence Thomas were great fun, with everybody in sight speaking in the Aesopian mode, their mouths saying one thing, their eyes something a little different. And our dear president was no exception.

George Bush said that the race of Clarence Thomas was "not the factor" in his selection, which is a little like saying that Cleopatra's body was not a factor in her selection by Antony. The president went further: "He is the best man."

We have got to assume that there is one other lawyer in America, maybe even two, who are "better" than Judge Thomas, according to generally acknowledged criteria—experience, learning, intelligence. Moreover, said Bush, Thomas is a "fiercely independent thinker."

That phrase, for reasons that don't come readily to mind, is supposed to be a high compliment. I don't know why. Hitler was a fiercely independent thinker; so was John Brown. I prefer the maxim that goes: If it's true, it's not new. If it's new, it's not true.

And then, among the instant critics of the choice of Thomas, Eleanor Holmes Norton was everywhere, National Public Radio, PBS—I am certain she was talking about the shortcomings of Judge Thomas to the sleepy bartender at five in the morning.

Her line is very interesting. You see, what we should want, in a black Supreme Court justice, is someone who has had the experience of an American black.

But isn't this exactly what Clarence Thomas has had? A very poor boy, deserted by his father? The only routine experience of an American black he hasn't had is a crush on Jesse Jackson.

Well, yes, but the point is that he hasn't had the kind of experience that led him to thinking like Thurgood Marshall or like Eleanor Holmes Norton, if you see what I mean, and Jim Lehrer did see what she meant when he said to her, "Would you rather have a white liberal on the court than a black conservative?" to which she answered, "Of course!"—releasing us from the logjam of her strictures about the ideal background for an American black going to the court.

Alan Keyes, the brilliant black intellectual who served as an assistant secretary of state for Ronald Reagan, punctured the quota argument. This was a little twist the liberals had been playing with, beginning at the presidential press conference at which Thomas was launched. It goes like this: A is opposed to quotas. A nominates a black to succeed a black on the court. Therefore, A is actually in the quota business. The distinction, said Keyes, is between representation and quotas. There is nothing un-American (or unconstitutional) in seeking variety, when the time comes to staff a government agency. It is perfectly rational to say, for example, that women are underrepresented in Congress. It is something quite different to say that Congress ought to be 51 percent female. The explanation need go no further than exactly that.

Bush has accomplished something quite other than bringing to the Supreme Court someone who appears to be a promising jurist. He has done more in one day to remind the nation, and above all to remind black Americans, that it is incorrect to think of the black population as a monolith. Blacks tend to vote the way they do because the Democratic Party has perfected instruments of seduction that tend to attract, dealing as they do in victimology.

Black leaders like Benjamin Hooks and Jesse Jackson are constantly engaged in stressing the black race's helplessness in the hands of the oppressive white race. But it is quite wrong to suppose that the situation is frozen, that blacks are immovable on the subject. Governor Thomas Kean had the support in New Jersey of the majority of the state's blacks. New York Representative Charles Rangel told me one night with impish glee how lucky the Democrats were that George Bush hadn't named another vice presidential candidate: "If he had named Colin Powell, the Democrats could have kissed the black vote goodbye."

Bush has picked a black man of true distinction, forever to divide the political monolith.

The point was best made in an Op-Ed piece appearing in the *Los Angeles Times* in 1985: "There seems to be an obsession with painting blacks as an unthinking group of automatons, with a common set of views, opinions and ideas. Anyone who dares suggest that this may not be the case or has a viewpoint that disagrees with the 'black viewpoint' is immediately cast as attacking the black leadership or as some kind of anti-black renegade. We certainly cannot claim to have progressed much in this country as long as it is insisted that our intellects are controlled entirely by our pigmentation." Those words were written by Clarence Thomas.

—THE REASONS THOMAS IS UNFIT

AUGUST 2, 1991

Why is Clarence Thomas thought by some to be ineligible to serve as an associate justice of the Supreme Court?

Well, he's a Catholic (or was). He is married to a white conservative (a woman). He is black (allegedly). He believes in something called a natural law (along with Thomas Jefferson). He once smoked marijuana (or was it twice?), and he hung a Confederate flag in his office in Georgia (only it was a Georgia state flag, it turns out).

The congressional Black Caucus, with the single distinguished exception of its only Republican, Gary Franks of Connecticut, voted within a matter of hours to reject Thomas. Then the black contumely began in earnest. Samples:

• Professor Derrick Bell of Harvard Law School: "The choice of a black like Clarence Thomas replicates the slave masters' practice of elevating to overseer (and other positions of quasipower) those slaves willing to mimic the masters' views, carry out orders and by their presence provide a perverse legitimacy to the oppression they aided and approved. Given what is arguably a First Amendment right to 'act the fool for white folks,' it would be regarded as unseemly for blacks who understand all too well why Thomas should not be seated on the Supreme Court to take the lead in opposing him." Read: No black man whose views are congruent with those of white conservatives is honest.

• Barbara Reynolds, columnist: "I still advocate his confirmation. . . . If Hugo Black, who once was a member of the KKK, could become a distinguished liberal justice, there is hope that a Negro can turn black. Maybe Thomas, who would have lifetime employment as a justice, could find his soul." Read: No black man whose views are congruent with those of white conservatives has a soul.

• Derrick Jackson, the *Boston Globe*: "Both [Booker T. Washington and Clarence Thomas] were showpieces for white conservatives eager to show off African-Americans who rise from poverty, mouthing the sole benefits of individual self-help while the U.S. gets off the hook for large, group injustice." Read: If individual blacks succeed, don't celebrate their success; it casts shadows on those who don't succeed.

• Dewayne Wickman, *USA Today*. "It's foolhardy to think there do not exist scoundrels who would attempt to foist the peculiar tenets of their church upon the rest of us. Such is the nature of the self-righteous. Doug Wilder [governor of Virginia] suggested Clarence Thomas may be such a person. He ought to know." Read: Clarence Thomas threatens the survival of the First Amendment.

• Haywood Burns, Dean, CCNY Law School at Queens: "If [Thomas] has 'made it,' he has at the expense of betraying those from whom he has come." Read: If President Bush appoints a black to high office, that person has betrayed his race—e.g., Colin Powell, or Louis Sullivan.

• An NAACP board member "who asked not to be identified": "Thomas is Bork in blackface. I don't see how we can support someone who stands against everything we stand for." Read: No black who disagrees with the NAACP's board, which disagrees with the 56 percent of American blacks who wish to see Thomas confirmed, should be confirmed.

• Representative Craig Washington, D-Texas: "Clarence Thomas is not fit to shine the shoes of Thurgood Marshall." Read: Go back and eat watermelon, Clarence.

• Barbara Reynolds: "[Clarence Thomas's rulings could be]

influenced by his wife, a white conservative." Read: No aspiring black judge should marry a white conservative.

• Vernon Jarrett, Chicago columnist: "[Clarence Thomas is] Willie Horton in reverse." Read: President Bush uses blacks merely as symbols. Thomas is a bad symbol. (Not clear whether Horton is good symbol.)

• Carl Rowan, columnist: "If they had put David Duke on, I wouldn't scream as much because they would look at David Duke for what he is. If you gave Clarence Thomas a little flour on his face, you'd think you had David Duke talking." Read: Only if you were as dumb as Carl Rowan.

Tens of thousands of blacks who are embarrassed by the extreme statements of some of their spokesmen can take comfort in the fact that they have company among white folks. When Robert Bork was nominated [as already noted above], Senator Edward Kennedy lost no time. "Robert Bork's America is a land in which women would be forced into back-alley abortions, blacks would sit at segregated lunch counters, rogue police could break down citizens' doors in midnight raids."

If you take comfort in being associated with Senator Kennedy, you can take comfort.

—The End of the Affair

October 16, 1991

It is sheer coincidence, but I happen to know someone who has worked side by side with Clarence Thomas since he became a judge, and this friend of incorruptible standards confided in me just days before the Anita Hill scandal broke that Clarence Thomas was a man who irradiated integrity and judicial insight. "You would not recognize the Clarence Thomas I know from his appearance before the Senate [Judiciary] Committee."

On the other hand, we had every reason to expect that the Thomas who would appear before the committee would be a contrivance of his handlers, beginning with President Bush. Mr. Bush launched the charade by saying that he had picked the person "best qualified" to serve on the court. (To begin with, there is no way to discover the person best qualified to serve on the court. This is not a tennis match at Wimbledon, where the best-qualified contestant simply wins.) And then the president said that the race of Clarence Thomas had nothing at all to do with his selection, a statement which, if Mr. Bush had there and then been strapped down to a polygraph, would have catapulted the quivering needles of the machine out of sight.

No wonder, then, that when Mr. Thomas appeared before the committee after six weeks of grooming by White House Procrusteanizers, he sounded like a trained fool. He had "never" discussed *Roe v. Wade* with anybody since its enunciation in 1973, which for a lawyer is rather on the order of saying he had never heard that John F. Kennedy had been shot in Dallas. And when the subject of the natural law arose, he made it sound as though it was a game people played from time to time, like Scrabble.

It was the dirty design of Senate left-ideologues to discover how Mr. Thomas would probably rule on issues that are supposed to be confronted by a man sworn to interpret the Constitution and the laws, not to rewrite either. And this predisposition of contemporary Senate Judiciary Committees brings out recesses of vacuousness in Supreme Court nominees, who if they speak their mind, like Robert Bork, get beaten, and if they give out the impression that they have no mind, like David Souter, get approved.

The lineup on Thomas was, roughly, what one might expect of a black candidate who had vigorously disapproved of racial preferences and was destined to win by a slim majority because enough senators are still inclined to honor the constitutional prerogative of the president to name members to the court.

Along came Hill. Her charges raised several questions, most of them unexamined. Unless I missed it, no senator examining Professor Hill said to her, "Professor, assuming that everything you say is correct, does it follow that Clarence Thomas is disqualified from serving as a Supreme Court justice?"

She might have begged the question by saying, "No, but his perjury about what happened does disqualify him." But the senator could have come back by saying, "Suppose that he had admitted having said to you what you recite?" If Ms. Hill had then said that obscene passes by a man to a woman disqualified someone from honorable service on the court, the interrogator might have gone on to say: "Why is sexual effrontery disqualifying for a member of the court, but not for a member of the Senate, or a president of the United States?"

I don't know what Professor Hill would have answered to that question. But the interrogator could have gone on to say, "Is Senator Ted Kennedy, in your judgment, qualified to vote on legislation for the United States? After all, a Supreme Court justice isn't supposed to pass laws, and for that reason is less important, under the Constitution, than the legislature. If it could be established that Senator Kennedy made a pass at a woman, should he be kicked out?"

Professor Hill might have hesitated to answer the question, giving the interrogator opportunity to press the point. "Are you aware, Professor Hill, of the extracurricular activities of the late Justice William O. Douglas? Ought he to have been confirmed; or, after that, impeached?" After continuing silence, the interrogator might have pressed on to say, "What about a president of the United States? Is he qualified to serve if he has used women in ways inconsistent with orthodox sexual convention? Should Grover Cleveland have been elected, after the discovery of his bastard child? Warren Harding, when his mistress was espied in the closet? John F. Kennedy, who endeavored to beat the record of Don Juan?"

They were all humiliated and humiliating—Bush, Thomas, and Biden and his Rockettes. And they wonder why only one half of the American people bother to vote.

5 THE GULF WAR

—THE UNITED NATIONS AS PARTNER
AUGUST 31, 1990

The sudden enthusiasm for the United Nations requires sober thought, lest we confuse that body with the prodigal son. Internationalists who have been pining for world government for two generations are wildly delighted by the behavior of the United Nations in bringing an all-but-unanimous vote in favor of U.S. initiatives against Iraq. What that vote establishes is not the plebiscitary strength of the United Nations, but its inherent weakness. You see, what it tells you is nothing more than that when the United Nations behaves, it behaves.

What is it that brought on this unanimous vote? Two and a half developments. The first was the decision of the Soviet Union to back the U.S. boycott. What caused the Soviet Union to do the correct thing? Not its correctness, obviously; the Soviet Government had a very great stake in the friendship of the United States during a period when it desperately needed U.S. credit, expertise, and influence.

In fact, the Soviet Union voted the right way against the tug of its own immediate interests, which were a rise in the price of oil. For every ten-dollar rise in the price of oil, the Soviet Union stood to make ten dollars in hard currency as a major oil exporter. The Soviet Union therefore calculated that a hegemony dominated by Iraq in the Persian Gulf, notwithstanding the huge rise in the price of oil such a unit would bring, was not worth defying the United States over.

Then—China. China saw nothing in the vote that damaged its own interests, and was clearly drawn by the opportunity to act in unison with democratic leaders who have been looking askance at the Chinese Government since the affair at Tiananmen Square fifteen months ago.

And then—this is the half—the third world straddlers. We know (the Heritage Foundation has accumulated the statistics) that these nations voted against the United States and in favor of the Soviet Union, back when our interests were clearly separated, about nine times out of ten. The Soviet direction is no longer so important as once it was, given its jettisoning of the ideological baggage. When the Soviet Union was the declared enemy of U.S. policy whatever it was and wherever it was being pursued, the third world amused itself by the twitter it added to the Soviet roar.

Without the Soviet Union to inspire it, it is no longer as inclined to moral infidelities. So the third world voted, for the most part, with the United States. Even Cuba abstained, rather than vote against us. Why? Because Cuba is vaguely angry at the Soviet Union over its bourgeoisification, but not to the point of registering solidarity with Iraq—against the balance of the entire Arab world.

The notion, then, needs to be resisted that the absorption of Kuwait by Iraq was the occasion for a moral epiphany that saved the soul of the United Nations. These are the folk who over the years have closed their eyes to most of the monstrosities committed in our time.

The current vote establishes absolutely nothing other than that the concatenation of elements in the current crisis is unusual. All the pressures, or practically all, have generated in favor of the U.S. position against that of Iraq.

It pays to ask the question: What if Iraq had a nuclear bomb, and threatened to use it? Suppose that it had a meager ballistic delivery system, but one capable of intermediate range, with which it threatened one missile dropped on Moscow, a second on Berlin, a third on Cairo. Would we then see such an amalgam of virtuous forces as have been heralded this time around?

The question is embarrassing because the answer is so obvious. After all, Iraq hasn't done anything that the Soviet Union didn't do as a matter of routine, acting on its own behalf or through a client state, for a generation. But in dealing with the Soviet Union, one dealt with a nation become a superpower if only because of its inventory of nuclear weapons. When a nation becomes nuclear, one calls it Sir.

If anyone approaches the United Nations in search of strategic moral sense, take only a lifetime's rations. If the United Nations were serious, it would have endorsed many years ago the development of anti-missile defense systems—SDI—to guard against the situation not today (all that Iraq has is poison bombs), but tomorrow, when Iraq will have nuclear bombs. That will leave the world with the alternative of intervening to destroy nuclear repositories, or encouraging the development of regional defense systems capable of guarding against incidental nuclear offensives.

But pending all that, beware of any hypnotic delusions about the United Nations.

—Is It Worth Joey's Life?

January 25, 1991

The anti-war people never really found a doctrine after the argument ran dry that we should continue with the sanctions. Some still hang in there with the cry, "We won't die for oil!" but that moral-geopolitical analysis is also tending to run dry as the perception widens that "oil" is simply the convenient symbol of the kind of worldwide aggression that Saddam Hussein had in mind when he overran Kuwait and dealt with it in ways that reminded old-timers of the Rape of Nanking (we hanged the Japanese general who supervised that operation).

"Oil" is or can be as pointed a weapon as bread or water: Industrial societies cannot operate without oil, and most Americans with any imagination acknowledge that they do not wish to engage in a massive retreat to Walden Pond, where they can live beautiful, pure and simple lives without phones, refrigeration, television sets, toasters, or Nintendo.

Perhaps in recognition of how straitened their arguments are, we hear now the personalization, the argument about human life. Anna Quindlen of *The New York Times,* scoffing at the low casualty figures in the Persian Gulf war, says sure, it doesn't matter that only six American aviators have been killed—unless one of them is "your father, your brother, your husband or your lover."

And from Arthur Schlesinger, Jr., no less—a renowned historian—the comment that the gulf war is "not worth one human life."

Now such formulations as these are perilously easy to use, and are guaranteed crowd pleasers. But they are, really, most dreadfully irresponsible. The uses of the argument about a single human life being worth more than everything else you can think of have the appeal of causing the listener to think of his wife or her husband or of their baby child, causing them to ask the question: Would I trade the life of my dear one in exchange for a return to eighteen-dollar oil? The answer, if not the reasoning process, is instantly clarified—or, rather, made more obscure. And the only way to fight it is by turning the melodrama upside down and asking the question: Was it reasonable for Patrick Henry to say, "Give me liberty or give me death"?

But back up for a moment. There are fifty thousand Americans who are killed every year driving their automobiles. Why doesn't Schlesinger say that automobiles should be banned, because the pleasures he takes from them—going to Americans for Democratic Action rallies, driving to the White House when he had offices there, driving down to Coney Island for an afternoon of fun—are all very well, but are they worth the life of his wife, child, sister, or Jackie?

I mean, stop and think of it: Let us suppose that I am addressing a thirty-year-old man with a little three-year-old girl and I say, "I am the god of justice and balance, and I ask you to choose between giving up for the rest of your life driving an automobile, or losing the life of your child." What will you say? Yes, me, too: The child will live, but the god who gave me the alternative I'll stick pins into for the rest of my life.

The attempt to answer military questions by asking the question, How much do you love the kid over there who just got married, the youngest son of proud and devoted parents? is a sentimentalization of important calculations that are necessarily made, so to speak, in cold blood. Liberty, Thomas Jefferson once said, needs to be watered regularly by the blood of tyrants and patriots. That is a little like saying it in Hollywoodese, but you can dry out that observation and ask: Is it or is it not historically the case that a society needs to defend its freedoms?

If the answer is that yes, this does need to be done, then you accost the second question: Does the threat to your freedom begin on the day that the Nazi trooper deposits you in a train to Buchenwald? Or does it begin a little bit before that time—say when Hitler took over the Rhineland and it was still possible to stop him? Or, for that matter, when Hitler seized absolute power in Germany a few years earlier and became visible, to the farsighted, as a genuine threat to European peace? It wasn't just Joey who died finally stopping Hitler, it was fifty million Joeys.

A mature society alert to timely action against destroyers of the peace makes its bid. It might say—to use a round figure—that one fifth of 1 percent of the population is going to die every generation in order to preserve freedom and sovereignty. That's 500,000 people—about what we lost in the three wars that spanned a single generation: World War II, Korea, and Vietnam. It is calculations of that order that arm us for the casualty figures ahead, and it doesn't mean that the death of Joey won't be heartbreaking to those who love him.

—Stop the U.S.S.R. Now
February 19, 1991

The Soviet Union, under the leadership of who-the-hell-knows, is getting into the Persian Gulf act big, and the time to stop this effrontery is right now. Unfortunately, in order to do so, George Bush is going to find himself running into himself, having in days gone by attached such great importance to the vote of the United Nations Security Council.

As a formal situation, this is what we are facing:

The Security Council, after several resolutions leading up to the final one, authorizes member nations to "use all necessary means" required to compel Iraq to abide by the U.N.'s several resolutions that it get out of Kuwait.

The Security Council was not foolish enough to suppose that it could describe exactly what military steps were or were not appropriate to the realization of its objective. But the whole process had to do with the distinction between sanctions, which began in August, and military action, which was sanctioned by the United Nations to begin on January 15 if Iraq hadn't by then complied with the directive to get out of Kuwait.

An entire week before our bombs inflicted casualties on 500 civilians who were taking shelter in a military installation, the Soviet Union began some heavy breathing on the matter of civilians dying in the war. Yevgeny Primakov was sent by the Kremlin to Baghdad to discuss with Saddam Hussein peaceful alternatives to the existing conflict. CNN showed the two gentlemen hugging each other. Indeed, we must assume they have a great deal in common, since Primakov is represented as a figure in what is so unfortunately and confusingly referred to as the "conservative" wing of the Soviet Government, meaning the Stalinist wing, which makes Stalin a conservative, but then, that's the way it goes.

Primakov returned to Moscow and Foreign Ministry spokesman Vitaly Churkin has given us the Solomonic judgment of his superiors. "We have no strategy that would go beyond the U.N. resolutions. Our objective is, as we see it, to persuade Iraq to withdraw from Kuwait."

Well, that is indeed the essence of the U.N. resolution backed by the United States, with this gloss: that in order to secure the safety of Kuwait, it will be necessary to gut the aggressive potential of the gentleman Primakov was hugging during their interview early in the week. Thanks to vigorous action by the allies, led by the United States, this exactly is what is going on.

Now the motives of the U.S.S.R. are not difficult to penetrate. It desires to be the superpower that, at the great moment of confrontation, leaned just enough on the other side to attract the devoted attention of the Muslim brotherhood who are aroused by the consequences of a war in which most of their leaders are engaged side by side with the United States. The Soviet Union counts on a backlash, and such a thing is entirely conceivable, not only in the Muslim world, but also in the Christian world.

The clerics at the World Council of Churches, at their meeting in Canberra, denounced the military action. It is no doubt a coincidence that total U.S. casualties to date are just about as many as the number of Mexicans who were trampled to death worshiping at a Mexican shrine several days ago, suggesting that God's designs are seldom so particularized as to call down moral thunder on well-motivated acts that result in human suffering.

Our intentions in the Persian Gulf are clear and unimpeachable. The Soviet Union's experience with that part of the world took on an aggressive salient against Afghanistan in which it managed to kill 1.2 million Afghans before retreating with 100,000 of its own dead. The U.N. resolutions objecting to Soviet behavior throughout the period went, of course, unheeded. As indeed Saddam, who looks now to the United Nations for relief, ignored its reproaches throughout the fall.

What Bush needs to do in very plain language is to inform the world that the Soviet Union has not been retained as a peacemaker perhaps because it will take a generation or so of expiation for its activities over the past to qualify it as a peacemaker. If the Soviet Government wants to reduce human suffering, it can do this overnight in the Baltics, and in the long term by renouncing Soviet conservatism at home. Meanwhile we should strip Moscow of its beguiling headlines as attempted peacemaker, and bear in mind always as entirely appropriate the image of the Soviet envoy and Saddam Hussein embracing, the celebration of affinities.

—GEORGE BUSH FACES DOWN INSTITUTIONAL
CHRISTIANITY

FEBRUARY 26, 1991

When President Bush went to the Episcopal church opposite the White House to attend services at 7 A.M. on the day after the ground war in the Middle East began, the headline in the *International Herald Tribune* read, FOR BUSH, A PACIFIST SERMON.

Those who weren't there and didn't hear the entire homily need to depend on the two passages quoted in the newspaper dispatch. The Reverend John C. Harper quoted a nineteenth-century Episcopal hymn with the refrain, "The wrath of nations now restrain/Give peace, O God, give peace again." And the sentence quoted from the sermon was to the effect that "restraining our wrath means restraining ourselves. In the end, we must find ways of making peace in our world by making peace in ourselves."

The reader is invited by the headline to suppose that Harper was rebuking Bush for the action he had taken at 8 P.M. the night before when he opened the gate and the tanks went racing north. But it is wrong, if that was the minister's intention, to suppose that he was transcribing Christian doctrine.

Most people who are interested in moral questions having to do with war are familiar with St. Thomas Aquinas' criteria, all of which are met in the current engagement. Fewer are familiar with C. S. Lewis's shrewd passage on anger. A *failure* to feel wrath can be morally emasculating. A call for justice is rightly fueled by wrath at injustice. The failure to react to such acts, on a scale small and large, of which Saddam Hussein is guilty, can be justified as geopolitical cool or isolationism; it cannot be justified to the extent that it reflects indifference.

At church on Sunday, Harper offered prayers for the president, for the armed forces, and "for our enemies." This is essential Christianity. We pray for our enemies in part because they may themselves be innocent of the purposes to which they are being put, in part because in taking such positions as they take, they may be invincibly ignorant, to use the theological term so comprehensive in its indulgence of error—a term, however, misused to the extent that it seeks to launder human misbehavior to the point of eliminating the stain of evil.

While Bush was at a Christian church praying for the enemy, Saddam Hussein was delivering his own sermon. While he had been seeking peace through the United Nations, Saddam told his people, "the treacherous Bush and his filthy agent Fahd, and others who have consorted with them in committing crimes, shame and aggression, committed the treachery. Those cowards who have perfected the act of treachery, treason, and vileness committed treachery after they departed from every path of virtue, goodness, and humanity."

So what should the Iraqi people do? "Fight them with your faith in God. Fight them in defense of every free and honorable woman and every innocent child, and in defense of the values of manhood and the military honor which you shoulder. . . . Fight them and show no mercy toward them. For this is how God wishes the faithful to fight the infidel."

Count as among the victims of Saddam Hussein, on top of the half million in his pointless war against Iran, on top of the Kurds he has gassed, the men and women he has tortured and killed within Iraq, the untold thousands killed and being killed in Kuwait, and the estimated 20,000 Iraqis already dead because Saddam Hussein would not obey the instructions of the same U.N. Security Council to which he was now appealing. Add to these victims God, whose name Saddam Hussein has surely taken in vain.

Whatever byways on the road to this final third act George Bush may have missed, this is the time to adjourn any complaints about them and to concentrate on an ennobling performance. Bush gave the reasons for the stand he took in August; he persuaded all but the unpersuadable (who will not settle for less than a devious motive, preferably mischievous, preferably evil) that the challenge posed by the aggression of Saddam Hussein threatened nothing less than the stability of the entire world. His success in marshaling the vote of the Security Council, which included acts of virtuoso hypnosis of the Soviet and Chinese delegates, is a feat that will live in diplomatic history. His understanding with his generals, with whom he has with exact correctness shared responsibilities—his political, theirs military—is exemplary.

And, finally, that little boot, quiet but resonant, that he finally gave to Mikhail Gorbachev was done adroitly, efficiently, with just the right touch of hauteur: "Gorby, you are getting in the way."

Bush is rightly the man of the hour.

—THE ABANDONMENT OF THE KURDS

APRIL 11, 1991

The events of the past two weeks have been as destructive of Western morale as anything that might have been conceived of during the ecstasy of early March short of a midnight raid by Iraq's Republican Guard that carried off General Norman Schwarzkopf and his principal aides.

The dissipation of the moral satisfaction earned by George Bush merits careful examination because it teaches us that rigid geopolitical formulas have to yield, in special circumstances, to moral considerations when these achieve transcendent importance.

The view of the Bush administration going in was that having effected the evacuation of the Iraqi army from Kuwait, we had done our job. Moreover, that it would be critically important not to pursue the enemy to Baghdad, because to do that would be a) to exceed our franchise, as written by the United Nations; b) to raise suspicions among Arab nations that we were back in the imperialist business, telling other countries what to do and what not to do; and c) to run the specific geopolitical risk of upsetting a balance of power in the area whose stability depended on an unfragmented Iraq, in the absence of which, to use the much-misused term, we would have the Lebanonization of a country with borders on Iran, Turkey, Syria, and Jordan.

That was the schematic that guided U.S. policy. It is, as previously recorded in this space, textbook stuff that, left standing on its own, could competently defend itself in any seminar.

But it was overwhelmed by events of the kind that influence Western thought. We do not know the casualty figures, but the context of them is 1.5 million Kurds destroyed by Iraq during the past eight years—and, in the south, the excuse to mobilize against members of the Shiite minority—which were the catapult that might have sprung Saddam Hussein out of office.

Suddenly all that the world could see was little Kuwait, slowly trying to put its house in order, well-protected in the south by Saudi Arabia, in the north by the diminishing ranks of the great coalition. And everywhere to the north, bloodshed and torture and threatened starvation for every enemy of Saddam Hussein.

If Schwarzkopf had been retained to destroy the opposition to Saddam Hussein, he could not have done better than he has been ordered to do, by standing immobile, while in some cases within the sight of his legions we witness attack helicopters manned by agents of Saddam Hussein shooting and killing the freedom fighters.

Is it too late? Probably. But Representative Stephen Solarz, whose voice was critical in the days that Congress debated whether to back Bush's military operation, is at it again. In the winter months he pleaded with his colleagues to heed political realities and back military opposition to Saddam Hussein. He did so as a politician who had opposed the Vietnam War with his special gift for omnipresence. (When Solarz decides to take on a cause, you read about it in *The New York Times, The New Republic,* view him pleading on the Sunday talk shows and on *Crossfire,* and hear him on the radio.) It was not possible, under the circumstances, for his critics to dismiss him as a perennial hawk.

Solarz plans now to call on the U.N. Security Council to consider a resolution that would instruct the government of Iraq to stop instantly the genocidal war against the Kurds and the rebels in the south. The failure to comply with such an order would constitute a call on the coalition to renew its military operations against Iraq.

It will not prove easy for those countries that voted in favor of the liberation of Kuwait to cavil on the Solarz resolution. No doubt it will be argued that to kill one's own citizens is an internal affair, by which standard the United Nations could not have interfered with Adolf Hitler, so long as his death camps were confined to the territorial boundaries of Germany.

Spokesmen for relief can argue that the renewal of the military operation is merely to complete what was begun in January: that the repulsion of the Iraqi forces from Kuwait served only to chop off a few tentacles from the monster that continues to wage aggressive war.

On Monday, European Community leaders called on the United Nations to establish, in effect, a new country out of a chunk of Iraq, a Kurdish enclave. If these statesmen find that action consistent with the U.N. charter, they should have no trouble with the Solarz resolution.

The best thing Bush could do would be on his own authority to destroy the destroyers, because time has very nearly run out; failing that, to back the Solarz resolution; failing that, to abandon any claim to the triumphant act of statesmanship we have all applauded.

—Causing Tears

June 7, 1991

I very much fear that the joke makers will very quickly make sport of President Bush's performance before the Southern Baptists on Thursday.

It is considered high sport to make fun of a man who breaks into tears, especially if he is a politician. It is generally assumed, and not without reason, that the performance is synthetic. One should begin any reflection on Bush's evidencing tears when he spoke of praying in January before pulling the final lever on war, that he is not a Huey Long, who could cry on the shortest notice.

(It is somewhere recorded that, reciting a speech written for him by one of his entourage, which speech he had not even read over before delivering it, Long reached a line in which he thought the trace of a tear theatrically appropriate. He engineered that tear without any difficulty, and later on casually commented on his proficiency in these dramaturgical matters.)

George Bush was stunningly eloquent in what he said. It is worth noting here that someone not given to rhetorical virtuosity is potentially more moving than the most finished orator. L'il Abner, saying just the right thing in just the right way in extraordinary circumstances, might move in ways even Cato, Henry V, Abraham Lincoln, and Martin Luther King could not. What reaches the listener is the raw agony of the effort to communicate emotion.

What the President of the United States told his audience was that he and his wife prayed together before making the final decision to send Americans in some cases to their deaths. As he recalled that on that evening in January he had broken into tears, tears came freshly to his face. Quickly he disposed of them—but, questioned on the airplane later, he did not deny them. He said that the decision had been one that tore at his emotions, and (he said this clumsily, which was reassuring) in describing his feelings on that historic night, once again he was moved to tears.

Whittaker Chambers wrote to me in 1959, "American men, who weep in droves in movie houses, over the woes of lovestruck shopgirls, hold that weeping in men is unmanly. I have found most men in whom there was depth of experience, or capacity for compassion, singularly apt to tears. How can it be otherwise? One looks and sees; and it would be a kind of impotence to be incapable of, or to grudge, the comment of tears, even while you struggle against them. I am immune to soap opera. But I cannot listen for any length of time to the speaking voice of Kirsten Flagstad, for example, without being done in by that magnificence of tone that seems to speak from the center of sorrow, even from the center of the earth."

When, during a presidential primary campaign in 1972, Senator Edmund Muskie broke down into tears in frustration over an ugly libel against his wife and was then and there judged unfit for presidential office by the tastemakers, I sent him that passage from Chambers, so blindingly beautiful, so incandescently true (though never having heard Kirsten Flagstad speak, I can say only that hearing her singing voice was a tremulous experience).

It is recorded that the night that Harry Truman authorized the *Enola Gay* to drop an atomic bomb over Hiroshima, he had his usual ho ho hearty dinner and went calmly to bed. It is admirable that Truman weighed the considerations and (characteristically) moved decisively, without any compunction about wrongdoing. But one must suppose that Abraham Lincoln—and George Bush —would have spent the night less calmly.

I am required to confess that some of the above is in part self-serving. I have never condemned soldiers to action and possible death, but I have once or twice been given the assignment of eulogist, and I remember two occasions when I was not able to finish words I had myself crafted, summoning as they did to the author of those words the palpable images of the men whose death I was mourning. I admire, but could not imitate, a man whose lachrymal glands could stand up against a eulogy over a departed child.

Milton wrote an elegy to a young man dead, and Bach wrote music searingly beautiful, his own tribute to a departed brother. One must suppose that Milton wept over his poetry, and Bach over his music.

George Bush's tears lent that special gravity that properly attaches to the act of condemning human beings to death. I can't believe that those soldiers who, on the following day, would march in triumph in Washington and, later, in New York, would think any less of their president, who was willing to recall the devout experience on the night he acted, speaking from the center of sorrow, as commander in chief.

THREE

COMMENTING

—OH, FOR THE SIMPLE TRANSACTION
MAY 6, 1986

Stepping out of a bookstore the other day, I drew back. While I was inside it had started to rain. There then happened one of those tiny, inconsequential transactions that go to the heart of commerce. A middle-aged black man was sitting on a stool just under a protective awning, and in a large portable wastebasket of sorts he had a collection of umbrellas. There is nothing one wants more than an umbrella when caught in the rain. How much? Five bucks, he said. I gave him five dollars and walked happily, securely, into the rain. I am glad there is no law that made it illegal for me to do what I did. (Curses! Is there one?) I didn't inspect the man's license to sell umbrellas on the street, did not inspect the umbrella for a union label, did not ask whether the seller or his wares had been approved by OSHA, and did not take the name of the seller, in order to report to the Internal Revenue Service that I had paid him five dollars.

The next problem was a bus. I spotted one and entered it. To my great relief I learned that the bus was asking for one dollar, instead of for ninety cents, inasmuch as people who carry packets of ninety cents around with them are blessed with more organized habits than I was born with. With exemplary panache I handed the driver a dollar bill—only to be told that buses do not accept bills. I wondered whether this was a drive against counterfeiters—for a while, during World War II, you could come in across the Mexican border only with two-dollar bills, because Nazi counterfeiters had flooded Mexico with U.S. dollars of every other denomination. But no, the idea, one learns, is to protect the bus driver from robbers.

The bureaucrats who write regulations and are so far removed from reality for some reason didn't in their planning acknowledge a very basic reality, namely that you can fold or roll up a dollar bill and insert it into the narrowest receptacle, causing the same security experienced by four quarters, or ten dimes, or twenty nickels. The driver told me I would need the change, and so I began one of those clumsy search-in-every-pocket rituals as slowly as possible, permitting as many city blocks as possible to glide by in the event I was finally ejected because I had on me only dollar bills. Sensing, finally, that I was engaged in a theatrical charade, the bus driver took pity and said in a voice loud enough for a half-dozen passengers nearby to hear, that perhaps someone would be willing to make change for me or to sell me a token, which an obliging gentleman proceeded to do.

I reflected, over the thirty-block bus ride, on the difference between free-spirited laissez-faire and the kind of laws that get passed by bodies of men and women who love central planning. In the one case, you simply fork out the money and buy the umbrella. In the other, you had to go through three motions, and unless you were lucky, you would be out on the street and the Metropolitan Transit Authority, which wants money from Washington to make up its deficit, would have been out one perfectly good dollar bill, usable as legal tender.

These microcosmic incidents hug the memory when one comes across fustian denunciations of Michael Deaver. Deaver was asked by one reporter what he thought he was doing, setting up a public relations firm when he left government, to which Deaver gave just the right answer: "Did you think after twenty years in government I was going into the ice cream business?" What Mike Deaver is doing for a living is changing people's dollar bills into tender negotiable in federal buses. Mr. William Safire advises us that the number of lobbyists assigned to the Senate has risen from 5,000 to 20,000 in the last five years. Well, somebody has to fence the opinion of legitimate merchandisers—some of them make umbrellas for entrepreneurs-in-the-rain to peddle—in legislative and executive quarters.

We should launder our minds every now and then, flush out the bureaucratic cobwebs, and get back to the umbrellas needed in the rain. Willing seller, willing buyer—beautiful.

—The Fight Against Ho-hum Anti-terrorism
June 3, 1986

The Israeli ambassador to the United Nations is, as most Israelis are on the vital questions, strictly no-nonsense on the matter of terrorism. His recently published book, *Terrorism: How the West Can Win,* has a sad-fascinating provenance. It almost slips the memory that in 1976 an Air France plane was hijacked and taken to Uganda.

What followed was the legendary Entebbe raid. A squadron of Israeli airplanes set out in the dead of night. Mission: rescue the passengers of the airplane. They did this but, as might have been expected, there were a few casualties. One of them was Lieutenant Jonathan Netanyahu. In his memory the Jonathan Foundation was founded. It is an Israeli think tank devoted to devising means of combating terrorism. And the book by the dead man's brother, Benjamin, is a keenly edited report of the most recent meeting of the Jonathan Foundation in Washington in 1904. Participating in the seminars that led to the book were, among others, Michael Ledeen of Georgetown University; Secretary of State George Shultz; Senators Daniel Patrick Moynihan, Alan Cranston, and Paul Laxalt; former U.N. ambassador Jeane Kirkpatrick; Yitzhak Rabin, George Will, Paul Johnson, and Jean-François Revel. Match that, if you are in the business of brainpower gathering.

It becomes important, along the line, to define terrorism. Mr. Netanyahu's definition is a very good start. He defines terrorism as "the deliberate and systematic murder, maiming and menacing of the innocent to inspire fear for political ends."

Flashback. In 1973, at the United Nations, the U.S. delegation, myself included, struggled to get the General Assembly to deplore terrorism in a comprehensive way. The great windbag of the U.N. in those days, and indeed every day during the quarter century in which he figured in the U.N.'s history, was Mr. Jamil Baroody, the ambassador of Saudi Arabia. I kid you not when I tell you that he offered the following amendment to the simpler definition of terrorism backed by the United States and a few allies. The resolution, Ambassador Baroody said, should read: "Measures to Prevent Terrorism and Other Forms of Violence Which Endanger or Take Innocent Human Lives or Jeopardize Fundamental Freedoms, and Study of the Underlying Causes of Those Forms of Terrorism and Acts of Violence Which Lie in Misery, Frustration, Grievance, and Despair and Which Cause Some People to Sacrifice Human Lives, Including Their Own in an Attempt to Effect Radical Changes."

Well, that will buy you a franchise to terrorize McDonald's, if you are Burger King. And, of course, the movement to condemn terrorism in a comprehensive way failed, even as it continues to fail today. The measure of the failure isn't the U.N.'s usual paralysis. It is the apparent paralysis of the free world in making common cause, the explosive example of which came when, in April, the United States did take modest action against Qaddafi in Libya only to awaken the next day to pronouncements in Western Europe that gave the impression that we had bombed not Libya but England, France, Spain, Italy, and West Germany, and maybe even Bethlehem.

Mr. Netanyahu believes it is a challenge of focus. His point is that it is creepingly self-evident that there is no excuse for terrorism, and that terrorism can't be dealt with by dilettantes. He says it right out: 1) No concessions: never acquiesce in terrorist demands. 2) No appeasement of easygoing countries that tolerate transient terrorists, let alone resident terrorist training. 3) Common policies among allies (he means, obviously, try to insist on common policies. 4) Diplomatic sanctions (close down the appropriate embassies). 5) Economic sanctions against terrorist sanctuaries, including boycott and embargo. 6) Increasing pressure on "neutral" countries, e.g., those that permit airlines from Syria or Libya to land in their territory. 7) Concentrating on what hurts the target countries economically. 8) Educating the media: The press "should treat terrorists the way it treats organized crime."

This commentator sees Ambassador Netanyahu, and raises him one. What are we going to do about the Soviet Union? It is conceded by all the authors who contribute to his volume that the Soviet Union is, really, the principal engine of international terrorism. So does that leave us chopping off the hydra's coils, leaving the head forever immune? Ah, but that is the challenge of the era, the challenge of how to deal with the evil empire.

—Making Policy as the Crow Flies

July 15, 1986

In French and Spanish the word "serious" has a meaning that doesn't correspond with any of the synonyms given for that word in English. It means responsible, reliable, trustworthy, reflective. The other day, James Jackson Kilpatrick, who is a serious man, made an unserious suggestion about how we should deal with dope traffickers. It repays hard attention to the meaning of the word to understand its ramifications in the current situation.

What we ought to do, said Mr. Kilpatrick, is catch a bunch of dope traders, try them, convict them, and then hang them in public squares.

Now if you heard that kind of talk from the mouth of, oh, the early or even the middle George Wallace, you would smile and say: there he goes again, the same man who suggested the best way to deal with protesters standing in the way of a bulldozer is to bulldoze them.

But Jack Kilpatrick really means it. It is an expression of high dudgeon and also a concrete recommendation. He has heard described, and he has witnessed, the tortures experienced by those taken in the biological and psychological death agonies of drug consumption. It is agony whether you go on to die or whether you go on to live. Kilpatrick's point is that if ever there was justification for executing a murderer, there is justification for executing those wanton murderers who distribute narcotics that cause worse pain by many leagues than any pain experienced by the mugger's pistol shot.

Ten days ago we saw happen almost exactly that in Malaysia. The executions were not, to my knowledge, public, but they might as well have been, given the attention paid them in the world press. Two Australians, caught with merchandisable quantities of heroin, were tried, convicted and, after due process using up almost three years, hanged.

There was the usual outcry from the anti-capital-punishment set and even a few others, but the government of Malaysia stood its ground, pointing out that there were signs all over the place warning potential drug merchants of the fate that would befall them. It is of passing interest that the local equivalent of the American Civil Liberties Union, which opposes capital punishment, announced that drug merchandising was a crime so heinous that opposition to capital punishment was officially suspended when applied to that crime.

But Mr. Kilpatrick's suggestion is not serious. It is not responsible. It is not reputable. It is not viable. Why? Because it is absolutely predictable that it will not happen.

This has nothing whatever to do with the entirely different question: Should it happen? If tomorrow I needed to vote yes or no on a national plebiscite, "Shall we adopt the Kilpatrick Proposition?" I would unflinchingly vote yes. And after, oh, a couple of hundred hangings, there would be a very sharp decrease in the merchandising of drugs. It wouldn't cease, any more than crime in Great Britain ceased when they used to hang you for stealing sixpence. But in modern America death sentences are taken much more seriously than they were two hundred years ago, when executions were commonplace and public floggings a regular feature of city life. There are still a lot of people out there who maintain that there are no figures to sustain the proposition that capital punishment reduces the incidence of murder. Well, let that one go. But it would be hard to find anyone who would dispute the conclusion that public hangings would dry up the assembly line of drugs passing under the eyes of the American public on a vibrant street corner.

But this is not going to happen. We are too frozen, institutionally, in our views about executions, let alone public executions. So then why make the suggestion? If it were done in the spirit of fantasy ("One day they passed a law . . . the next day, the consumption of drugs dropped by 90 percent"), that would be one thing. But Mr. Kilpatrick was being—in the American usage—serious. But not serious in the continental sense.

Cocaine consumption is up 600 percent in many American cities. In Pakistan, the morning paper advises us, the growth of poppies is up 400 percent over last year. A lot of that stuff is destined for American blood vessels. And we can't stop it, and aren't stopping it. We are subsidizing a criminal class, overflowing our prisons, corrupting the police and the courts, depleting our reserves of detectives and judges, and accomplishing nothing. Either bring on the scaffold (which we aren't going to do), or legalize (which we probably aren't going to do either). We can, then, look for more of the same. Much more of the same.

—MORE OF THE SAME

SEPTEMBER 7, 1989

If I were a Constitutional Convention, I swear I would make it illegal for politicians to compare the costs of apples to the cost of false teeth. The whole of the official reply to President Bush's (anemic) drug crusade consisted of that kind of thing. Here he is, spending a mere $8 billion on the drug war, but he's willing to spend $166 billion in bailing out the savings and loan crowd, and $300 billion on defense. Ad nauseam.

The bailout of the S&L industry can take this form or that form, but it consists essentially of redeeming the pledge of the U.S. Government to protect the savings of depositors. If Senator Biden and the Democratic wailing wall think that drugs preoccupy the American people, they should try repealing the law pledging the security of individual depositors, give that $166 billion to the drug program instead, and then prepare to retire from public life, which would come shortly after, or shortly before, they were hauled out of Congress and tarred and feathered on Pennsylvania Avenue.

In respect of what we spend on the military, the idea, dear senator, is to protect the United States from nuclear devastation, which, believe it or not, is a higher priority even than the drug problem. But (sigh) no doubt as long as we live, we'll hear a politician complain that we are spending less on research for muscular dystrophy than we are on interstate highways. Just promise me to tune out when you hear somebody say that kind of thing, OK? As noisily as possible.

Now both Bush and Biden said one truly interesting thing. Let us agree that it is obviously interesting to mobilize public pressure against drugs. But although it's nice to have a pep talk from the Oval Office on the subject, it isn't all that necessary. If there is one day that goes by without the newspaper or the television or the radio or the comic strips or the pulpiteer telling us about the danger of drugs, it is a coincidence similar to a simultaneous eclipse of the sun, moon, and planets. What was interesting in what Bush said wasn't that we were going to spend more money (everybody knew we would spend more money), or that we would be tougher on the user (that has been making the rounds for a year or so), or that we need more jail space (we've needed it for six years). It was that glancing sentence about how the drug kings would be—executed. Yes, executed.

Now the electric chair is pretty serious business. If indeed President Bush is going to begin a movement to hang drug merchants, what is the legislative scenario for such legislation, beyond the 1988 law which makes it technically possible to get the death sentence for a drug merchant involved in a transaction that resulted in people getting killed? What are we going to do about getting the Supreme Court to OK it? Are we confident that we will be able to cope with the anti-capital-punishment lobby, which is not without its reserves? What are the prospects that one offender will actually be executed before, oh, the end of Bush's second term?

And then Senator Biden is talking—again, glancingly—about a "strike force" commissioned to go to wherever drugs are being grown and processed. Presumably this would exclude Vietnam, since we can't go back to Vietnam under any circumstances; but short of there, is Senator Biden suggesting that our strike force should be prepared to descend into the prairies, jungles, and tundras of Bolivia, Peru, Chile, Pakistan, India, Cambodia, Burma, and China, not to say the fifteen or twenty states within our own borders which glow with pride over the quality of their golden grass? Strike forces with that kind of a mandate will certainly eliminate whatever unemployment problem we have left. But one wonders whether the Democratic Party will stick with Senator Rambo's expeditionary forces.

One can only hope that the not-very-new federal program bears fruit. As President Bush pointed out, in the last five years the number of dilettante drug users has decreased by more than one third, which is splendid news. But the hard users are growing in number, and their victims crowd graveyards and hospitals. The beginning of wisdom about the evil of addiction to something as compelling as crack is that the user cares only that he get it. If it is available, he will get it. If there is a woman with a handbag standing between him and crack, that woman will lose her handbag. If it is a cop, he will be a dead cop, or else the user will begin his tortuous way to nonexistent jail cells. We will have, unless President Bush's genocide-for-merchants bill gets written into the law, or Senator Biden's army conquers the world, more of the same.

—THE EXQUISITE PHILANTHROPY OF MR. LANG

AUGUST 7, 1986

Herewith a report on an enterprise that gives out one of those Fourth of July tingles that occasionally remind us that: a) the United States is a pretty special place; and b) it could be a lot better.

The story begins with a highly successful New York businessman, Mr. Gene Lang, who some years ago was asked to address the eighth grade graduating ceremonies held in the high school he had attended. He prepared one of those pretty speeches, what one might call Horatio Alger boilerplate, about how glorious was the future of the young American graduating from junior high. But on the way to the ceremony he surveyed the figures. Of 100 children who matriculate in New York City high schools, 25 will graduate. And only one half of those graduates will qualify to go on to a city university.

Mr. Lang threw away his speech and said to the students: Here are the statistics you face. Now if you bring yourself to overcome the odds, I will pay your college tuition. He is now financing the college tuition of the overwhelming majority.

Peter Flanigan, a cosmopolitan banker associated with the firm of Dillon, Read and sometime assistant to President Nixon, pondered the story and came upon an extraordinary anomaly. Whereas 75 percent of public-school children don't graduate, 96 percent of those who attend the Catholic-run schools do graduate, and three quarters of them go on to college. Is this effected by expelling all backward or unruly children? It turns out that the parochial schools expel a smaller percentage of students than the public schools send to correctional institutes.

Well then, surely there is a line ten miles long of applicants for admission to the parochial schools? Negative. There are hundreds of empty seats: The parents—or rather the parent in most cases—don't have the money.

An organization called Student/Sponsor Partnership was born. Individual New Yorkers are invited to sponsor a student selected by the administrators of Cardinal Hayes High School (for boys), or Cathedral High School (for girls). Requirements: The selected student must not be a genius (geniuses can take care of themselves) or an imbecile (waste of any school's time). The student must come from a single-parent home, the parent on welfare. The sponsor contracts a) to put up $1,500 per year for his student; b) to make himself (or herself) accessible to encourage the student and to keep an eye on the student's progress; and c) to consult periodically with a special counselor whom the schools bring in to monitor the student's progress, get him out of bed if he is playing hookey, advise him on his work, and make provisions for extra work as required.

Now the ethnic mix in the schools we speak of is indistinguishable. Roughly, they are 55 percent black, 45 percent Hispanic. One third of the students attending the two Catholic high schools are non-Catholic. The program, which will be tax-deductible, is nonsectarian. It is a brand-new idea, but already the Student/Sponsor organization has lined up sponsors for twenty boys and twelve girls beginning next September. Some sponsors who cannot afford the $1,500 put up a part of it, the balance coming from someone else, the question of who will act as the personal sponsor left open for Solomonic dispensation.

So there we are. There is the ugly residue left in one's thinking on this matter, namely why on earth are the high schools, given the identical raw material, doing such a lousy job? But the invitation is not to invidious comparison, rather to the satisfaction of knowing how, by relatively small exertions, individual lives can be changed. The difference between graduating from high school and going on to college, and dropping out of school at age fifteen or sixteen can mean the difference between a lifetime spoiled and a lifetime consummated. Mr. Flanigan recalls that many affluent

New Yorkers drive right by the Bronx every day. They have it within their power to pull an individual human being away from the ghetto.

And the problems of New York, in this respect, are not so different from the problems of other great municipal centers in America.

—Is There a Role for the Moralist?

March 17, 1987

A couple of years ago I received a letter from a married woman, name undisclosed. Her husband was sterile and, at age thirty-nine, she wished a child and asked me to be its father. Her letter, transmitted through her lawyer, described her as a professional working woman and an active Christian who wished to mother and bring up a child. The covering letter from the lawyer confirmed her factual statements, and confirmed also that the mother and father would have no difficulty in supporting the child. The mother proposed that the child be begotten by artificial insemination.

I paused over that request longer, probably, than most people would have done. Providence decreed that my wife and I would have only a single child. I wondered, of course, what kind of satisfaction could an absentee, let alone an anonymous, father take from mere procreation. What appealed uniquely, under the circumstances, was the prospect of helping a woman, who desired this seed, to become a mother. And then my thoughts turned to the question: Is there a moral right and wrong in the situation?

Now, I am a Roman Catholic, though by no means unique among those who believe that that which is right or that which is wrong is not necessarily the outcome of one's own moral ratiocination. The Catholic Church most conspicuously administers something called the magisterium, which addresses difficult moral questions and advises on them. Christian teaching tells you that you cannot override your own conscience—so that, for instance, if your conscience tells you that it is wrong under any circumstances to kill, then the church's authorization of the act of killing in a just war is subordinated to the verdict of your own conscience.

Christian teaching would distinguish between the active conscience that took direct moral issue over a church teaching, and the conscience engaged in self-indulgence. It is widely known, for instance, that perhaps a majority of Catholics practice some form of birth control. It is widely supposed that a small minority of those who do, do so because they object to the proscriptions by the Vatican on birth control on moral grounds.

Along come the massive declarations of the Vatican on the whole matter of the uses of technology in respect of birth. The Vatican's ruling is that such a step as I once considered would be wrong. More: that *in vitro* fertilizations are wrong. More: that medical intervention of any sort in the process of fetal growth is wrong.

Now, the instinctive reaction of a world grown morally solipsistic is: Do I like that ruling? Does that ruling serve my interests? My own inclinations? It is unusual for the citizen to defer presumptively to the moral authority of others. It is one thing for the citizen to accept democratic legislation. If a law is passed tomorrow that requires you to surrender an extra 3 percent of your income to the Treasury, why, you simply do exactly that. Because among the things that might otherwise happen if you don't do exactly that is that the police will arrive at your door. But there are no clerical police anymore.

We have now a front-page story in *The New York Times* the lead sentence of which is a marvelously innocent party to the relevant questions.

"The Vatican's recent proposals urging governments to ban medical intervention in human reproduction," writes the *Times*'s Marcia Chambers, "raise serious constitutional issues that could soon emerge in state legislatures and the courts, legal scholars say. The experts say that if laws supporting the Vatican's position are adopted, challenges to them would center on two legal doctrines: the right to privacy in decisions controlling a human's body and church and state separation under the First Amendment to the Constitution."

There is a lot of unmeditated thought in that paragraph. Presumably if the Vatican came out against racial discrimination in

1854, the U.S. Supreme Court would nevertheless have felt free to wait until 1954 to prohibit Jim Crow. But the silly business apart— the suggestion that a codification by the American democratic process of ideas that originated with a church somehow makes those laws fragile—we really ought to acknowledge (within reason) the role of the professional moralist.

There are moral quandaries, and we need guidance. And those who believe that the Judeo-Christian narrative is God's narrative should give special attention to the personal relevance of a body of men whose lifelong concern is the study of right and wrong, and how to tell the difference between the two.

—QUICK! GET MILTON FRIEDMAN ON THE LINE!
OCTOBER 22, 1987

So the stock market goes to hell; what do you do? First you eliminate jumping out of the window, which is reactionary. Then you mull over your resources, foremost of which, in my case, is Professor Milton Friedman, who will answer my telephone call. He is, after all, a Nobel Prize winner, the most celebrated living economist in the world, and if you catch him with his mouth open you can bet that an opinion has just come out of it. If you catch him with his mouth closed, you can bet that he has just bitten an opinion in two. And he is my beloved friend.

How are you, Milton?

We're fine, how are you?

I was wondering whether you could do me a favor. I would like nine hundred words for *National Review* on the market breakdown. We would need it by Thursday, noon.

Nope.

Why not?

I have never written an economic analysis tailored to the market, and I'm not going to start doing that now.

Why?

Because the behavior of the market doesn't correlate in any significant way with the behavior of the economy. It's a mistake to imply that it does, and that's what would be inferred if I wrote about it.

Well, why don't you write precisely on that theme? And it wouldn't be cheating, would it, if you were to suggest what the investor might expect from the market, given the condition of the economy?

Yes, it would—I would be in the business of vetting the market, and I just told you, I'm not going to do that. I make my own decisions about the market, but not for public instruction. I sold all my stocks during the summer.

You did!

I did. And I'm going back into the market tomorrow. Bulls can make money, and bears can make money, but hogs can't make money. The hog is the man who insists on waiting until the stock market is at rock bottom. He will be left behind.

Well, it seems to me you've already said something interesting, right there.

The only thing you can say about the market is what J. P. Morgan said about it. He was asked and said, "The market will fluctuate."

But this has got to be more than fluctuation, doesn't it? The talk is of another 1929 depression.

Nonsense. I have been predicting for quite a while a recession in the next six to nine months, but that's a long way from a depression. Remember that the economy, this time around, has not peaked. In 1929, the economy had peaked in August. So that the two events are not comparable in the most important way.

Well, do you go along with the proposition that there are safeguards built into the system that would prevent a depression on a 1929 scale?

In 1954, I delivered a lecture in Sweden under the title, "Why the American Economy Is Depression-Proof." I have seen no reason since then, and see none now, to change that conclusion.

But your position all along has been that even the Great Depression was avoidable, correct? Even without the Federal Deposit Insurance Corp., and the SEC, and Social Security, et cetera?

Yes. The economic downturn from August 1929 to the end of 1930 was more severe than during the first year of most recessions, but if an upturn had come shortly after, the episode would have been classified as a garden-variety recession. It was converted into the Great Depression by the collapse of the financial system in successive waves. In 1931, 1932, and 1933. The stock market played no significant role in this collapse. The argument that the 1929 market crash produced the 1931 to 1933 economic contraction is a prime example of *post hoc, ergo propter hoc.*

You're saying that it could all have been avoided?

Yes. The financial collapse of 1931 to 1933 need not have occurred and would have been avoided if the Fed had never been established, or if it had behaved differently. The Fed's inept performance led to changes in the financial system that make a similar financial collapse highly unlikely.

Well, that's good news, isn't it?

Yes, that's good news.

I still don't see why you won't write nine hundred words on just what you've said for *National Review*.

You've got nine hundred words in what I've just said.

Good point. Thanks a lot, Milton, and good night.

Good night, Bill.

Anytime.

This is Bill Buckley, saying good night.

WE'LL SEE YOU FOR $100 BILLION
SEPTEMBER 19, 1989

The question most often asked is, "Do you hope that Gorbachev will succeed?" The formulation that typically follows is, "Do you think Gorbachev will succeed?"

It is illuminating to organize one's mind to answer these questions by contemplating what it is we do not want. Clearly, what we don't want is an economically reconstituted Soviet Union braced to renew its seventy-year offensive against the free world.

The evidence is great that, finally, the Marxist-Leninist afflatus, which commanded the Soviet Union, arm-in-arm with history, to spearhead a drive against the free world, is intellectually and spiritually dead. Although we recognize the abundant signs of an

exhausted historical imperative, we know also that there are the-
aters in the world in which activity goes forward of exactly the
same character as went forward under the leadership of Stalin and
Khrushchev and Brezhnev. That Mikhail Gorbachev has tacitly
renounced his own pledge to communize the world, even though it
was reiterated as recently as 1988, is meaningless to many non-
Russians, for instance in North Korea, China, Vietnam, and Cuba.

We do not know whether the sound of the Marxist tocsin is
completely stilled, and we certainly don't know whether historical
Russian expansionism is dying with the twentieth century. We do
know one thing of salient importance.

It is that the Soviet Union is in dire economic straits. Last
June, Deputy Prime Minister Leonid Abalkin, who serves directly
under Gorbachev, addressed a meeting of his fellow economists
and declared flatly that the Soviet Union as presently constituted
had two years left to live; that if economic reforms had not by then
taken hold, anything might happen. Specifically, Abalkin mentioned the possibility of a "rightward swing," by which is meant, in
Soviet terminology, a Stalinist swing.

Professor Richard Pipes of Harvard, the distinguished historian who has just completed a monumental work on Russia, advances the interesting point that Gorbachev's immunity resides
largely from the recognition by all conceivable alternative rulers of
the Soviet Union that were they to take power, they would end by
being powerless themselves. The shortage of housing, food, medicine, and basic materials is not something that can be provided by
any change in leadership or by any fresh dogmatical brew. There is
only one thing that can save the Soviet Union economically, and
that is hard currency.

In 1988 the Soviet Union spent, in constant dollars, 3 percent
more than it had ever spent before on its armament industry. We
know that today, even after the INF Treaty, the Soviets are more
powerful as a nuclear nation than ever they were before. And of
course we know that the strength of their conventional forces outweighs that which NATO commands by roughly two and a half to
one.

I would propose a purchase of (nonreplenishable) Soviet military equipment, nuclear and non-nuclear, of $100 billion per year
for the next three years. A carefully tabulated catalogue of Soviet

military hardware should be compiled calculating that which is redundant to a purely defensive conventional force and a deterrent nuclear force. The missiles and warheads and tanks and submarines and armed carriers would file out of Soviet ports onto U.S. shipping and, upon reaching the continental shelf, be jettisoned out to sea.

Three years of such activity would accomplish two goals. The first is the economic rejuvenation of the Soviet Union, with the huge capital investment of $300 billion. The second is the destruction of that incremental inventory of Soviet weapons that endangers peace on earth. The financing of the enterprise would be done by reducing our own military budget by $100 billion per year for three years, which under these special circumstances we could afford to do.

I don't deny that the proposal is complicated in detail, but it is simple in conception. The outcry that the Soviet Union would never consent to such an arrangement leaves it for us to say only that it is not inconceivable, given the pressures on the Soviet economy. To which we add: If the Soviet Union refuses the exchange, we will have learned much that is useful for us to know. Indeed, much that is vital for us to know.

—The Slow Death of Princess Di

June 23, 1992

The scene in Great Britain is very sad, and is nicely captured by the headline in the current *National Review,* WILL THE BRITISH MONARCHY SURVIVE THE ROYAL FAMILY? There are several aspects of the Cinderella story that have especially captured the British.

There is, to begin with, the absolutely chimerical quality of Princess Diana. If a more beautiful woman ever existed, she was never photographed. Inevitably, the very thought that such a woman as she has been mistreated gives rise to questions about the tortfeasor.

How is it humanly possible, people are quite naturally asking themselves, that such a creature as Lady Diana Spencer should be neglected by the Prince of Wales? If the biographer is to be believed, and his credentials appear to be pretty reliable, the relations between Him & Her aren't merely a matter of minor incompatibilities. They appear to loathe each other's company.

Explanations for this are given that don't really make much sense: She likes rock music and soaps and fashion and stuff, and he likes serious-minded matters, is something of an evangelist at heart, and thinks her quite impossibly trivial.

The trouble with that explanation is that some of the most wonderful marriages in the whole world unite just such women with just such men. They engender a love that transcends these disjunctures, and live dreamy lives—in the case of the current attractions, surrounded by palaces and banquets and jewels and adoring multitudes.

The setback at this point is very serious for Prince Charles, because people are asking themselves: What's the matter with him? He's not queer, they say, because in fact he has Another Woman. But it is certainly queer, they are saying, to prefer any other woman to Princess Di.

A second point has to do with a sense of shock that the story should be so widely told. A book and the tabloids, sure; but serialized in London's _Sunday Times_? If you were to marry _The New York Times_ with the _Congressional Quarterly_ and the annual publication of the Bureau of Weights and Measures, you would have some idea of the . . . sanctity of the serious British press. Granted, much of its gravity is gone in recent years, and Rupert Murdoch has made the _Times,_ by contrast with the _Times_ of twenty years ago, a relative swinger. But for _The Sunday Times_ to serialize the inside story of the decomposition of the marriage of the heir to the throne!

Sir Peregrine Worsthorne, a distinguished journalist and columnist, has (seriously?) suggested that the time has come in Great Britain to restore horsewhipping. Yes, he would horsewhip the owner of _The Sunday Times,_ the said Mr. Murdoch, and also the editor, Andrew Neil. His idea is that only such exemplary treatment of the malefactors could adequately portray the sense of national outrage at publishing the inside story of a private marriage.

But a third current of thought is much more relaxed. There

are observers of the scene who are saying to themselves that it is really a most awful pity that the dream lady and, as princes go, an OK heir have gotten themselves into a two-scorpions-in-a-bottle situation. If she leaves him, which appears inevitable, and he ascends to the throne (which is not inevitable: Monarchs live forever —Louis XIV was succeeded by his great-grandson), it will make for a bloody awkward situation.

This isn't the way the royal dream world is supposed to go, and inevitably the question occurs to some people: Ought an end to be put to the whole charade?

No doubt if Ross Perot were to announce that after serving as president for a while he will agree to act as prime minister of Great Britain, that would put an end to all those fancy-dress anachronisms. A Texan who says that if elected president he wouldn't allow "Hail to the Chief" to be played in his presence would hardly put up with all that royal festoonery, which is the iron bodice that binds such as Princess Margaret, Prince Andrew, Princess Anne, and now the poor Prince of Wales to standards they simply aren't prepared to meet.

But there is another school of thought, held by a diminishing minority. It says: Look, you may be wretchedly unhappy as a human being, but you have elected to serve in a position that has normative responsibilities. Bite your lip, weep at night, and pray that God will lift the weight from your shoulders, but accept it that you are a prince/princess and that as you betray your weaknesses, so others are minded to yield to theirs, and the consequences can be as disastrous as those that followed the dissolute courts of Charles II and Louis XVI and—up to a point—Alexander II.

There are those who like to think that if you cannot prevent yourself from committing suicide, why then do it in the manner of Robert Maxwell. But don't protract the pain and disappointment and disillusion for a whole people for so very long a period.

—RESTORATION TIME?

JULY 3, 1992

We learn that on the death of that Romanov who was generally accepted as the pretender, there was a meeting of the surviving Romanovs, at which Nicholas, who is sixty-nine and lives in Rougemont in Switzerland, proclaimed himself the head of the Romanov clan.

The only other plausible contender is the daughter of the expired Romanov, but there are reasons why, in the estimate of Nicholas of Rougemont, she is not qualified. They are too technical to set down, but are very persuasive to those who follow the warp and woof of dynastic legitimacy.

I ought to add that I am personally acquainted with Nicholas of Rougemont, and can certify that he is not a gentleman given to idle fancies. So that, Nicholas having asserted himself as head Romanov, the question instantly arises: Might he be useful to the sometime Soviet Union, particularly at this moment?

But no sooner does Romanov of Rougemont announce that he is No. 1, he goes on to say that he does not believe in restoration! He believes that the country we are talking about ought to have a "constitutional president." In other words, he wants for the former Soviet Union nothing very different from what we settle for here in America.

In doing so, it occurs to a great many people, he is undermining one of the principal purposes of a monarch, which is, surely, to transcend politics.

A year or so back, King Constantine of Greece was on *Firing Line*, and the program looked into the question: Is there a role for the monarch? Constantine is an anointed king, which is why he is referred to as "King" Constantine. What happened to him, however, is that a coup he engineered against the colonels who had come to power in 1967 failed. He fled the country, and when the coup came that overthrew the colonels, the incoming prime minister organized a hasty referendum that voted to abolish the monarchy.

Even so, the dream of restoration is never far from his fancy, or from that of a great many Greeks who believe that exactly what Greece needs now is a figure who is above the politics that have made that ancient, inspiring country something of a tatterdemalion economic and political embarrassment. On *Firing Line*, panelist Michael Kinsley said to him, "King Constantine, why don't you go back to Greece and run for office?" His answer: "It isn't my role to run for office."

That put it nicely, I thought. Kings (and queens) precisely shouldn't "run" for office. They should run from any prospect of running for office.

What they should do, when serving, is of course to uplift the country whose sovereign they are. That is the problem, right now, of Great Britain. Certainly not that of Queen Elizabeth, who appears to be exemplary in all matters, but the problem of the House of Windsor, even as hemophilia was for so long a problem of the Romanovs.

But if we could forget the distractions of Fergie–Di–Margaret et al., we'd see that the Queen serves as a cohesive force at just the moment when cohesive forces are very badly needed. If the day after tomorrow we are to discover that Czechoslovakia is now two countries, even as Yugoslavia is three, perhaps four, perhaps even five countries, why should we be surprised if the Scots were to assert their independence? And if so, should Wales be left grafted onto England, notwithstanding those polarities of history and culture?

What got the name of "Balkanization" after World War I is very much the rage in Europe right now, and such comfort as we can take from the scene has to do with the providential fact that no power in Europe is bent on conquering its neighbors. Within conventional borders, that kind of thing is going on, and the entire world is steamed up attempting to help victims of the Serbs, who wish more territory than that to which they appear entitled. But in the eastern Ukraine there is a heavy concentration of Russians, as there is a heavy concentration of them in two of the Baltic states.

It is a time to engage in extrapolitical figures, and it would be healthy to see a commission within the United Nations consider— as a peacemaking measure, precisely—restoration. In Ethiopia, for example, riven as it is by ethnic antagonisms, what better than a Haile Selassie who, however, would be constitutionally bound?

It is probably inconceivable that a sovereign could be extruded who would be acceptable to the Zulus and to the Xhosas. But it is not inconceivable. And who, at the moment, is talking about more practical solutions?

So let's get on with it: The Restoration Society for Peace.

—AN AGENDA FOR CONSERVATIVES

JANUARY 1990

We eschew the recital of our credenda. In our first issue (November 19, 1955), we thought of ourselves as young David with his slingshot, proclaiming that our role at *National Review* was to "stand athwart history, yelling Stop!" History has done that, ground to a stop. The Marxist dialectic is dead, and as the occasions warrant, we will recite again our creed. But today, we seek merely to enunciate an agenda for the nineties. If we succeed in the next ten years, and American liberals adopt the position that it was inevitable that the goals here suggested should have been realized, even as they have spoken recently in accents suggesting that they have a proprietary hold on history, we will satisfy ourselves, as we do here, to say merely: We welcome the changes, and will not dwell on their etiology.

Political developments in the final year of the last decade give grounds for profound satisfaction. Communism continues to be a threat but has ceased to be a creed. And since political cosmologies require faith in order to prosper, the menace of communism diminishes, though it can hardly be said to have ended. Using less than 20 percent of its inventory of nuclear weapons, the Soviet Union could tomorrow destroy the United States, never mind that you-should-have-seen what we did to the Soviet Union.

Direct threats to the United States during this decade are of several orders. The first and most obvious threat is that posed by the strategic nuclear arsenal of the Soviet Union. An intermediate threat is posed by the capabilities of China, which, were it to pursue aggressive preparations, could by mid-decade acquire a menacing nuclear capability. And then there is the threat, down the line, associated with the proliferation of intermediate and long-range missile launchers that can transport nuclear explosives, as also chemical and biological weapons. We know that there are six nations today that have intermediate launch capability, so that, for instance, a missile fired from Iraq could reach Great Britain. There are two problems posed by these developments. The first is to deter proliferation. An unsmilingly direct move in that direction was made by Israel in 1981 when it bombed Iraqi plants plainly designed to create nuclear-explosive material. When the United States detected plants in Libya as plainly designed to produce poison gas, we took no military action, satisfying ourselves with putting pressure on Libya's suppliers, though the year before, we had declared ourselves plainspokenly on the threat to international law and order posed by Qaddafi, dotting our i's and crossing our t's with a military strike that, however, failed to destroy Qaddafi. The lesson: we need to be continuously alert to the problems posed by such weapons, and prepared and equipped to make surgical strikes as required.

We will need to guard against *n*th-power aggression in the event anti-proliferation fails. In the long run we are going to have to explore the possibilities of an anti-nuclear technology, which means that we need to take appropriate action in the short run, now. The quarrel over SDI got mixed up, during the 1980s, with strategic ideology. The accommodationists feared, above everything else, disequilibrium, and although they did not succeed in killing SDI, they enfeebled it to the point of delaying until at least the middle of the decade an accumulation of empirical knowledge on whether an anti-missile system would give us effective protection against vagrant missiles. Ideally, we envision a new, universal nuclear umbrella, an enterprise undertaken in partnership with Europe, an enterprise dramatically collusive with the [former] Soviet Union. In any event, the development of protective technology against what used to be called ABC (for "atomic, bacteriological, chemical") aggression is high on our agenda.

During the seventies, in ambiguous language, we were coaxed back in the Wilsonian direction on America's responsibility for human rights throughout the world by President Carter, and subsequently, though less explicitly, by presidents Reagan and Bush. During the sixties, prompted by the tribulation of Vietnam, a significant group of influential Americans abandoned not only our national afflatus as the country whose manifest destiny was to bring democracy to every country in the world, but also any subjective pride in living in a better society than that of Ho Chi Minh, who was bound to win in part because his society was more just than our own, more enviable—who were we to suggest that our way of life was superior?

That self-hatred/self-doubt has substantially modified, though there is a hard academic undertow that continues to disparage America. When we supported democratic forces in the Philippines, effecting the replacement of Ferdinand Marcos, and, several years later, when by a show of military power we prolonged Mrs. Aquino's tenure as democratically elected president, we were not directly engaging in cold-war theater. It was different from our landing the Marines in the Dominican Republic in 1965. The justification given by President Johnson at the time was the same as that given by President Reagan twenty years later when he landed the Marines in Grenada: We would not tolerate another Soviet satellite in the hemisphere over which, as an imperial power, we have primary responsibility, however diplomatic it is to appear at international conferences wearing egalitarian dress. The national anxiety over Nicaragua was based on cold-war reasoning: i.e., we saw in Nicaragua the attempted Sovietization of a small Central American country, an act of imperialism made possible by arms shipped from Cuba, which arms had been shipped there by the Soviet Union or one of its Eastern European satellites.

Now, if the chain, Moscow–Havana–Managua, is broken in the immediate future, we will adjust our foreign policy accordingly. It is at least predictable that neo-isolationist forces in the United States, mobilized into action by the globalist communist threat, will now ask the question: Why—if Nicaragua is no longer a salient of an imperialist enemy—should we *care* if its people consent to be enslaved?

The question is one that invites both moral and strategic attention. Moral, in that we have it in our power to prevent a country such as Nicaragua from "enslaving itself" (nicely handled in Spanish usage, by the way, in which the reflexive mode is regularly used, for instance, to inform us that "the teacup broke itself," finessing the question whether it was clumsily pushed over the edge of the table, or whether it decided, entirely on its own, to commit suicide. *Se perdió Nicaragua).* Possessing that power, should we use it? One important element in the American tradition flows from John Quincy Adams's famous statement to the effect that the American people are friends of liberty everywhere, but custodians only of their own. Assuming that the historical coroner gives us, in the 1990s, an authoritative reading of the death of a [nuclear] threat, we will be left facing directly the Wilsonian question: What is the nature of our responsibilities for human freedom in the rest of the world? There are people in the United States, though they are not numerous or influential, who would go to the remotest beaches of the world to midwife democracy, most ardently to South Africa. American conservatives are likelier to take differentiated positions on the question. We should continue to distinguish between those nations that can be helped by the exercise of diplomatic muscle (for instance, the Philippines at the time of the Aquino-Marcos crisis), and those that can be helped only by the expenditure of blood and muscle. In general, there has been approval of our effort in Panama, though no very large lessons can be drawn from this venture inasmuch as we were clearly motivated by our dislike of one provocatively offensive and ugly dictator (there was no serious movement to replace Omar Torrijos ten years ago). And although we face a Latin American backlash reflecting traditional opposition to gringo intervention, we are probably vindicated in hemispheric sentiment by the rhapsodic gratitude of the Panamanian people, what one might call the "Grenada effect."

In dealing with other nations, we should temper our rhetoric and adjust our trade policies with some reference to the way in which the governors treat the governed. My own suggestion, published ten years ago in *Foreign Affairs,* is to detach official human-rights groups (the Third Committee members within the U.N., the U.S. representative on the U.N.'s Human Rights Commission, the Assistant Secretary of State for Human Rights) from government, to which they would cease to have direct accountability, leaving it to them merely to report on the status of freedom in the nations of the world (much as is now done by Freedom House, Amnesty International, and others). In any event, we should be guided by realistic priorities. They are that the safety of our own nation is of paramount concern, and that the strategic relevance of other nations to that concern has to be the operative consideration. But our interest in human rights elsewhere in the world must be manifest and enthusiastic, leaving us the task of developing the appropriate vehicles for expressing our humane involvement in mankind.

Although it is arresting to hear the professional futurist of *The Economist* exclaim that the problems of Great Britain have almost always turned out to be different from those forecast twenty years earlier, there are, visible, a number of staples. Although it is possible that if oil were to return to the thirty-dollars-plus level, accessible reserves of oil shale would double or even triple existing reserves, a nation as heavily dependent on energy as our own cannot safely count on such a development. We need to encourage a substitute for fossil fuel, not only because we are running out of oil, whatever the touted reserves of the Middle East, but because a wider use of coal as a substitute is offensive to ecology. The way forward would appear to be nuclear power. The most binding scientific superstition of the 1970s had to do with the ineluctable toxicity of nuclear power. The success of the anti-nuclear-power movement has been the most momentous Luddite extravagance of the century. We need to rub our scientists' noses in the consequences of prolonging our ostracism of nuclear power. To do this requires not only the dissemination of knowledge, but cooperative legal action, such as would immunize nuclear-power producers against legal harassment by ideologues.

In this same connection, we will need to keep our eyes on the metaphysical—yes, metaphysical—implications of the environmental movement. It is essentially conservative to conserve, whether we speak of energy or timberland, elephants or bald eagles. But the conservationist movement, in the hands of some who appear to dominate it, sometimes sounds as though the creation of man was an act of aggression against the animal and mineral kingdoms. We know that the regulation of hunting and fishing and mining and timber cutting is prudent and in most cases necessary. But the creeping imperialism of environmentalism and its hardening axioms are moving us in the direction of a prohibition against everything from the wearing of fur coats to the use of the gas-powered automobile, a form of fanaticism that lies athwart the natural relationships between man, animal, and nature. Against such reductionism conservatives need to contend, by propping up the natural order of priorities while of course remaining sensible to our obligation to preserve the vital organs of our planet.

This is the primary international economic question. We must cherish the benefits to which we are entitled as a nation, which are the result of a free-market system, an abundance of resources, and a resident population for the most part animated by the work ethic. But it is vital not to identify these factors, which have led to our prosperity, with any divine warrant granting the United States perpetual economic ascendancy. The most reliable means of measuring our economic slippage is by consulting the marketplace, whose rankings are impersonal. The temptation to tamper with the indices of the market should remind us of the necessity to resist such tampering. The temptation will increase, during the nineties, to "protect" native industry. To do this is wrong for three reasons. The first is that the cultural effects of protectionism tend to encourage such anomalies as we are familiar with in Japan, a rich nation with poor inhabitants: the perverse effect of protectionist policies. The second is that protectionism cannot, in the long run, work, given that any net economic satisfaction has to reflect the value of the dollar in competition with other currencies. To hide depreciated production behind the veil of tariffs is to subsidize the attrition of the dollar; the results of this are inevitably mischievous, and can be tragic. A third reason for opposing protectionism is moral: to mobilize against the economic ascendancy of poor nations by attempting to exclude their products from the home market is inhibiting not only to the United States consumer but also to prospective economic growth in lands inhabited by fellow human beings. Tariffs are a form of economic warfare, and it is fortunate that the arguments against protectionism blend prudential and moral considerations.

. . .

During the eighties it was established that the high hopes of the sixties for developing policies that would do away with the American underclass have failed us. They have failed us for reasons most systematically (and eloquently) chronicled by Charles Murray, who goes so far as to speculate that the people we speak of would probably have been better off, using conventional criteria (education, health, obedience to the law, preservation of the family unit), if the government in Washington had taken no measures whatever to federalize welfare.

Whether that is so we can never know, but we do know that although there are many exceptions, an underclass is developing which appears to be more static than any other with which, in its lifetime, the United States has contended—with uniform success, excepting only the intransigent problem of the American Indian. In the South Bronx, 83 percent of the babies born last year were born to unwed mothers in families for which the father takes no responsibility, and some of them lose their mothers weeks, days—even hours—after their birth, to be raised as orphans, if they are not adopted. The phenomenon has got to be viewed as the fruit of policies fueled by a combination of moral liberalism and state compassion.

It is a conservative challenge to fasten concentratedly on the advent of what threatens to be a stationary underclass, and to take measures against the consolidation of that condition. Much that is of an experimental nature needs to be done to encourage upward mobility, but already there are data that would appear to justify two approaches. One is a heavy reorientation of educational policy at the grade school and high school levels in the direction of choice. More and more, states are beginning to permit parents to send their children to public schools of their choice. But this is not accomplishing the needed reforms. The alternative of private schooling appears to be essential in order to test the final resources of our system. The "voucher" plan is widely deprecated, both by citizens of egalitarian conviction and by educators who, among other things, quite correctly see in the voucher system a challenge to their own security. The reform needs to be pressed doggedly, and this is especially difficult to accomplish in a society as impatient, as achievement-oriented as our own. We are a people who want to see the recapture of Danang on Monday, the immobilization of the DMZ on Tuesday, and the surrender of North Vietnam on Wednesday. Ask the boat people. But to examine the fruits of alternative education requires several high school generations. Here and there, on a very small scale, such comparisons have begun, or are being made. It is a duty to celebrate those successes and to widen the experience to include more members of a class that appears now to be tethered to the deteriorated condition of so many of today's public schools.

Whatever else is responsible for the breakup of the family, it is inescapably the case that the official prejudice against religion in education has played a large, perhaps even a decisive role. The *Playboy* philosophy, explicitly regnant in the sixties, may have appealed to the younger generation as the key to hedonism, but hedonism is not the key to happiness, and the wretchedness that blights so many families—white certainly, but predominantly black —has much to do with the nakedness of the public square, in which for generations there were men and women who spoke the language of duty and morality, of loyalty and obligation. And licentious engagements in hedonism are more readily outgrown in the more disciplined classes than in those less self-reliant.

The church/state clause in the First Amendment has effectively been transformed into an instrument of secularization. The time has come, for those who deplore present trends and wish to resist them, to invoke their knowledge of history sufficiently to proclaim that fanatical interpretations of the separation clause of the First Amendment are unrelated to protecting the public from the illusory threat of an established religion. And to go further, to note that the effect of the fanatical interpretation of the separation clause has been to insulate two generations of urban youth from exposure to an ethos whose advocates would have been celebrated as prophetic benefactors of the lower class, if only what they spoke hadn't already been spoken under the aegis of the Bible. Conservatives should be adamant about the need for the reappearance of Judeo-Christianity in the public square.

. . .

A politics related to the view of man as a transcendent creature cannot avoid addressing the fundamental questions of human life, which have to do, obviously, with the preservation of life during its normal span. The questions raised in hot dispute around the world focus on the beginning and on the end of life.

The question of abortion divides Americans, and the appropriate means of proceeding politically also divides Americans. Among those who oppose abortion, for instance, there are the latitudinarians who believe that effective moral pressure can only be generated internally. At the other end, there are those who believe that the higher moral perception should be written into the law, even as there were those who believed 150 years ago that a flat-out prohibition against slavery was the only tolerable moral mandate. Abraham Lincoln, as we all know, was not among them. And in between are those who believe that existing political mechanisms need to feel pressure, of whatever kind, to move in the correct direction.

Disagreement as to means is not only tolerable but welcome, sharpening the argument as it does, and exploring, to good end, different epistemological techniques. But that there should be an end in common is plain, that end being to gain acceptance of the assertion that some time before the child is born, the child _is,_ and that to close out his life is a morally aggressive act, inconsistent with the dignity of life which is the foundation of conservative politics.

The same consideration should guide us in respect of life at the other end of the compass. This problem is already acute and will grow more so, given the pace at which science succeeds in elongating the time between when man is, so to speak, ready to die, and the time when man will die. The great quarrel will deal with the responsibility of society when there is the clearly expressed will of someone who deems life on earth under his current condition worse than death. We are aware that self-inflicted euthanasia is becoming conventional in the Low Countries of Europe, and we are progressively made aware that medical journeymen often surreptitiously practice euthanasia on their own initiative. What we have not arrived at is an understanding suitable to conservatives who believe in the sacredness of life, but who believe also that there is a point where its prolongation becomes fetishistic, rather than humane. Lively arguments on where the line is, how it is to be drawn, and what are the reasonable presumptions in the absence of coherent instructions from the patient will take place. Conservatives must once again be willing to listen, and to accommodate themselves to reasonable moral compromises provided they are assured that the only agents whose voices will give guidance are those directly involved with the individual as an individual, rather than the individual as a state statistic.

The rising crime rate is substantially related to the consumption of drugs and the continuing prohibition against their sale and purchase. Conservatives do well to be skeptical of radical proposals (the most notable of them in this area: to legalize the sale of drugs). But they should be curious and open-minded as data accumulate, data skeptical about the prospects of our war on drugs, and inquisitive about how the situation would unfold in the event that our war against drugs (because it would still be that, a war against drug abuse) were to proceed under the aegis of legalization. Social hostility to the abuse of drugs (whether alcohol or cocaine) should continue, with the question left open whether more damage—or less—would be done under legalization. At the very least, conservatives should forthrightly reject the proposition that to favor legalization is the equivalent of favoring the use of drugs. It is, moreover, a duty of conservatives to give running attention to the loss of derivative liberties as a result of the general mayhem caused by traffic in illegal drugs, even as it was a duty, and still is, to acknowledge the implicit effects of racial discrimination on the liberty of people discriminated against. The question of how to deal with the drug problem should therefore be considered open, with data reviewed dispassionately.

During the coldest days of the cold war, conservatives were frequently taunted as closet statists, opportunizing on their hospitality to joint enterprise of the state and industry, now become a vassal to a military-industrial complex. The taunt was always empty, in that it was never a feature of the conservative faith that the military establishment could efficiently be conducted as private enterprise; and the size of the military was, and continues to be, a response to the perceived threat against the nation, rather than the expression of a gestating appetite for statist growth.

Still, we did get used to large federal numbers, and although Ronald Reagan's presidency is justly celebrated for having reduced the rate at which federal growth increased, it did in fact continue to increase. Some of that increase was an aspect of federal "entitlements," written into the law by Democratic Congresses and irreversible under Democratic Congresses. Notwithstanding, it is a fair criticism that, with few exceptions, less attention was paid than should have been paid to the creeping acquiescence of conservative monitors to the continuing growth of the federal government. With this derivative indulgence came a corresponding evanescence of any recognition of, let alone loyalty to, the Ninth and Tenth Amendments, which are there as constitutional beacons warning against shoal waters in approaching omnipotent central government.

Few of the major political problems we face are unrelated to the size, unmanageability, and roguishness of statist policies. The federal deficit is entirely a product of state activity. The huge subventions we give out (to farmers, to carefree patrons of thrift and banking institutions, to American manufacturers) are deeds of the federal government. Child care is now on the starting line of federal offensives. The implicit rationale of state-to-state income transfers has got to be that the relatively affluent states (there are seventeen) should provide help to the less affluent states (there are thirty-three). That idea is completely lost in a sky made black by crisscrossing dollars. The renewed presumption against centralized government, a presumption reiterated in the doctrine of subsidiarity, needs to be reinvigorated. Conservatives need to guard against the kind of anarchy that sometimes detaches conservative analysis from the real world, bringing on the ridicule fully earned by political solipsists. But if anyone is to warn against the presumptive absorption by the federal government of social and federated activity, who questions that this ought to be the responsibility of American conservatives?

· · ·

And who, if not the courts, is responsible for the disappearance of the great constitutional brakes explicit and implicit in the Ninth and Tenth Amendments? The analysis and demonstrations offered by Robert Bork in his book *The Tempting of America* are central to the understanding of a wayward judiciary, whose improvisations led Judge Bork to share the fate of the two discarded amendments. It is difficult to deny that the courts are looked upon by ideologically ambitious legislators, academicians, and journalists as the agents through which they can hope to advance their policies when it proves impossible democratically to do so by mobilizing an electoral majority. The division brought on by the nomination of Judge Bork, unlike the divisions brought on by the nominations of a half-dozen other judges rejected in recent memory, stays in the mind and will be the locus of constitutional discussion at least through the forthcoming decade, during which the question of original understanding and self-government must be faced on the only possible rational understanding, namely that in the absence of the former, we cannot have the latter. We are self-governed, or we are governed by the courts. A commitment to circumspect behavior by the courts does not, one mentions in passing, endorse a court system instructed only by legal realism, according to which the legislature can ordain the suicide of individual freedom, in contradiction of the implied covenant given us by the Declaration, and the Constitution.

Chief executives have tended during the past generation to be Republican, and they have on many issues been at loggerheads with a Democratic Congress. The result has been that many conservatives have developed a dangerous attachment to executive supremacy. We need to remind ourselves of the hypothetical possibility that there might someday be a military adventure that we do not endorse. In a federal republic, Congress is the likeliest repository of conservative affinity, the more so since the distribution of power is designed to work to the benefit of the democratic dissenter. The coexistence of equal senatorial rights for Rhode Island and California with the Supreme Court's doctrine of one man, one vote suggests the tension at the constitutional level. The inertial domination of Congress by the Democratic Party has done much to confuse conservative thought, causing it to be spastically pro-executive, which is a misdirection of energy that should be going into electoral reform and a vigorous loyalty to sound congressional representation of conservative views and analyses.

Even as we need to tame the Court, we need to beware the inclination to side with the executive in matters of public dispute over policy. We all know that there is a tendency to be enthusiastic about the authority of the Supreme Court, or less than enthusiastic about that authority, depending on the direction in which the Supreme Court opines. Just as we need to guard against judicial usurpation, we need to guard against executive usurpation. A strong executive can be a necessary, galvanizing force in a pluralistic and cantankerously divided republic, and be especially important in an age in which decisive military or paramilitary action can only issue from a commander in chief. But the executive's authority cannot be supreme, let alone unchallenged. Just as it happened during the fifties that the Court became an instrument of leftist ideology, so it has happened that the executive, most notably under Franklin Delano Roosevelt, became an instrument of leftist ideology. Conservatives need to revisit such works as James Burnham's *Congress and the American Tradition* and to remind themselves that providential absenteeism might at some point in the future result in the election of a Democratic president who will enter office citing paeans by conservatives to executive supremacy.

The plight of so many of our colleges and universities reflects the nescience that grips the academic world. It is distressing to reflect that the near-universal rejection of Marxist structure and methods by Eastern European workers and intellectuals is not emulated by our faculties of social science. There is a near-paralysis of reason evident throughout the academic world. The proposition that a college matriculant should be referred to as a "freshperson" suggests the utter imbalance, sociological and aesthetic, of the sponsoring academic class. That a first-rank college should feel obliged to sponsor "Gay–Lesbian Awareness Days" suggests the kind of cultural diffidence that testifies not to tolerance, but to helplessness.

The movements that have closed in around comparable worth,

affirmative action, and feminist demands testify not to the whole-some latitudinarianism of the open society, so much as they do to the refusal of society to make wholesome commitments: to natural distinctions and natural inclinations to meritocratic priorities. At the level of higher education, the critique needs urgently to be encouraged, to dissociate genuine tolerance from the kind of fad-dism that denotes intellectual emptiness and a surrender to ideo-logical academic warlordism. In this struggle the role of the alumni is critical. They must be encouraged to take an intelligent interest in the policies of the colleges they support, infusing jolts of sanity and realism into campuses in which academic and even social mores appear to be uninformed by deliberate thought.

Conservatives should explore with concern, all the more so as the threat to the national security reduces and with it the need for a military of two million young Americans, the dissipating bonds of social cohesion. It has been thirty years since Robert Nisbet pos-ited the need of the quest for community. The factionalism of modern politics militates against the recognition of common inter-ests. These interests conservatives need to investigate, in search of the attenuating ties that bind us together. Whether the time has come to revisit the idea of national service is a question that should be explored without the rancor associated with traditional-ist opposition. That any such service, if adopted, should be volun-tary, and substantially the creature of individual states, should be conservative stipulations. But the idea should be explored, in par-ticular at a time when high and illegal immigration, and the fac-tionalism elsewhere spoken of, encourage centrifugal forces in our culture. The republic we give our loyalty to, which many Ameri-cans have died defending, has to attract continuing affection and pride, and such affection and pride are nurtured by reciprocal service. The republic guarantees us our liberty, and we revivify the spirit that generates the desire for liberty. To do this it is required that the sense of community be stimulated. A conservative chal-lenge is to seek out ways by which the beneficiaries of our patri-mony acknowledge their debt to it and feel the need to requite that which we enjoy. As some would put it, there is no such thing as a free lunch. Neither is there such a thing as free liberty.

FOUR

REFLECTING

1

Remembering Communism

The hassle over the itinerary of Mr. Reagan when he journeys to Europe invites reflection on anniversaries and what they reveal.

Ten years after V-E Day, we had just finished telling the Soviet Union, our wartime ally, that we didn't give a damn what they thought about it, we were going to conclude a peace treaty with West Germany (our wartime enemy), which we proceeded to do. We had been intimate friends of Adenauer, the leader of West Germany, from virtually the beginning. We wrote some stiff laws—no Germans would be allowed to publish and circulate Nazi propaganda. We hanged a few criminals (and were a little unhappy about doing so, since there were jurists who said we were violating our own constitutional guarantees against ex post facto justice).

At the other end of the world we also did a spot of hanging, but then propped up the same emperor under whose divine benediction the Japanese bombed Pearl Harbor and launched their ravenous war against Manchuria, China, the Philippines, and Southeast Asia. But a few years of Douglas MacArthur and we were the fastest of friends, and five years after V-J Day we were sending American troops to defend, to their death, the South Koreans and the Japanese against communist aggression from North Korea.

How much easier it is to reconcile oneself with countries one has defeated, than with countries that have defeated us. True, the Germans and the Japanese, though defeated, came around quickly, but that was because in order to reconcile themselves with their own defeat it was necessary that they should publicly abominate their older leaders. So that it was all but impossible, a year or two after the war's end, to find a German who professed veneration for Hitler, or a Japanese who professed veneration for Tojo. And so we became friends with people we struggled so hard to kill, in a war that brought death to 55 million people.

But ten years after the Vietnam War, we do not recognize the government of Vietnam. And our own government has not changed: They are still Republicans, and Democrats run Congress, not communists or Maoists.

No one, on the tenth anniversary of the fall of South Vietnam, is suggesting that we have anything in common with the people who conquered South Vietnam, Laos, and Cambodia—and, incidentally, defeated the United States. Nor were we wrong in predicting what would happen if the North Vietnamese took over the South. Peter Berger, the sociologist and philosopher, has said resonantly that anyone who can't tell the difference between authoritarianism and totalitarianism could not tell the difference between Saigon and Ho Chi Minh City.

But the introspection to which we have been given, on this tenth anniversary of our defeat in Southeast Asia, devotes very little time—have you noticed?—to the awful betrayal of 1975. We no longer stood to lose American soldiers in 1975. They were long since gone. But Congress stood there. President Ford begged it to act. Congress all but laughed at the call to redeem the pledges we had so solemnly made to the South Vietnamese after—as well as before—the Treaty of Paris. The general fit of iconoclasm, brought on by the unpopular war and exacerbated by the apparent moral insouciance of Richard Nixon in the matter of Watergate, coarsened our sensibilities, so that instead of worrying about how to redeem promises made, we worried about executive initiatives that might be taken to redeem those programs. In 1973 we voted $2.3 billion in aid of South Vietnam's armed forces. In 1974 we cut the figure in half; in 1975, by another third. Southeast Asia learned what it can mean to rely on the United States. And other countries have learned, though most of them have no alternative than to hope that the United States will live up to its obligations.

"Finally, however tragic the outcome," writes Professor John Roche, who served Lyndon Johnson during his Vietnam years, "I will argue to my dying day that this was the most idealistic war we have ever fought, fundamentally a war for an abstraction: the freedom of a bunch of unfamiliar Asians at the end of the world." How strange those sounds, which antedated the period during which the American intelligentsia for the most part persuaded itself that the Vietnam War was the high moment of immorality. But that high moment came not while we were fighting, but when we abandoned our wounded. For that reason the focus will be on Europe this season, not on Saigon, or Da Nang, or any cemetery in South Vietnam where the bones lie of men who trusted us.

—WHAT IF THEY WERE NAZIS?

MAY 11, 1985

A colleague remarked, apropos of the whole Bitburg business, "What if Daniel Ortega and his Sandinistas were Nazis?"

It is a riveting observation. It informs us deeply about the moral scramble of our time, in which as we struggle to remember how hideous was Hitler, we struggle equally to forget how hideous is communism.

Consider, for instance, the calm revelations of the past few years concerning the Cultural Revolution in Mao's China.

When eighty top journalists went into Shanghai in 1972 with President Nixon, there was something on the order of elation: Here, finally, we all were. In the Great Kingdom. Mao Tse-tung was a hero. True, he was a tough man, but you needed a tough man to create Mao men. En route to China we all read the glowing accounts of Mao's accomplishments, written by Ross Terrill of Harvard and published in *The Atlantic Monthly*. Theodore White, the distinguished American journalist and sinologist who was an early enthusiast for Mao, nowadays shakes his head and says, "We did not recognize just how bad it was." Yes, it was that bad. Brutal killings, torture, categorical imprisonments of everyone associated with the old Communist Party, a despoliation of college life, burned books, anti-intellectualism rife. All the details are painstakingly collected in the meticulous, resourceful book of Fox Butterfield, *China: Alive in the Bitter Sea.*

We welcome, of course, the regime of Deng Xiaoping, who has

studiedly attempted to institute reforms, economic and political—without, however, altering the totalitarian nature of life in China. But there is detectable no sense of horror among Americans who visit there, either at what happened in China under the banner of Deng's old boss and mentor Mao Tse-tung, or of Deng's other boss, Chou En-lai. We treat it as merely an unpleasant episode, on which we do not choose to dwell. It is inconceivable that any American traveling in China would exhibit moral hesitation at fraternizing with surviving members of the Old Guard, those who had a hand in implementing the Bolshevik Revolution. All but inconceivable that any American staying at home would loudly protest such fraternization as a betrayal of the victims of the regime of Mao Tse-tung, the Great Helmsman.

But all this is also true, though perhaps a little less so, of the Soviet Union, is it not? Two rulers back, less than two years ago, the head of the Soviet Union had been the counterpart of Himmler in Nazi Germany. But about Mr. Andropov we were all tacitly urged to speak in civil accents, and of course there was considerable dismay when President Reagan elected not to attend his funeral, although he did drop by the Soviet Embassy to write his signature into the official book of condolences.

How come this disparity in how we feel about evil regimes indistinguishable from one another?

Probably the difference is not much more complicated than that the Soviet Union has The Bomb. If the Soviet Union so elected, there would be a world war, conceivably the terminal experience of the planet Earth.

Well now, suppose that Hitler had got himself a bomb, which as a matter of fact he came very close to doing. Imagine that that bomb had exploded over Liverpool in the early spring of 1945: exit Liverpool and, by the way, four little baby Beatles. Suppose Hitler had then said that the next bomb would fall on London and the third on Paris, unless we came to terms with him. What would have happened? Yes, precisely that. Just as Japan reacted to Hiroshima, so would London have reacted to Liverpool.

So Hitler lived on—in 1945 he was only fifty-six years old. Say that he lived on to approximately the same age as Churchill, and Mao, and Adenauer, dying a natural death in 1975. There were 300,000 Jews left in the concentration camps when Hitler's bomb ended World War II, so he polished them off, and of course continued to torture and kill and otherwise persecute any dissidents, even as Stalin did. But before he died, he had amassed in Germany the equivalent nuclear throw-weight amassed by the Soviet Union. Wouldn't our diplomats be attending anniversaries of Hitler's rise to power, even as they attend, in Moscow, anniversaries of the October Revolution?

One fears that that is the case. That considerations of self-concern govern our moral attitudes. Evidently we need to defeat a totalitarian power before we can settle down to despising it. If Daniel Ortega wore a swastika on his sleeve, the liberals in Congress would be calling for an American Expeditionary Force to crush him. As it stands, he is relatively safe.

—TERRORISM AT THE EXPENSE OF THE SOVIETS?

OCTOBER 5, 1985

Well, what do you know. Soviet victims of terrorism. For years, those Soviet citizens allowed to roam the world have done so with the equivalent of the laissez-passer sign that two thousand years ago permitted a Roman citizen to go anywhere in the world certain that he would not be molested. *"Romanus sum"*—"I am a Roman." That was it. The passport to security. This morning's paper shows upper-torso pictures of four Soviet diplomats somewhere in Lebanon. There is nothing like undressing a diplomat to make your squalid point. One of the victims is dressed in what looks like fatigue pajamas. Two have on T-shirts. The fourth has on nothing. All of them have pistols pointed at their heads. None is smiling.

And not one but two Muslim fundamentalist sects claim credit for abducting the Soviet diplomats. Both cite as their reason for doing so Soviet-backed Syrian attacks on the Lebanese port of Tripoli. Whether the salient the terrorists complain of is actually a Soviet operation is not the point of this inquiry. Rather, that for the first time in memory the Soviet Union is facing up to the kind of thing non-Soviets have been facing up to for years and years.

Never at Soviet gunpoint, almost always at the gunpoint of those who without Soviet backing would have no guns to point.

The mind turned to a rundown six years old of the activities of the Soviet Union involving terrorism. The study was done by Mr. Brian Crozier, director of London's Institute for the Study of Conflict.

Just to begin with, the two wars in Indochina were for the most part fought by acts of terrorism—i.e., the use of violence for political ends. It was so in the war against South Vietnam, and subsequently in the war within Cambodia.

Libya's Qaddafi gave refuge to the world's most wanted terrorist, Carlos ("The Jackal"). Carlos, it was alleged, was given $2 million as reward money for kidnaping the OPEC oil ministers in Vienna. Carlos was recruited by the KGB in Venezuela, trained in Cuba, and received, so to speak, graduate training in Moscow before being turned loose on the world. Arafat, who narrowly missed the retaliatory bombings of Israel in Tunisia, was invited by Moscow to open an office there in August 1974. Ten years earlier, the Vietcong's political wing had been issued a similar invitation, auguring the Soviet commitment to the final drive against the noncommunist Vietnamese.

On and on it goes, the most spectacular recent terrorist events including the attack on our Marines, the killing of the novelist Georgi Markov on Waterloo Bridge by a Bulgarian assassin, the attempted assassination of the pope. One would not be surprised to learn that Judge Crater was whisked off in a Soviet freighter.

The programming must have been done by the Great Impresario in the Sky. Consider: Ever since our Marines were slaughtered in 1983 in Beirut, Washington has been saying: You watch now, you watch. We watched, nothing happened. Then came the great June 1985, Beirut airport hostage crisis, and Washington told us: You watch now, you watch, and all America watched, and nothing happened.

On September 25, three holiday-minded Israelis, on a little sailboat in Cyprus, were killed by Palestinian terrorists. It required exactly six days for a squadron of Israeli fighters to go a huge 1,500 miles to the headquarters of the PLO in Tunisia and destroy those headquarters, killing upward of sixty people. And that happened within twenty-four hours of the abduction of the Soviet diplomats, together with the ultimatum concerning Tripoli.

How has the Soviet Union responded? As expected. The terrorists are counterrevolutionary reactionaries, etc., etc. But if we have learned anything about the psychology of modern terrorists, it is that only sticks and stones will break their bones. There are no words in the Soviet inventory that will frighten them in the least. We even tried to drum up some Muslim holy words with which to scare off the terrorists who held our hostages in the embassy in Iran, to no effect. These people listen only to dive-bombers.

So whom will the Soviets bomb? One of their problems is that they are being asked to bomb their own children, because terrorism as we know it is not the bastard child of communism, quite the contrary: It is the beautiful child of communism, the flower of the union of political ambition and ethical depravity. Stand by.

—Ronald Reagan at the U.N.
October 29, 1985

The president's speech to the United Nations was a joy. It antagonized both the Soviet Union and American liberals, a sure sign that on October 24 God was in his heaven, and all was right with the world.

Here is the point to keep one's eyes on. It is that our strategic posture vis-à-vis the Soviet Union has for a generation been defensive. We have always, or almost always, left it to them to determine the theater of combat. Obviously, when that happens the enemy will choose favorable terrain. During the past period, the Soviet Union has posed as the suitor for an arms agreement that will leave the world safer from war. What never comes up is why there should be any danger of war in the first place.

But the Western specialty, dating back to the 1948 crisis in Berlin, has been the countersalient. The Soviets block Berlin, so what do we do? Block Vladivostok? No, we airlift to Berlin. The Soviets threaten Lebanon, so we land troops in Lebanon. The Soviets mastermind (there is a historical question here) the invasion of South Korea, we land troops in South Korea. They move nuclear missiles into Cuba, we chase them out of Cuba. They invade Vietnam, we defend Vietnam. They attempt to colonize Grenada, we liberate Grenada.

The theme of Mr. Reagan's talk can then be defined as: What is it that's going on in the world that gives rise to international tensions? As I say, it isn't the existence of a huge inventory of nuclear weapons—weapons aren't inherently frightening; it is the will to use them as weapons that frightens. The president pointed to four areas of the world in which there is a great deal of tension —indeed, in which people are killing each other. Because of what Moscow has done, in Afghanistan. Because of what Moscow has done, in Nicaragua. Because of what Moscow has done, in Ethiopia. Because of what Moscow has done, in Angola. Subtract Soviet support of these revolutionary governments, and suddenly a great stillness would come. That is the kind of stillness that accompanies true rapprochement.

Sure, there was in the speech an element of national pride. Mr. Reagan referred to the United States as a country that occupies no land abroad except—a lovely metaphor—"beneath the graves where our heroes rest." But that isn't bombast, and although some of the editorial writers cringe at any expression of pride in the record of America, it is fairer to say that the difference between our record of conduct abroad since World War II and that of the Soviet Union is rather too infrequently remarked, than so frequently remarked as to elide into chauvinism. We have every reason to call to the attention of the world, as Mr. Reagan did, that we have given $300 billion of aid to the world's needy: a figure ten times as much as the request we have outstanding for research into a space shield.

And why not recall, as Reagan did, what Premier Kosygin said in 1967 when we suggested a moratorium on ABM technology? Kosygin said, "I believe that defensive systems, which prevent attack, are not the cause of the arms race, but constitute a factor preventing the death of people. Maybe an anti-missile system is more expensive than an offensive system, but it is designed not to kill people but to preserve human lives." The New York Times editorial writer sniffed at quoting an "eighteen-year-old statement." Well, the Bill of Rights is older than that.

They didn't interrupt Mr. Reagan, not once, to applaud him

this time around. Last year he was applauded every time he mentioned the need for arms control. It is a key to how things work in
the United Nations that when you inquire as to why you need
arms control, there is silence. There is applause only when you
deal with the obvious threats posed by international tension. By
analogy, they would applaud a speech about stopping AIDS, but
not a speech about stopping dirty-needle use or aberrant sexual
habits.

Mr. Reagan may surprise the skeptics in Geneva. He has certainly not approached the disarmament talks in the spirit of someone who is willing, in exchange for ephemeral trades in arms
reduction, to give up on the important things. And these important things are those that distinguish life in the West from life
behind the Iron Curtain.

—How to Deal with One's Dissidents

June 12, 1986

On the same day that Kurt Waldheim was elected President of
Austria, Ricardo Montero Duque arrived in Miami after twenty-
five years in Fidel Castro's prisons. How did he get out? Well,
Senator Edward Kennedy arranged it. He asked Fidel Castro, and
Fidel gave a seigneurial response.

That morning Ronald Radosh, a professor of history at City
University of New York, reviewed for *The New York Times* a book
by a sometime fellow prisoner of Montero Duque, the difference
being that Armando Valladares was in prison only twenty-two
years, not twenty-five. And how did he get out? President François
Mitterrand asked Fidel Castro to let him out, and Fidel gave a
seigneurial response.

For some reason, Professor Radosh announces that "it has
taken us twenty-five years to find out the terrible reality—Mr.
Castro has created a new despotism that has institutionalized torture as a mechanism of social control." It is not clear why it took
"us" twenty-five years to find out that Castro has been systematically torturing people. Some of "us" have known this for about

twenty-four years, reporting on such torture regularly, for instance in *National Review.*

But back to Mr. Valladares's book, which is called *Against All Hope: The Prison Memoirs of Armando Valladares.* Valladares was a young employee of the Postal Savings Bank in Cuba when Castro came to power, and he expressed misgivings about the communization of Cuba and was therefore arrested. That was when it began.

In prison he was tortured. Here is how Professor Radosh paraphrases life in the prison of Fidel Castro: "Mr. Valladares and other prisoners who refused 'political rehabilitation' were forced to live in the greatest heat and the dampest cold without clothes. They were regularly beaten, shot at and sometimes killed; they were thrown into punishment cells, including the dreaded 'drawer cells,' specially constructed units that make South Vietnam's infamous tiger cages seem like homey quarters."

He tried once to escape, but unsuccessfully. Retribution was swift. We quote now directly from the author. "Guards returned us to the cells and stripped us again. They didn't close the cell door, and that detail caught my attention. I was sitting on the floor; outside I heard the voices of several approaching soldiers . . . they were going to settle accounts with us, collect what we owed them for having tried to escape. . . . They were armed with thick twisted electric cables and truncheons. Suddenly, everything was a whirl—my head spun around in terrible vertigo. They beat me as I lay on the floor. One of them pulled at my arm to turn me over and expose my back so he could beat me more easily. And the cables fell more directly on me. The beating felt as if they were branding me with a red-hot branding iron, but then suddenly I experienced the most intense, unbearable, and brutal pain of my life. One of the guards had jumped with all his weight on my broken, throbbing leg."

Back to Professor Radosh: "That treatment was typical. In the punishment cells, prisoners were kept in total darkness. Guards dumped buckets of urine and feces over the prisoners who warded off rats and roaches as they tried to sleep. Fungus grew on Mr. Valladares because he was not allowed to wash off the filth. Sleep was impossible. Guards constantly woke the men with long poles to insure they got no rest. . . . Even at the end, when the authorities were approving his release, Mr. Valladares was held in solitary confinement in a barren room with fluorescent lights turned on twenty-four hours a day. By then he was partially paralyzed through malnutrition intensified by the lack of medical attention."

Valladares speculates that when the truth is known about Castro's political prisoners, "mankind will feel the revulsion it felt when the crimes of Stalin were brought to light." Professor Radosh evaluates this: "It is not too tough a judgment."

The world is aflame at Austria's having elected as president a man suspected of having cooperated with a German Nazi war criminal in Yugoslavia thirty-six years ago. Much of that world accepts Fidel Castro with equanimity; some of the world, with enthusiasm. To do so is the equivalent of waiting until every Jew was killed by Hitler before discovering the evils of Nazism. Diplomats who present their credentials to Fidel Castro should spend the evening before reading Valladares's book. The man they will meet, the governor of Cuba, is the Hitler Stalin of today.

—Killed in Nicaragua

May 15, 1987

The poignant—and infuriating—appearance of the parents of Benjamin Linder before a congressional committee requires us to ask: What on earth is going on? Representative Connie Mack, R-Fla., tried to tell the grieving parents that the moment was not ideal for discussing the circumstances of their son's death; but no, the parents yanked across the exchange that huge tapestry of historical disorder that is making it all but impossible to recognize what the essential story line is.

The tapestry in question shows the Contras as a demonic force, fed by mean-minded cold warriors bent on killing innocent people engaged in pastoral reforms. I swear, anyone watching the nightly news on CBS would never think to associate the Contras with the idea of liberation. There is not, on CBS, a moment given over to the idea of the Contras, or to the iniquities of the government they are fighting. Hollywood could go no further than Dan Rather in polarizing the principals: Ortega, bowing his head reverentially, mourning the death of Benjamin Linder, Mrs. Ortega kissing the weeping mother. Then rat-tat-tat machine gun bursts of Contras, preparing with their illegal arms to kill more Benjamin Linders, more innocent Nicaraguans.

And we get further personalizations. Eugene Hasenfus, like Benjamin Linder, was involved in Nicaragua. What he did was to get shot down by the Sandinistas, caught trying to get arms to the Contras. He became the object of media ignominy. The reckless merchant of death, helping on a voluntary basis to bring more misery to a torture-ridden people. He is the complement of Benjamin Linder.

It is ironic that, one continent removed, a trial proceeds against Klaus Barbie. There it is absolutely clear who are the heroes, who the villains. The villains were those Frenchmen who simply went along. The heroes were the men and women of the night who struggled to save one Jew here, one there; one innocent child on Monday, another on Friday. These were people headed for death camps at the hands of a totalitarian regime. Nicaragua's regime has not reached the level of intensity in its war against its own people reached, say, in Cambodia by Pol Pot and the Khmer Rouge, but the question to ask is, In what direction is it headed?

The 200,000 Nicaraguans who have fled Nicaragua during the past eight years, preferring to do it while they can rather than to leave as the boat people left Indochina, know the direction in which Ortega is taking Nicaragua; in the direction that Castro—so volubly admired by Ortega—has taken Cuba: toward a totalitarian, militarized state. The heroes, in an orderly canvas, are hardly the Benjamin Linders who travel to Nicaragua primarily to encourage the regime rather than merely to build dams. But try, just try, to get that story via CBS—or, indeed, via the most talkative Democratic spokesmen.

The frustration is brilliantly captured by Joseph Sobran, who writes: "Was Benjamin Linder, the young American engineer killed by anti-communist forces in Nicaragua, a communist? He was, says the columnist Richard Cohen, 'a man whose intent was to make life a bit better for Nicaraguan peasants . . . a dreamer out to bring a little light to a dark corner of the world.' Yeah, but was he a communist? *The New York Times* reports that his friends described him as a 'political activist interested in Central American causes.' Well, was he a communist? He was 'a founder of a campus group called Committee in Solidarity with the People of El Salvador.' And was he a communist? 'He was a self-effacing, gentle person with a twinkle in his eye and a laugh,' says his friend Millie Thayer. The nearest thing to a straight answer is provided by *The Washington Post*: Linder and other foreigners in Nicaragua 'are among the thousands of *internacionalistas* who have come to Nicaragua to work for the Sandinista cause. Many are Cubans or East Europeans sent by their governments, but a larger number are American and West European volunteers.' "

The Sandinistas have given their people genocide (of the Miskito Indians), poverty (national income down about 40 percent), a one-party press (the opposition for all intents and purposes does not exist), an end to press freedom *(La Prensa* is finally shut down completely), an end to civil rights ("suspended"), and compulsory military service (75,000 men under arms). There have always been some Americans who sympathize with the communists, but not many of them have been lionized.

—THE U.N. TURNS TO HUMAN RIGHTS IN CUBA
MARCH 11, 1988

Even though the 8:30 A.M. English-language news issues from Geneva, there was no mention on March 11 of the developments the day before in Geneva at the United Nations Commission on Human Rights. It was the big day of the U.N. Human Rights season; Maureen Reagan was in town as a member of the U.S. delegation, and also Vernon Walters, our ambassador to the United Nations. The chairman of this year's delegation to that commission is Armando Valladares (now a U.S. citizen), and if he is not an expert on human rights in Cuba, then Rudolf Hess knew nothing about life inside Spandau Prison. What happened? Let the suspense reign. . . .

The United States was fervently backing the most modest human rights resolution ever formulated. It followed the conventional form of those resolutions, which come in U.N.-sonnet form. The first eight or ten or twelve batches of prose describe the motives of the resolution's originator ("Aware of its responsibility to promote and encourage respect for human rights and fundamental freedoms; recalling Economic and Social Council resolution 1235 . . .") until staggereth the patience of any nonbureaucratic reader. After that are the three or four patches of prose that state the resolution.

In this case, all the United States was asking for was that Cuba be urged by the Secretary-General of the United Nations to permit the Red Cross to travel to Cuba to examine its prisons. One would think this a reasonable request. In the first place, Cuba could always say no, the Red Cross can't examine our prisons. And what then would happen? Nothing.

But in the surrealistic world of the United Nations, these things achieve their own importance, so that intensive lobbying went on for weeks. As one might expect, a vicious campaign was mounted against Armando Valladares's *Against All Hope,* a brilliant, devastating exposé of twenty-two years of life in Castro's prisons. It was charged that Valladares had been—oh, a member of the Nazi Youth Guild, or whatever: Even the most fastidious clerks tend to forget what was today's distortion extruded by the Castro propaganda machine.

One unusual development was embarrassing not so much to Castro, who is not easily embarrassed (he wasn't embarrassed in 1962 when the Soviet Union was detected having moved one half of its nuclear missiles into Cuba), but embarrassing to Felipe González, the prime minister of Spain. The Madrid daily *ABC* got hold of an official, confidential report on human rights in Cuba conducted for the Spanish government by Spaniards, which report concluded, to use language more economically than the United Nations, that there *are* no human rights in Cuba. But such is the fraternal feeling of socialist prime minister Felipe González for Castro (they exchanged, a couple of years ago, on Castro's first and only trip to Europe, the biggest public smooch in the history of osculation), that the government managed to suppress the report's circulation. Spain determined to vote against the U.S. resolution and was left pretending to be ignorant of the state of human liberties in Cuba.

If you can follow a little Byzantine thought, it went as follows: If a) the Red Cross were to enter Cuba and report that the prisons

and psychological institutions were in fact torturing political prisoners, then b) the report of Spain's secret commission investigating human rights would indeed be verified; but c) since that report
had been suppressed, the result of that verification would be embarrassing to the Spanish Government. That is a specimen of U.N.
logic.

In any event, tension mounted greatly, and huge efforts were
made to line up the votes. One arithmetician figured that the deciding vote might be cast by São Tomé. The Europeans, with the
exception of Spain, were with us. The communist bloc and its
fellow travelers, against—of course. The big effort was not to persuade the Latin American states to vote for us—that would be too
much to expect—but to abstain. Our representatives in Geneva
know that most Latin American countries do not dare to show
hostility to Cuba. Castro might send Che Guevara, Jr., to do a
little terrorizing in return. On the other hand, to abstain or to vote
in favor of Cuba costs nobody anything.

The great moment came, and *flash!* the Cuban Government
proposed that a delegation from the Human Rights Commission
travel to Cuba to see for themselves how squeaky-clean Cuban
prisons are and how secure Cuban rights are. There was instant
commotion, and the Senegalese chairman said he wanted to mod-
ify the invitation at least to the extent of turning it around: The
United Nations investigators' trip to Cuba would be paid for by
the United Nations Commission on Human Rights, not by Castro.
That seemed a major concession, when Castro said OK. And so?
The Cuban proposal was carried, unanimously.

That is the kind of thing that has been passing for a concern
for human rights by the United Nations for forty-three years.

—TIANANMEN: A CRACK IN THE CONCRETE?

MAY 19, 1989

On an off-duty morning in Hangchow pursuing Mr. Nixon about
on his historic trip to China in 1972, four journalists set out toward
the marketplace for a stroll. We came upon a little one-woman
stand where embroidered handkerchiefs were being sold. Teddy

White trotted out his thirty-year-old Chinese to converse with the pretty, middle-aged saleswoman, asking discursive questions. Suddenly James Michener broke in, and he was all business. White translated for him.

"Do you have any children?"

"Yes, I have a boy and a girl."

"How old is your boy?"

"Sixteen."

"What do you want him to do when he grows up?"

"I want him to do whatever Chairman Mao wants him to do."

"But what do *you* want him to do?"

"Whatever Chairman Mao wants him to do."

"If Chairman Mao asked you what you wanted your son to do, what would you say?"

"I would say, 'I hope it will please Chairman Mao that I wish him to join the People's Army to continue the struggle against the imperialists.' "

The scene was vivid in the mind when on Thursday one saw and heard the television reporter inside a bus among the protesting students in Shanghai:

"What do you want to do when you finish school?" one boy in his late teens was asked.

"I want to be an artist. Maybe a writer."

To another young man, "And you?"

"I want to be"—slight giggle—"a VIP."

Mao Man!

And then on Thursday in Beijing there was a meeting between a student leader and Zhao Ziyang, the successor to Mao Tse-tung as chairman of the Communist Party, and also Li Peng, the premier. In days gone by a student given such an honor would have reacted with slavish awe. This student, representing the hunger strikers, began by reproaching Li Peng for being late. The student then went on to ask for genuine negotiations. The premier replied that unless the students retreated, there would be "chaos—worse even than the Cultural Revolution." The student leader was adamant, refraining only from voicing one of the students' most emphatic demands, namely that Li Peng resign his office.

That student needed to be helped when leaving the room, so weakened was he by his fast. He was returned either to the hospital or to the trenches in the middle of Tiananmen Square, where history is being written as resonantly, one prays, as the history that was written in Paris on the fourteenth of July when the Bastille was overrun, or in November of 1917, when the Winter Palace was stormed. A great monsoon rain came down, outrageously unseasonable, and the sheer force of it dissipated the protesting crowds; but not for long. They were back, protecting themselves from the rain's fury as best they could. The hunger strikers prostrate on the pavement in the center of the square did not move, except those who were taken on stretchers to the hospital for intravenous feeding.

The delegations walked through the square carrying banners, all of them calling for reforming the system. Much was spoken about "corruption," which is an extra-ideological vice, on the scale of the afflictions brought by the communists to the Chinese people, as vexing as Tammany Hall up against the Holocaust. And one student leader said that his legions did not wish to overthrow the Communist Party; they merely wanted to reform it. One wondered whether they know that the only way to reform the Communist Party is either to replace it or to transmute it into an unrecognizable shape even as, traveling in the opposite direction, the East Germans came up with the German Democratic Republic as a name for their totalitarian state.

No, they do not have an explicit program of reforms, which is why they reach out for symbolic reforms, the resignation of two of the principal figures in Chinese official life. Whatever then happens, China must be different, they insist. And as the student leaders cry out with one voice, exhibiting a desire for the kind of freedom they have never experienced, one is dazzled with hope.

All that was required to produce this change was an estimated 30 to 55 million killed, thirty-five years of repression, a revolution seeking to overturn the cultural coordinates of Chinese life, and a foreign policy of which the sponsorship of Pol Pot is symbolic. One is reminded of the one great line of the Russian writer Ilya Ehrenburg: "If the whole world were to be covered with asphalt, one day a crack would appear in the asphalt; and in that crack grass would grow."

—TIANANMEN: SO WHAT DO WE DO NOW?
JUNE 6, 1989

Pundits who need to opine on the developments in China and fear that what we write on Monday will be obsolete on Tuesday can take comfort, even if the National Security Council, the State Department, and the Pentagon can't, over the extraordinary failure of our sinological cadre, in the academies here in America and in our diplomatic outposts in China and elsewhere, to have predicted anything. They did not sense the latent resentment of the population at large, did not foresee the initial success of the demonstrators; they predicted a crackdown when it did not happen, did not predict a crackdown when it did happen, and did not predict the severity of the crackdown when it did happen.

Mrs. Bette Bao Lord, born in China—a brilliant analyst and novelist—said on CBS that she didn't think "anyone would have guessed they [the authorities] would be so brutal." Lacking in historical perspective? The executors of the Cultural Revolution were ten times more brutal, and they were, well, also Chinese. And her husband, Winston Lord, the learned professional and our most recent ambassador-on-the-scene in China, announced that the Chinese Government had "lost all legitimacy," raising the question: When, and just how, did the Chinese Government acquire legitimacy, other than by exercising de facto authority over Chinese life? If that is all it takes, who is to say that the government of Deng-Peng will lose its legitimacy? All it needs to do is to continue governing, and precisely that is their manifest objective.

It is revealing to study the ways of our professional diplomatic and journalistic managers. At this writing, the estimate (of Britain's BBC) is that 2,600 people have been killed in the first thirty-six hours of Deng's repression. That is a lot of people, by one perspective. It is almost as many people as the United States has executed for capital offenses since Chiang Kai-shek came to power in 1927. So we have graduating perspectives: 1) Killing somebody because he is guilty of murder. 2) Killing somebody because he is, in the judgment of the authorities, creating, as Deng charged, "anarchy." And then, 3) killing somebody because he stands in your aggressive path. The Ayatollah Khomeini, whom the Prophet permitted to die before Salman Rushdie, killed one million Iranians in his pointless war against Iraq, and he is mourned by a multitude equal at least to the multitude we saw at Tiananmen Square on the most exuberant day. Mikhail Gorbachev stepped into the Afghan invasion, appointed a fiercer general than the incumbent, and the rate of killing increased, reaching 1.2 million Afghans before the decision was made to pull out.

One of ABC's China correspondents said that the Chinese Government had forever "lost its credibility." An interesting question: If tomorrow, or the day after tomorrow, the government of Gorbachev were to slaughter 2,600 Lithuanians, or Armenians, or Ukrainians—would it lose its credibility? An ABC correspondent on *This Week with David Brinkley* accosted guest Henry Kissinger and said: Look, this is the country of Thomas Jefferson. Can't we do something more to the Chinese than merely "deplore"—he managed a facial condescension in giving out the word used by President Bush—the action of the Chinese Government? Another interesting question: What did we do other than to deplore the action by the Soviets in 1956 in Hungary when they ran their tanks over students and hanged their premier? Or twelve years later, when they took comparable action against Czechoslovakia? The answer is: You don't get really and truly mad at superpowers that dispose of nuclear weapons. What they do you deplore in the sanctuaries of editorial offices or in the Security Council of the United Nations.

We should rue the awful ignorance from which we all suffer about what really goes on in the mind of the tyrants. Kissinger is right—Deng Xiaoping hardly welcomed a situation similar to one of which he was the victim: The Cultural Revolution put him in jail for ten years and made a paraplegic of his son. And now he is seized, in Karl Wittfogel's phrase, with the megalomania of the aging despot, and rather than acknowledge the right of his citizens peaceably to assemble in order to petition the government for a redress of grievances—a right guaranteed to Americans by the First Amendment—he shoots them, and tomorrow may hang those his fusiliers missed.

The only thing we can reasonably do isn't, at this point, fustian retaliation. A moral freeze is in order. Then wait. Wait to see what happens. Whom will we be dealing with? What might be the effect of sanctions withheld? And—finally—do we really have effective, usable sanctions against the third superpower in an age where we seek a triangular disposition of power, rather than the pre-1960 hegemony, China–U.S.S.R. _v._—us?

We can loathe what was done, and learn from it. Do not be surprised, Virginia. That kind of thing can happen in countries like that, and regularly does.

—TO BIND THE WOUNDS
DECEMBER 13, 1991

It's a bad time to be asking Americans to give money to foreign countries, and there is of course a special irony that tends to undermine the request for help to a country that in pledging to bury us cost us a few trillion dollars in self-defense.

All of this Secretary of State James Baker was aware of when he spoke at Princeton, which is why he was careful not to mention money to be shipped to "Russia et al.," as we may as well agree to call that conglomerate. Instead, he put it this way, that he had in mind agricultural and medical relief that would cost every American the sum total of two dollars.

Even though the arithmetic is easy in this case, and an absolute breeze for a Princeton audience, he didn't do it for them. To have said "$500 million" would have caused every television network on Thursday night to have presented a dozen stricken men and women in a dozen towns, claiming how much they could benefit from a very small fraction of that $500 million.

There is no denying the stress of the times, dramatized by the television news shot of the upscale pawnshop in Beverly Hills. You drive in your Rolls-Royce and walk out without your Rolls, but with a check for fifty grand or so. The Rolls will stay where it is for exactly four months. During each of those four months you must send in 4 percent interest. That means $2,000 per month. If you're lucky, in April you can get back your car and you are out only $8,000, but the $50,000 you borrowed may have been just exactly critical in saving your real estate business or your funeral parlor enterprise, or keeping your two kids in college by paying the bills.

It is in times like these that one needs to think back on the great structures of Europe, so many of them diadems celebrating the artistic explosion of faith in the twelfth and thirteenth centuries. It was then that the four "great ladies" of France were built, at Chartres, Notre Dame, Rouen, and Reims. The four cathedrals make anything built since that time appear to be wistful acts of architectural pettifoggery: One can't walk into the cathedral of Chartres without knowing that one has seen the most beautiful creation in the world. And, in quieter moments, one asks: How is it that such a monument was paid for?

It is worth repeating to oneself the generality an economics historian made a few years ago—namely, that the level of income did not change much between the time of Christ and the beginning of the Industrial Revolution. In current terms, that would have meant that approximately 99 percent of all human beings lived below the poverty level. And yet they willingly contributed their savings to create such as the great ladies of France.

Mr. Baker is not suggesting that the United States alone bear the burden of seeing Russia et al. through the forthcoming agricultural depression. There are wealthy countries and many of them have much more to lose should the anarchy and fascism described by Baker take hold in that desolate part of the world where one third of the airports are closed because they can't find enough fuel in the greatest oil-exporting country in the world, where 30,000 nuclear missiles bask in the highest-quality fuel sufficient to propel them to every city in the West with a population of more than 500,000.

What Europe reasonably fears most in the months immediately ahead isn't a nuclear attack from rogue scientists in Kazakhstan. What it fears most is a wave of immigrants that would make the Mexican irruption into the American Southwest look like an orderly afternoon outing. East Germany could find itself seeking to block 10 million Russians who want—who demand—food, as every human being alive demands food, unless he is an Irish terrorist bent on suicide. There is no way the United States can say no in such a situation.

It has been a crazy year, a voluptuary feast for the historians of the future, the year in which the Union of Soviet Socialist Republics outlawed the Communist Party, in which Mikhail Gorbachev, *Time* magazine's Man of the Decade, began to fade into insignificance; in which Saddam Hussein challenged the greatest power on earth, was humiliated by the greatest power on earth, and somehow ended the year with a higher prestige than the American president who brought him to his knees, but forgot to behead him.

It must not be the year in which America's concern for itself forces human beings whose entire lives have been a wretched struggle against the totalitarianism of their ideologized elite to suffer now the fate of starvation, or the whiplash of reaction.

—LENIN'S GETTING OLD

JUNE 25, 1991

The people at *60 Minutes* devoted the entire hour on Sunday to excerpts from programs done over the last decade in and about the Soviet Union. It was a galvanizing hour, reminding us of many things, among them the tenacity of our illusions even in the very recent past about Soviet communism.

In this respect, much credit goes to the producers of *60 Minutes* who were not shamed to let us all see the glowing tributes paid to the communist state as recently as 1972. Morley Safer is there, and he speaks about the huge material abundances of Soviet life, about the gaiety of Soviet dress, the color, the general animation. We are introduced to a society that seems to be, finally, working, a dream coming true.

True, Safer concluded that segment, the Russian people don't have freedom; on the other hand, they never did.

It seems a million years ago, but that is the way so many of our journalists and intellectuals saw the Soviet Union. It was so in China; indeed, 1972 was the year in which Richard Nixon led so many journalists to China, to see and to adore.

The program went on to introduce us to an eighty-year-old woman, married to a writer who was taken in 1936 by the GPU, a predecessor of the KGB. What had he done? Nothing. He was executed. His brother was then imprisoned. And his father. And now the old lady, talking in fluent English to *60 Minutes*.

Flash to several Russians, among them young people, who say quite frankly and enthusiastically that they very much wish that Stalin were still alive. Yes, it is important to recall that such neural disorders exist. There are those (mostly in the closet) who wish Hitler were alive. The people of Moscow wept when Ivan the Terrible said he might abdicate his office.

On my first visit to Russia in 1970, on behalf of the United States Information Agency, I was extensively briefed about what was unsafe. Watch the booze—there are Soviet officials who will attempt to exchange toasts at a velocity visiting foreigners can't control. No sex—Mata Haris are everywhere. Don't under any circumstances accept a letter from anyone with the request that it be mailed when you get back to the States. And then the supreme commandment: Under no circumstances derogate Lenin in any way. He is the redeemer in the view of almost everybody in the Soviet Union.

Twenty years later, the majority of the people who live in Leningrad opt to change the name of the city. Back to St. Petersburg, bypassing its former name of Petrograd. Lenin hated saints.

Here and there there had been evidence of anti-Leninist popular thinking: a statue defaced, a wisecrack about the old man. But the gravity of the action of the voters of Leningrad was quickly understood by the Kremlin, which announced that the change in name could not take place.

Many reasons for this were given, among them that it would be extremely expensive to change the name on all the relevant maps and brochures and road signs. But the fear expressed by Mikhail Gorbachev reflects the awful insecurity one would experience on learning that the legitimizing instrument of your faith is crumbling.

If (however inconceivable) it were established that the Constitution was illegitimate, by what would the courts and the legislators and the executive be guided? If (however inconceivable) it were established that Christ was a paid actor and the crucifixion a venture in black theater, what would the Christian world do? Perhaps the YMCA would replace the Vatican.

But now the revolution is decomposing. Lenin instructed us

that "Orthodox Marxism requires no revision of any kind either in the field of philosophy, in its theory of political economy, or in its theory of historical development." But that is never true. Lenin's sole virtue was a relative indifference to adulation. It was only after he died that Petrograd's name was changed.

But Lenin, himself as close as any man could be to heartlessness, understood intellectually the need for icons. And as a political matter, he'd have approved the hagiography of communism, not because he believed in the elevation of ideological saints, but because he'd have found it useful to accelerate the revolution.

60 Minutes showed us a slice of today's Moscow. And there we see—the can-can. Nikita Khrushchev, in 1957, saw it done in Los Angeles and railed against it as evidence of bourgeois degeneracy. All of this in twenty years. Enough to make a man a Couéist ("Every day, in every way, I am getting better and better").

—A History of the Cold War?

March 13, 1990

A distinguished British historian, an old personal friend (we were roommates at school), suggested seriously that I undertake to write a history of the Cold War. I told him my book-writing time was mortgaged through 1994, and I don't intend to embark on such a venture at that point (one can reasonably expect a forest of Cold War R.I.P. books in the interval). But the proposition stayed with me overnight, and bore fruit as follows:

1) Any book on the Cold War should take seriously the thought and analysis of those who participated in the Cold War and agonizingly predicted the defeat of the West. Most widely recognized among these was Whittaker Chambers. His lament, widely quoted and anthologizable in the literature of despair, was phrased in a personal letter to me written in 1954. He said: "The enemy—he is ourselves. That is why we can hope to do little more now than snatch a fingernail of a saint from the rack or a handful of ashes from the faggots, and bury them secretly in a flowerpot against the day, ages hence, when a few men begin again to dare to believe that there was once something else, that something else

is thinkable, and need some evidence of what it was, and the fortifying knowledge that there were those who, at the great nightfall,
took loving thought to preserve the tokens of hope and truth."

And there was Aleksandr Solzhenitsyn, who wrote that over a
very few years he had witnessed the collapse of the will of the
West. That for a period, during the fifties and sixties, the uncoor-
dinated resistance within the Soviet Union—a spiritual fraternity,
really—had reason to think of the West as an immovable wall
against which the Soviet Union would not, could not prevail; but
that after our retreat from Vietnam, and our insensitivity to so
much that the communists were engaged in, culminating with the
declaration of martial law in Poland, there was little reason to
hope that we would prevail.

The historian must examine the thought of such as Chambers
and Solzhenitsyn without donning a pathologist's robe. Their concern was deeply rooted in objective analysis—but objective analysis of Western weakness, not of communist weakness. This is a
point to stress.

2) Whereas we can proudly say that the Western powers will
presented formidable obstacles to Soviet expansionism, we need
to say this carefully. The last successful Soviet diplomatic offensive
brought them the INF treaty. We think little of it at this point
because the prospect of a Soviet military drive across Eastern Europe has all but faded, with the dissolution of the Soviet empire in
the region.

But the Soviet offensive was dramatically and frighteningly
successful. Any future general at a war exercise, studying the political culture of the late 1980s, would be justified in concluding that
the disappearance from Europe of theater nuclear weapons of a
range extensive enough to reach the Soviet Union left our potential enemy with a measure of security it had not dreamed of getting in early negotiations.

The West was left with strategic weapons, at closest range
from submarines in the Baltic Sea. But the firing of such weapons,
aimed at slowing down or aborting a Soviet blitzkrieg, would have
been seen by the Kremlin as the equivalent of weapons fired from
Omaha. And our knowledge that such would be the Soviet reaction would have resulted in preventing the submarines from firing.
The Europe of 1989 might well have been converted, as little as

one year later, into a neutralist Europe headed by an anti-nuclear political party in East Germany, to be joined by an anti-nuclear political party winning in Great Britain. Meanwhile, the United States had acquiesced in what seems like a permanent satellite government in Afghanistan, had refused to take decisive action in Nicaragua. And then—

3) And then, as some of us believers might put it, God cleared his throat. And lo, on March 11, 1990, the little state of Lithuania declared that it was independent of the Soviet Union. It is reasonably expected that Latvia and Estonia will follow—in the footsteps of Poland, and East Germany, and Czechoslovakia, Romania, and Bulgaria. A triumph of Western policy?

Only if one chooses to believe that the mere survival of the West was itself triumphant. It is forever to the credit of the West that it elected to remain a nuclear power, exercising the deterrent club, the shield which so many Westerners argued we should do without,

But it was the agony of life under communism that dictated the outcome. The West might have reason to bask in its diplomatic prowess if it had taken less than forty-five years to liberate the swollen kingdom of the slaves. They were liberated primarily by the shortage of bread in the motherland of the proletariat, rather than by the abundance of it in the West. No history of the Cold War will successfully assert that the demise of the Soviet empire was a triumph of Western diplomacy. What we did, essentially, was to stand still. And, in the case of some, to pray for divine intercession.

2

Combat Duty for Women?

AUGUST 6, 1991

T he Senate has now passed a bill permitting women who volunteer to fly combat aircraft to do so, and the movement to extend the rights of women to equality in the trenches is growing. Have a thought, please, to this demurral.

1) The practical arguments, in favor and against, have occupied most of the time of the jurists brought in to decide the question. It is observed that, on an average, a man is 40 percent stronger than a woman. Does that sound decisive to you? Perhaps, in which case you have given the subject insufficient thought for the simple reason that there is little correlation between human strength and military skill.

This is not to say that there are no situations in which sheer brute physical force isn't critically useful: Of course there are such situations, but they are put in place by recalling that Napoleon was 5 feet 3 inches, and that T. E. Lawrence weighed less than 150 pounds.

2) A corollary of the above is the argument that women's reflexes are every bit as fast as those of men, and that success or failure as a modern soldier, particularly in a fighter aircraft, depends on the speed of response. If Amy can read the dials and do the correct thing just as fast as Roger, why should the Air Force discriminate against her?

The answer, of course, is that the Air Force should not discriminate against her, if speed of response is the only criterion relevant.

3) To the argument that in combat conditions it is a burden to provide two sets of washroom facilities, the pleaders for what they

call women's rights argue to the effect that in combat situations, antimacassar niceties become simply irrelevant, and that, after all, even in the narrow confines of a foxhole it is possible to make token adjustments.

Both men and women go up in spacecraft, and mixed company has made long passages, plotted and unplotted, on small boats and even on rafts. Primitive cultures simply ignore biological differences at this level, and war making has a great deal to learn from primitive cultures, where the objective is the thing that rules, not the taboo, which is properly relegated to insignificance.

Very well then, the arguments in favor of women in the military are in. Here is the side to which I belong:

1) The attempt to equalize the sexes is going to be asymptotic. You think you have reached equality, but there is still a tiny difference there. That difference bespeaks an insight that is a hallmark of civilization.

2) It is a pity that the useless word "equality" ever got into the act, because one cannot in the nature of things make "equal" that which is not the same. You can play around with other words if you wish. Fungible? No, the sexes aren't fungible. Miscible? Yes, but miscible elements retain their identity: If the sexes weren't miscible, life together would be impossible.

But the point is overwhelmed, and that point is that men and women are different, and that it is *of nature* (*ex natura*) that one sex should be drawn to one pursuit (among many), the other to another pursuit (among many).

That a woman should aspire to be a poet or an architect, a doctor or an engineer, does no violation to the critical insight of separateness of nature. But that a woman should ignore what binds her to the newborn child or enjoins her to comfort men who cannot adequately be comforted by other men is a tug against nature. And that a man, himself a poet or a doctor or an engineer or an architect, should cease instinctively to gravitate to his responsibility to protect the home is a violation of his nature.

The awful, fanatical compulsion to perfect interchangeable sexes does violence to primary instincts that are wrong when abused. But to overcorrect an abuse is to commit a fresh abuse.

Because we know that women should be educated and should vote and should exercise their capacity to lead does not dissipate that tropism that assigns to the woman primary responsibility for the care of the child, and to the man, primary responsibility for the care of the woman.

Transplanting it all onto the battle scene, we need to wonder whether the machine gunner exposing his life to effect a mission isn't dismayed at the thought of a young woman firing away at his side, causing him to wonder whether the fight he is fighting reflects a civilized order.

3

Three Critical Views of Democratic Fetishism

A) DEMOCRACY—A CURE-ALL?
JULY 16, 1991

When, at a television seminar in Berlin a year ago, Ambassador Vernon Walters said in passing that no democracy in this century had initiated an aggressive war, my memory churned in search of the exception. Unsuccessfully, because the ambassador was right.

Granted, he was saved by the tolling of the nineteenth-century bell. His figure was hallowed by only a year or so, given the Spanish–American War of 1898, which is difficult to view other than as an offensive war by the United States against the Spanish empire, never mind whether it was justified.

So then, that is certainly one up for democracy. But the enthusiasm for democracy seems incautiously optimistic. Moreover, it runs into its own difficulties, because of course it requires the crystallization of acceptable boundaries. It is jarring to recall that as recently as during this century, Wales and even Scotland were discussing the kind of "devolution" that would have meant, in effect, self-rule.

A few miles to the west, the disorder and the killings go on in Ulster and Ireland over the dogged question of self-rule: Ulster wants to hold on to its independence as a part of Great Britain, while substantial elements within Ireland want irredentism.

At this particular moment the odds that Canada will split open are very good: Quebec appears adamant in its insistence on Québec Libre, a movement abetted by Charles de Gaulle when he visited Canada twenty-four years ago.

Ten years ago Chile and Argentina very nearly went to war over the question of who should govern the region around Tierra del Fuego. India is continually rent on the question of Kashmir.

And, of course, holding center stage are Yugoslavia and the Soviet Union.

These, granted, are not democracies, but the question to ponder is: If they gave everyone a vote tomorrow, and the vote included the right to define boundaries, how many countries would evolve from that fissiparous mess? Five? Ten? And on whose side should the grown-up nations be? Should we pull for independence for the Baltic states?

Surely the answer is yes, though the official position in Washington is no. But how about Slovenia? Or Georgia?

The dogmatists' assumption that democracy tends to wash away the exorbitant sins of its people is otherwise disturbed by a knowledge of history. India is in a state of high combustion, and has assassinated two leaders in recent history. In a way, it is comparable to Portugal before World War I and immediately after, until Antonio Salazar took charge. (Salazar took charge! But he was a dictator. That's right, he was.)

And a decade after that, Spain all but fell apart, suffering more than a million casualties in one of the goriest civil wars in modern times. What then happened was that Francisco Franco took charge. (Franco took charge! But he was a dictator. That's right, he was.)

In Chile in 1970, Salvador Allende was elected president, never mind that in a three-part election he garnered only 36 percent of the vote. What then happened was three years of ripening strife. In the summer of 1973 Chile's Supreme Court declared unconstitutional two of the actions of Allende, and the country was headed for civil war and Augusto Pinochet took charge. (Pinochet took charge! But he was a dictator . . .)

What would you do if you were Alberto Fujimori, the democratically elected president of Peru? The figures, as of the weekend, are that the terrorists, supplemented by the counterterrorists, last year killed what in the United States would be the equivalent of 50,000 people. "Democracy" in Peru does only the dainty service of legitimizing the role of the president and the legislature. But democracy does not have the power to do anything effective to curb the terrorists, and the army does not seem to have the strength, or the resources, that were finally mobilized by the Filipinos to quell their terrorists in 1954.

Meanwhile, Colombia, which is off and on again as a democracy, but has been one now for thirty-three years, seems to have two governments. The drug government lays down the terms under which they will agree to stop killing Colombian candidates for the presidency and other folk. And these terms include the power to alter the constitution, so as to forbid (for instance) extraditing Colombians to the United States.

Which brings to mind the interesting metaphor: Is a democracy that exports a huge volume of drugs to another country engaged in "aggressive action" against that country? If not, what exactly do you call it?

Enthusiasts though we are for self-rule, it pays to scale down our faith in its magical properties. What we need to do is go much further in refining what it is that marks civilized life, and self-rule is only one part of it.

B) DEMOCRACY IN HAITI

DECEMBER 1, 1987

Roger Allan Moore, Esquire, with a sizable delegation, was dispatched by the State Department to Haiti with the mandate to report back to the government whether the election on Sunday had been fair.

This is a fairly recent tradition: the political version of what in arms control lingo we call "verification." An example was the delegation sent to Saigon in 1971 to depose that the election of President Thieu had been fair. Memory is vague about the exact report of that commission, but not at all vague about the report of one of its members, a professor at Harvard. He gave birth to one of the most memorable ambiguities in recent political history: "The elections in South Vietnam were every bit as fair as those in Massachusetts."

The chairman of the Haiti commission, Mr. Moore, was a Bostonian of such elegance and bearing as one would associate with the chairman of a State Department commission to investigate democratic procedures in the House of Lords. Poor Roger Moore, his trip to Haiti puts one in mind of Scott-King's tour of modern

Europe: He and his commission went to see another candle lighted in the democratic world. Instead, they found themselves in the jungle. I am especially thankful that Roger Moore is safely back, because I love him like a brother, and because he is the chairman of the board of directors of the magazine I serve as editor.

But will we never learn? It was way back that we were informed about the tentative character of political democracies. "Democracy arises out of the notion that those who are equal in any respect are equal in all respects; because men are equally free, they claim to be absolutely equal." That was Aristotle, and twenty-five hundred years of history would appear to be sufficient confirmation of this axiom about democracy and democracy failed. But just as Woodrow Wilson was set on making the world safe for democracy, breeding instead Stalin and Hitler, we rail against despotism and breed public chaos.

Now, the kindest thing anyone could have done for the people of Haiti between 1957 and 1971 would have been to shoot Papa Doc. He was a superstitious sadist high on guile and corruption. His son was an affront to political and social aesthetics, but in fact he was less inclined to rule by violence than his father. Few Haitians wish him back, save possibly those who cannot speak today because they were killed on Sunday in the effort to replace Baby Doc. But getting rid of Duvalier doesn't tell us democracy is the next step.

Representative Stephen Solarz of Brooklyn has a wonderful idea what to do about Haiti. First, you ask the "government" of Haiti to invite a regional force to come in and enforce "free and fair" elections. But if the government—the same government, the democratic pieties of Lieutenant General Henri Namphy notwithstanding, that stood by while the butchers did their work—declines to invite a "regional force" (including Cuba?) to come in and impose democracy on Haiti, we send one in anyway.

Leaving us with?

Utter mockery. The notion that, after the Solarz-democratic regional army comes in and supervises elections, political hygiene will come to a country that has been ruled by dictators for thirty years is voodoo politics. If you will permit a dirty word, what Haiti needs right now is a twenty-year dose of benevolent colonialism.

Except that it affronts his sense of what is proper, I should suggest that Mr. Solarz volunteer to act as Emperor of Haiti for a dozen years, or if the title puts him off, Procurator of Haiti—whatever. Then go ahead with the elections, but hope that when the time comes to do so, elections will not be likened to the holocaust of last Sunday. In Spain, Franco stepped in. One million casualties later, Spain began a very long road back to a democracy that was forty years in gestation. Perhaps Franco could have let his country go earlier. We will never know.

But we should know that to go directly from Duvalier to one-man, one-vote is the kind of thing best done in think tanks at Harvard, where when it doesn't work, people don't get killed.

---

c) Overtaxing Democracy

February 13, 1986

It is time, thanks largely to developments in the Philippines, to say some unkind things about democracy. The first of these is that democracy does not necessarily usher in virtuous governments or tolerable human conditions. The second is that democracy, particularly in its currently accepted, fanatical application (one-man, one-vote), is nothing more than a Western superstition. We are entitled to our superstitions and to our taboos, but it does not make much sense to assume that they are readily universalized.

Two episodes, illustrative in purpose. The movie, a dozen years ago, and the startled reaction to it by an American who saw it in Lagos, Nigeria. Scene: an eighteenth-century American slave ship, engaged in transporting West Africans for sale in the slave markets of Charleston, South Carolina. There is a mutiny by the blacks against the white captain and his white crew. But it is suppressed, the ringleaders of the mutiny are segregated and are made to walk the plank. Wild cheering from the audience. What goes on here? the American asked himself.

His host, a native Nigerian and a professor of anthropology, explained that Africans are trained to believe in the absolute authority of the chief. And the chief, in this picture, was the slave-trading captain of the vessel, and that mattered more than that he was corralling Africans into lives of slavery in the New World.

Proceed to deplore this blind allegiance to authority, as we all do, but stow it away as a fact of life in many parts of the world. It certainly has its manifestations when the Hitlers and the Stalins find it easy to conscript maintenance men to administer the Holocaust and gulag.

Next: An American scholar, doing research into the balloting after one of those elections we in effect presided over in South Vietnam during that country's brief interregnum with self-rule, elicited from the majority of the peasants he interviewed an attitude toward what they were doing that amounted to condescension over Western eccentricities. The idea, as one man put it, that by dropping a piece of paper in that box, over against that other box, you were substantially or even intelligently guiding your own future was—well, he just laughed.

It was certainly self-serving when President Marcos told me eight years ago on television that the American legacy of democracy had not been firmly enough rooted in the Philippines. But at the same time he was absolutely right. One does not deduce from his being right that he should also be president-for-life, but it is true that democracy had become a sham before President Marcos invoked martial law in 1972. Contenders were hiring private armies, and were then—as now—refusing to abide by the apparent results of elections. It is safe to say simply that democracy was not working, and democracy has hardly had a workout under Mr. Marcos of the kind that gives us confidence that it is now ready to work.

Democracy is primarily valuable, the late Max Eastman wisely summarized in a book on political philosophy, as a negative instrument, a way for a people to say: We do not desire the existing rulers to continue to rule. The notion that democracy is actually an instrument by which the people can fine-tune public policy is a Western superstition, along with the notion that anyone eighteen years old, whether literate or illiterate, instructed or dumb, should participate in political decision-making.

They are talking now about elections in Haiti where 80 percent of the people are illiterate, and about one-man, one-vote in South Africa. *The Washington Post* editorializes, with reference to

Subic Bay and Clark Field in the Philippines and the implied threat against them if Mrs. Aquino should win: "He is right: The bases are important to the United States. But they are not more important than the condition of democracy in the Philippines." What utter nonsense. We hope that ordered self-rule will come to the Philippines, but whether or not it does, we have imperial responsibilities in the Western Pacific that have nothing whatever to do with civic progress in that country.

What matters most is the constitution of liberty. John Stuart Mill, the primary bard of Western democracy, conceded this when he opted for autocracy well intentioned, rather than democracy as an instrument of totalitarianism and chaos. Ask not, in Africa or in Latin America, how many people voted for the incumbent governor; ask what kind of life are the people permitted to live. Are they free? Are they protected from arbitrary rule? Are their holdings safe from inflation and theft? Can they leave the country with their savings?

"Democracy" may triumph in the Philippines, and life may become intolerable as the result.

4

How Dangerous Is the Voters' Ignorance?

AUGUST 27, 1987

I have been upbraided by a friend of hard critical intelligence. Years ago, in a public exchange with Robert Maynard Hutchins, former president of the University of Chicago, I pronounced that "I would sooner be governed by the first two thousand names in the Boston telephone directory than by the two thousand members of the faculty of Harvard." But on another occasion I scoffed at the idea of the universal franchise. Asked to be more specific, I replied in one interview that a recent finding by the Gallup organization revealed (this was twenty years ago) that 20 percent of the American people didn't know what the United Nations was. The question now raised is: How can anyone take the two positions simultaneously, the first populist, the second elitist?

I do not find the apparent paradox self-destructive. If you take the first two thousand names in the Boston telephone directory, you might find that 20 percent of them (four hundred) had never heard of the United Nations. But subtract those four hundred votes from the two thousand and it doesn't follow that a vote on a public issue would result in a different verdict. This would not be so if the plebiscite were directly on the matter of the United Nations. If you asked the question, Do you believe in withdrawing from the United Nations? you would not get a rational answer from those Bostonians who did not know what the United Nations was.

On the other hand, among academics there is a syndrome, identifiable even if it isn't easy to describe. I remember the straw poll taken in Princeton some years ago which revealed that the faculty was divided as among McGovern (George), Nixon (Richard), and Gregory (Dick) for president. My recollection may be slightly inexact, but the poll came out approximately 65 McGovern, 8 Nixon, and 8 Gregory.

This may be dismissed as academic humor, in which case the obvious commentary is that one would be uneasy being governed by such folk as are given to academic humor. But one readily sees that 20 percent anomalies subtracted from both bodies leave you safer with the telephone directory than with the faculty directory. Raw ignorance, provided it is blended with something less than that, is less dangerous than raw hubris, all but unadulterated.

Still, you get isolated exposures to raw ignorance that are truly unsettling. In the recent trial in which Captain Jeffrey MacDonald sued author Joseph McGinniss, one saw such ignorance actively at work. MacDonald is the convicted killer of one pregnant wife, two daughters; McGinniss the author of _Fatal Vision,_ an intimate account of the murders. The lawsuit was initiated by the killer, who claimed that the author had defrauded him by writing an unsympathetic book, citing a contract that, he claimed, had been violated.

One juror, reacting to the argument that you cannot expect an author to write something he knows on investigation not to be true, did so violently. What rights should an author have that other, plain folk do not have? The answer, of course, is those rights distinctive to authorship, even as a policeman should have rights distinctive to police work and a house painter rights distinctive to house painting. She wanted to award the killer "millions of dollars"—an inflationary wish to begin with, since the author does not dispose of millions of dollars, but alarming in the lack of definitional intelligence.

The lady, by the way, when pressed, admitted that she had not read a book since she had graduated from high school. People who do not read books are less likely to be concerned about the rights of authors than people who do read books.

I was myself involved in a lawsuit a couple of years ago against a kooky racist publication, and we sat before six jurors. The attorney for the defendant (the kook) petitioned, on the second day, for a mistrial, on the grounds that the _Washington Times_ had published a story that morning on the trial, remarking the piquancy that the lawyer representing the racist kook had been the same lawyer who represented James Earl Ray, the convicted killer of Martin Luther King. The lawyer claimed that this would discredit him in the eyes of the six black jurors.

The judge interrogated the jurors one at a time, and then ordered the trial to proceed. None of the jurors had read the *Washington Times* that morning. None of the jurors had read a newspaper that morning. None of the jurors ever read a newspaper. When polled after the verdict came in, one of them said it was all this simple: Both parties had voted for Reagan, and anyone who voted for Reagan was racist.

So the point is to deprive ignorance of special, critical leverage. And that is a continuing problem for a democracy that takes pride in itself.

5

Poor Jim Baker

OCTOBER 3, 1989

T he vicissitudes of foreign affairs are so overwhelming as to leave breathless critics with the sole alternative of complaining that President Bush and James Baker have no "strategy." That criticism can be made in a polemical courtroom, but we should look at some of the problems they are facing before plunking down a facile answer to all of them.

• There is China. China, celebrating the fortieth anniversary of its people's revolution, lacking only people to celebrate it. Those who came close enough to Tiananmen Square to qualify for admission needed to be searched and identified. There they could ponder forty years including the period during which a hundred flowers were supposed to bloom, for every one of which about 10,000 Chinese were killed. Then the Cultural Revolution, which was the greatest assault on culture up until Pol Pot decided to eliminate literacy from Cambodia. Followed by a general relaxation of controls, which came to a sharp end last June when young Chinese began to take literally what they had thought of as encouragement to democratize their revolution.

The United States has simultaneously to paw the ground with legitimate indignation at the brutality of the June repression while studiously avoiding any geopolitical rupture of the kind that would accelerate the banns of Sino-Soviet affection. Not at all easy, not at all.

• The Israelis invented the word *chutzpah,* and there ain't anybody in the world who can practice it the way they can. The sequence goes as follows: Our secretary of state gives a speech telling the Israelis that they must really cut out planting fresh settlers in the West Bank, against the terms of the Camp David Accords. The United States then puts extra pressure on the Soviet Union to release Russian Jews who are anxious to leave. But once the Jews receive their visas, the great majority express a wish to settle—not in Israel, but in the United States. Israel does not like this, because it needs a Jewish population to guard against being dysgenically overwhelmed by Arabs, who procreate with the speed of light.

So . . . we contrive to reroute the Russian Jews to Israel, and Israel tells them to go settle in the West Bank, and then turns to the State Department and says: Please send us $400 million more to help build houses for the Russian Jews to settle in the West Bank. We can only assume that when Jim Baker heard that one, he stomped out of his office and ordered a hot dog.

• And then there is Colombia. Two weeks ago, President Bush tells all the world that in his war on drugs, Colombia will figure critically. After all, Colombia is the hotbed of the cocaine export trade, and Colombia has suffered most drastically from the effort to reduce, indeed to eliminate, that export. The man who would be president, and had a good chance of becoming president, was assassinated. The minister of justice finally, well, just plain gave up, after her family was threatened several times. There is, in much of metropolitan Colombia, something like a de facto curfew, so militantly in control of the streets is the drug merchant class.

And last weekend the news came in that the Colombian population is tiring of the fight. That there are politicians there, increasingly popular, who are saying: the hell with it. "Let's grow the stuff and ship it out and let the United States worry about Americans who want to poison themselves by paying for it. That's their concern, not ours. Ours is to do what we can to save our republic." What do Bush–Baker–Bennett say in reply to that?

• Now the Soviet Union seems to be coming apart. It can't feed its own population, or clothe it, or, for that matter, keep it sober. And then there is the centrifugal dynamism, growing, growing, to the point where little Latvia simply announces that it is going to go independent, which is something like Nantucket announcing that it is going to leave the Union.

This, plus thousands upon thousands of East German refugees

—and the East Germans are the spoiled men of the satellite empire—rushing through the hole in the Wall, via Hungary et al., to breathe freedom in West Germany. We can't stop them and won't, obviously; but the State Department does worry that the deterioration in Gorbachev's control of his own country could convulse Eastern Europe, and after that? After that what? What is our strategy for that? If you have the answer to this, call Jim Baker, collect.

6

On Resisting Temptation

AUGUST 12, 1988

A few years ago a request came in to the office of my television program, *Firing Line*. Would I have on Harry Reems and his lawyer, Alan Dershowitz? Harry Reems was being prosecuted under the federal obscenity laws for, in effect, being the Fanny Hill of the movie *Deep Throat*. The feds were going after him in Tennessee, for the same tactical reasons that motivate defense lawyers when they try to get a sympathetic jury. Tennessee jurors were less likely to be amused by wide-screen fellatio than New Yorkers or San Franciscans.

Well, of course this engaged the resourceful wit of Alan Dershowitz, professor of law at Harvard and standby advocate for front-page criminals. Mr. Dershowitz (who down the line won the case) objected on several grounds: the first, the selection of Tennessee as the locus for the trial; the second, the broad question of civil liberties (you can make any movie you want except a snuff film is Mr. Dershowitz's position). But in the course of the discussion I asked him about a particular feature of the film and he said he had not seen it. Not only had he not seen the movie whose star he was defending, as a matter of principle he did not intend to see it, because although he is prepared to defend the legal rights of pornographers, he does not want to encourage them in their trade.

The episode comes to mind in the current tumult involving *The Last Temptation of Christ*. Like most Americans I am a Christian, and therefore believe that Jesus Christ was the Incarnation— i.e., that he was at once man and God. For God, one exercises special reverence. We do not tell dirty jokes in church. And it is something of a dirty artistic joke to take such liberties as Martin Scorsese has taken in his movie. It tells us something about current perspectives that you could never get away with showing a fictional treatment of the life of Martin Luther King imputing to him the impurities, *mutatis mutandis,* imputed by Scorsese to Christ.

Now, it is entirely within the biblical tradition to understand that that part of Christ that was human flesh and blood suffered greatly during his ordeal on earth. Christ, the night before he died, asked God the Father whether that cup might not be taken from him. That is, in contemplation of the horrors that lay ahead, he hoped finally, desperately, to be spared them. That illumination of the human side of the duality of Christ is inspiring to Christians, reminding them of the true suffering of their savior.

But Scorsese helps himself to the remaking of Christ. He gives us a figure who, among other things, serves as a carpenter engaged in the making of crosses on which other dissenters from Roman law were crucified: the equivalent, two thousand years ago, of being the manufacturer of the gas pellets used to kill the Jews of Nazi Germany. On the cross, he gives us a Christ whose mind is distracted by lechery, fancying himself not the celibate of history, but the swinger in the arms of the prostitute Mary Magdalene. The blend of the ultimate altruist seeking in primal agony the fantasy of hot sex is something far from what a Senator Bilbo would have dared to do at the expense of Stepin Fetchit, bad-mouthing blacks in a smoker in the thirties, let alone on huge Hollywood screens with hawkers outside shilling for big juicy audiences to get a shot of impiety while protecting Artistic License.

In a way, Alan Dershowitz had it right. A truly civilized society is judged by the extent that it succeeds in governing its own appetites without the need of the law. Drug taking is also illegal, but everybody knows that anyone with a few dollars and an I.Q. of 100 can get all the drugs he can buy. To the extent that we are a civilized society we reject the use of drugs, as we seek to reject— and mostly succeed in doing so—the improvident use of alcohol and, increasingly, tobacco.

Even as we resist, to some degree, pornography, never mind the erotic satisfactions it can give. Professor Dershowitz was saying that in a free society, people will produce such a movie as *Deep Throat,* and people will go to see such a movie, even as, two thousand years ago, people went to the circus to amuse themselves by seeing lions and tigers and gladiators kill and dismember Christians.

But Dershowitz made a fine point when he said that he would not personally view the film made famous by his client. I shan't see Mr. Scorsese's film, any more than I would go to see a movie featuring George Washington as a drug trafficker or St. Francis of Assisi as a slave trader. Mr. Scorsese has given the Christian community a little opportunity to show their loyalty to our God.

7

Can a Tax-Deductible Church Take Sides?

AUGUST 11, 1988

There are three reasonable approaches to the whole idea of tax exemption for religious institutions. The first is: There shouldn't be any tax exemptions for anybody or anything. Not for the little church around the corner, not for Harvard University, not for the Olympic Laser Sailboat Committee. That position is so defensible that it happens to be my own: The government should stop using tax policy to encourage or discourage particular activities.

The second way is to say: OK, here is your tax exemption, and here is a list of things you can't do. In days gone by, they used to call these "prohibited transactions." But they were full of holes. Tax-exempt publications could not spend "substantial" time urging legislation, and on no account could come flat-out in favor of a political candidate.

But the business of denial or non-denial of tax exemption can become an instrument of harassment, and that is happening right now to the Catholic Church. One doubts it will ever come to a question of actually withdrawing tax exemption from the church. I have no doubt that if that day approached, the church would contrive to meet that challenge by having a great hand reach down from the skies, pick up the U.S. Capitol, and drop it into the Potomac.

But the attempt is worth considering. It is backed, of course, by the American Civil Liberties Union, something called the National Association of Laity and a couple of dozen other pro-abortion organizations and, yes, the alleged infraction of the church is its stand on abortion—specifically, Cardinal Humberto Medeiros of Boston, who attacked two pro-choice congressional candidates;

a 1984 statement by then-Archbishop Bernard Law and seventeen other bishops defining abortion as the critical issue of that year's presidential campaign; and a television appearance, also in 1984, by Archbishop John O'Connor of New York urging voters not to support candidates who take a pro-choice stance.

As it happens, the courts are winding their arguments around a technicality, namely, whether the plaintiffs have "standing"— i.e., have they suffered or will they suffer as the result of the court's verdict, and do they therefore have the right to bring a grievance before the courts? The defense claims that any future ruling by the courts cannot do or undo anything done in 1984. The plaintiffs argue that the removal of tax exemption is the only way to guard against future infractions.

But the interesting question is extrabureaucratic. It is: Should a church have the right, while enjoying conventional tax protections, to urge the incorporation into law of a deeply held moral belief? We don't believe in polygamy; should a church be penalized for advocating anti-polygamy laws?

During the nineteenth century, the case against slavery crystallized above all in the churches, even as it had done in Great Britain. Was it incorrect for churches to press the case for emancipation among their parishioners? "Incorrect" in the sense that to do so would be to violate the (then nonexistent) tax code?

Insight into the question comes by asking oneself: Doesn't the constitutional prohibition against denying the freedom of religion subdue the case against the IRS code? *Christian Century* magazine lost its tax exemption in 1964 for a few years because it came out for Lyndon Johnson for president. One could understand if it had lost its soul for making that argument, but the secular punishment, in order to be plausible, should have been based on the extramoral character of the partisan position. If a Catholic bishop were to say, "Vote for any Republican," one might properly raise the objection. But in saying, "Vote for any candidate, irrespective of whether he is Republican or Democrat, who believes in protecting the life of the unborn," surely you are arguing a moral position distinguishable from the kind of partisanship the IRS is seeking to discourage.

The churches were prime movers in the civil rights legislation of the 1960s, and one hears no complaints against Martin Luther King's sermons.

But of course, it's as simple as this. You crank up all these eristic arguments against this organization or that one depending on what positions are being taken. I'd like to see action by the anti-Catholic team taken against a church that recommended voting only for candidates who believed in gay rights. But that won't happen. How come? Easy. Hypocrisy.

8

On Having Fun with the Fundamentalists

I t is the season to be jolly at the expense of the television/ radio preachers. Oh my, how those saintly television commentators are enjoying it all! And the press in and around Washington has not had so much fun since Congressman Robert Bauman was caught in mid-speech denouncing juvenile delinquency, while furthering it.

The implied notion here, of course, is that the whole idea—the idea of preaching the word of Christ on television—is discredited. How is that? Well, because a preacher called Jim Bakker (pronounced, to the eternal distress of the secretary of the treasury, "Jim Baker") engaged in an act of adultery and then paid blackmail money to prevent his transgression's getting out.

Implicit in the handling of the story is the notion that those who do not practice what they preach invalidate that which they preach. To suggest such a thing is to betray a most awful misunderstanding of Christian teaching. The man whom Christ designated as the rock on which he would found his church sinned three times before the cock crowed. It is testimony to the profoundest understanding of Christian teaching that such generalities as "Physician, heal thyself" are utterly empty of moral and empirical meaning. If a doctor himself smokes cigarettes or drinks alcohol to excess, his failings do not invalidate his medical advice to others not to yield to weaknesses he cannot dominate. (After receiving a scolding from his physician for drinking too much, a character in Rabelais responds, "Forsooth, I do believe I know more old drunkards than I do old doctors.")

It has not been noticed in any account I have seen that we are dealing with a communion of people among whom an act of adultery is a Watergate-gravity offense. There is a certain irony in beholding the mirth among people for whom an act of adultery is no more offensive than, say, serving white wine with red meat, over the distress caused by a single act of adultery by a preacher who preaches against adultery. We tend to be much more understanding of politicians who preach thrift and practice prodigality.

Whatever virtues Mr. Bakker does regularly practice, asceticism is certainly not one of them. That paradox is as old as the first effort by the first pilgrim in the first catacomb to make a sacrifice in order to adorn an altar. That habit, in 1,100 years, produced the Cathedral of Chartres, whose incomparable beauty gladdened not only the heart of Henry Adams, but also the millennium of peasants who made sacrifices to create it. The adornment of the altar grew, almost inevitably, to the adornment of the house of the ministers of the altars, and the bejeweled palaces in which the popes and the cardinals and the archbishops lived. In some, the paradox (despite the things of this world) is never jarring. Pope Pius XII could be wearing the Hope diamond and still, beholding him, one saw a man wearing the simplest cassock, pursuing the vision of Christ.

Nothing Christ taught requires despising beautiful surroundings. But he did teach that priorities must inform the Christian, and it is not easy for anyone to judge whether the apparent vulgarity of the physical surroundings of the Reverend Jim Bakker reflects a disorder in his spiritual discipline. That he did not, at a crucial point, succeed in resisting temptation merely confirms that he was a sinner. That he expressed contrition invokes the extrasecular promise of forgiveness, seventy times seven times. But even granted divine forgiveness, there is the penance to be paid, and he is paying it by losing his exalted position in the public ministry.

There is great sport in catching up the hypocrite, but the cliché —"Hypocrisy is the tribute that vice pays to virtue"—must never get lost in the exercise. A few years ago, such hypocrisy transpired in what might well have been a scene from a play by Neil Simon. On their wedding night, two graduates of a fundamentalist Baptist college resolved to come clean, and first she, then he, admitted to not being a virgin. Further exploration revealed that they had both lost their virginity at play with Billy James Hargis, the president of their fundamentalist college.

The point is that Christianity not only survives such enormities, it takes strength from them because the abiding lessons of Christianity are reaffirmed: Man is a sinner. Man can repent. God will forgive. That is so very different from the fashionable secular complement, which is: What is sin?

9

Opportunizing on Chernobyl

MAY 3, 1986

I t took the Soviet Union four days to advise the world (five days to advise its own citizens) that there was a meltdown, and it took somewhere between four and five hours for the U.S. ideologues to seize on Chernobyl as an answer to their prayers. One can only suppose that Jane Fonda looked up at the celestial clouds and thought fleetingly that maybe there is a God there after all. If you pray long and persistently enough, God will give you the China Syndrome. To be sure, he gave it to us in the Soviet Union, but so what? We can rally the troops and have it out for good and all, and rid America of nuclear power.

The assembly mobilized to welcome Chernobyl calls itself the Coalition of Environmental/Safe Energy Organizations. It includes, obviously, the Union of Concerned Scientists, whose concern over the possible success of our space shield, which concerns them most of the time, gave room for concern over our nuclear electrical plants. They seize on Chernobyl as a reason once and for all to phase out all the atomic fuel plants in the United States. They are joined in this by some of the conservationist groups, who if they had their way would rip up all transcontinental highways to protect the peripatetic rights of meandering buffalo. One expects the Sierra Club nowadays and, alas, the National Audubon Society to prefer the preservation of the lousewort over the preservation of free people enjoying an industrialized leverage on life.

But it is the first time some of us were made aware of the Christic Institute, and so help me, the very first time one came across something called Blacks Against Nukes. One would think that there are enough issues around to divide us without having to worry about why it is that blacks should have more or less to worry about in the matter of nukes than whites or reds or, for that matter, mulattoes.

When one thinks back on Three Mile Island and how it succeeded in intimidating an entire post-industrial demarche, one is grateful that the trepidations that now stop us dead in our tracks didn't arrest our forefathers. If so, the *Niña,* the *Pinta,* and the *Santa María* would have turned around and headed back to Spain if one bo'sun had become seasick. The relevant facts distinguishing Chernobyl from nearly all A-plants in America are visible even to extreme non-scientists. The Soviets used a graphite moderator, and were without the protective dome we have been insisting upon since well before Three Mile Island. By common standards, this is primitive stuff; in the words of one observer, Soviet safety measures were at the "Bhopal level."

It is instructive that on the very day the Soviet nuclear accident was revealed, the presidential commission on the space shuttle explosion reported that its searches into the causes of the tragedy of last January are now positively concluded. The *Challenger* was destroyed because of a design failure in the shuttle seal and because of the temperature of the weather. Four months, and we have the answer. The technicians can go back and redesign the seal, and it should be possible to launch again before the end of the year. By contrast, no new nuclear energy plants have even been spudded since Three Mile Island, never mind the progress in that industry in Europe.

It will be interesting to see how Europe reacts to Chernobyl. Clearly no plant will any longer be tolerated that duplicates the flimsy protective devices of Chernobyl. But the Europeans are not going to stop nuclear energy. They have their mad scientists over there, too, but Europeans tend to have an eye out for commercial progress, and ideology tends to be gently but firmly shoved aside when there is a threat to it.

We should reflect seriously on the figures. The Soviet Union already relies on nuclear fuel for 10 percent of its electricity, and has in mind greatly increasing this figure, not so much because it is running out of oil, but because it likes to sell its oil for hard currency. Japan, which has to import all its sources of energy, derives 25 percent of its electricity from nuclear power. The truly impressive figure is France's: 65 percent of French electricity comes from nuclear sources, and even now France is selling electricity to Great Britain, an island of coal in the North Atlantic.

It is calculated that every American expends per day the same amount of energy as would be expended if each one of us had ninety-nine slaves working for us full-time. Oil and gas, for all that they appear ubiquitous at this moment, are diminishing universal assets. Nuclear power is going to give our grandchildren mechanical leverage in an intractable universe—or else it is going to emancipate those slaves, leaving us all the joys of caveman existence.

10

There Is Danger in Honoring Evil Men

JANUARY 2, 1986

W
e read a great deal about the troubled world we live in, and we should read more about it as we contemplate 1986 and the challenge ahead in this century. Organized communism is of course the principal agent of human evil, but there is a great deal of this evil that springs, so to speak, from the very soul of man, and it is everywhere—in Central Park, in the South Bronx, in West Hollywood, and around the corner, true; but in America its force is not organized, and this is a critical difference.

Doing some light reading over the Christmas holidays, I learned more about Colonel Idi Amin than I had known, from the hugely rewarding *Modern Times* of Paul Johnson, the British historian. And reflection on Amin is by no means out of order, inasmuch as he is alive and well, looked after by the sheiks of Araby in Jedda.

Listen to this: Idi Amin became a Muslim when he was sixteen. He hired out as a Ugandan mercenary to fight cattle rustlers in Kenya. "It was discovered," writes Johnson, "he had murdered Pokot tribesmen and left them to be eaten by hyenas, got information from Karamajog tribesmen by threatening to cut off their penises with a panga, and had actually sliced off the genitals of eight of them to obtain confessions." All of this and much more the British knew, but were reluctant to prosecute on the eve of independence for Uganda, so they referred the case to Obote. "Obote settled for a 'severe reprimand,' a curious punishment for mass-murder."

Sometime later, Qaddafi egged Amin on to ousting Obote because he had a few Israeli advisers about. Amin then began massacre on a he-man scale. "Amin often participated in atrocities, sometimes of a private nature. Kyemba's wife Teresa, matron-in-charge of Mulago Hospital, was present when the fragmented body of Amin's wife Kay was brought in: Amin appears not only to have murdered but dismembered her, for he kept collections of plates from anatomical manuals. He is also said to have killed his son and eaten his heart, as advised by a witch-doctor he flew in from Stanleyville. There can be little doubt he was a ritual cannibal, keeping selected organs in his refrigerator."

Well after most of this was known to all political insiders in Africa, the Organization of African Unity elected him as their president, and all chiefs of state, with three exceptions, attended the summit conference held in Kampala. "The heads of state showered Amin with congratulations during the summit when, having consumed parts of his earlier wife, he married a new one," Johnson comments. As chairman of the OAU, he addressed the General Assembly of the United Nations in 1975 in a rabid speech in which he denounced a "Zionist–U.S. conspiracy" and called not only for the expulsion of Israel but for its extinction (i.e., genocide). "The Assembly gave him a standing ovation when he arrived, applauded him throughout, and again rose to its feet when he left. The following day, the U.N. Secretary-General and the President of the General Assembly gave a public dinner in Amin's honor."

Historian Johnson summarizes: "Amin was not just a case of reversion to African primitivism. In some respects his regime was a characteristic reflection of the 1970s. His terror was a Muslim-Arab phenomenon; his regime was in many ways a foreign one, run by Nubians, Palestinians and Libyans."

George Shultz made a dramatic gesture when in Yugoslavia he banged his fist down on the desk of the foreign minister and cut short the explanation of the hijacking and killing on the *Achille Lauro* as a mere expression of Palestinian earnestness in the search for a homeland. The terrorist let go by the president of Italy, given hospitality in Yugoslavia, protected now in Iraq, is one more testimony to the willingness of world leaders, even leaders of relatively civilized states, to handle matter-of-factly men who deserve execution. They deserve that not merely because moral poetry is served by punishing them. It is, rather, a need for an assertion of will against outlawry by states that try to govern themselves by the rules of law.

You cannot at one and the same time generate a heated and purposive disgust with Idi Amin and also give him state dinners in New York, and protect him from mosquito bites in Saudi Arabia. Diplomacy can be the great innovator of moral realism. The United Nations is of course the very worst laboratory for the development of anti-anti-totalitarian vaccines. Sometimes it is simply necessary to confront Genghis Khan across the bargaining table. But beware the ceremony. It weakens the blood of free men.

11

The United Nations' Fortieth Anniversary, 1985

OCTOBER 24, 1985

NEW YORK—This is U.N. week here in New York, an event most of the country will be spared, even unto the reporting of what the princes of the third world tell us. There is a certain amount of color to it all, no denying that. Monday morning the dictator of Nicaragua went jogging in Central Park, followed by Secret Service guards carrying hidden submachine guns. The day before, Mr. Mobutu of Zaire hired two private railroad cars to take him and his staff to Washington. En route they were served caviar and champagne, among other things, and perhaps pondered the plight of the poor nations.

The frugality of Mr. Mobutu is in contrast with his appearance at the United Nations in 1973, when he a) denounced America and the West in general, and b) traveled here aboard the S.S. *France,* where he had eighty first-class staterooms for his entourage, including his private photographer and his wife's hairdresser. So, in twelve years, Mobutu is reduced to fifty attendants and the S.S. *France* to none. The government in Paris said, in effect, that it couldn't afford to keep up the *France* as long as Mobutu traveled on it only once a year.

There is a lot of that kind of sniping against the third worlders, whose economic profligacy at home is quite simply a scandal: Mengistu of Ethiopia spending $50 million on a new building in Addis Ababa while American middle-class citizens send dollars to relief agencies for Ethiopia, and musicians sing rock round the clock to raise money. There is that part of the United Nations that strains charity, but it is probably fair to say that most New Yorkers have got used to it, and not many speeches these days are devoted to it.

They talk about other things. Charles Lichenstein, the bright political scientist who served on the staff of Ambassador Jeane Kirkpatrick at the U.N., electrified the world when, provoked, he reminded a U.N. official that the United Nations was always free to pack up and head out to sea, with a whole lot of Americans waving it goodbye as it sailed off into the sunset. Never mind that sailing into the sunset from Manhattan would end the U.N. up in Hoboken; nobody ever said Chuck Lichenstein was a cartographer. It was the thought that counted, and that thought had great and deep echo chambers in the American spirit, because the United Nations has outraged every ideal enunciated at its founding.

That is what worries the thoughtful residents of New York. I mean, the idea of a celebration. Celebrate is what you do when you run the four-minute mile, or when you win a world war, or when Christ is risen. The problem with this week in New York City is that everyone is here to celebrate the fortieth anniversary of the United Nations, but there is nothing to celebrate, unless you take the position that anything forty years old is worth celebrating, in which case AIDS has about thirty-seven years to go before we celebrate it.

The United Nations is the greatest distillery of anti-Americanism outside the Kremlin. It is the greatest distillery of anti-Semitism—even including the Kremlin. It is, to quote myself, the greatest assault on moral realism of any institution in the world today. The reason for this is that within the United Nations the assumption is that statesmen are concerting to advance liberty and comity. That underlying assumption is traduced by the behavior of the men who, in the United Nations, spread falsehoods, encourage hostilities, and deplore and restrict the growth of freedom, while excusing and indirectly encouraging the increase in terrorism.

Can it really be all that bad? No. Nothing is all that bad. There are fine men and women associated with the enterprise, who labor mightily to surface a clean thought every now and then. And, every now and then, the delegates are exposed to intelligent and resourceful research, even to a good speech. There is no doubting that there is a felt hunger in the world for peace and just a little liberty for oppressed peoples. And an adventurous spelunker willing to delve into the depths of U.N. oratory will every now and then bump into a little stalagmite expressing the deeply hidden ideals of the United Nations.

But there is precious little to celebrate. If ever it were relevant that the background of the President of the United States is that of an actor, it will be relevant on the day he arrives in New York to celebrate the U.N.'s fortieth anniversary.

12

As We Get Older, Do We See More?

MARCH 1987 ISSUE OF *50Plus* MAGAZINE

This essay is written on a day in which 300,000 young men and women, their age estimated at between eighteen and twenty-two, have made a most fearful ruckus in the streets of Paris. What is marvelous about the whole thing—to this mature observer—is that although I have read about these riots in the newspapers, and viewed depictions of them on the evening news, I have found it extremely hard to know what it is that the young people are rioting about. There is talk about how this is a right wing riot, not a left-wing riot. But I swear, if I had to sit down and write a column about what exactly it is that is exercising the young people of France, I would need to call two or three old friends in Paris to ask: "Tell me, what in the hell is going on?" And whereas fifteen years ago this lack of particular knowledge would greatly have vexed me, it no longer does.

There is, in maturity, a crystallization of perspective. The overwhelming majority of those who buy beer and munch hungrily the television news while eating pizzas are—young people. There is a sense in which they bring to the news their theatrical demands for perspective, for apocalyptic confrontations.

Every now and again, we learn from reading history, what seems at first a trivial episode—the charge against the Winter Palace in January 1917—becomes the trigger of a new (in the cited case, new and bloody) epoch. But mostly such phenomena as the French students' demonstration are trivial historical skirmishes, as remarkable as a grain of brownish sand, moments after it is flicked onto a yellow-white beach: you will need to hover over the area, magnifying glass in hand, in order merely to find it. You have, well, grown up. And the kind of thing that caused freshman riots at college brings now less a concern for the causes of the riots than a concern that the rioters will not cause damage to themselves, to others, or to that membrane of civility that, after all, permits us to call America a community.

In that sense, I think, it is true that we all become more conservative with age. The graduation of perspective. What is good about this graduation is very good: we continue, so to speak, to do our knitting and smile when youth tortures itself over events that —we know, we know—are of no greater historical importance than the flash flood's cosmic importance, down Mississippi way, last spring (however harsh its impact at the time). In that sense, the conservative is viewed as someone who accepts the day's news with a sense of history. My favorite of recent genre was the reporting *Time* magazine did two or three years ago. A journalist was interrogating Frenchmen in portions of France that had been occupied during the war. He asked what was life like under the Nazi occupation. One farmer replied, "Terrible, terrible . . . but nothing like what it was under the Spanish."

The *Spanish*!

He was referring to the Thirty Years' War, three hundred years earlier.

The problem of trying to cope with history with the perspective of maturity is that there is the danger that you will pass over not merely the frivolous things but also the weighty things. I found myself recently, writing a book review for *The New York Times,* asking the question: How many books per year on the subject should I find myself required to read in order to discharge my obligation to those who suffer from the oppressions of the Soviet Union? If you are sixty, and have been alert to the question, you will have read ten?—twenty?—one hundred books describing the tortures of life over there? There is a temptation to think the one hundred and first book, well—redundant. "We know all about that. What more is there to say about it?"

This is the special challenge to the mature. To be able to distinguish between the appropriate smile over the histrionics of those who are merely releasing political energy, and unending indignation over the studied capacity of men and women, young and old, consciously to impose misery on others. A fascinating recent study, the meaning of which is more obvious to older people than younger people, informs us that since the turn of the century, of the 155 million people who have been killed, 120 million have died at the hands not of foreign governments but of their own governments.

These are data that the older generation, reflecting on its experience, is adjured to reflect on. How is it that the state—the protector, in our case, of our Bill of Rights—is so frequently the executioner of its own citizens?

There is no ready answer to the question, none to the problem. But it is safe to say that the older viewer, sifting through his own experience, is better equipped to distinguish between the ephemeral and the scourge; and that a knowledge of the appropriate means to deal with the scourge will, if publicly articulated, commend itself. The Declaration of Independence was a catalytic document in the sense that a letter to the editor is not

I never fully understood a letter I received when I was a relatively young man (thirty-five) and furiously energetic. I turn to it now, twenty-five years later, because it begins to have meaning for me. The circumstances were these.

Whittaker Chambers, then sixty-one and still a central figure in America (it was he who put the finger on Alger Hiss and exposed a scandalous Soviet spy ring which—it was commonly said —launched the whole age of McCarthyism), had become a close personal and professional friend. He told me one day that he wished to travel in the South with his wife, and I made the arrangements for him. But these arrangements expanded. They began with a simple invitation to sojourn at my mother's house in Camden, South Carolina. But before long, the whisper that he was about to be in town evolved into the planning of a major dinner party for his admirers, followed by invitations to visit the gardens in Charleston—the whole shebang. Then suddenly, from Chambers, a telegram: "Cancel all plans to visit South. Regards Whittaker."

I was both dismayed and alarmed—alarmed at the possibility that his delicate health was failing him. I called him, and he said on the phone that he had written to me—I should wait for the letter. It arrived, and began:

"You meant to do something generous and beautiful, and we seemed to dash it back in your face. It was bound to seem that way. Weariness, Bill—you cannot yet know literally what it means. I wish no time would come when you do know, but the balance of experience is against it. One day, long hence, you will know true weariness and will say: 'That was it.' "

The weariness Chambers spoke of was not the kind of thing that brings to mind the immediate need for rectifying sleep, or nutrition, or even companionship. Weariness, for him, was something else: a disposition to do with less and less and abjure that which required physical and social energy. His letter went on, recalling the tribulations of historical and mythical figures; and soon he was explaining, in greater detail, the practical meaning for him of weariness. "One must have got rid of great loads of encumbering nonsense and irrelevance to get there; must have learned to travel quite light—one razor, one change. . . ."

I think now, also, of Bergen Evans, the lexicographer who wrote so authoritatively and entertainingly. Interviewed at age sixty-five (he died at seventy-three), he was asked by a reporter where next he wished to travel. His answer was that he wished to travel nowhere. I have seen, he said, most of what I would wish to see. And I have reached the age when it becomes clear to me what it is that I enjoy doing most.

Mr. Evans concluded his self-examination: he most enjoyed reading, enjoyed reading more than he enjoyed viewing. The imagination, he seemed to be saying, does not dull in later age, but the stimulus to it is more readily self-generated. Bergen Evans could read a book about Venice, and Venice was from that moment on his mind, in his memory. Even the sounds and the smell. He was oh-so-happy with just his books. And then there was Henry David Thoreau, the great ascetic. He said that he tried every day to do with less and less.

Now that is the ambition of the anchorite. For that kind of self-control I have no appetite, nor even a prospective appetite. I respect greatly the contemplative calling. But after all, the monks have to have somebody to pray for, and I am resolutely one of them.

Self-isolation, for me, is not the thing to pursue—not at all. I have long since maintained that television is the greatest boon of

the electronic age for elderly people. It is a source of visual distraction and, with the advent of the videocassette, more than just a
means of random access to the world. You need not even count on
cultivating such an imagination as Bergen Evans's. If you wish to
see Venice, why, you can locate Thomas Mann's *Death in Venice*
and, for all I know, a dozen documentaries on Venice. The point,
however, remains: At a certain age, after a certain amount of
experience, Venice can come to you rather than you to Venice.

My late mother-in-law is much quoted by her surviving friends for
having at one point extemporized it all to a contemporary suffering from, oh, fallen arches. "After the age of fifty," she clacked,
"why, dear, it's all patch-patch-patch." But this essay has nothing
to do with physical health, addressing instead psychological positions that crystallize with age, and one of these is what the editor
of this journal calls "conservative with a small *c* "

You may be old, Father William, and a lot of the abrasions of
youth will pass you by, but some of the wisdom of maturity gives
abiding comfort, even that which is fatalistic. We may not be able
to battle against true weariness, but we can savor some of the true
sweetness of a complaisant farewell to the hectic life. We leave it
to others. Oh, perhaps with a little nostalgia, but without any wish
to relive it. The rocking chair brings different pleasures from the
rocking horse, but they are just what one wants, when weariness
becomes, gradually, welcome.

13

Can We Resurrect the Idea of Sin?
Sinfulness?

APRIL 6, 1986, ISSUE OF *The New York Times Magazine*

A while ago, I advocated licensing drug sales alongside a national educational effort to persuade potential users, on purely utilitarian grounds, that, on the whole, they were better off not amputating mind and body in exchange for quick nervous highs. None of the reactions to my suggestion surprised me, save one, by Dr. Mitchell Rosenthal. He is the head of Phoenix House, and he said that drugs should continue to be illegal, pending the day when they were universally shunned. He explained that the only way to lick marijuana, targeted merely as an example, was to engender "societal disapproval" and bring on "informal social sanctions" of a kind that would make marijuana simply not accepted. His objective is nothing less than to "revive an ethos." Make drug-taking . . . "sinful"? What exactly is that?

The development of an ethos can work, and two examples come to mind. I do not tire of recalling the distinguished and scholarly Bostonian who told me one day at lunch that he would leave the table if he heard uttered any of the casual anti-Semitic remarks he routinely had heard uttered as a boy in the dining room of his equally distinguished father. Americans sixty years old or older have lived through a period during which lackadaisical anti-Semitism all but disappeared. It happened almost as suddenly as the anachronization of the word "Negro." Nobody uses the word Negro anymore, except maybe the United Negro College Fund. Another example of an evolutionized taboo has to do with garbage on coastal waters. It isn't yet universal, but it has graduated, in my lifetime, from a folkway to a *mos*. You can take the most disorderly, self-indulgent twenty-one-year-old sailing; he may smoke pot in his cabin while fornicating, but he will not throw the trash overboard. How come?

Something moral in character seems to have been vitalized, or revitalized. Why, and by what? In the matter of anti-Semitism, one can hardly ask for a more melodramatic propulsive agent of racial tolerance than the Holocaust. With the exception of the Arab and the communist worlds, the impact of anti-Semitism, run rampant under the Nazis, has burrowed itself into the sensibilities of the moral style setters in our culture and, through them, pretty much the population at large, always excepting, well, always excepting the exceptions—redneckery never goes away. In the matter of a respect for conservation, the idea of the vulnerable planet worked its way into the agenda of common concerns. It became, to be sure, one part fad, but also one part dogma. And dogmas, strictly defined, tend to reflect attitudes about sin.

The moral theologians of yesteryear used the term *ut in pluribus* (perceptible by all) to tell us that moral laws, if they hoped to grip the moral imagination, needed to be popularly plausible, and I am here saying that the prospect of racial genocide, as of a ravaged planet, has actually engaged the moral attention even of easily distracted people, forming a habit of mind. And such habits of mind, because they come down to us without mere reference to pain-pleasure criteria, are of a character that qualifies as moral-theological, entitling us to say that we feel it is somehow "sinful" to transgress on what one might call commandments: Thou shalt not discriminate against someone because he is Jewish. Thou shalt not heedlessly exploit nature.

So then, reflection on what it is that "happened" begins, I think, by acknowledging that the *capacity* to recognize particular habits of conduct as sinful continues to reside in us. Perhaps I say this as an act of faith, speaking as a believing Christian. But non-Christians, and even atheists, are, for the most part, prepared to acknowledge that, whatever the epistemology by which they reach moral decisions, most people are potential clients of argumentation that is extra-instrumentally moral. For instance, thoughtful folk will ponder the moral question whether a fetus is a human being, an intellectual acknowledgment of which would obviously overwhelm utilitarian arguments about the sovereignty of maternal inclinations having to do with life or death questions. What causes us to wonder is the desuetude of the word "sin." It is as infrequently heard, outside our churches, as the word "God," and, of course, the terms tend to be associated.

The three generic sanctions that cause societies to cohere are social, legal, and divine. It is hardly difficult to give examples of a deed that offends one of the sanctions but not the other two. One can arrive tieless at a formal party without arousing the police or, one supposes, divine displeasure. One can, illegally, transport bottles of Scotch for sale from Connecticut to New York without affronting one's neighbors or one's God. And one can take in vain the name of the Lord without incurring civil or social disapproval.

On the other hand, the three sanctions often make common cause. Murder, rape, theft are only the most obvious examples. The question before the house, however, has to do with that category of offenses against which social, and even legal, sanctions are deliquescent. In most municipalities one can smoke marijuana with de facto legal impunity; and in most middle- and upper-class ("progressive") households, the weed is smoked with scant social opprobrium. The use of marijuana is not, to my knowledge, specifically proscribed by Judeo-Christianity, but this is so, one supposes, only because no episcopal authority of note has got around to the particularization of the generic law against gluttony: it reasonably follows that to dope the mind is in the same category of excess as to stuff the body, and, therefore, a deadly sin.

But what if religious sanctions against the use of marijuana were to be made explicit? Would we . . . well . . . notice it? When Dr. Rosenthal talks about vitalizing an ethos against the use of marijuana—made explicit by declining to tolerate young junkies coming to your house to smoke there—he does not mean that our ministers, rabbis, and priests, inveighing against drug-taking, would breathe life into a social sanction, much as the sanction against throwing refuse into the water was vivified by the work of Rachel Carson and those others of the natural ministry who made us conscious of the tenderness of the planet. If the pope, speaking ex cathedra, were to declare sinful the use of marijuana, its use by Catholics would diminish. But in general, an effective ethos needs nowadays to be engineered by extratheological asseverations. Whatever became of sin?

The highly touted *Playboy* philosophy is ever so much in point here. Some years ago, the chaplain to Yale University, the Reverend William Sloane Coffin, was asked to comment on the rampantly free sex that characterized the Woodstock generation. Mr. Coffin would rather have bombed the dikes in North Vietnam than answer the question by saying that the Judeo-Christian code specifies monogamy as, well, the "code" by which one measures sexual behavior which is "right," distinguishing it from that which is "wrong."

What Mr. Coffin said was that anything—*anything*—can be overdone. For instance, he explained, drinking a beer won't hurt you, but you have got to guard against becoming an alcoholic. The questioner was supposed to derive from this that a Yale student should not have more than one concubine at a time, because out there in the murky psychological world that is the equivalent of alcoholism of the mind. Take too many lovers or mistresses and you deprive sex of its sublimer meaning, much as if you chug-a-lug a bottle of Mouton-Rothschild 1959 you dilute the pleasure of it. The reverend had, of course, some very good points here—psychological, sociological, and even biological—but they didn't have very much to do with sin.

In his essay on sin in *The Great Ideas, a Syntopicon of Great Books of the Western World,* Mortimer J. Adler gives us this conspectus: "In the pagan and Judeo-Christian conceptions of sin, the fundamental meaning seems to depend upon the relation of man to the gods or to God, whether that itself be considered in terms of law or love. The vicious act may be conceived as one which is contrary to nature or reason. The criminal act may be conceived as a violation of the law of man, injurious to the welfare of the state or to its members. Both may involve the notions of responsibility and fault. Both may involve evil and wrongdoing. But unless the act transgresses the law of God, it is not sinful. The divine law which is transgressed may be the natural law that God instills in human reason, but the act is sinful if the person who commits the act turns away from God to the worship or love of other things."

That is pretty straightforward stuff, and would certainly account for the disappearance of "sin" when the word is used other than as a metaphor. It is, however, worth noting as a sign of latent life in the word that, reaching for final gravity with which to denounce or describe a particular situation, one hears such things as, "John's treatment of Jane was really . . . sinful." We are here suggesting that behavior ultimately offensive is properly described not merely as illegal or antisocial, but, verily, as opposed to the laws of God Himself.

And then, too, the idea of expiation is not entirely foreign to our culture. In formal religious circumstances, Catholics go to confession. There they enumerate their sins, plead contrition, and are given a "penance" and contingent forgiveness. That penance dissipates their sin partially, and in all cases removes from the penitent the mortal burden of a mortal sin that would consign him to eternal damnation. By Catholic arithmetic, there is left owing expiation in another world—the time spent in purgatory—before one is fit to enter into the company of God. Judges in criminal law, under pressure to lighten the prison load and to mete out more imaginative punishments than time in jail, have recently shown signs of inventiveness—a hundred hours of community service, that kind of thing. Perhaps one day not far off a judge will give a young man caught defacing a synagogue, as an alternative to the statutorily permissible one year in jail, an assignment of a half-dozen books of holy Jewish literature to study, from which it would be hoped that the meaning of his desecration would dawn on him. That would be an example of the secular law reaching out to help the divine law.

What has happened to sin is the evanescence of the religious sanction. Irving Kristol has written that the most important *political* development of the nineteenth century was the wholesale loss of religious faith, the implication of which was that man's natural idealism turned to utopianism, which always boils down to ideology. Enter the twentieth century. The loss of religious sanctions imposes on the remaining sanctions a heavier weight than they are designed to handle, and when that happens, and society gets serious about something, it has recourse only to force. Nelson A.

Rockefeller's solution to drugs was to take a drug user, put him in jail, and throw away the keys. The great totalitarian triumvirate—Hitler, Stalin, Mao—took the legal sanction further than Cotton Mather took hellfire; or, put another way, in imposing their sanctions they reified hellfire on earth.

And, elsewhere, Kristol touched a grace note of piquancy wonderfully, awesomely grave in its implications. As far as he could figure out, he said, in the United States a man could have sexual intercourse with an eighteen-year-old girl on a public stage just so long as she was being paid the minimum wage. Social sanctions against disgusting behavior—*disgusting?*—lose vigor if they go uncodified, and even then they lose vigor if the ethos that supports the laws is attenuated. "When one asks how a sense of guilt arises in anyone," Freud said in *Civilization and Its Discontents,* "one is told something one cannot dispute: people feel guilty—pious people call it 'sinful'—when they have done something they know to be 'bad.' But then one sees how little this answer tells one." Legal constraints surrender, up against the force of massive contumacy. As well, at this point, as stopping the spread of pornography in America as during Prohibition one could hope to stop the use of liquor.

Sin sits in the back of the bus. But it is still there, a presence in the conscience, and this is so probably because it was so intended, by the First Mover, that man—*in pluribus*—should harbor the capacity to distinguish between right and wrong, and that he should feel something between an itch and a compulsion to exercise that capacity:

There is a famine in the land, and you harbor a supply of grain. But you harbor, also, a secret: You happen to know that a caravan of supplies is on its way and will arrive within a few days.

Can you charge for your supply of grain a very high price, as if it alone stood between your client and starvation?

Yes, you are at liberty to do it, St. Thomas Aquinas said, but it would be wrong.

Wrong?

Why?

Because it is *wrong,* sinful; *Res ipsa loquitur*! (The matter speaks for itself.) And you shouldn't need Immanuel Kant to explain it to you. I said over the air not too long ago that I believed in metaphysical equality, that otherwise there was *no way* I could be made to believe that Mother Teresa and Sister Boom Boom were equal. I have a letter from someone who says he does not understand, and cannot find in any dictionary, the use of the word "metaphysical" to define in any intelligible way the word "equality." Why, I will write him, it means, here, *equal in the eyes of God,* and that is all the explanation *I* need: equal beyond measurement. I'd find it sinful to reason otherwise, even about Sister Boom Boom.

It isn't only Pope John Paul II who speaks of the necessity of a spiritual revival in order to forward civilized life. Years ago, the late Professor Richard M. Weaver pointed out the obvious, which so often so much needs pointing out: namely, that Marxism and communism are redemptive creeds, while liberalism has no eschatology, no ultimate sense of consummation. Lacking that, it is at a grave disadvantage contending with secular religions which offer absolute achievements to their flock. The rediscovery of sin would cause us to look up and note the infinite horizons that beckon us toward better conduct, better lives, nobler visions.

14

The West Has to Believe in Its Uniqueness

EXCERPTS FROM A SPEECH ACKNOWLEDGING AN AWARD,
NOVEMBER 18, 1986

I guess what I need to say is that however grateful I am for your generosity, I have no illusions of having earned it. I remember as a boy hearing of the young man who applied to the traveling carnival for a job. Asked by the skeptical manager just what he could do, he said that he could dive from a hundred-foot ladder into a barrel of sawdust. The manager was much intrigued by the young supply-side acrobat and ordered the ladder hoisted, from the distant top of which, moments later, the young applicant dove, to the astonishment of wide-eyed attendants, right into the barrel. The excited manager approached him, as the applicant crawled out, dusting himself off, and offered him a hundred dollars a week. But catching the expression of a Yankee bargainer, he quickly raised that to two hundred dollars and, after much sweat, to the unheard-of sum of three hundred dollars. He demanded, finally, an explanation of the acrobat's unverbalized shaking of his head. . . . "Well," the young man finally spoke, "you see, before just now, I never did this thing before, and to tell you the truth, I don't like it."

But I do like it. It just happens—I can only think that grace is responsible for this, while also singling me out as a baby who survived my mother's constitutional Freedom to Choose—that I was born inclined toward the service of my own opinions which, happily, tend to coincide with those of our Founding Fathers and, however inexactly I am guided by them and deficiently disciplined in exercising them, to those of my Maker. I would deserve a medal if I got up one day and spoke out for progressive taxation, or détente, or protectionism, or socialized medicine for louseworts. But then the medal would come from such people as award them for successful screen tests by those who act out of character. . . .

But I have solemn duties to discharge tonight. For all that he has a capacity for sport and games, Dr. Ernest W. Lefever does not fool around, not around the clock. This summer he wrote to me to say that I was to deliver what he carefully called, quote unquote, a "serious address" on the quote unquote "Future of the Atlantic Alliance." I had just about got it figured out how this Alliance was to be held together, including which arms and how many we should ship off to Iran, when last week I received a typewritten copy of the program, which had me down as speaking on, quote unquote, "the Role of Ideas in the Survival of the West."

I hadn't known, until a couple of weeks ago, that we would be honored by the presence of Our Leader. In soliciting his presence, Dr. Lefever reminded me of the durability of the parable that counsels throwing out a very large net and trusting to faith. On the other hand, invitations to others to attend this festive affair were not universally successful, I have reason to know. Last Friday I received a letter from Professor John Kenneth Galbraith. "Dear Bill," it began. "I've now had two invitations and a telegram from James Goldsmith asking me to attend a dinner later this month celebrating your public ethic. The price, $7,500, seems entirely appropriate for so rare a commodity." I am sorry he did not elect to come. It would have made for a fine symbolic rebirth. We conservatives make way for late vocations, as President Reagan's career reminds us.

Any discussion of the role of ideas inevitably brings to mind the paradigm: How ought things to be, if things were as we wished they might be? But of course the concern of the Ethics and Public Policy Center is to explore the bridge between the paradigm and the particular: the criterion and actuality. Although they are separate, the one ought never to shrink from its authority to inform the other, even as the latter should never proceed as though Providence and the morally informed intellect had not posted, however distant and obscure on the horizon, lights to guide our thought and conduct. Woodrow Wilson and John F. Kennedy spoke as if it were our responsibility to send the United States Marines to bring

freedom to the wretched of the Central African Republic. We
know we can't do this and won't therefore do this, but that does
not mean that freedom *ought* not to come to the Central African
Republic. It is immensely heartening to hear from the president,
as we have just done, that we are engaged in attempting to help
freedom fighters, even if we are not ourselves taking an active role
in these struggles, using American manpower.

Yes, such countries as we speak of ought to be free. That is the
distinction we need to bear in mind. That which ought to be, and
that which is, are always different, but the relationship between
the two should be kinetic: we should know that we *ought* to strive,
and what *for*. And although the president tells us that we have
recovered from the period when, as he put it, "too many had lost
all sight of [such an] enduring truth," we need to acknowledge,
fatalistically, that the assault on the very idea of permanent things
is by no means something that happened only yesterday, nor
something done only by infamous names. Historians of relativism
can reflect on the implications of the thought of William of Oc-
cam, or they can look to the true founder of legal realism in the
United States, the venerable Oliver Wendell Holmes. In many of
his opinions, as Walter Berns has reminded us, he reflected his
redundant refusal to find in our Constitution anything that suggested enduring ideals. Indeed his notion of fidelity to the Constitution was to expedite the popular will: "If my fellow citizens want
to go to hell," he said, "I will help them. It's my job." Unsurprising
in a jurist who could elsewhere write that he saw "no reason for
attributing to man a significance different in kind from that which
belongs to a baboon or to a grain of sand."

Many leaders of thought in America are constrained by a dogmatic egalitarianism to accept the notion that the toleration of
pluralism commits us to the proposition that all ideas are equal.
We see this in the philosophical outreach of academic freedom,
which was defined idiomatically, when I was in college, by the use
of the metaphor that all ideas should start out even in the race:
that—by derivation—the teacher of integrity must not reveal any
preference for the Bill of Rights over, say, the Communist Mani-
festo, let alone permit himself the asseveration that the one document is an approach toward the just society, while the other is a
howl in the opposite direction. Our devotion to pluralism is nowa-

days translated by the professionally tolerant into the notion that in exercising his right to attend a black mass, a citizen can consecrate a profanation. That in exercising the freedom to do so, the right of the mother to kill an unborn child becomes the full-grown partner of the right of the human being to be protected from the oppressor, whether the act of aggression takes place in a concentration camp or in a clinic.

The difficulty is magnified by organizational impulses to humility in international assemblies, the United Nations acting as the principal distillery of civil egalitarianism. There the representative of the Soviet Union is deferred to as often as the representative of the United States, even when the subject under discussion is human rights. One reason for our philosophical abjectness is that the retreat from colonialism left us with the compulsion to believe that such a retreat enjoined upon us a retreat from the postulated superiority of one idea over against an antithetical idea. If infanticide, or euthanasia, or torture, is condoned by a society, as indeed each is here and there practiced, if not officially condoned, then our democratists, expansively adhering to their commitment to pluralism at home, tacitly acknowledge that that is how it is: Cultural variations, in this view, reflect not differences in the refinement of civil sensibility. They reflect, rather, what we should happily confirm, that after all, no enduring truths are finally knowable. Under the banner of pluralism, all we can with philosophical confidence say is that Khomeini's Islamic fundamentalism is simply their version of our Judeo-Christian faith. We are familiar with the vernacular turns such self-mutilating modesty takes. My favorite was the ecumenical conference in Tokyo twenty-five years ago at which, during dinner, one Oriental gentleman turned to his Western counterpart and broke the ice by saying, "My miserable superstition is Buddhism. What is your religion?"

We live in an age most awfully precarious, threatening as it does the survival of the West, and Dr. Lefever, our host, correctly intuits that only ideas will bring us through—ideas backed up, as needed, by a nuclear arsenal, pending its replacement by a space shield. I like to think that I share the ultimate confidence of Joe Louis in the divine order, as described by the president. But I am sometimes reminded of the little boy with precocious horticultural skills who tended a tiny twenty-foot-square garden in a corner of the slum where he lived. He was visited one day by a priest who exclaimed over the little floral enclave. "That is a beautiful garden you and God built," he commented. "Yeah," said the boy, "but you should have seen it when only God was taking care of it." We need the Bible, and we need our Minutemen. And—the point I want to stress—we need to refine the appropriate protocols. Medical doctors manage, when for whatever reason consorting with witch doctors, at once not to give offense while at the same time declining tacitly to agree that bat-turd is a satisfactory substitute for penicillin. Beware the tug of relativism. Jeffrey Hart commented recently on the aggregate achievements of Professor Mel Bradford. Hart began by recalling that, as he put it, "A most decent and friendly Dartmouth professor of religion was quoted the other day to the effect that 'many of us'—he meant college professors—develop a long-range historical perspective. We know that America's existence is brief in a long-range historical perspective."

Mel Bradford, Jeff Hart reminds us, knows that this opinion is false. "The settlers who arrived in Massachusetts and Virginia and elsewhere did not travel culturally naked or devoid of memory," Hart wrote, "nor did America begin in 1787 or even in 1776. The Founding documents grow out of the lived experience of the colonists not least in the colonial legislatures. They go back to the Old Whigs of 1688 and much further back still: to Coke and Brackton and the growth of the common law, to the long development of the traditions of English and Scottish legal practice; the medieval patrimony of Christiandom and *romanitas.* The Mayflower Compact of 1620 was not, to quote Bradford, a 'bright thought.' America is not the short light of a November day. Its fathers are Aeneas and Moses, its predecessors Rome and Jerusalem."

Yes, Rome, for Bradford, not Athens . . .

"Roman history," Bradford wrote, "taught that all of this was natural; a commonwealth 'grown' not 'made'; a definition by history, not by doctrine or lofty intent; and a general recognition, negotiated in the dialect of experience, that all Americans had together a corporate destiny and would henceforth depend upon each other for their individual liberties; . . . [dignity], under a piously regarded common law, is a check upon ideology, not a source."

There is much room left over for argument, even as there is

room left over, under this roof, for divisions about the imperma-
nent things. But I tender you, Dr. Lefever, and your distinguished
board of directors and associates, this challenge: Deliberate the
means of saying it in our public philosophy, saying that however
much respect we owe to those who hold other ideas than those
that are central to Judeo-Christian postulates, we mustn't confuse
any respect for the preternatural dignity of other human beings,
other minds, with a respect for the fruit of their reason. How at
once to do both these things—to respect a difference of opinion
without undertaking a respect for different opinions? It is a searing challenge, in a world sensitive to cultural condescension, a
world inflamed by the notion that one-man one-vote presupposes
one-culture any-culture, one-philosophy any-philosophy, one-God
any-God. The survival of the West depends entirely on the ascendancy of Western ideas, the vessel of true civil progress. The West
is witness to the irreversible proposition that to be free is forever
and eternally different from being unfree, and therefore that
much preferred to being unfree. So that to fashion our conduct,
and always our thought, with reference to the imperatives of the
decalogue becomes an expression not of cultural jingoism, but a
humble acknowledgment of the debt we owe to Providence.

It isn't inappropriate, Ernie, to take satisfaction from the
progress made in this direction by our initial speaker. Oh yes, he
needs to rein himself in when the protocols stand up as dragons'
teeth blocking the passage of a liberating candor. But such truths
as we ought to cherish come repeatedly from Mr. Reagan, came
from him tonight in profusion; come from him in greater density
than, at any time in my lifetime, from the lips of any other leader
of the West. It is implicit in what he says that America is by no
means prepared to think of its founding ideas as ephemeral. You
do not proudly defend ephemeral ideas with a nuclear arsenal,
which we pray will always be sedentary. But the mobility of those
weapons is the ultimate witness to the conclusiveness of our faith
in the ideas we gather tonight to honor, taking satisfaction from
each other's company, and from the high fraternal voltage generated by our belief in God and man, bringing to us that distinctive
serenity that makes us simultaneously servants of God and masters of ourselves. I am proud to be in your company, and I thank
you for giving thought to my work.

15

Redefining "Smart"

JANUARY 1985 ISSUE OF *Playboy*

This year, we subscribed to cable television, mostly because when cable television comes around, subscribe to it is one of the things with-it households do, even as, fifty years ago, they would have subscribed eventually to larger encyclopedias, larger dictionaries; bought more magazines.

But suddenly I realized the subscribing—to encyclopedias, dictionaries, magazines, newspapers, newsletters, book clubs, catalogues, still other cable networks, etc.—had to stop. Go to a large newsstand. Do you know there are more than 400 magazines devoted to computing alone? More than 40,000 books published per year? More television played commercially in one year than movies produced since the industry began? And, through all this flood of information, occasionally you will want to take time to remind yourself that the sky is blue, the grass green, the waters pure.

Which brings us to the question at hand: How is it possible to keep up in today's world?

The answer is that it *isn't* possible to "keep up," not even at a rudimentary level. To which dismaying observation one reasonably asks, "What do you mean by a rudimentary level?" To which I answer—why not?—*People* magazine. It is rudimentary, isn't it, to have a working knowledge of the stars and the starlets of the society we live in?

Well, hear this. Last Christmas, my wife and I sailed in the Caribbean with a couple with whom we have for many years shared the season. Richard Clurman is my best-informed friend in the entire world. When serving as chief of correspondents for *Time* and *Life,* he cultivated and developed those habits that required that he know everything about everything going on. So he arrived, as usual, with his heavy rucksack of books and magazines. Among the latter, I remember offhand *Scientific American, The Economist, The Atlantic, Harper's, The New Republic, The Nation, National Review, Esquire, Time, Newsweek, Playboy, Business Week, Foreign Affairs,* and I am certain to have forgotten a supplementary dozen. He reads at a rate that would leave the ordinary computer puffing to keep up. After a day or two, he had gone through the magazines and started in on the books.

One week later, in the Virgin Islands, I sauntered about an old colonial town in search of periodical matter, finding, at the drugstore, only *People,* for a copy of which I exchanged a dollar and a quarter.

It was the year-end issue, and thumbing through it in the cockpit that night, sipping a planter's punch, I came upon what is evidently a yearly feature, enumerating sixteen persons who had committed renowned gaffes of one type or other, twenty-five persons who had committed extraordinary feats of one kind or other. My eyes traveled down the list with progressive dismay in search of a name I recognized. I did discover one, finally, in each category, and paused for a moment, taking a deep draft of rum to console myself over my confirmed deracination from my own culture.

It struck me to recite the names I had just read to Richard Clurman. So I gave them out, one after another. He scored better than I did, recognizing three out of forty-one. (Neither one of us —this was December 1983—had ever heard the name Michael Jackson.) I am fifty-nine, Clurman a year older. Was this merely a generational gap? Is it that each of us develops habits of mind, perhaps needing to do so for self-protection, winnowing the flood of information that comes at us so that certain phenomena become, for all that they are ubiquitous, for all intents and purposes imperceptible?

Or was it sheer chance? Individual lacunae? But I told the story of going over the names of the featured galaxy of *People* to Henry Grunwald at a party a few months later, and he shrugged his shoulders. He is, after all, among other things the editor in chief of *People,* even as he is editor in chief of all the publications put out by Time, Inc. "I know what you mean," Grunwald said.

"When they tell me who they have scheduled for the cover of the next issue of *People,* half the time I never heard of him or her."

Someone once said that Erasmus (1466–1536) was the last man on earth about whom it could more or less safely be said that he knew everything there was to know. But even in the sixteenth century, "everything" was defined as everything common to Western culture. Erasmus could hardly have known very much about cultures whose existence neither he nor anyone else in the Western world had written about. What they meant to say was that Erasmus had probably read every book then existing in those Western languages in which books were then written. The library at the University of Salamanca, founded in the thirteenth century, still has, framed and hanging over the little arched doorway that leads into the room in which all of the books of one of the oldest universities in Europe were once housed, a papal bull of excommunication directed automatically at any scholar who left the room with one of those scarce, sacred volumes hidden in his vestments. Books copied out by hand can be very valuable. The tradition is not dead, thanks to the Russian *samizdat,* by which Soviet dissenters communicate with one another, even as early Christians communicated by passing about tablets in the catacombs. Knowledge in those days, in the early years of movable type, was difficult to come by. But then there was not so much of it as to overwhelm. In that relatively small room in Salamanca were housed all the books an Erasmus might be expected to read—granted that his mind was singular and his memory copious. So had been Thomas Aquinas's, a man modest except when laying down certitudes, who admitted, sheepishly one must suppose, that he had never come across a single page he had not completely and instantly understood. If, *per impossibile,* Thomas was required to linger a few days in purgatory for committing the sin of pride, I am certain that the torturers stood over him demanding that he render the meaning of the typical "documentation" (that is what they call instructions) of a modern computer.

Never mind the exceptional intelligence. It is sufficient to meditate that in the sixteenth century it was acknowledged as humanly possible to be familiar with *all* the facts and theories then discovered or developed, to read all the literature and poetry then set down, to know the library of Western thought.

Move forward now 250 years and ask whether or not Benjamin Franklin could have been surprised by an eldritch scientific datum, an arcane mythological allusion, a recondite historical anecdote, an idiosyncratic philosophical proposition. Of course he could have been, even bearing in mind that Benjamin Franklin was a singular intelligence, eclectically educated, and that he was surrounded, at the convention in Philadelphia, by men most of whom moved sure-footedly in the disciplines then thought appropriate to the background of statesmen. The standards at Philadelphia were high; indeed, it has been opined that at no other deliberative assembly in history was there such a concentration of learning and talent.

But these are anomalies. We ask, and continue to do so, How much was there lying about to be learned? Two hundred and fifty years having passed since the last man died who "knew" everything, then by definition it follows that there were "things" Ben Franklin didn't know. Perhaps we are circling the target. "Things." What things?

It is said that twice as much "knowledge" was charted in 1980 as in 1970. How can one make an assertion of that kind? At a purely technical level, it isn't all that hard to conceive. Suppose, as an example, that every decade the penetrating reach of a telescope doubles. In that case, you begin the decade knowing X about astronomic phenomena. At the end of the first decade, you know 2X; at the end of the second decade, 4X; and so on.

It is so (the epistemologists tell us) primarily because computer science advances us (we fall back on ancient metaphors) at an astronomic rate. It was somewhere reported that when George Bernard Shaw was advised that the speed of light was equal to 186,000 miles per second, he greeted that finding as a madcap effrontery—either that or a plain, bald lie.

Such sullen resistance to the advancement of physical knowledge is behind us; indeed, it has left us blasé rather than awed. When we pick up the telephone and lackadaisically dial Hong Kong, we simply submit—to a kind of magic we never presume to understand. The inquisitive minority among those who use such instruments for such purposes is mindful that something quite extraordinary is going on, triggered by rudimentary digital exertions by one finger of one hand, the result of which is to rouse a friend (he had better be a friend, considering that it's midnight in Hong Kong) by ringing his telephone eight thousand miles away: a process that combines a knowledge of "things"—things such as transistors, transmitters, radio beams, oscilloscopes, etc., etc., etc.— they will simply never understand and are unlikely to burden themselves with the challenge of attempting to understand.

So it is that the knowledge explosion, as we have come to refer to it, is acquiescently and routinely accepted by both the thoughtful and the thoughtless, the grateful and the insouciant. Every now and then one identifies a little cry of frustrated resentment. Ten years ago, I took to Bermuda a self-effacing boatwright in his mid-sixties to give expert testimony in a lawsuit. He was asked by the defendant's lawyer how he could presume to qualify as an expert in all that had to do with the construction of a seagoing boat— woodwork, electricity, engine, rigging, plumbing, sail, William Muzzio answered diffidently that, in fact, he knew as much as any of the specialists who worked for him who had mastered only the expertise in their separate fields.

He then paused for a brief moment in the little, attentive courtroom. . . .

He did not, he corrected himself, know—himself—how to fabricate transistors for ships' radio gear. Thus the sometime complete boatwright formally acknowledged the progressive relative finiteness even of his own very wide expert knowledge of all that used to be required to launch a seagoing yacht. Others acknowledge their progressive relative ignorance by the simpler expedient of paying no attention to it whatever.

Consider, in the light of our general concern about our increasing ignorance, the obsessive interest in the working habits of the President of the United States. It is widely acknowledged that Ronald Reagan devotes fewer hours to studying the data that flow into the executive cockpit than his predecessor did. But two questions are begged by those who stress invidiously the comparison. The first is: Is this difference reflected in the quality of Reagan's performance as Chief Executive? And the second, How could his predecessor, Jimmy Carter, reasonably assume that he had mastered all the data conceivably relevant to the formulation of the most enlightened decision? How do we correlate—or do we?—knowledge and performance in nonscientific situations? Unflattering things have been said about Carter's handling of the presidency, but nobody ever accused him of dereliction at the homework level. And then again, five presidents back, John F. Kennedy was once overheard to say that the presidential work load was entirely tolerable. Notwithstanding this nonchalant evaluation of arguably the most taxing job in the world, Kennedy, as Chief Executive, had probably more full-time bards working to apotheosize him than any president since, oh, Abraham Lincoln after he was shot.

What are we to make of all this confusion on the matter of time devoted to the acquisition of knowledge?

So we move in on an intimation of the painless acclimation of our culture to an unspoken proposition: that every day, in every way, man knows more and more, while every day, in every way, individual men know less and less. The question arises whether we give in, by our behavior, to complacency, or acknowledge philosophically, even stoically, *force majeure,* much as we acknowledge biological aging and, eventually, death. There is, after all, nothing an epistemological reactionary can do to erase human knowledge. Buckminster Fuller remarked that it is impossible to learn less. Valiant efforts at Luddite nescience have been made, most notably by Pol Pot, who recently set out to kill everyone in Cambodia who was literate—save, presumably, those in his circle who needed to read his instructions to kill everyone else who could read his instructions. He was stopped, finally, after he had killed somewhere between one quarter and one third (the estimates vary) of all Cambodians. But poor Pol Pot, all he ultimately accomplished was the premature death of millions of people and a testimonial dinner in his honor by Communist China.

Given, then, that we cannot hope to read, however much time we give over to the effort, one one-hundredth of the books published in America alone every year, nor read one periodical out of every hundred published, and all of this to say nothing of catching up with those masterpieces written yesterday that silt up into public recognition, some of them ten, twenty, even fifty years after first published, how can we hope to get about with any sense of—self-satisfaction isn't quite the right word, because self-satisfaction is not something we ought ever to strive after—rather, well: *composure* is probably as good a word for it as comes readily to mind?

Nothing I have ventured until now is, I think, controversial. Is it controversial to bridge over to the final point: namely, that inhabitants of a common culture need to have a common vocabulary, the word vocabulary here used in the most formal sense as the instrument of intercommunication?

It is probably not a culturally disqualifying civic delinquency, or even civic abnegation, to come late, say six months or even a year late, to the recognition of Who is Michael Jackson? and What exactly is it that makes him, after two hours at a studio, create something the price of which Picasso would not have dared to ask after twenty hours' work at his easel? But I do think it hovers on civic disqualification not to know what is meant, even if the formulation is unfamiliar, when someone says, "Even Homer nodded."

Now, any time anybody comes up with something everybody ought to know on the refined side of, say, *The world is round, not flat,* or, *A day comprises twenty-four hours,* you will encounter an argument over whether knowledge of that particular datum is really necessary to integration as a member of a culture. So that what I just said about Homer's nodding will be objected to by some as not intrinsic to a "common vocabulary" in the same way that, let us say, it is intrinsic to know the answer to the question: What was Hitler's Holocaust? Subgroups within a culture will always feel that a knowledge of certain "things"—even of certain forms, certain recitations—is indispensable to a common knowledge and that without them, intercourse (social intercourse, I suppose I should specify, writing for *Playboy*) is not possible. These "things" go by various names and are of varying degrees of contemporary interest. For instance, there is "consciousness enhancement" as regards, oh, black studies, or malnutrition, or Reagan's favoritism toward the rich. But these are, I think, faddist in any large historical perspective. Not so much more remote "things," such as Homer's nodding.

With the rise of democracy and the ascendancy of myth-breaking science, the need arose to acknowledge man's fallibility, preferably in a way that also acknowledged man's vanity. This was the period during which a belief in the divine right of kings began to wither on the overburdened wings of certitude. So that it became common in the seventeenth century, the lexicographers tell us, to reflect that if it—i.e., human fallibility—could strike out at Homer, the more so could it overtake us. Homer was the symbol for the poet universally regarded as unerring (the divine Homer); yet objectivity raises its obdurate voice to point to errors (mostly factual inconsistencies) committed by the presumptively unerring. Only just before the beginning of the Christian era, Horace had written that "even Homer sometimes nods." And as recently as 1900, Samuel Butler spotted a picture of a ship in the *Odyssey* with the rudder at the front.

And so an entire complexion of social understanding unfolds before us: so that by recalling that even Homer nodded, we are reminded of the vulnerable performance of lesser human beings— indeed, of *all* human beings. And if we acknowledge our weaknesses, then we inherit insight into such terms as "government by laws, not by men"; of such propositions as that "nobody is above the law"; and of such derivative things as checks and balances; insights, even, into the dark side, and black potential, of human nature.

In the age of the knowledge explosion, the struggle, by this reckoning, should be not so much to increase our knowledge (though that is commendable even if we recognize, fatalistically, that we fall further behind every day) as to isolate those things that no data that have been discovered have ever persuasively challenged and—here we approach an act of faith—no data will ever plausibly challenge. These are known, sometimes, as the "eternal verities." A secular version of one of these verities is that no one has the right to deprive another man of his rights. Let the discussion proceed over exactly what that man's rights are but not over the question of whether or not he has rights. But in order to carry on that discussion intelligibly, we need to share that common vocabulary that reaches out and folds protectively into a common social bosom those common verities. If, next Monday, all Americans were to suffer an amnestic stroke, forgetting everything we had ever known, what is it that would be required before we reassembled—if ever—around such propositions as are asseverated in the Declaration of Independence and in Lincoln's Gettysburg Address?

Western culture is merely a beachhead in space, Whittaker Chambers reminds us. That insight is what distinguishes today the Renaissance man. He is not the man who, with aplomb, can fault the Béarnaise sauce at Maxim's before attending a concert at which he detects a musical solecism, returning to write an imperishable sonnet before preparing a lecture on civics that the next day will enthrall an auditorium. No: The Renaissance man is, I think, someone who bows his head before the great unthreatened truths and, while admitting and even encouraging all advances in science, nevertheless knows enough to know that the computer does not now exist, nor ever shall, that has the power to repeal the basic formulas of civilization. "We know," Edmund Burke wrote, "that we have made no discoveries; and we think that no discoveries are to be made, in morality—nor many in the great principles of government, nor in the ideas of liberty, which were understood long before we were born, altogether as well as they will be after the grave has heaped its mold upon our presumption, and the silent tomb shall have imposed its law on our pert loquacity."

16

Reflections on the Perils of the Holiday Season

JANUARY 1993 ISSUE OF *Playboy*

The party season! Rapturously welcomed by some; by others greeted with fear and loathing. But everyone understands that in some social situations there are shoals, and these have to be navigated with care. Some demand of you a facility for small talk, which some of us simply don't have, requiring us to make do with what we have, or to veer sharply to one side or another of the reef. Then there are those special perils, the awful bores. These are all the more difficult to circumvent because—unlike the shoals that lurk hidden by at least a few inches of water—the bores are more like stalagmites, rising directly between you and your objective: the bar, the beautiful widow, your best friend.

The questions arise: How to maneuver? What to do? What to stress?

I had a professor who took to writing me four or five times a week for several years, many of his letters seven or eight pages long and almost all of them describing his then current plight. One of his plights lasted about nine months and had to do with his failure to pay enough money to the IRS a year or two earlier. I don't think Dante devoted more pages to *The Inferno* than my professor did to whether, how, at whose expense, and with what recrimination he should come up with the $1,300, plus interest and maybe a penalty, to pay Internal Revenue.

His obsessive quandary became amusing enough, after six or seven months, to cause me to make mention of it at lunch to a friend in common. My tax-torn professor knew the great French political philosopher Bertrand de Jouvenel intimately, I only in my capacity as a protégé of the professor. I recounted at lunch the agonies with which my friend belabored in his letters the question of his taxes. And M. Jouvenel smiled and said yes, he knew the professor was that way about all matters, had always been that way. "And it astonishes me, for so intelligent a man. Because every subject in the whole world is more interesting than oneself," said M. Jouvenel, some years before writing his autobiography.

In fact, I think him quite wrong. I don't pretend that my friend mightn't have seized on a more interesting subject than his tax delinquency, but I remember reading all those letters with fascination because they composed, really, a portrait of his mind, which—it happened, happily—was among the most interesting I have ever encountered. It was all there: extraordinary analytical skills, extraordinary capacity for self-justification; paranoia, an innocent perplexity, dependence, a capacity to exfoliate from a routine problem a comprehensive *Weltschmerz* about our life and times.

But for some reason, the general social rule—don't talk about your personal concerns continues to govern, especially at large parties where social contacts are fleeting and especially at large parties of the kind that generally abound at holiday time. These parties are an institutional imperative, so that just as the blossoms come out in May, so do the large parties constellate about the holiday season. It is then that it is likelier that the ratio between the people you know and the people who are simply there becomes smaller and smaller. It is then that, entering the auditorium, you scan the horizon anxiously in search of a familiar face. And having found one, what do you talk about?

Here is my point! Talk about *his* affairs. M. Jouvenel is wrong in this matter, and I will give you a hypothetical example. The man you recognize is a banker. Yesterday the Labor Party beat the Likud Party in a general election in Israel. The day before that, Gerald Ranck played thirty-one Scarlatti sonatas at the New York Society for Ethical Culture auditorium, the same day that John McEnroe defeated Ivan Lendl at the French Open in Paris. Hypothetical question: Unless you know your mark extremely well, what reason do you have to suppose that he will discourse on any of these events authoritatively, originally, or amusingly?

The answer is, you have no grounds for faith in the matter. You do know that the man you have just approached is interested in banking. If it happens that he is a banker only because his father made him vice president at the age of twenty-two and he has secretly hated banking ever since, my rule still applies: You are in rare luck, because he can confide to you how much he hates his profession, how filthy, rotten, boring, and exploitative it is, and that makes for interesting banter. More likely he is a banker because banking is his thing, so that you can come up with something that encourages him to expatiate there and then on a subject he knows a great deal about, and your question will inflame his didactic spirit.

"Say, Elmore, about the discount rate—is it possible in the futures market to gamble on the discount rate down the line, say, six months or maybe a year?"

I don't happen to know the answer to that question, but I can promise you, sight unseen, that a banker—or, for that matter, a broker, or an economist, or an informed businessman—will gambol off that question for just about as long as you want him to. By this I mean that if he tries to give you an objurgatory reply ("Course not!"), you are still left free to draw him out ("But explain to me exactly why not. It seems to me that . . .").

As he winds into the subject, you can keep him wound up. The subject at hand will inevitably abut on another question and you skate right along with him. One thing you absolutely know is that he will be saying more interesting things to you than in answer to the question "How do you account for Ross Perot's appeal?" The reason for this is that you have, in the past eight months, read more about Perot than about AIDS, the rich, and the homeless. So the chances are infinitesimal that you will hear anything new or engaging on the subject. But you are talking to a banker and he *does* know about the vagaries of the discount rate. Moreover, he can illustrate his points by recounting personal experiences. And the most interesting experiences are, really, personal. Would you rather read an account of the Battle of Austerlitz or an account of what Napoleon was thinking during that battle?

However, some people are manifestly incapable of saying anything interesting, even about themselves. On the other hand, some people famously dull by reputation can surprise you. It may happen that the dullard you are talking to will decide that this is the moment to confide that during his youth he was a serial murderer.

It is unlikely that in recounting whom he murdered, how and why, he can bore you.

But it is true, as I said, that some people can be boring when talking about any subject. I know someone who would cause my mind to wander between the moment he told me he spotted those funny fighter planes coming in over the hills in Honolulu and the moment, only two minutes later, that they were dropping their bombs on Pearl Harbor. With people such as these, either you are or are not qualified to defend yourself.

The British historian and diplomat Harold Nicolson was famous for, among other things, observing in his diaries that ninety-nine people out of one hundred are interesting, and the hundredth is interesting because he is the exception. Well, if you have the lepidopterist's interest in the rare butterfly, you can manage—by saying to yourself: I will interest myself in this encounter by analyzing and committing to memory the reasons why he or she is such an infernal bore. You begin, in your mind, to frame the list of his vacuities: He is inarticulate. He is repetitious. He laughs incessantly. He tells you in such excruciating detail how many ducks went by before he shot for the first time, that you find yourself toying with stupid tangents. (Is duck overpopulation something of an ecological problem?)

But most of us aren't well developed as bore taxonomists. It is therefore a good idea to develop means of self-defense when, at a party, you find yourself locked in with the great bore. The first line of defense is, of course, to train your face to register appropriate responses: the half-smile, following on his little wink; the eyebrows raised in suspense, as his voice indicates that what he is about to say is a revelation; and the barely enunciated "I'll be damned!" when it is clear that he is saying something he accounts unusual. The French have the all-purpose word, *tiens,* that is appropriate in absolutely every situation. Depending on the lilt you give it, you can use it to respond to news that your interlocutor's wife has just died of cancer *("Tieeeeeens"),* or that he just married Miss America *("Tiens!").* The closest equivalent in English is "I'll be damned." ("I'll be daaaaaamned." "I'llbedamned!")

These are the rudimentary skills to develop—some kind of facial and spoken reaction to what has been said—and if you have had a lot of practice, which, given the unfortunate incidence of bores, almost everybody has had, you can become very good at it. But there has to be a second line of defense.

You catch the word Mabel, and you jump in. Now, you have to be dogged about this. "Mabel?" you interrupt. "Is she related to Susan Mercer?" He looks at you, surprised—he's never even heard of Susan Mercer (nor have you). He is maybe just slightly annoyed, because his narrative was interrupted. You need to dig in.

"Who is Susan Mercer? She was Mabel's half sister, wasn't she? You remember, of course, the famous lawsuit? God, what a case! One of my best friends was working at the law firm that took Susan's case. He spent over a year on it, he said, tracking down all the evidence, what with the disappearance of the will and the stepmother's refusal to confirm that Susan had been legally adopted. I remember the lawyer saying that it—the case, *Mercer v. Mabel What's-her-name*—introduced the legal concept of 'pleading in the alternative.' You know: Lawyer stands up, addresses the court and says 1) Mabel didn't have the money, 2) Mabel had the money and it was her right to have it, or 3) Mabel had the money but gave it back to Susan." You look up in turn for a reaction. Ah, but your friend has dematerialized.

But that course of action, needless to say, requires a certain histrionic resolve, and most of us don't have it and need then to go to another line of defense. There are several of these, but the easiest to get away with is to gulp down your drink and then confess you must go to the bar and fetch another, but you'll be right back, har-har.

There is the special problem raised by the party at which you have a social objective. There are difficulties here because it may be necessary, having spotted your mark, for you to move over to him or her, passing by eleven people with whom, in the normal course, you would feel obliged to dally, even if only for a moment. And then in the pursuit of your quarry you may find yourself guilty of behavior if not exactly boring, certainly boorish.

I have a memory of this. Along with my wife, I arrived at a boat party with Mrs. Dolly Schiff, whom I liked, who was among my employers (she published my syndicated column in the *New York Post,* the newspaper she owned) and who was an important political presence in New York at a time when my brother James was its junior senator, preparing to run for reelection. Boarding the boat, Mrs. Schiff said to me: "Do you know, I have never even met your brother?" Well, said I, I shall certainly cure that tonight —I knew that my brother was among the invited guests.

A half hour later, chatting with my brother on the crowded deck, I spotted at the extreme other end the imperious forehead of Dolly Schiff. I grabbed my brother and told him we must forthwith go to the other end of the deck, past the eighty-odd people sipping champagne, so that he could be introduced to Mrs. Schiff. Ignoring a dozen old friends, we reached her—at a moment when her head was slightly bent down, exchanging conversation with a petite woman whose back was to us. I charged in, "Dolly, this is my brother Jim, whom you wanted to meet. Jim, Dolly Schiff." The little woman we had interrupted turned around slowly to us and smiled.

She was our hostess, the Queen of England, but it was too late to undo the damage, so I proceeded with the introduction to Mrs. Schiff (Jim had sat next to the queen at dinner and needed no introduction to her; the rest of us had been through the receiving line). Jim said he was sorry to interrupt Mrs. Schiff, who smiled down at Her Majesty. I thought I'd break the ice by suggesting that the entire company join me in pleading with Mrs. Schiff to give me a raise. The queen reacted with a half smile and excused herself to greet another of her guests. There can be casualties of a determined mission at a party.

It is, of course, the objective of some guests to mingle with absolutely everybody at the party. I remember at the casual cocktail hour in California talking quietly at the edge of a social congregation with the president-elect of Yale University. I told him that a year earlier the outgoing president, Kingman Brewster, had been at this same affair. "The difference between King and me," Bart Giamatti said, "is that when he walks into a social gathering, his eyes fix instinctively on the center of the densest social activity and he homes right in on it, the true social animal. My own instinct is to look to the farthermost edges of the gathering and head softly in that direction. Where I am standing right now," he said, smiling.

Yes, and that raises the question of one's *querencia,* a favorite word of mine, one that I learned many years ago from Barnaby Conrad and have tirelessly used. The word describes a tiny area in the bullring, maybe fifty square feet, within which the fighting bull fancies himself entirely safe. The difficulty lies in that each bull has his own idea exactly where his *querencia* is, and it is up to the matador to divine, from a ferociously concentrated study of the bull's movements as he charges into the ring, its location; because the matador must, at peril to life and limb, stay well clear of it when executing his critical passes. The bull who finds himself close to his *querencia* and is pained or perplexed will suddenly head for it, and in doing so jerk his horns in an unpredictable direction, the same direction the matador's groin or abdomen might find itself.

We all have, in any social situation, an undefined *querencia,* and we instinctively seek it out immediately upon entering the crowded room. Most usually, it is where one's spouse is—but that is a difficult sanctuary to avail yourself of because it is deemed socially backward at a party to glue yourself to your spouse. So you look elsewhere for your *querencia.* Generally, it is one human being, someone with whom you feel entirely comfortable, whom you can trust to greet you as if your company were the highlight of his day. You have tons to tell him, and he has tons to tell you, all of it of common interest. Is he . . . she . . . there? You look around.

No.

Is there an alternative *querencia* anywhere about?

Well, yes. Somebody told you that Algernon MacNair was going to be there. Not quite the company you most looked forward to attaching yourself to, but quite good enough to avoid the high stilt of tonight's social affair, and there is a specific point of interest. Maybe his Op-Ed piece this morning, in which he took those peculiar positions about taxation. But no. He is not there, nor is anyone else who will fill the bill in the same way.

Ah, but then the *querencia* can be greatly elastic. You can develop a consuming interest in the appointments of the sumptuous apartment. Every picture deserves close attention, worth at least three minutes of your time, as you look first this way at it, then that way, then examine the artist's signature. And the books! You pick up one from the fourth shelf and open it with delight transfiguring your face. How is it that this neglected volume found its place into this library? How discriminating the taste of our hostess! By the time you have examined that book, perhaps two or three others and a dozen pictures and a score of family photographs—it is time for dinner!

With some apprehension you look down at your card and wonder who will be seated on your right, who on your left; and it is at such moments, as when in a foxhole, or on a sinking boat, that you rediscover God and the need to utter a silent prayer.

FIVE

SNAPSHOTS

—GOP Convention Notes, 1992

September 14, 1992, issue of *National Review*

T he general assumption was that the issue of "character," for a while defined as how many extramarital liaisons Bill Clinton had had, was out of the way, settled; *res judicata.* It was very evident on Monday that this isn't the case, not at all. And it is also plain that the ticket-leaders, Bush–Quayle, are not depending on lesser lights to stress the point. They are thoroughly engaged themselves in the practice of saying to the American voter: "Forget everything else, if you like. Forget the Democrats' predilection for the lousewort over the American worker. Forget their sullen dislike for a strong American military. But do not forget this, that we are fit to lead, they are not."

Mr. Quayle began it quite early when he said, "Did you notice how much time Bill Clinton spent on the subject of American values? The first fifteen minutes of his hour-long speech was on the subject. Well, it's a great thing for America when Bill Clinton comes out for family values." That statement has only a single meaning. It places, in the center of the political ring, Clinton's spotted personal record.

George Bush came on. He attempted to provide his own cover in respect of his renowned weakness as an orator. "I am no wordsmith," he said, slightly mispronouncing the word. "For me, eloquence is action." (Rambo becomes more eloquent than Socrates.) But the president was en route to what appears to be gestating as the planted axiom of the Republican Convention: the proposition that Republican leaders are better people. Mr. Bush did not go as far as GOP chief Rich Bond, who attempted an extraordinary disjunction—"We are America, they are not America"—but he said it: "Who do you trust to do what is right for the U.S.A.?"

Speaker after speaker chimed in. Alan Simpson repeated five words Clinton had used to open his letter to his mentor at age twenty-three: "To maintain my political viability"—the letter in which he proposed to join the Reserves as a means of avoiding the draft. Pat Buchanan said it directly: George Bush volunteered and "at seventeen was the youngest fighter pilot in the war. When Bill Clinton's time came, he sat up in a dormitory room in Oxford and figured out how to dodge the draft. Which of these two men has won the moral authority to send American young men to battle?"

The point here is not idle. William Bennett, tackled on the subject on *Crossfire,* reminded the interlocutor that character was the only qualification enumerated by the Founding Fathers for serving in public office. But along the way at Houston one got the idea that character was surfacing in part because other matters were not. The only public issue that got genuine ventilation was free trade, ably handled by Carla Hills and Governor Jim Edgar of Illinois. Abortion was kept behind the scenes, with the illusory recommendation of a Constitutional Amendment. Taxes were not stressed for the obvious reason that President Bush was rendered forever vulnerable on the subject in 1990.

A kind of dreamy optimism was the hallmark of an eloquent plea by Ronald Reagan, enlivened by his singular aptitude to amuse while deriding ("They kept telling us with straight faces that they were for family values, and they call *me* an actor!"). But what Mr. Reagan was saying was that all the beauties we have experienced in the past in America are as nothing beside those that lie ahead for us. This is an unadorned biblical metaphor ("Eye hath not seen, nor ear heard, . . . the things which God hath prepared for them that love him"). Ronald Reagan did not give the impression that he was programmed to end the evening with this wistful vision of an even greater America. Reagan's voice was nothing if not heartfelt. He has been around a very long time—after all, he reminded us, he and Thomas Jefferson were friends, and Clinton is no Thomas Jefferson. He has addressed six conventions, and the laws of probability suggested that this would be his final appearance, and he wished to leave his fingerprint indelibly in the memory of his flock: America is unique. America was born to be exceptionalist. But you know, folks, this does require character.

How big a tent should a political party have? Pat Buchanan was roundly condemned in various accents. John Chancellor said that the convention floor was abuzz with concern over Buchanan's tribute to force. What Buchanan said was that in the last analysis it was "force" that stayed the hand of the marauders of Los Angeles. The militia, using "force, rooted in courage, backed by justice," protected the old people's home. Chancellor didn't say it in exactly these words, but listeners knew what he was thinking: that we had been listening to Mussolini.

Senator John Chafee said that the Republican Party of Pat Buchanan was one that desired gay-bashing and holding up to obloquy women who chose to have an abortion, and he thought this "distasteful." Barbara Bush, reiterating her previously announced position that she didn't think abortion should figure in the Republican platform in any way, confessed that she found certain aspects of Pat Buchanan's speech to be "judgmental." That word, by the way, has acquired a negative meaning of a kind that leaves the language without an appropriate word to describe opposition based on moral grounds. The result is that we become a nation of moral castrates, "afraid to say a good word about Camels, for fear of offending Lucky Strikes," as the late Willi Schlamm once termed the creeping relativism of the 1950s.

The interview with Pat Buchanan conducted by Tom Brokaw was hilarious for the social distance Mr. Brokaw attempted to put between him and his guest. He referred to him, I kid thee not, as "Mr. Buchanan." The regnant familiarity among media moguls is so pronounced, the chances are Tom Brokaw would have referred to, oh, Walter Lippmann as "Walter." "Mr." Buchanan suggested the kind of formality one invokes in order to convey that you are perfectly well aware that you are talking to somebody who lives in a moral sanitarium. Thus you would expect Dan Rather or Peter Jennings or Brokaw to refer to "Mr. Duke" when/if interviewing

David Duke; but to "Jesse" when talking with the Reverend J. Jackson.

What Buchanan said to Mr. Brokaw was that when he watched the proceedings at Madison Square Garden, he "never felt so alienated" from his own society. Why? Because he felt he was watching the deliberations of a political party that refused to weigh the question of right and wrong. Thus homosexuals had the same right to "marriage" as heterosexuals, which is like saying that baseball players have the same right to play football as football players. He said that the Democratic Party was all for choice, but not for those who wished to send their children to religious schools. Freedom of speech for pornographers, but not for rabbis to deliver a benediction at a public-school graduation.

The Big Tent theory of inclusiveness has a hard time making distinctions. Franklin Delano Roosevelt let slip in 1944 that he had no objection to members of the Communist Party voting for him—because, after all, they had a vote. Modern readers will find it difficult to imagine the shock experienced by some over *that* Big Tent, because although we were fighting as allies with the Soviets, we knew a great deal about Stalin's practices, and about the practices of his agents in the United States, sworn to advance an anti-democratic, anti-capitalist revolution by force or any other means. . . . How would Democratic inclusionists have reacted to hospitality shown to David Duke? Why is it so difficult to understand those who believe that one can't seriously advance family values and homosexual marriages at one and the same time? Or that there really are Americans, by no means fanatical in disposition, who believe that to kill unborn children is at least as offensive as to bar blacks from a country club?

But the evening ended with a glow. There was Newt Gingrich, tough but genial. Jack Kemp, with his roaring enthusiasm for life and for opportunity for the underdog. And Phil Gramm, with his country-and-western paean to the land of opportunity, with heavy emphasis on the salient opportunity of the season, which is to vote Republican in November.

The effort was made here and there to define family values. Not an easy thing to do, by the way—over the weekend, brainy essayist

Lance Morrow of *Time* magazine was fretting over a professional assignment to do exactly that. Barbara Bush reached for metaphors. Well, she said, when the children were growing up, we went to church, we cheered the Fourth of July, we sang carols at Christmas. And accepted, and learned to accept, that life is not necessarily easy. "Thank heavens we didn't expect our kids to be perfect: they weren't."

But, said the First Lady, ask George what it is he is proudest of, his record in college, his success as an entrepreneur, his public career, his election as president and service in that role, and he'll answer that what he is truly proud of is that "his children still come home." Those who heard her can't have suspected that Mrs. Bush was alleging that the children of Bill Clinton and Al Gore had become refugees of their parents' households, inasmuch as they are underage for that kind of thing. And if they suspected that the reference was to the Reagan family and the much publicized alienation of daughter Patti, who makes a living by badmouthing her parents, that contingency was covered by Mrs. Bush's acknowledgment that tragedy is a part of human existence. "We lost a daughter, almost lost a son, and another child had a learning disability."

But there it was, family values as defined by the First Lady. Sure, she engages in hyperbole. Her husband is not only the best husband, president, and statesman in the world, he is also the "healthiest" man. Some delegates might have permitted themselves to wonder whether Arnold Schwarzenegger wasn't perhaps at least as healthy, but then what is a political convention supposed to celebrate, if not the supremacy of its candidate, even if a little transmogrification is required?

On top of it all there were celebrations, inside the Astrodome and outside the Astrodome. Among other things, Bill Clinton became forty-six years old on Wednesday, which reminded some of us old fogeys that that was exactly Napoleon Bonaparte's age when it was all but universally determined in Europe that the best thing to do with him was to send him to St. Helena to live.

. . .

Jackie Gleason complained twenty-five years ago that as of the moment it was announced that CBS would pay him five million dollars a year (at the time a record-breaking sum), he knew that he faced failure. "People will ask themselves after each of my programs, 'Was he five million dollars funny?' and they will say to themselves, 'No. Not *that* funny.'" Mr. Bush faced problems of that order after all the talk about the need for him to deliver the "speech of his life." On the other hand if he *had* delivered the Speech of His Life, defined as something transcending anything he had ever before done, he probably would have guaranteed the loss of the election. The delegates would have been puzzled to hear from Mr. Bush something on the order of a Cooper Union address.

Although the president had a sprinkle of innovative ideas, notably the notion that taxpayers should be given the right to assign 10 percent of their income taxes to debt-reduction, on the whole it was pretty much the same thing; and the same thing is a whole lot better than other-than-the-same-thing, at the hands of mad-dog government interventionists. There was, however, the one difficulty, the brooding omnipresence to which no Republican analyst has prescribed a plausible cure; that problem is Congress.

If it is true, as Mr. Bush and 121 other speakers (the count of senior campaign adviser Charlie Black) claim, that Congress is responsible for the paralysis of legislative action, exactly what is going to persuade Americans this time around to stop voting for Democratic senators and representatives? Mr. Bush's speech?

It worked for Eisenhower in 1952—he got a Republican Congress for a couple of years; and twenty-eight years later Mr. Reagan brought in a GOP Senate. But as the delegates were powerfully told, for forty-two years by and large the Congress has been Democratic, and with such a Congress—and Mr. Bush—no progress can be made.

What is the thoughtful voter to conclude? Either a) that there ought not to be a Democratic Congress; or else b) that there ought not to be a Republican president. The rational voter might be tempted to conclude that it is easier for him to vote No to a Republican president than it is for him to persuade fifty first-cousins in fifty states not to vote for Democratic congressmen. This is a point that Mr. Bush might dramatically have highlighted if he had said: Look, four more years of the kind we have just had—with me proposing appropriate legislation and the Congress refusing to act —would result in bad government. If bad government is reendorsed by the voters in November, my patriotic duty would be to withdraw. Let the Electoral College designate a Democrat as president if the people once again immobilize a Republican president with a Democratic Congress.

The late Professor Willmoore Kendall in his famous essay "The Two Majorities" said that the American voter tended to speak in two voices. In the first, he toyed with high and idealistic theory: vote for Woodrow Wilson, thrilling the world with his high harmonic serenities about freedom and democracy for everybody, guaranteed by the United States. In the other mode, the same voter would look at the congressional choices and incline to the one who promised to shield young Americans from any mandate to die fighting for democracy on the shores of Tripoli. In textbook democratic schematics it looks nice, a reflection of the division of powers. Congress says Yes, the Executive says No, and the voter has rhetorical satisfaction and practical relief.

The popular sense that the political picture is not, in Mr. Bush's words, "in place" underlies the malaise of the current mood; and although in high spirits George Bush hacked away at the ideological pyre designed by his critics to cremate him as responsible for everything that has disappointed Americans during the past four years, he did not face up to the consequences of the problem he described: a paralysis in government. He was engagingly feisty, kindling the enthusiasm of the delegates. But had he said, "Let's deport any citizen who has voted Democratic more than twice," he could probably have got a standing ovation. What he did not satisfy was the appetite of Americans who feel that indeed something of a structural significance has to be done about the American political system.

—THE KGB EXONERATES ALGER HISS
NOVEMBER 6, 1992

The news story all but spoke of Alger Hiss as having been definitively cleared. By the U.S. Supreme Court? Oh no. By a Russian general-historian, General Dmitri A. Volkogonov. A man of high reputation, who however in "clearing" Alger Hiss of having served as a spy for the Soviet Union takes rather unusual liberties.

Americans may assume that the general has access to KGB or the GRU files, because the general is chairman of the supreme council commission on KGB and military-intelligence archives. But to assume that after four or five weeks he established that Alger Hiss was never a communist agent for the Soviet Union a) says odd things about him as a historian (you can't begin to go through KGB files thoroughly in five years, let alone five weeks), and b) makes him suddenly an expert on American judicial history.

You see, said the general at his interview with Hiss emissary John Lowenthal, during the Cold War people were quick to suspect other people of complicity with the enemy. "The fact that [Alger Hiss] was convicted in the fifties was a result of either false information or judicial error." Suddenly, we are listening to a Russian general to find out whether Alger Hiss was fairly tried and convicted.

The following day on CNN the reporter identified Alger Hiss as "having gone to jail for allegedly committing perjury." Yes, and Ted Bundy was executed for allegedly murdering ten women.

A letter from historian Gertrude Himmelfarb: "As a former grubber in archives (better organized archives, on less secretive and sensitive subjects), I assure you that one month of searching and inspecting is no time at all—certainly not enough time to produce the categorical judgment attributed to the general. In fact, a categorical judgment of this kind is itself suspect; historians always qualify their conclusions, cover themselves lest subsequent findings refute them. There is something very odd about this whole story. . . . Remember Trevor Roper's gaffe about Hitler's secret diaries?"

Indeed. But the movement to exonerate Hiss has run into so many obstacles over so many decades that to declare him innocent is on the order of declaring Dreyfus guilty. *Newsweek* reports:

"Alger Hiss is still on trial in America. Was he a spy, a member of a secret communist cell who passed along confidential State Department reports to the Soviets? Or was he a statesman framed by the fanatical right, a wanton sacrifice to the careers of Senator Joseph McCarthy and Representative Richard Nixon? The legal system never resolved the question."

Those sentences are historical travesties of a major order. (The legal system absolutely resolved the question.) Yet they appear in the current issue of a national American newsweekly.

The overwhelming case against Alger Hiss is documented by Professor Allen Weinstein in his book *Perjury*. That book was judged as dispositive of the Hiss case by historian Arthur Schlesinger, Jr., who was not a McCarthyite. Every legal maneuver, effort, caprice, and effrontery was attempted on behalf of Alger Hiss, and always these efforts to turn history around came to naught. The incriminating papers were typed on Hiss's typewriter, they were given to Whittaker Chambers, and he sent them up the espionage assembly line to his Soviet superiors.

And it isn't as though all evidence against Hiss died with Chambers in 1961. Only two years ago Oleg Gordievsky, the Soviet Union's spy chief in London from 1982 until his defection in 1985, published a book: *KGB: The Inside Story.* In a mere footnote in the book, Gordievsky referred to Iskhak A. Akhmerov as "Hiss's wartime [KGB] controller." And U.S. writer and spy-watcher Thomas Powers, writing in *The New York Review of Books* on August 17, 1989, advises us that the code name for Alger Hiss in the Soviet Union was "Ales."

There is more to be said about the Chambers story, and a gifted young historian (Sam Tanenhaus) is working on a comprehensive biography of one of the most fascinating and talented writers of the century, the great witness who gave us *Witness.*

General Volkogonov is a nice man, but it really was a little odd when in Moscow last month he turned into a bitter-end defender of Hiss with his certification that Alger Hiss was a victim of McCarthyism and said: "I would like to hand this document over

. . . and believe that you can tell Mr. Alger Hiss that the heavy weight should be lifted from his heart."

How nice. All we need to do, in order to lift that heavy weight from Alger Hiss's heart, is to defame the American system of justice, classify as libelous dozens of witnesses who built the case against him, and reject as a sadistic liar a great man who, unlike his old spymate Alger Hiss, tried to make it up to the country he betrayed.

—GEORGE WILL OVERBOARD
JANUARY 20, 1987

My esteemed friend George Will has gone not-quite-right on the matter of Palestinians–Israel–The Vatican–Cardinal O'Connor–history. It all began with a vituperative attack on the Vatican at the end of *This Week with David Brinkley* on Sunday January 11. Will referred to the "Vatican's contemptible behavior toward the Holocaust" and its "continuing contemptible behavior toward Israel." He voiced his suspicion "that there is a residual anti-Semitism at work in Vatican policy" and suggested that the appropriate remedy was for the United States instantly to establish its embassy "not just in Jerusalem, but in East Jerusalem . . . thereby underscoring the fact that a united Jerusalem is and forever shall be the capital of Israel."

And then in his syndicated column for January 15 he ripped into Cardinal John O'Connor's innocent tribute to the Holocaust Museum—the cardinal, whose emotions are copiously expressed, had said reverently that the Holocaust "may be an enormous gift that Judaism has given the world." Will transformed those words into an endorsement of the Holocaust on the grounds that it gives us something to grieve over. Such perverse readings of the meaning of an impulsive response by a transparently good man should bear in mind that Christendom celebrates as its primary day of joy the day of the Resurrection, which could not have happened save for Christ crucified. If the analogy was inappropriate, the sentiments clearly were not.

But George Will is losing sight of rather a lot of things, the first of them that it was Israel that invited Cardinal O'Connor to the Mideast, encouraging him to use his resources as a cleric in order to advance the possibility of peace. The problem with devising peaceful solutions in the Mideast, where George Will is concerned, is that there he sees only a single position: Israel's—at all times, in all places. George sometimes sounds a little like Rabbi Kahane, who is properly scorned by the majority of the Israelis for his anti-Palestinian fundamentalism. If progress of any kind is going to be made in that part of the world, you don't begin by siding with Israel on every single point.

The overwhelming majority of the governments of the world do not recognize Jerusalem as the capital of Israel. This is not a collective venture in anti-Semitism. It has to do with the U.N. resolution that gave birth to the State of Israel. That resolution, which the United States and much of the world backed, called for the internationalization of Jerusalem. In the ensuing hostilities, the western half of Jerusalem was occupied by the Israelis, the eastern half by Jordan; and nineteen years later Israel won the eastern half by force of arms.

There is no pressing need for the United States (or for the Vatican) to overrule the U.N. verdict when dealing with the most sacred acreage in the world, sacred to Moslem, Jew, and Christian. On the matter of recognition of Israel by the Vatican, Mr. Will is simply incorrect. According to going rules (set down in *Satow's Guide to Diplomatic Practice,* Section 199), the formal exchanges between the Vatican and Israel over the years amount to de facto diplomatic recognition.

In 1963, Rolf Hochhuth's play *The Deputy* accused Pope Pius XII of indifference to the Holocaust. Ever since, scholars have probed to define his role. We know that in his Christmas message in 1942 the pope urged all Catholics to give shelter wherever they could: "Humanity should help the Jews who for reason of their faith have been marked for death." When Pius XII died, Israeli U.N. representative and future prime minister Golda Meir said of him on the floor of the United Nations, "During the ten years of Nazi terror, when our people went through the horrors of martyrdom, the pope raised his voice to condemn the persecutors and to commiserate with their victims."

There was one line—the final line in Will's column—that

causes true pain. Concerning Cardinal O'Connor's statement that obviously he needed to obey the Vatican on the matter of where he could meet with Israeli officials, George Will commented: "Israelis have heard his alibi before: He was only obeying orders." George Will seems to be saying that at the next Nuremburg trial, Cardinal O'Connor would be up for a crime against humanity. He must know (he does; I am merely reminding him) that rhetorical abuses can also be crimes against humanity.

—SEVER DIPLOMATIC RELATIONS WITH NICARAGUA?

APRIL 2, 1985

Q. We do, do we not, have diplomatic relations with the government of Nicaragua?

A. Yes.

Q. That being the case, how can we, under international law, give aid and comfort to armed militants whose stated intention is to overthrow the government we are recognizing?

A. Our official rationale, in giving aid to the Contras, has been to help the government of El Salvador. That government has been assaulted by rebels who are supplied by Nicaragua, indeed whose headquarters for a long period of time were in Managua.

Q. What business is it of the United States, party No. 1, to help El Salvador, party No. 2, from an act of aggression by Nicaragua, party No. 3?

A. It has always been recognized in the community of nations that any nation can lawfully aid any other nation to defend itself against aggression. That was the exclusive rationale of our intervention in South Korea. We had no treaty obligations respecting South Korea, we simply intervened under the umbrella of the United Nations as it happened, to help in a war against aggression.

Q. But doesn't intervention of that sort normally lead to a declaration of war against the aggressor power?

A. No, as a matter of fact. Professor Eugene Rostow from time to time reminds us of the *Caroline* incident.

Q. Well, would you remind us of the *Caroline* incident?

A. In 1837, a bunch of aggressive Yankees in upstate New York decided to send a few soldiers and supplies to Canadians involved in an insurrection against Canada, i.e., Great Britain. Great Britain retaliated most ingeniously. It didn't suspend diplomatic relations, let alone declare war. But it did seize an American vessel called the *Caroline*, which had been used to transport the American aggressors. Having seized the vessel, the British simply let it loose a little way upriver from Niagara Falls. You can imagine what happened to the good ship *Caroline*.

Q. You mean, with people aboard it went down the falls?

A. I mean with people aboard it went down the falls.

Q. But suppose that El Salvador did not even exist, and therefore we had no way to depend on Nicaraguan aggression against El Salvador to motivate our aid to the Contras. What would we then do?

A. Secretary of State George Shultz, in his speech a fortnight ago in San Francisco, edged the government over in the direction of the argument that our aid to the Contras is in and of itself a proper response to the militarization and totalitarianization of Nicaragua. You remember, he said that if the Soviet Union asserts the right under the Brezhnev Doctrine to intervene in any country to prevent democracy from taking root, so do we have the right to intervene to help democracy.

Q. Would it then make sense to sever diplomatic relations with Nicaragua?

A. Clearly this would be a sensible psychological move. There is a paradox in simultaneously recognizing a government and giving aid to those who seek to destroy it. It breeds a lot of schizophrenia in Congress, for instance.

Q. Does the president have absolute authority in this field?

A. Absolute authority is exactly the way to put it. No one contests that the chief executive has the right a) to recognize a government, and b) to sever relations with a government. Tomorrow morning, President Reagan could sever relations with Nicaragua. He would have sufficient cause to do so: namely, Nicaragua's disturbing the peace in the area. And as we have discussed, even if Nicaragua were not aggressing against its neighbors, the president could sever relations, giving as a reason for doing so the tyrannical

nature of its government and the claim by the Contras to participate in a government they fought to create.

Q. Surely you aren't advocating that the president sever relations with all tyrannical governments?

A. No. But Nicaragua is a state in which totalitarian control is
not fully consolidated. It is fighting a war against its own people in
order to stay in power. We can think of it as less than a de facto—
let alone de jure—government. If we are helping the Contras it
must be because we hold out hope that they might prevail against
the tyrants. That being the case, we should stand by to recognize
the new government.

Q. Why, then, doesn't President Reagan sever diplomatic relations?

A. The tyranny of the status quo. That, plus an anxiety to
persuade other Latin American governments to go along with us,
as they did when we severed relations with Castro's Cuba. But de-
recognition should definitely be put on our agenda.

Q. You are very persuasive on the subject.

A. Thank you. I shall see that you are not aboard the *Caroline*
next time out.

—WELCOME TO THE SEVEN O'CLOCK NEWS

JULY 21, 1987

Good evening. This is Dan Blather with the evening news.

Today in Washington, Admiral John Poindexter testified that
President Reagan knew nothing about the diversion of funds from
the sale of arms to Iran to the Contras. In testifying to this effect,
he left the congressional investigating committee with a hard task
in any effort to establish that President Reagan had committed an
impeachable offense. But let's get the story from Bill Grant at the
White House. Bill?

Yes, Dan, it was a devastating development, viewed in one
way. But several committee members have told us that the principal question they are investigating is the management style of
President Reagan. They are asking: Is he actually in charge of the
White House? As one member said, the people elected Reagan

president, but what they got was an admiral and a colonel writing foreign policy. So Mr. Reagan isn't exactly out of the woods.

Thank you, Bill. Thank you ever so much. Let's hear from Leslie Stowe about the public reaction to the admiral's testimony. Come in, Leslie.

Thank you, Dan. Well, Dan, the people are saying something to the effect that you can't fool all the people all the time. Although Admiral Poindexter has denied that the president had any knowledge of the diversion of funds, a test sampling of six hundred and fifty New Yorkers establishes that 52 percent of the people simply do not believe that the president is telling the truth. And, of course, New Yorkers tend to be more sophisticated than non–New Yorkers. Out there, there are people who actually believe Ronald Reagan. Let's meet Mrs. Stilton in Indiana:

(*Interview*): Do you believe Mr. Reagan is telling the truth, Mrs. Stilton?

Uh-huh.

Why do you believe he is telling the truth, Mrs. Stilton?

Santa Claus told me so.

Thank you very much, Mrs. Stilton. Back to you, Dan.

Oh, thank you so much, Leslie. That was very illuminating. We turn now to Chris Dallas, who has a report on what was done with the funds diverted by the White House to the Contras. Come in, Chris.

Thank you, Dan. Well, a recent survey has shown that those funds were responsible for weapons and hand grenades with which the Contras are reported to have killed somewhere between two and three hundred innocent peasants, mostly senior citizens over sixty-five and children under fifteen. Here is a report from Managua, from a Red Cross volunteer, a young American college student, Ben Rudman.

(*Close-up, interview*): Ben, what exactly are the Contras doing with the money illegally given to them by the Reagan administration?

Well, Chris, as you know, the Contras are mostly former followers of the dictator Somoza, and they obviously want to get back into power, and they frankly don't care how they do it. If they have to destroy the entire civilian population of Nicaragua, that's just fine by them.

Thank you, Ben. Back to you, Dan.

Oh Ben, how can I thank you enough? Well, we have now a report from Senator Orrin Hatch, a senior Republican who has all along defended President Reagan. Senator Hatch, may I ask you, sir, how it is possible for a national security adviser to engage in such an operation without the knowledge of the president?

Well, Dan, look at it this way—

Thank you very much, Senator Hatch.

That, ladies and gentlemen, was Senator Hatch, defending President Reagan and Admiral Poindexter. Tomorrow's witness will be Robert McFarlane. He has asked to testify again, even though he testified last week. There are reports that he is very disturbed by the testimony of Admiral Poindexter and the testimony of Colonel North. It is possible that Mr. McFarlane will come in with evidence that will contradict the testimony of Admiral Poindexter. Let's have a word with the senator in charge of the investigation, Senator Inouye. Senator Inouye, what is your opinion of the credibility of Admiral Poindexter?

(*Close-up, interview*): Well, Dan, Admiral Poindexter took an oath when he was in the Naval Academy. In that oath he promised he would not lie and he would not cheat and he would not obey unlawful orders. But he has told the committee that he has done exactly that—lied, cheated, and obeyed unlawful orders.

Would you say, senator, that it all reminds us of—Nuremberg?

Those are your words, Dan, not mine.

Oh, thank you, Senator Inouye. Thank you very much. And Bill, and Leslie, and Chris. Thank you all very much. You've made my day.

—————

—ANTHONY LEWIS, REPORTER

OCTOBER 26, 1985

You are the jurors. Now hear this:

One night back in November 1982, a middle-aged black policeman, Officer X, was visiting with relatives during the early evening. At about eight, he said good night and headed home. He had just entered the gates to his little house when, from behind, there was the rat-a-tat of an automatic rifle. Twenty slugs into the policeman. A waiting car whisked the murderer away.

But after the murderer got home, he became intimate with his roommate and in due course told her that he had "shot the dog," Officer X. She listened, and after a while decided she'd better take her information over to the police. The police arrested the murderer, questioned him, and got from him a confession. Moreover, the murderer took them to the scene of the crime, reenacted everything that had happened, even indicating where he had hidden, and where the victim had fallen. He said that he had acted against Officer X because he was under orders from a terrorist organization to which he belonged to shoot him.

When the following spring the trial was held, the murderer suddenly recanted. He said in fact he hadn't killed Officer X. But it was much too late. Not only was the evidence circumstantially overwhelming, there were independent witnesses who corroborated every detail of that confession. When his lawyer pleaded that the confession was not valid, a court heard the complaint and ruled that the confession had complied with the Criminal Procedure Act of 1977. The murderer was accordingly sentenced to death, and denied appeal on the grounds that there were no extenuating circumstances, the precondition for appeal in that country. A date was set for the execution two years later.

Shortly before the scheduled execution, the murderer's lawyers came in with an entirely different appeal. Yes, they said, it was true that the murderer had killed Officer X. But they wanted to have a fresh trial at which they could establish that the mental condition of the murderer at the time of the killing was indeed an extenuating circumstance. The court put off the execution, which had been scheduled for the following day, heard out the fresh appeal, ruled in due course that it was not substantial, and rescheduled the execution.

Which execution took place on October 18 of this year.

Now listen to what you can do to that story—if you are Anthony Lewis of *The New York Times* and you are determined to put a hideous construction on literally anything the South African government does. Here is Mr. Lewis:

"President Botha and his officials have sent the message [that there will be no changes in South Africa] with uncommon clarity.

Their recent actions have had the character of not only rejection but provocation.

"Consider, for example, the decision to execute a poet [Question: What does it matter that the murderer was a poet?] and supporter of the outlawed African National Congress [that is the Marxist terrorist group that declines to disavow violence. Notice, no description by Mr. Lewis of the character of the ANC, which gave the murderer the instructions to kill the policeman]. . . . It was more than two years since [the murderer] was sentenced to death for allegedly [get that "allegedly." He was convicted, by his own confession, by circumstantial evidence, and by the confirmation of other witnesses] participating [you like that? You fire twenty slugs into someone and you are "participating" in a murder] in the murder of a policeman. The government granted a stay in August; it appeared to be responding to new evidence and to worldwide appeals for clemency. Then, suddenly, it proceeded with the execution." [The government commuted five death sentences at the same time that it considered, and denied, the appeal of the murderer in question.]

And, finally, Lewis continues: "[The murderer's mother] is an elderly, nonpolitical woman who said she once 'felt sympathy' for those in power. But now she said: 'This government is cruel. It is really, really, cruel.' "

So those are Mr. Lewis's rules. The murderer who fired into the back of an innocent black policeman, on the orders of a terrorist organization, is the character we are propped up to sympathize with. Not the police, judges, and government officials who brought him to justice. Mr. Lewis, like so many critics of South Africa, has got to the point where he can't even bring himself to call the act of a murderer cruel.

Weep, if you can still figure out whom to weep for, and whom to weep over.

SIX

CORRESPONDING

—A Dozen or So Letters Exchanged with Readers
of *National Review* on Divers Subjects.

Memo to: WFB
   From: McF
Bill, *hanc scriptionem vidisti*?
   From *Fort Pierce* (Fla.) *Tribune,* Q & A column by editor, Lee
Barnes.
   " 'Why don't you print William F. Buckley's political col-
umns?'
   " 'We have a policy here that we will only use columnists who
write in English.' "

McF: *Qualis anus equi!*   Bill

Dear Mr. Buckley:
   In the editorial "Cruelest Month" [May 8, 1987], *NR* has it
"shoures soote." Has Chaucer been revised since the 1929 edition
of *The Student's Chaucer* (The Clarendon Press, Oxford), which
has it *"shoures sote,"* or has someone been guilty of carelessness?
                                 Cordially,
                                 Robert E. Kohler
                                 Kohler, Wisc.

Dear Mr. Kohler: It is an old rivalry (Oxford *v.* Cambridge). The
Chaucer we use around here (at *National Review* we always speak
in Middle English until noon) we get from the New Cambridge
Edition, ed. F. N. Robinson (Houghton Mifflin), a fine book in
which all *shoures* are *soote.* Cordially,   WFB

Dear Mr. Buckley:

You can't imagine my excitement upon reading, when you visited the *Titanic* in 1989, of your descent two and a half miles into the ocean! If only you hadn't come up.

Sincerely,
Thomas J. Sinsky
Madison, Wisc.

Dear Mr. Sinsky: Did you not know that I was irrepressible? Cordially,   WFB

Dear Mr. Buckley:

Re your *Firing Line* interview with Henry Kissinger, from a qualified TV professional objectively concerned American:

1. The manner in which you sit is rude. Can't you sit upright in an adult fashion? In single shots you appear tilted. In two shots you sit as if your guest has BO.

2. Even in questioning you appear rude. You don't ask questions of a guest (even one whose opinion you favor) but your questions come in a long form of . . . interrogation.

3. You always come up with the personal insecurity of a long preface attempting to show what . . . you . . . know.

4. Finally, we have tried the Liberal Way and it has not worked. We have tried the Conservative Road, and neither has that worked . . . although conservatives are still attempting to force a square peg into a round hole.

Sincerely,
Hamilton Morgen
Harrison, N.Y.

P.S. In my book, the professed Liberals and Conservatives have been the most anti-American.

Dear Mr. Morgen: 1) No, I can't sit straight. Congenital. Most people *don't talk about it out loud!* 2) If you think my questions are long, try Socrates. 3) Of course I want to share what I know about the subject: After all, I spend three hours reading up on it the night before. Have you ever jumped out of an airplane at midnight with a parachute? With the mission of eliminating the guard at the end of a bridge? Well, I haven't either, but if I did, I would certainly want detailed introductory instructions. 4) The trick, Morgen, when you run into that problem, is to make the hole a little larger in diameter—and plop! in goes the square peg. Cordially,   WFB

Dear Mr. Buckley:
    Re Richard Brookhiser's "Why Dole Can't Do It?" [Dec. 4]— he forgot one major factor. The Democratic cross-over vote. Democratic? Yes, the Democrats have worshiped the Dole for years.
                                                                    Truly,
                                                                    Russ Shank
                                                                    Waynesboro, Va.

Dear Mr. Shank: I dunno . . . Either my standards are slipping by publishing this, or yours are by writing it. Cordially,   WFB

Dear Mr. Buckley:
    Early this morning, whilst discussing with my husband which of us should take the garbage out, I realized that if said quickly enough, "garbage out" sounds much like Gorbachev. Can you tell me if there is any meaning in this?
                                                                    Sincerely,
                                                                    Patti Devlin
                                                                    Lafayette, Calif.

Dear Mrs. Devlin: Sure. The hacksters call it GIGO. As with computers, it is true of Summit conferences: Garbage In, Garbage Out. Cordially,   WFB

Dear Mr. Buckley:
    Attached is an article from today's *Philadelphia Inquirer,* which you may find interesting:

Indian Scalping Out of Sight
WASHINGTON, Oct. 9—For more than a century, the oil painting—a scene of an Indian holding aloft a white man's scalp— had hung without apparent complaint in hearing rooms of the House Interior and Insular Affairs Committee.
    The silence lasted until freshman Representative Ben

Nighthorse Campbell (D., Colo.) spied the painting, *Death Whoop,* early this year as he took his committee seat facing the work of art.

"It's a depressing painting," said Campbell, a Northern Cheyenne who is the only Native American serving in Congress. "It's out of touch with the sensitivity of Indians. It plays on the prejudice of man."

Campbell complained to a sympathetic Interior Chairman Morris K. Udall (D., Ariz.), and the result yesterday was a formal unhanging of the painting, one of a series of Indian scenes done in 1868 by retired General Seth Eastman.

"This is one of the great historical moments of the House Interior Committee," Udall said at the brief ceremony that ended with two workers unceremoniously hauling away *Death Whoop* on a dolly.

The removal of the painting was yet another change brought by Campbell, an artist and silversmith, to the traditions of Capitol Hill.

House rules require male members to wear neckties. Campbell wears only neckerchiefs held in place by rings bearing Indian designs. He persuaded Speaker Jim Wright (D., Tex.) to make an exception for his neckwear.

Aside from the article's content, there is one thing which does puzzle me: the mention of a "formal hanging."

Now, I'm just an ordinary working slob—not one to be invited to formal anythings. I have had the honor of attending *informal* unhangings (shirt and shoes a must; socks optional); but the upper crust shuns me.

But *you,* sir—surely you have attended a formal unhanging! If it wouldn't be telling tales out of school, could you describe what goes on at a formal unhanging?

> Very truly yours,
> Vincent P. Benedict
> Ardmore, Pa.

Dear Mr. Benedict: Well, it's a dark suit, of course, and non-flamboyant tie. There is silence when the formal unhanger comes in. Some people like drums when he mounts the stepladder; personally I think that's overdoing it—silence is enough. When the picture comes down, there is a diseulogy, brief, on the painter.

And then, silently, in pairs, you troop out. It is followed by refreshments. Cordially,   WFB

Mr. Michael Kramer
New York magazine
Dear Mike:

You write (incredibly) in your mag, May 12, "Having neatly rebuked [Charles] Murray, whom he [Daniel Patrick Moynihan, in his book *Disintegration Blues*] calls a serious scholar despite Murray's support of William F. Buckley Jr.'s proposal for 'taking away the right to vote from anyone who [has] no source of income except welfare,' Moynihan is less helpful in shaping a future . . ."

I have seen non sequiturs in my life, baby ones, middle-sized ones, and great big ones, but they all stand aside in awe at yours. A policy recommendation has nothing to do with scholarship, serious or nonserious. And if it did, I take the occasion to remind you that the proposal attributed to me was first made by John Stuart Mill, whose scholarly credentials are generally accepted.

Yours cordially,
Bill

Dear Mr. Buckley:

While in the bookstore last week to pick up the latest *NR*, I espied a copy of the English translation of *Pravda*, and curiosity took hold. Having purchased and read it cover to cover, I now suffer from guilt, despite having enjoyed some chuckles and not a few guffaws along the way. I feel that what I did was the political equivalent of an evangelical reading Aleister Crowley just to see if the reality matches the bad reputation. What's worse, now I feel tempted to pick up an issue of *The Nation*.

I repent of the former error and shall struggle mightily against the latter temptation. I feel that the least I could do to atone is finally to make a commitment to *National Review,* so I am sending a check for my first subscription. However, I shall not feel cleansed until I receive forgiveness and guidance from the venerable WFB. . . .

Yours in Conservatism,
Kevin O'Hare
San Francisco, Calif.

Dear Mr. O'Hare: *Ego te exculpo.* Your penance is a two-year subscription. You should avoid occasions of sin—i.e., the larger newsstands. Hum "The Star-Spangled Banner" before meals. If tempted, call our hot line, number available to anyone with a three-year subscription. Cordially,   WFB

Dear Mr. Buckley:

I have one brother who went to Harvard and another who went to the electric chair. My mother died in an insane asylum when I was three, and my father is serving a life sentence for narcotics trafficking. My sister is a prosperous and respected prostitute in Boston.

Recently I met, and fell in love with, a girl just out of reform school where she served time for smothering her illegitimate newborn baby. We plan to marry soon.

Should I tell her about my brother who went to Harvard?

J. Bute
Houston, Tex.

Dear Mr. Bute: Why not just economize your biography by saying you have a brother who went to Harvard and to the electric chair? Cordially,   WFB

Dear Mr. Buckley:

In the course of conversation at my son's twenty-fifth birthday party, a recent girl graduate of Yale (econ) queries, "What are the Ten Commandments? I've never heard of them."

Cordially,
(Mrs.) J. Neubeiser Thompson
Long Beach, Calif.

Dear Mrs. Thompson: I am told the Rare Book Room of the Yale Library has a copy, but I can't vouch for it. Cordially,   WFB

To the Editor of *Esquire*:

For your information, from John Gregory Dunne, *Esquire,* February 1987:

. . . Mr. Buckley makes a habit of that sort of reply. . . . I was less infatuated with his *Overdrive* than he thought I should be, and he responded to *The New York Review of Books* (where my piece appeared) with a letter . . . [He] finally delivered the kayo punch: "Dunne begins his review by reporting that he and I have had a 'fitful' correspondence over the years. But you see, those notes, while perhaps addressed to the couple, were really directed to his wife, who, of the two, was my friend."

From WFB's answer to Dunne in *The New York Review of Books,* November 10, 1983 (the material italicized is omitted by Dunne's reprise in *Esquire*):

Dunne begins his review by reporting that he and I have had a 'fitful' correspondence over the years *and that during the 1960s I would end my epistles, "Pots of love."* But you see, those notes, while perhaps addressed to the couple, were really directed to his wife, who, of the two, was my friend, *and signed off her infrequent notes to me, "Love."*

We await eagerly further installments of Mr. Dunne's manual on how writers should behave.

Yours truly,
Wm. F. Buckley, Jr.

Dear Bill:
    The damnedest thing happened the other day. I received from Hertz a package wrapped in platinum paper. When I opened it, there was the most beautiful leather Cartier wallet. But wait—there's more. In the wallet were ninety one-hundred-dollar bills, plus a Hertz platinum service card. I assume you got the same. It's a great club we belong to, particularly since it's so rare that we rent cars.
    See you in the Hertz Club men's bar one of these days.

Cheers,
Art [Buchwald]
Washington, D.C.

Dear Art: I wouldn't be proud of those ninety one-hundred-dollar bills. That means Hertz thinks you're for sale. I got the wallet and the platinum card, but no bills. They know I'm not for sale. They know I'm a conservative, and you're—let's go somewhere one of these days in a Hertz. Shall we use your card or your cash? Cordially,   Bill

Frank A. Olson
Chairman
The Hertz Corporation
Dear Frank:

Thank you so much for sending me the Christmas card wishing me and my Hertz platinum card a Merry Christmas and a prosperous New Year.

I heard through the grapevine that you gave Bill Buckley a seat on the New York Stock Exchange for having driven ten thousand miles in one of your cars. I was curious whether you are handing these out to all Platinum Service clients, or just to Buckley because of his television show. Buckley is always one-upping me and I was wondering if he invented the tale of the Stock Exchange seat to get me mad.

Sincerely,
Art [Buchwald]
Washington, D.C.

DEAR MR. OLSON: GOT YOUR SELL ORDER—HERTZCO, 100,000 SHARES—FLOOR GOING CRAZY, HAVING A WONDERFUL TIME, LET'S DO SOMETHING ONE OF THESE DAYS FOR ART, WHAT DO YOU SAY?   BUCKLEY

Dear Bill:

Please help me with a problem that is driving me to despair. Several years ago I trained my dog to turn on the TV and to bark when she sensed a tone of *joie de vivre* on the evening news, in return for a jelly-bean reward.

A few days ago she began to camp in front of our set and bark incessantly at such words as "disarray," "hypocrisy," and "credibility," and she is getting so fat that I am concerned about her health.

Quick—can you tell me what is going on and what I can do about it?

Yours truly,
J. Z. Menard
Granville, Ohio

Dear Mr. Menard: Why not send the jelly beans to Dan Rather, Tom Brokaw, and Peter Jennings? As a return address, give "HQ, The Contras, c/o The White House." That should take care of the barking at both ends. Cordially,   WFB

Channel 13
N.Y.C., N.Y. 10019
Attn: Managing Director
Dear Sir:

It has bothered me sufficient times to warrant my taking pen in hand and ask for your assistance.

Mr. Buckley seems to be listing to the "left" (a side on which he feels most uncomfortable) all the time. To me it has a disturbing value, for I keep questioning—"Is the chair broken? Can it be so every week?"

Perhaps he has concluded this peculiar position allows for a unique camera angle and gives him an advantage.

"Is it possible," I ask myself, "he has a problem with his back?"

Maybe he never sat up straight at Yale or even before that!

Hasn't any other viewer noticed it? Or am I seeing his "position" incorrectly?

Respectfully,
Mack Rapp, Senior Consultant
Rapp & Rapp & Associates, Inc.
Port Washington, N.Y.

Dear Mr. Rapp: Channel 13 forwarded your kind letter in which you are concerned about my back. I suffer no pains, so I have no excuse other than my natural slouchiness. Might I make a suggestion? Why don't you tilt over when you watch the program until the long axis of your body and that of mine are exactly parallel? Try that and I think you will find that the only thing that then distracts you is my main guest, who will appear to be at an angle. But since each guest adopts a slightly different posture, there will unquestionably be an agreeable variety to compensate for this. Yours cordially,   WFB

Dear WFB:

It is my understanding that Janeski Fondavich, prima ballerina, has been rewarded for her performance in the Afghan countryside—by being furnished an all-expenses-paid five-year visit to a modern medical facility in the Ural Mountain region of Siberia. Why aren't we as generous with our artists?

Sincerely,
Gerald J. Urpschot
New Orleans, La.

Dear Mr. Urpschot: Because the Reagan administration is lacking in compassion and in an appreciation of the arts. Yours cordially,   WFB

AND THE PROPHET LOOKED ON THE TEMPTATION OF MALACHEY IN THE BOOK OF BUCKLEY AND HE SAW THAT IT WAS VERY GOOD.

STILL, HIS HEART STIRRED WITHIN HIM. HE WAXED WROTH, AND HE SAID TO THE LORD GOD, "HOW SHALL IT BE, LORD, THAT THIS SCRIBE SHALL BE SO SMOOTH OF TONGUE THAT HE SHALL HIMSELF SPEAK TO THE PEOPLE? THAT IS MY TASK, LORD, THAT THOU HAST LAID UPON ME LONG AGO."

AND THE LORD SAID UNTO MOSES, "BE THOU FIRM OF SPIRIT. I AM THE LORD, THY GOD. I KNOW ALL THAT HATH BEEN AND ALL THAT SHALL COME TO PASS. DO THOU MY BIDDING. WHATSOEVER THY HAND FINDETH TO DO, THEREFORE DO IT WITH ALL THY MIGHT.

AND IT WAS SO.

C.
Beverly Hills, Calif.

Dear Charlton Heston: If you think you can fool me by trying to play Moses this side of Hollywood, why you have a surprise coming to you. . . . By the way, er, what did . . . He . . . think of

my *Temptation of Wilfred Malachey* tape?* I mean, as if you knew.
Best,   Bill

Dear Mr. Buckley:
    Don't you think it's about time you sent Blacky to Tripoli?

Regards,
Joel F. Schnoor
Schenectady, N.Y.

Dear Mr. Schnoor: Blackford Oakes, Yale 1951, is a professional
engineer who has traveled extensively—to London, Berlin, Stockholm, Moscow, Mexico, and Havana, practicing his profession,
and has no idea what on earth you are talking about that would
take him to Tripoli, save to build a bridge, or oversee, say, the
construction of a monument to the then-late Mr. Qaddafi. Yours
cordially,   WFB

Dear Mr. Buckley:
    Help! My international relations professor claims I suffer
from cognitive dissonance because I cannot sympathize with the
Soviet viewpoint. I don't believe the Soviet Union and the United
States are on a spiral of aggression causing each to misperceive
the other as the aggressor. I actually think the Soviets are the
aggressors. I don't think Soviet insecurity is the cause of its behavior in the Third World. I even believe in a Soviet Grand Strategy.
In fact, my favorite expletive is: "Communist." What can I do to
change? Perhaps I should undertake electroshock treatment or,
worse yet, maybe I should cancel my subscription to *National Review* and subscribe to *Pravda.* Do you have any suggestions?

Cordially,
James H. Boardman, Jr.
APO New York

Dear Mr. Boardman: Why not subscribe your international-rela-
tions professor to *NR*? Electroshock treatment would then become relevant. Cordially,   WFB

---

* A children's book by WFB. New York: Workman Publishing Co., 1985.

WFB—

Quick question. Why is Qaddafi (Quadaffi, Kadafy, etc.) the megalomaniac Svengali, only a colonel?

Lee Wasserman
Cleveland, Ohio

Dear Mr. Wasserman: Because Colonel Qaddafi shot all the generals. Cordially,   WFB

Dear Mr. Buckley:

Mrs. Moses and I spent two weeks in New Guinea early this year, and learned that the crocodile is a central figure in the natives' worship of the rivers. The pidgin word for crocodile is "puk-puk." There are no alligators in New Guinea, so, logically, the pidgin word for alligators is also "puk-puk."

I thought you'd like to know.

I enjoyed *See You Later, Alligator.*

Very truly,
Raphael J. Moses
Boulder, Colo.

Dear Mr. Moses: You are thoughtful not to have told us what the pidgin New Guinean word is for "See you later." We are, after all, a family journal. Yours cordially,   WFB

Memo to: WFB
From: Linda

I hope you noticed the *Parade* magazine Special Intelligence Report (Jan. 5) which lists you (behind Carl Sagan and Norman Schwarzkopf) as the third most intelligent man in America in the opinion of *Parade*'s readers. Congratulations. . . . (Who is Carl Sagan?)   XX Linda

Dear Linda: What I like best about the Intelligence Report is that it lists John Kenneth Galbraith as seventeenth. I have sent him the clipping with the notation: "Dear Ken: Congratulations! You are a monument to upward mobility!"   XX Bill

The Editor
Baltimore Sun
Baltimore, Md.
Dear Sir:

I have two objections to your editorial, "Buckley, ex Cathedra" (September 24).

You write of my calling Reagan's refusal to lay down tariffs to protect U.S. steel "the correct Christian decision," and you state, "We trust that Jewish, Moslem, Hindu, and Buddhist teachings on the religious aspects of international commerce in steel were considered and dismissed as 'incorrect.' "

If you will consult Webster III, you will find that under "syn." for the adjective *Christian* is given, "decent, civilized." The example cited is, "act in a Christian fashion."

And then you write, "William F. Buckley, Jr., whose elegant arrogance and affectations of a British accent has won him fame and fortune . . ." Arrogance and affectations being separate modifiers, they require the use of the plural verb.

Yours faithfully,
Wm. F. Buckley, Jr.

Dear Mr. Buckley:

I have invented two words for you to add to your vocabulary. If you use them you are guaranteed to seem both intelligent and unintelligible: BABIFEROUS: *adj.*—like an infant. INDERELIGUALISM: *n.*—I have no idea what this is, but I think the ACLU is in favor of it.

Hope you like them.

Sincerely,
Fred "Funnytoons" Stesney
Van Nuys, Calif.

Dear Funnytoons: No. Indereligualism, no matter how sophisticated the case for it, is in flagrant violation of the multiculturalist commandment. Cordially,   WFB

Dear Mr. Buckley:

In your review of *The Tenth Man* in *The New York Times Book Review*, you wrote: "And early on in the book . . ." I've come to expect from you a certain care with the language. I don't understand this usage. I've noticed its regular occurrence lately and assumed it was incorrectly modeled on "later on," and was just another of the linguistic fads which come and go like pop songs. I thought Howard Cosell was responsible for it. Like him, it seems redundant.

I don't mean to be a *noodge*. I understand that mixing levels of usage can be part of style. I can live with "OK" and "guy" for that reason. But please explain why a man who respects infinitives (correctly) would feel comfortable with "early on in."

Sincerely,
Richard Hill
Linville Falls, N.C.

Dear Mr. Hill: A couple of things. First, you cheated a little by asking whether I really liked the sound of "early on in," which sounds awful but entirely begs the question whether "early on" is legitimately used. The "in" would need to be there irrespective of whether the "on" was there: The "on" neither legitimized nor illegitimized the ensuing "in"—you with me, Mr. Hill? . . . Anyway, as you know, American idiom tends to add the redundant preposition; thus Americans will often "lift it up off the table," and "enter into the fray." There is a sense in which, by using the preposition, you induce a sense of languor, desirable in a situation described in the book review from which you quote. "Early in life, John showed an interest in Shakespeare" tells you something just a little different from "Early on in life, John showed an interest . . ." A little overtone of precocity in the latter, missing from the former: and a sense of easing into Shakespeare from the cradle, rather than discovering Shakespeare one fine day as, one fine day, I discovered Red Wing Peanut Butter. Enough? Cordially,   WFB

Dear Mr. Buckley:

I agree with conservatives who want to make English the official language of America. But while we're at it, how about making English the official language of *National Review*?

Maybe it was a bad fortnight, but in the December 31 issue, we see *perestroika* (p. 20); *ad nauseam* (p. 26); *vere dignum et justum est* (p. 29); *ad infinitum, cogito ergo sum, Märchen, sum ergo cogito* (all on p. 31); *credo quia absurdum est* and *anima* (p. 32); *nomenklatura* and *glasnost* (p. 40); *magnum opus* (p. 41); *soi-disant* (pp. 41, 42); *de haut en bas* (p. 42); *a fortiori* (p. 44); *Kraft durch Freude, Ordnung,* and *Achtung* (p. 46); *jeu d'esprit* (p. 49); *tour de force* (p. 50); and *billets-doux* (p. 53).

Now, I consider myself reasonably well educated in languages: I have a degree in Russian with minors in German and French, and am fluent in legalese and nineteenth-century American English. But I confess that some of these phrases are Greek to me. I'm not advocating eliminating foreign words from the lexicon. But if you cannot persuade your erudite writers to use English, could you at least provide translations for your harried readers?

Yours truly,
John Braden
Fremont, Mich.

Dear Mr. Braden: It is an old complaint, the use of foreign words. I would even quote to you from Fowler, except that I can't find anything under "foreign words" in my Fowler here and I am isolated in Switzerland at the moment. However, delicately used, they do bring little piquancies and with them—well, *aperçus* which, because they are extra-idiomatic, give you a fresh view of the subject. As if, in a gallery, you could rise—or descend—ten feet, and look at the picture from that fresh perspective. Don't you think? Or is mine a *fausse idée claire*? . . . By the way, knowing no German, Russian, or Greek, I often experience your frustration; but when I do, I bite my tongue on the grounds that somebody out there is getting pleasure. *Noblesse oblige.* Yours cordially, WFB

Dear Mr. Buckley:

I have invented a new verb: *Buckley.*

Definition: To dress up a falsehood with eloquent language, with the result that it *appears* to be true.

Thus, if Conservative A and Conservative B are discussing plans to publish a falsehood.

Conservative A might say: "Wait a minute. We can't print that in its present form: It's clearly and obviously false."

Then Conservative B could say: "Don't worry. We'll *Buckley* it: Then it'll appear to be true. Then whoever reads it will believe it." Then Conservative A could say: "Oh. Good idea. Wonderful."

Cordially,
Hank Green
Denver, Colo.

Dear Mr. Green: You have it almost right. What's missing is only that if it is Buckleyed, it not only appears correct, it *becomes* correct! So you get a B plus. Cordially,   WFB

Editor
The New York Times Book Review
Dear Sir:

For the record, I had nothing to do with the choice of the two headlines ("Joy of Sesquipedality" and "I Am Lapidary but Not Eristic When I Use Big Words") imposed on my essay on the use of long words and foreign phrases *(TNYTBR,* Nov. 30, 1986).

Yours faithfully,
Wm. F. Buckley, Jr.

—A Defense of the Use of Unusual Words and
Foreign Words

November 30, 1986

One day in May I found on my desk my column, clipped from that morning's *Washington Post,* a red arrow—courtesy of my secretary —pointing to an editorial underneath it. It read, "ERISTIC: (i ris/ tik) *adj* [Gr. *eristikos,* d. *erizein,* to strive, dispute d. *eris,* strife] of or provoking controversy, or given to sophistical argument and specious reasoning." I looked up to the corresponding asterisk in the text and there saw my sentence, "The action by Judge Robert Carter [in fining the National Conference of Catholic Bishops for contempt] has brought out a lot of smiles in judicial political circles (as a rule, you don't step up and fine the Catholic or the Protestant churches—or the Jewish synogogues) for failure to comply with eristic complaints." (The Abortion Rights Mobilization was suing to deny the bishops their tax deductibility, to which end it had persuaded the judge to subpoena the bishops' internal memos on abortion.) *Washington Post* editor Meg Greenfield was rapping me on the knuckles, a quite unusual public reproach: I couldn't remember when last she had thought to help the readers of the *Post* to understand unusual words, however much time she needs to spend explaining unusual editorial positions. Dear Meg, I thought. The instincts of the Jewish Mother just took her over this time.

And then, a week or two later, another clipping on my desk, red arrow, footnote, only this time it was the *Charlotte Observer,* explaining to its readers the meaning of "lapidary." (Their footnote: "Lapidary. Having the elegance and precision associated with inscriptions on monumental stones.") Presently there appeared a letter of explanation from Mr. Ed Williams, Associate Editor of the *Charlotte Observer,* and the challenge was now, well, lapidary. Mr. Williams wrote me:

"I oversee the *Observer*'s daily Viewpoint page, and in that capacity am in charge of preparing syndicated columns for publication in this newspaper. Sometimes I insert aids to the reader, such as the definition of 'lapidary' in your recent column, enclosed. A fellow editor asked why I didn't also define *à outrance.* I replied that I thought you use foreign words and phrases in your columns because 1) you like to show off, and 2) you take delight in irritating people. Far be it for me, I said, to deny you those pleasures. Then I realized I shouldn't presume to answer for you. So let me ask. Why do you use, in your column, foreign words and phrases, and unfamiliar English words, that are unlikely to be understood by the average reader, or at least the average editor? Surrounded by dictionaries, I await your reply."

The point here raised—When is it okay to use an unfamiliar word? When is it not okay?—is endlessly argued, yet even so, fresh insights and original formulations continue to be coined. One of these, I think, was Dwight Macdonald's distinction, made in his marvelous survey of Webster III for *The New Yorker* (March 10, 1962), in which he distinguished between unusual words (okay) and words that "belong in the zoo sections of the dictionary" (not okay). I should think most people would agree, for instance, that "arachibutyrophobia" would be an example of the latter (the word is said to define the fear of peanut butter's sticking to the roof of your mouth). James Jackson Kilpatrick (in his book *The Writer's Art*) takes a position on the dogmatic side against the use of unfamiliar words and cites me, however kindly, as a prodigious offender (as it happened, the Lord delivered Kilpatrick into my hands, because his proscriptive passage against long and usual words contained four long and unusual words). Kilpatrick likes to quote Westbrook Pegler, who denounced the use of what he called "out-of-town words."

The question, under the proximate prodding of Mr. Williams, is worth revisiting. And an easy way to begin is to examine the two words singled out for attention: the first one the word Mr. Williams thought that courtesy required him to translate for the benefit of his readers; the second, the French, which he let pass as arrant and provocative exhibitionism.

What happens when Mr. A. and Ms. B. flatly disagree about whether a word is "unusual"? Well, there is a problem there of an obvious order, namely that some words are unusual but widely recognized, while others are unusual and widely unrecognized. Returning to the general theme a few weeks ago, Mr. Kilpatrick wrote in his column that he had recently published the sentence "The *Miami Herald* carried a 72-point four-column head, DADE-LAND IS DOYEN OF AREA MALLS." Whereafter he received a letter from a Floridian who wanted to know "How many people know what 'doyen' means?" Observed K.: "The more pertinent question: How many of the *Herald*'s 450,000 readers know what doyen means? Ten percent? 20 percent? 80 percent?" Kilpatrick is a man of troubled conscience. He goes right on to say that here he himself has just finished making reference to "72-point" type. That is workaday prose of the John-Jane-Gyp order for anyone who has ever engaged in editorial enterprises—but what about those 450,000 readers? Might they not have preferred, K. tortures himself, "inch-high type"?

Nobody is going to pay Mr. Gallup a lot of money to find out how many people in Florida know what the word "doyen" means. And not many people would be willing to come up with a threshold percentage: *More than X know doyen?—Okay to use. Less than X, verboten* (forbidden). That's on the order of defining the line where obscenity begins.

All of which brings me to say that I do not think of "lapidary" as a word so unrecognizable as to interrupt the reading flow of the average college graduate. But in saying this it is important to reiterate one of the points I made in the public argument I had with Kilpatrick (in the introduction to his book, which he assigned me to write). It is quite simply this, that people with vocabularies of the same size are by no means people who know the same words. A while ago I reviewed a book by John Updike (*The Coup*), discovering over twenty words the meaning of which I didn't know. Knocking these words around at an editors' session in my office one afternoon, I would find that, cumulatively, my five colleagues knew them all. Sam Johnson's apothegm, "In lapidary inscriptions a man is not upon oath," if it is not in the anthologies that circle Mr. Williams's desk, it ought to be.

But then let's take the tougher one. Here is what I wrote in a column on Professor Paul Weiss, the philosopher whose eighty-fifth birthday was something of a national event. "At Yale [Professor Weiss] was the political liberal *à outrance,* but his orderly mind made it hard for him to defend some of liberalism's zanier forms."

This, now, is concession time. How many people are familiar with "à outrance"? It is, no question about it, an out-of-town word, though Pegler certainly ran into it when he was out of town covering the war in France in 1918, where the Germans faced the French, British, and Americans, fighting their trench warfare à outrance. But the French word is given in Webster, an English dictionary. First, the inquirer gets plain "outrance," in English ("the last extremity"), and then is invited to look at "à outrance," a separate entry, that gives: "to the death, unsparingly." The *OED* also lists it in French, and cites uses of it by Tobias Smollet and Walter Scott. . . .

But why should a syndicated columnist use the word? I can hear Mr. Williams re-asking. Well, not really, just to show off— one doesn't "show off" one's workaday equipment. You see, that word, and a hundred or so others, are a part of my *working* vocabulary, even as a C augmented 11th chord with a raised ninth can be said to be an operative resource of the performing jazz pianist.

Are we now closing in on the question, by using the exclusivist word "performing"?

Yes, in a way we are, I suppose. Because just as the discriminating ear greets gladly the C augmented 11th, when just the right harmonic moment has come for it, so the fastidious eye encounters happily the word that says exactly what the writer wished not only said but conveyed, here defined as a performing writer sensitive to cadence, variety, marksmanship, accent, nuance, and drama.

What of the reader who misses the refinement? Well, what of the listener deaf to the special reach of the C augmented 11th? That reader has the usual choices: he can ignore the word; attempt, from the context, to divine its meaning precisely or roughly (not hard, in the narrative above, on Professor Weiss's liberal politics); or he can look it up. Are these alternatives an imposition? Yes, if the newspaper's columnist that day is giving instructions on how to treat a rattlesnake bite. You would not instruct the reader to fight the poison *à outrance*.

But newspapers, in particular in one-paper cities, tend to acknowledge an obligation beyond merely reporting the news. The very idea of a "feature," whether designed to advise (Ann Landers), amuse (Art Buchwald), satirize (G. R. Trudeau), or opine (the syndicated columnist), presupposes that the performer should use the full range of his relevant skills, even if the percentage of readers who turn to that feature is reduced. Surely there is a corner, in spacy papers that carry five pages on sports, for Addison and Steele? It required a Pulitzer Prize to alert some editors to the very existence of Murray Kempton, the most entertaining analytical belletrist in town, and now we read him, hungrily, in the *Stamford Advocate*. Readers have diverse interests, resources, skills, appetites. The Latin Mass Committee in London petitioned for the resumption of a single mass to be said in Latin after the postconciliar ban of 1965, and was turned down—on the grounds that Latin was only "for the educated few." Evelyn Waugh said it all in a letter to the *Times*: "Surely," he wrote, "in all her charity, Mother Church can make a little room, even for the educated few?"

SEVEN

PLAYING

SEVEN

1

See You Later

JUNE 11, 1985

Five years ago, setting out from Bermuda to the Azores on a sailboat, I advised friends and critics of this space that for the first time I would take two weeks' holiday at one time, instead of the customary one week at Christmas, the second in midsummer. The experience apparently entered my bloodstream because, however unremarked, there were building within me seeds great and strong in effrontery, blossoming one month ago in outright contumacy. What happened one month ago ranks with the day that Oliver Twist held out his porridge plate to the Beadle and asked for "more."

I asked my editor for one month's leave.

It isn't exactly sloth. It is that a month ago I addressed myself to the question of how to transmit my wisdom from where I would be to Kansas City, home of Universal Press Syndicate. I will be on a sailboat wending my way through Micronesia, propelled by the trade winds. I shall be pausing only four times in a five-thousand-mile journey, in exotic atolls where telephones function irregularly. One of these atolls is unfriendly to visiting yachtsmen, allowing them to disembark only if wearing gas masks, because the island in question is one of the places where the arsenal of democracy, as we used to call what now goes by the name of the military-industrial complex, stores its toxic gases, manufactured back at Bitburg time in case the Axis powers decided to use poison gas against American troops. Evidently there are leaks from time to time from those old rusty tanks, so one goes about in gas masks. The prospect of telephoning in my instructions through a gas mask proved the conclusive argument, my spies tell me, in this unusual act of indulgence by my friendly editors, one of whom is said to have remarked, "He's hard enough to understand speaking through plain ether; I wouldn't want to listen to him through a gas mask."

And so it is that this is the final column. Final, that is, for four weeks, after which, if the Pacific is pacific, they will resume. And the Pacific Ocean, from north latitude twenty degrees in Honolulu to south latitude five degrees in New Guinea, tends to dawdle pretty gently during the summer months, and if we have wind of a typhoon we shall show it great respect. I do not believe in accosting natural irruptions under the rubric of mutual assured destruction.

To get out of the way of a storm whose location you have established requires of course that you know where you are. Well, I will have on board two secret instruments, one conceived by me, a second by a conglomerate of geniuses. This last permits the measurement of one millionth of a second, and this translates, or will by the year 1989, into a little box that tells you where you are so exactly that you can double-park by following its instructions. The other is computer software that permits the navigator—which is me, a sometime columnist—to inform the computer where I think I am, within thirty miles, in which direction that star I just shot is, within thirty degrees, what second, minute, hour, and day it is in Greenwich, England, exactly how high up from the horizon it was—and lo! the heavens vouchsafe you the star's identity. The computer will say, "By Jove, that was Arcturus!" And you will know where you are.

Our preoccupations during this period will be with the nitty-gritty. Heat, for instance. We shall be hovering over the Equator, propelled by winds that come astern, as we travel at seven or eight knots. If the wind behind you is sixteen miles per hour and you are moving forward eight miles per hour, the net impact of the wind on your back is a mere eight miles per hour. I have never measured the velocity of the wind from a house fan perched at the corner of your desk, as it used to be before God gave us air conditioning, but I would guess the wind comes out at twenty or thirty miles per hour, which is why the skin stays tolerably cool. It will be otherwise when the sun is more or less directly above you, the temperature is hour after hour in the high eighties, and your ocean fan dribbles out only one quarter of the air you get from an electric fan. As though the motor had a speed marked Extra Special Slow. In such moments, sailors dream less of wine, women, and song than of Frigidaire.

Do such concerns get wished away, under the category of Problems of the Idle Rich? Well, the case can be made: Nobody is forcing me to sail from the United States to the East Indies. But it is the human way to exert oneself every now and again in eccentric enterprises. Last week I listened to a classmate describe his ascent of Everest and wondered how it is that anyone should engage in such madcappery; but then Dick Bass was taking risks I do not contemplate in my irenic passage with my son, and my friends, and books, and music, across the great Pacific Ocean.

2

Playing a Duet with Isaac Stern

JANUARY 15, 1985

Book writers are, to a certain extent, troupers. The way the publishers put it to us—only much more tactfully—boils down to this: "Look, Hemingway old shoe, you can't expect us to plunk out ten grand in advertising your next book if you even refuse to appear, at no cost at all, on the David Letterman show, eh?" The publishers have a point. But if you appear on the David Letterman show—or, for that matter, the comparatively staid *Today* show—you may find yourself put on the spot, the spot here defined as doing something other than merely explaining what public policies we need to pursue in order to have peace, plenty, and universal health, these being the subjects of my books.

So there I was on the *Today* show a couple of weeks ago, facing two hours with five intimidatingly talented people, with Gene Shalit acting as impresario.

Now, Gene Shalit combines those human qualities—wit, exuberance, gentility, hangdoggism—that make it quite impossible to deny him anything he asks for. So that when, ten minutes before we went on, Shalit said, "Bill, do I have to get down on my knees to ask you a special favor, or will you let me, as a gentleman, ask you that favor standing up?" I said, OK, Gene, godammit. What do you want?

"Well," he said, "I was talking with Isaac Stern last night. I had to talk to him—to get him to bring in his violin this morning. We both decided I shouldn't call you on the telephone, because you would say no. But it's harder for you to say no now, right?"

It came to me as on a midnight clear.

The design was for me to play the piano while Isaac Stern played the violin.

Now, my piano playing is on the style of Harry Truman's, except my impression is that he could play by ear, while I can't. Isaac Stern! Maybe the premier living violinist!

I told Gene all I could manage by heart was "Twinkle, Twinkle, Little Star," the fancy version of which, written by Mozart, is called "Variations on *Ah! Vous Dirais-Je Maman!*"

Perfect! Gene Shalit's face looked like a full moon of rapture. Absolutely perfect!

And so, for a couple of hours, I am sitting there opposite Abe Rosenthal, the editorial boss of *The New York Times,* who knows things even Erasmus didn't know. And on my right is beautiful Liv Ullman, who is very worried about hunger, not in Ethiopia but in America. Opposite is Betty Allen, the gorgeous retired black operatic soprano, now head of the Harlem School of the Arts. Next to her is Isaac Stern, who is also a brilliant and articulate man, with maybe just a touch of fuzz in his politics; and opposite him is Stephen Jay Gould of Harvard, the greatest paleontologist since Charles Darwin.

We are having moderate good cheer together talking about this and that between the commercials when the dread moment comes, and Gene Shalit beams and says, "I have a wonderful New Year's Day surprise for you. We are going to hear a duet with Bill Buckley and Isaac Stern." Now, I'm a guy who once showed a couple of my paintings to Marc Chagall—I don't mind that kind of thing, so long as the auspices are clear: this is hiding-inside-the-birthday-cake stuff.

So off I went, manfully, to the piano. Mind you, the TV cameras are rolling. And then suddenly the great Stern says:

"I don't want to play 'Twinkle, Twinkle, Little Star.' I want to play 'Auld Lang Syne.' "

But I can't play by ear, I say.

Aw, come on, says Isaac Stern. Everybody can play "Auld Lang Syne."

And off we go. But the chords I played must have intensified New Year's Day hangovers from coast to coast.

After it was over, the great Stern looked at me and said, "Well, Bill, you must make a New Year's pledge to practice the piano."

I mumbled something about how my piano was a perfect accompaniment to his politics.

And we all beamed, and dispersed, and went back to our solitary study of where, exactly, the line is drawn between good sportsmanship and making an arse of oneself.

Still, I have a feeling if next time around Gene Shalit asked me, would I please go up on a space launch for him, I probably would do just that, and listen up there in space to Isaac Stern on my Walkman, and think how lonely I was without my musical partner.

3

An Attempt at Explaining . . .

OCTOBER 1, 1989—*The New York Times*

*W*illiam F. Buckley, Jr., the editor, author, and amateur harpsichord player, will perform with the Phoenix Symphony Orchestra later this month. As the date of his guest appearance approached, he agreed to submit to an interview, by himself, on how he prepared for his orchestral debut.

BUCKLEY: What made you decide to play a concerto with the Phoenix Symphony Orchestra?

BUCKLEY: That's easy—I was invited. The interesting question is, what made the Phoenix Symphony Orchestra decide to invite me?

Q. Well, do you have the answer to that?

A. After my first few months of shock, little hints drifted in on the disorderly beach of my correspondence. Yes, I now know how the idea began. In one of my autobiographical books, I apparently made some reference to the singular pleasures it must give a musician to be able to play, night after night, masterpieces written by great composers, by contrast with the fate of the contemporary public speaker who needs to be satisfied with reiterations of his own invention. But that blissful alternative, I commented, is available only to the artist, which is what I hoped to be up until about the age of fifteen when I was precocious enough to recognize that I didn't have the talent to become one.

Q. But you decided at age sixty-three that you had enough talent, after all, to play with a symphony orchestra?

A. Well put. But we need to make distinctions. If the letter I received from the managing director of the Phoenix Symphony in

September 1988 had invited me to take up a career as a performing keyboard artist, I'd have replied without any difficulty.

But he didn't do that. His challenge was excruciatingly finite.
What he said, and the words are engraved in my memory, was,
"Would you play any Bach concerto any time in 1989 or 1990 with
the Phoenix Symphony?"

That was not an invitation for me to take on a profession at
which I knew I would be a failure. It was a challenge which, tran-
scribed into the language in which I read it, said: "Do you think
you could manage to cultivate the technique and the savoir-faire
to play any one Bach concerto with a professional orchestra on a
public occasion if we give you two entire years in which to practice?"

That was a different invitation.

Q. What was your immediate reaction?

A. At first I thought, no, it is quite simply impossible. My
fingers have been rusty for generations, the butterfly-in-the-
stomach problem is not one I could predictably overcome, and
anyway, the endeavor would consume entirely too much time. I
wake up and, roughly speaking, work until I go to bed—there is
never any time just "left over," let alone the kind of time it takes
to attack the keyboard at a professional level.

Q. So then what did you do?

A. I called Fernando Valenti. You don't hear his name as a
recitalist so often nowadays, as he has retired from the professional circuit owing to health problems. But I first heard him play
when he was a senior at Yale University, only a few years before
Time magazine made a casual reference to him as the "best living
harpsichordist." Years later we became very good friends, so I
called and told him about this crazy offer. I had the advantage of
talking to someone who knows, a) that I revere music, and, b) that
I am lucky if I get through chopsticks without playing a wrong
note.

Q. What did he say?

A. Well, he said it was a very "interesting challenge"—nobody
was going to say anything different from that, by the way, right up
to the present moment. So then I asked him which was the briefest
concerto Bach ever wrote, and he said, "The F Minor takes only
eight and one-half minutes."

Eight and one-half minutes! I was being given, potentially, twenty-eight months to discipline my fingers to play eight and one-half minutes, which comes down to about three and a half months per minute, or about one week per note. Figuring it out that way, I could perform the "Flight of the Bumblebee" in a couple of years!

Q. What was Mr. Valenti's reaction?

A. He said: Why don't you try working on it for a month or two and see if anything happens? Well, that is exactly what I did, only first I called Rosalyn Tureck, who is also a very close friend. She knows by heart everything Bach ever wrote for the keyboard and is as incomparable at Bach as Valenti is at Scarlatti. And I said: What do you think about the F Minor Concerto? And she said, "Well, everybody knows the famous Largo, the slow movement from the concerto. But my advice to anyone who sets out to conquer it is: Start with the third movement. Then go to the first movement. If you can manage those, you can manage the second movement.

Q. Did you follow her advice?

A. No, actually, I lined up my teacher. Rick Tripodi is an organ virtuoso at a local church whom I had come to know and who is a very gifted musician. Together we listened to a recording by Trevor Pinnock, and I decided the first movement was as difficult as the third. So . . . we set out. My idea was to give the experiment a two months' trial, practicing one-half hour a day, and taking a one-hour lesson every week. Getting to hit the right notes was sheer hell.

Q. But obviously, you didn't give up?

A. No. But I came close to doing so. After working on the first movement for about three months a friend told me about a musician who lived in the neighborhood with whom my friend was studying. "The wonderful thing about Mrs. Radcliffe," she said to me, "is that every five or six lessons, she just stops me and re-teaches me how to practice. She's great on teaching you how to practice."

Mrs. Radcliffe was genial and quite stern and told me to play the first movement no faster than speed 90 on the metronome until New Year's Day—that was six weeks off. I had been playing it at about speed 110.

I persuaded her to give me a second lesson during which I

played the first few bars of the third movement. She listened patiently. And then she said, "Have you made a commitment to the Phoenix people?" And I said: Well, I had a telephone conversation just a week ago with the managing director and I told him I was practicing every day and I had a premonition that I would be accepting his challenge.

I told her rather excitedly that I had asked him one specific question: How late in the day could I actually pull out? His answer was: "Ninety days." They would not schedule the concert until ninety days before. If I said yes at that time, I would need to go ahead with it. So, I said exuberantly, I've decided I can't possibly devote two years of my time to learning the F Minor concerto so I am going to perform it in mid-October, thirteen months after attacking it, which means that I have until mid-August to say yes or no definitively to Phoenix.

That was in January.

"You may as well say no now," said Mrs. Radcliffe.

"Oh?" I asked, probingly.

"You will never be able to play the F Minor Concerto. Not ever. Not unless you stop everything and practice three hours minimum per day, for two years."

That was a very sobering statement, and I recounted it not only to my first teacher, Rick Tripodi, but to my second teacher, Barbara Cadranel (Mrs. Fernando Valenti No. 2), herself a harpsichord recitalist, who had undertaken to coach me an additional one hour per week. She was indignant at this sign of negative fatalism and flatly contradicted it. The following day I had a telephone call from Fernando Valenti in his sickbed—he too was passionately aroused by the categorical pessimism of Mrs. Radcliffe. I felt suddenly as though I were listening to Knute Rockne during the half of a Notre Dame football game, when Slippery Rock U. was leading 50 to 0.

Q. So what did you do?

A. I persevered. I resolved that a day would not pass without my giving the concerto at least the half hour. Now this, for a peripatetic Modern Man, was a considerable commitment. I had to buy, of course, a Yamaha traveling five-octave keyboard instrument, which is designed for rock bands but which will give your fingers the requisite daily workout. Let me see. In the months ahead, I played bits and pieces of the F Minor Concerto in Antigua, St. Lucia, Martinique, Bequia, Switzerland, England, Mexico, Greece, Turkey, California, Hawaii, Tahiti, New Zealand, Australia, Sri Lanka, Kenya, South Africa, aboard my little sloop en route to Bermuda, and on a ketch touring Corsica and Sardinia. As I say, not a day went by . . .

Q. Had you at that time decided whether to perform on the piano or the harpsichord?

A. I was amused early on, struggling through the first movement in front of my original piano teacher, Marjorie Otis Gifford, age eighty-five, whom I adore above all living people. She suggested I play it on the harpsichord. When next I played it for my harpsichord teacher, she suggested perhaps I ought to play it on the piano. Amusing. But I came early on to the decision to do it on the harpsichord, for two reasons. The first that Bach wrote it for the harpsichord, which is also the instrument I love beyond all others; the second that my fingers, which are structurally weak, can handle the muscular requirements of the harpsichord with less strain—the harpsichord key depressed more easily than most piano keys. The disadvantages, on the other hand, are manifest.

Q. What are they?

A. There simply isn't any doubt that there is less room for dynamic interpretation when playing the harpsichord with a chamber orchestra than when playing the piano. You cannot control the volume, and your articulation of the notes is less easily discerned. You are entirely at the mercy of tiny gradations in timing which the listener needs to struggle to detect when there are other instruments playing.

I discussed the whole question with Trevor Pinnock, who is a great performer and scholar. He had recently played the F Minor in Berlin and had recorded it. He dismayed me by referring to it as "a treacherous body of music." Which it is, by the way: your fingers never get any time off, and if your fingering goes askew, it can only be compared to your parachute failing to open.

Q. What is in it for Phoenix?

A. I have pondered that. There are two extreme possibilities, from either of which Phoenix would profit. Suppose I go out there and freeze. Or, perhaps, hit a few notes and then dismember the

rest. Just turn in an absolutely memorable, god-awful performance.

Now that wouldn't be all bad for Phoenix, frankly. People
would remember it, and write about it: "Were you there when the
Phoenix Symphony Orchestra gave Buckley that chance-in-a-life-
time and he fell on his right-wing arse? It was speck-*tac*ular!" You
don't really get mad at Barnum and Bailey when one of its trapeze
artists misses and goes down, down, down to . . . Exactly.

Now the other possibility—I'd say the first possibility is infinitely more likely than the second—is that the local critic will say
that last night was definite proof that all those years spent by Mr.
Buckley writing and speaking were wasted, given what he might
have given the world as a harpsichordist.

Now even if I perform creditably, no critic is likely to say this
who knows what I have been through, because it would take me
longer than I expect to live to be able to perform Bach's other half
dozen concertos, at the rate at which I learn, let alone the whole
of the harpsichord literature.

In between the two extremes, if I hit most of the right notes
and prove that I understand what Bach was trying to do, people
will say: That was a nice little stunt Phoenix pulled off. They ran
risks, granted; but they weren't embarrassed. And it was fun finding out that a lapsed amateur can, if he is willing to spend lots and
lots of time on the problem, manage to draw on a lifetime of
devotion to a composer and play creditably for eight and one-half
minutes one of his beautiful concertos. Besides, think of all the
books and articles and speeches Buckley might have done in the
hundreds of hours otherwise devoted to solitary practice! We may
have been spared the equivalent of another six months of Reaganomics.

Who knows?—The Phoenix Caper might become an annual
event. If anybody wants to start a scholarship that would make it
possible for John Kenneth Galbraith to devote all his spare time
to mastering the Minuet in G, why I will contribute to that fund,
and maybe even organize a picket line around his house in Cambridge to guard against any distraction. You know, don't you, that
he has pledged never to cross a picket line?

4

The Indenture of the Dog Lovers

SEPTEMBER 1, 1985—*Family Weekly*

My father bred English setters, and there were around the house, at any typical moment, five or six, half of them kept at the farm where we used them in pheasant hunting, two or three around the house and, when I was twelve, one of these became my own, my first doggie. He was a tall, handsome black-and-white freckled beauty, whose pedigreed papers called him Sultan something or other followed by his patronymic, which I have long since forgotten, though I have not forgotten the pride I took in knowing that he had been bred of champions. At first I attempted with some formality to call him by his name, Sultan, but soon gave up, and for some reason found myself calling him Ducky.

In respect of my liking for dogs, as in other respects, I tended to be taken by enthusiasms. I shared, in those days, a bedroom with my youngest brother, from one window of which a porch began that led along the length of the huge colonial house to a staircase descending to the grounds below. I persuaded the caretaker to substitute for the fixed screen that shielded my brother and me from the mosquitoes and fireflies of New England summers a screen dislodgeable by the merest exertion of a dog's nose. The screen, the dog having passed through it, would return to perform its conventional function through gravity. Ducky could now vault the radiator along the window stool and, knocking the screen out of his way, land on the porch whenever inclined, during the night, to leave my bedside or, more commonly, my bed. When he returned, he would bound up on my bed, and elect to sleep always with his head either over my rump or over my neck.

Oh how we loved each other, Ducky and I. I had nine brothers and sisters, and my oldest sister, who was sixteen and far gone in cultivated sarcasm, noting the guileful habits of Ducky, who knew instinctively how to endear himself to those who could do him favors—take him hunting, give him food, or simply sit and stroke him—decided one day to refer to him as "Unducky." Some of my brothers and sisters thought this extremely funny. I did not. I managed to rise above it, however, and if anyone, in the course of the day, would say to me, "Bill, where's Unducky?" I would simply continue doing what I was doing, as though I had not heard the effrontery directed at my affectionate, noble doggie, who died one cold night, many years later, when I was a freshman at college.

My first experience with True Grief came when an older sister's cocker spaniel, who was called Peter, was killed by an oil delivery truck one summer afternoon. We rushed him to the vet's, but he was DOA. The caterwauling in the household was not surpassed in any Spanish nunnery on Good Friday. It was years later that I heard the awful story, apparently a commonplace in German folklore, which communicates the seriousness of a child's engrossment with his dog. Skipping home late in the afternoon from school, the story has it, seven-year-old Gretel asks her mother, "Where is Dada?" Her mother has spent the entire afternoon bracing herself for this encounter, because the awful truth of the matter is that Dada was tragically run over shortly after the little girl went off to school. Her mother, consulting friends and professionals, had decided to tell her daughter the plain truth, and take the consequences. Accordingly, she replied, in sober tones, "Darling, I must tell you something: Dada has been killed." The little girl looked up, wrinkled her nose, and then said, "Where are my cookies and milk?" Vastly relieved at her daughter's stoicism, the mother bounded to the kitchen to give her daughter her snack, after which Gretel said, "Mummy, where is Dada?"

"I told you dear, Dada had an accident and was killed."

There followed a lachrymose pandemonium which the mother could not arrest. Finally she blurted out, "Darling, I told you when you came home from school that Dada had been killed."

Little girl: "I thought you said *Papa* had been killed."

I am not saying it was so when our cocker spaniel Peter was killed, that we'd have gratefully exchanged the news that our beloved Father had been run over. But I intend to suggest the intensity of a child's grief, when something happens to the doggie.

My wife also grew up with dogs, and I don't think there was ever a moment when, during our married life, we were without a dog. The highlight of our doggie life together was being introduced to a dog, a dog so special that he and his "heirs," as I delicately call them (in fact, Rowley disdained female company), have brightened our lives consistently for fifteen years now.

The breed is called Cavalier King Charles Spaniel, and thereby hangs a tale.

Rowley came to us in Switzerland. He arrived in a lady's purse: the British gentlewoman, who had bred her own bitch, brought her little puppy as a house present, and it was love at first sight. He was ten weeks old, and when he was twelve weeks old I flew him back to New York, receiving permission from Swissair to keep him on my lap during the flight. There was something about Rowley that absolutely never failed, at least not during the first two or three years of his lifetime. It was that he was irresistible, and all rules pertaining to dogs and their governance were simply waived when otherwise inflexible executors of the law came face to face with—Rowley.

It happened that the Swissair flight landed at Shannon on that trip, and I decided Rowley needed to be taken off the plane to give him an opportunity to relieve himself. But I was no sooner down the gangplank than four men zoomed up in a jeep with a machine gun mounted on it. I had committed a most awful transgression. Because Ireland, you see, is like England in only one respect: It has the same rules against dogs landing on native territory without first putting in six months in Coventry in order to discover whether the dog is rabid. When the four Sumo wrestlers skidded to a stop telling me brusquely to take the dog back up into the airplane I said to them, How could they treat a little dog in this way? They looked down at little Rowley, and—of course—it worked. They permitted me to mount the jeep, Rowley in my arms, and were driven to a compound. That was the compound where, apparently, immigrating dogs were segregated, before going off to the hygienic dungeons where they sit, forlorn, for six months, before being designated as safe to mingle with the pacific breed of human beings who govern Ireland.

Anyway, there we were, and the leader of the detachment, his eyes furtively looking down at Rowley, waiting for him to do his business, made talk with me. I tried to keep the conversational fires burning, and we talked about politics, communism, the pope, and eternal salvation. All Rowley would do was bound about and look endearing. Finally the crisis came: The plane was about to leave. With some embarrassment, I having pleaded the distress of Rowley to the Irish paramilitary, I said we would obviously need to return to the aircraft, never mind that Rowley's little bladder, or come to think of it, immense bladder, was unrelieved. By the time we had got back to the airplane, each of the officials insisted on having a personal valedictory with Rowley, which affectionate embraces Rowley affectionately returned.

Rowley went everywhere with me, but as the years went by I had to acknowledge that there was just that slight estrangement that men with such keen perception as mine are bound to notice. He loved Someone Else more than he loved me. He loved Jerry Garvey, who drives for us, better. The seduction of Rowley began when first he rode in the car with Jerry. Sometimes in the front seat, sometimes burrowed in the cavity next to Jerry's legs, sometimes on the magazine shelf behind the back seat, from which he would peer out the back window or, occasionally, down at us: but most often, longingly, toward the front, where Jerry dwelled. But every year, for thirteen years, he was with us in Switzerland, without Jerry, and there his enchantment became legendary.

We welcomed a new little Cavalier King Charles, about whom something very odd needs to be confessed. It is this, that for the first eighteen months, he was a lovely and refined dog, much like Rowley, but there grew a coarsening of body and spirit which my wife identified with the spiritual depression that came on when Beepee, as he was (is) called, was succeeded by Blenhie (after "Blenheim"), the breed colored white and brown. Failing to be the center of attention, and unreconciled to the senior citizenship status of Rowley, Beepee became rather bulbous, and his hair turned matty: and when a Spanish friend who always loved him told us that he would love to give Beepee to his freshly widowed mother to console her, we acquiesced, and as I write, Beepee lives a charmed life in Bilbao.

Blenhie inherited the charms of Rowley, but in due course he, too, faced competition. The circumstances of the new acquisition will amuse all couples, the male member of which is regularly accused of extravagance.

I had come upon a gentleman who lived in Greenwich, Connecticut, and was advised that his wife bred Cavalier King Charles Spaniels. I was informed that they had just bred a fresh litter of beautiful Blenheims. Since, living in Greenwich, they were our neighbors (we live in Stamford), I prevailed on my wife to drive over and have a look at the little six-week-old puppies. She agreed, but on the way to Greenwich cautioned me: She reminded me we were under no obligation to buy a dog and certainly did not need yet another dog.

All six were brought out—about the size of a man's shoe—and began curling and playing on the carpet in the living room. At one point the breeders left the room, and my wife looked up at me from the other end of the room on the floor of which the puppies were playing, and raised her hand inquiringly . . . ? She had two fingers raised, and I nodded, and we have been happy ever after, with Sam and Fred.

I have never understood why, when there are beautiful dogs one can acquire, people should go out of their way to acquire non-beautiful dogs. But I know better than to give an example, because nothing arouses owners more than the suggestion that their breed is less than the most desirable in the world. And, of course, it is true that a dog objectively ugly—a cur, a mongrel, a you-name-it —can capture the heart and mind of its owner. I don't know why this shouldn't be true of dogs, come to think of it, since it is certainly true of people: I would rather have spent my days with the Hunchback of Notre Dame, who was very ugly, than with Tallulah Bankhead, who was very beautiful.

But admit it, the Cavaliers are strikingly attractive. And just as one feels the impulse to stroke them, they feel the impulse to be stroked. Sam and Fred can spend hours being fondled, as you read your book or talk to your guest. But then they will exhibit their independence. It disappoints me only that they do not like my study. Rowley used to come to my study once every hour or so, to have an extended love-in, during which we would re-exchange our eternal vows. Sam and Fred will accompany me to my study and then leave, to play elsewhere: or simply to lie, hours and hours on end, in the kitchen, or, preferably—always, if she is there—with Pat. We have constructed those little doggie-doors that give them all but total access to any part of the house, confining them only when they reach a gate outside the pantry compound, where they are barred from frolicking with incoming trucks and revisiting on my household the trauma I experienced as a little boy when first Peter, and then Brownie, went off to their greener pastures.

Oh Ducky, how I loved you! And you, Rowley! and Blenhie! And Sam and Fred! Did you know that in China under Mao Tse-tung, owning a dog was a crime? The idea was as simple as this, that if there were dogs about, there would be less food, because dogs consume food. Laid out thus schematically (do you want starving children, or no dogs?), one recognizes the legitimacy of the reasoning. But any constitution that says that children can't have a Ducky in the house, or oldsters a Rowley, a Sam, or a Fred, is a regime whose constitution is a fraud, a humbug. Do you need to say anything more about the curse of ideology? Ah, if only my doggies knew the battles I have waged on their behalf! If they did, they would hardly scorn my company in my study, where I ex-coriate the evil people who do not tolerate dogs in their kingdom!

5

Down to the Great Ship

OCTOBER 18, 1987—*The New York Times Magazine*

There comes a time when the nature of one's interest in a tragedy becomes historical, to use the word loosely; not human, to use that word loosely. When I was thirteen I was taken to Pompeii, and the guide spoke about the phenomenon and dealt only macrocosmically with the human tragedy. The people who died because Vesuvius belched up its firestorm of molten lava were entirely anonymous "victims," like the victims of Napoleon's march on Russia, the men slaughtered day after festive day in the Roman Colosseum, or the cavalrymen who charged in the Light Brigade.

That doesn't mean any of these events is wrenched forever from the creative attentions of the artist whose design is to reconstruct the human story and therefore to reevoke sympathy: for the suffering at Pompeii, for the artist who declares eternal war against the routinization of death that followed in the wake of Napoleon's retreat, for the writer who strives to capture the majestic nobility of the naked Christian, praying as he is prepared for the lion, for the historian who with mordant scorn portrays the bureaucratically homicidal idiocy of General Cardigan, who ordered his men to charge into suicide.

But the time comes when one's interest is taken by other aspects of the phenomenon. Such times must come, else we'd be drowned—every one of us—by preoccupation with our personal sorrows and by our knowledge of the suffering we know to have been endured in so many historical events. Zero Mostel could not have given us his version of *Fiddler on the Roof* if the audience had been permitted to ponder only the pogroms in Russia, and the ultimate solution they would lead to in Nazi Germany. If I went tomorrow to the mausoleum at Verona, I would probably find myself asking the guide whether there actually existed such a drug as Juliet took, brilliantly to feign death while all that was really happening was a moribund sleep, pending her reanimation by Romeo. I would not, by asking that question, deaden myself to the poetry of one of the great romances in literature.

If you want one item (there are thousands to choose from) that will recall the awful poignancy of the death of the *Titanic,* I offer you this. A day before the *Carpathia* reached New York, on April 18, 1912, with the 705 survivors it had picked up from the lifeboats a few hours after the *Titanic* had gone down, the *Mackay–Bennett,* a cable ship, set out from Halifax in search of corpses: men and women and children floating on the Atlantic in life preservers dead from exposure (this is how most of the *Titanic*'s victims died). Several hundred were retrieved. Some, because of decomposition, were thereupon buried at sea, but efforts were made to identify them and, when successful, to advise relatives of their fate and to itemize any special effects that had been retrieved with the corpse. Notification went to one couple concerning their young son. This is the text of the letter received back by the authorities in Halifax:

I have been inform by Mr. F Blake Superintendent Engineer of the White Star Line Trafalgar Chambers on the 10th that the Body of my Beloved Son Herbert Jupe which was Electrical Engineer No. 3 on the Ill-Fatted Titanic has been recovered and Burried at Sea by the Cable Steamer "Mackey-Bennett" and that his Silver Watch and Handkerchief marked H.J. is in your Possession. He bought him half a doz of the same when he was at Belfast with the R.M.S. Olympic to have a new blade put to one of her Perpellors we are extremely oblidged for all your Kindness to my Precious Boy. He was not married and was the Love of our Hearts and he loved his Home But God gave and God has taken Him Blessed be the Name of the Lord. He has Left an Aceing Void in our Home which cannot be filled.

Please Send along the Watch and Handkerchief marked H.J.

Yours Truly C. Jupe.
His Mother is 72 Last april 4th.
His Father is 68 Last Feb 9th.

Reading that letter, in the summer of 1912 (if indeed the letter was read other than by the recipients—it is unearthed in Michael Davie's *Titanic: The Death and Life of a Legend,* outstandingly, along with Walter Lord's, the best book afloat on the *Titanic*), one could be expected to feel sheer civic rage against the executioners of Herbert Jupe; and moral historians are ever free to cry out that justice was never really done after the great ship went down.

True, the White Star Line had to pay out $2.5 million, which is a lot more than it sounds, if you close your eyes for perspective: Captain Edward J. Smith of the *Titanic* was the highest-paid seaman in the world, receiving £1,250 per year.

Oh yes, Captain Smith. He paid a stiff price for ignoring four Marconigrams (as they then called wireless messages) warning of circumambient ice. After all, he went down with his ship. But, in fact, that was incomplete consolation to the relatives of the other 1,500 who went down.

Captain Stanley Lord of the nearby *California* chose to ignore eight distress flares on the extraordinary grounds (a judgment he reached from his cabin, half asleep) that the color of the sighted flares probably meant that they had been touched off as a sort of celebratory handshake in midocean, a merchant vessel spotting another from the same line somewhere in the distance. Captain Lord turned over and went back to sleep in his immobilized liner (he had ordered the engines stopped because of ice conditions). Captain Lord, who might have saved 1,500 people from drowning, walked into historical obloquy, though his professional career was unobstructed, and indeed there rose to defend him what appropriately were called "Lordites," who stressed inconsistencies here and there to justify Captain Lord's insouciance.

Who else was punished? Not Harland & Wolff, which had built the largest moving object ever created: the great Belfast shipyard had complied with the nautical specifications of the British Board of Trade, and no one at H&W had ever said the *Titanic* was "unsinkable." That unsinkable business was nothing more than the creeping vainglory of a jingoistic age in which the leading sea power in the world was trying to make a public demonstration of her infinite resources in order to assert her clear dominance over the brash competitor on the other side of the Atlantic, and to impress the Kaiser. It was not advertised that the British champion was financed, and in effect owned by, American bankers.

What about the Board of Trade itself? Why were there lifeboats for only 1,200 people, given that there were 2,227 on board? Well you see, the Board of Trade reasoned that any ship that had watertight bulkheads that could be raised to sequester an accidental inflow of water didn't need the traditional 10 cubic feet of lifeboat space per passenger. The contingency simply hadn't been considered that raising the bulkheads wasn't enough if the bulkheads weren't designed to rise to the ceiling of the topmost deck. As it was, what happened in the *Titanic* was that water under pressure flowed merrily uphill, even as water flows from one cube in a tilted ice tray into the next, and so on.

What was one to do to the Board of Trade?

You could give it a little rhetorical hell, and certainly Senator William Alden Smith and his investigating committee did so. If Senator Smith was a moral slouch, then so was Cotton Mather. He subpoenaed all the surviving officers of the *Titanic* and twenty-nine members of the crew. When he learned that five other crew members, ducking the subpoena, had sailed furtively out of New York aboard the *Lapland,* Smith responded by sending a vessel to bring them back. (Senator Smith simply asked President Taft for a naval ship: request granted; *Lapland* stopped.) The tenacity with which he challenged the behavior of British officers, British architects, and British administrators was undiminished by Senator Smith's ingenuous ignorance of the sea or of shipboard terminology (he did not know that a ship's "bow" was different from a ship's "head"). The investigation so provoked (and titillated) the popular press in Britain that a derisory invitation was issued to the senator to come to London to lecture at the Hippodrome on "any maritime subject."

And, of course, the British had their own investigation, conducted by Lord Mersey. It is fair to generalize that the Mersey board concluded in effect that although the North Atlantic route taken by the *Titanic* on its fateful passage ought not to have been taken, in fact it was the workaday steamer route; that binoculars should have been available to the lookouts, though binoculars are not necessarily aids to spotting objects at a distance; that more lifeboats should have been available, though it was not justified to indict the Board of Trade for failure to foresee that which was unforeseeable; that the behavior of the officers and crew would have been more orderly if clearer instructions had been given, but that under the circumstances they performed well, indeed in some cases heroically.

Leaving the parents of Herbert Jupe with what? Concretely, with £100, the per-seaman settlement from the civil lawsuit concluded in 1916. Civic rage had to satisfy itself by other means, and to that rough end an entire literature sprang up, each book, or article, with a slightly redistributed gravamen. There came, early on, the philosophizing of it all. By conceiving a vessel of such arrant luxury and size, we Lilliputians had stirred the attention of the gods, who stretched out an admonitory finger, casually but sternly to remind us that we are mortals, and ought not to engage in extrahuman conceits.

The Great War came, and gradually the memory of the *Titanic* receded, though always there were the full-time practitioners, however sparse at times they seemed (the first issue of the journal issued by the Titanic Historical Society got only forty-five subscribers). But the legend was rekindled by Walter Lord's stirring *A Night to Remember,* and by the movies and the television reenactments of that night to remember. The Philadelphia Maritime Museum became the formal showcase of Titaniana.

And then, in 1985, the great bell rang. First, a French research vessel, and then the little, pilotless submariner *Argo,* under the direction of the naval exploratory vessel *Knorr* from Woods Hole, Massachusetts, were "mowing the lawn" over an area 150 square miles in the neighborhood of where it was calculated the ship had actually gone down. The anxious operation was conducted under the direction of a French and an American scientist. The process had been going on tediously, day and night, ever since July 11. In mid-August, the fancy little sub, with its congeries of surrealistic technological devices designed to sound and permit to be seen objects on the ocean floor, began its slow sweep. At 1:40 A.M. on September 1, the excited French scientist found himself staring at a ship's boiler. The *Titanic* had been found.

. . .

Two years later, at eleven in the morning on the identical site, 963 miles northeast of New York City, 453 miles south of Newfoundland, after being asked one final time whether I suffered from claustrophobia, I was directed to the shoulder-wide opening of the little submarine, leading to vertical iron railing steps descending into the tubular control center of the *Nautile.*

It is the $20 million diadem of IFERMER, a scientific offshoot of the French Government—an underwater exploratory vessel built with titanium, six feet in diameter at its widest point and weighing only eighteen tons. It can descend to depths of 20,000 feet. The chief pilot occupies the berth on the port side. Behind him, sitting on an abbreviated chair, is the copilot. The starboard berth is for the "observer," in this case me. Each of us has a porthole built of one-foot-thick plastic. The copilot, in addition, has two sets of eight-inch television screens. The first set looks ahead via remote video, one camera video trained to look dead ahead, the other to pivot. The second set of videos portrays at close range and at longer range the exact operation of the mechanical arms operating from the side of the *Nautile,* designed to pick up objects from the sea bed. With aid of the video, the operator can exactly instruct the arms.

The overhead hatch is now tightly sealed and as you look about you, you close your eyes slowly, hoping this will not be the moment you contract claustrophobia. Once lifted and positioned by crane and halyard, the *Nautile* is dragged by cable to the launching end of the *Nadir,* the mother ship, dropped into the ocean, and towed by the *Nadir* and by frogmen on a rubber Zodiac a short distance through the water. The descent begins.

At about 2:20 A.M., losing finally its fight to stay afloat, two hours and forty minutes after it glanced the iceberg, the *Titanic's* stern rose up so high that the huge ship was almost vertical over the water. It paused there, appeared, in the description of some witnesses in their lifeboats, to shudder, and then eased back to an angle of about 45 degrees, as if cocking itself to spring ahead on its long descent. Seconds later it catapulted into its plunge, with its live company of some 1,500 people, including the eight-piece band, which had been performing for the condemned right up until it was no longer possible to stand up. Like everyone else, they were wearing life preservers. It is calculated that it took the

Titanic approximately ten minutes to reach bottom and that it was traveling, when it hit the ocean floor, at a speed of twenty miles per hour.

To descend the same distance, two and a half miles to the ocean floor, the *Nautile* takes ninety minutes, which means a descent at just less than 1.66 miles per hour. You try to sit up, which requires you to raise your knees six inches or so—there is no room to stretch them out. You have been advised not to eat breakfast, and dutifully you have not.

It is 11:30 A.M., thirty minutes after our descent began, lunch time aboard the *Nautile*. The copilot, Pierre Yves, brings out the two little packages wrapped in aluminum foil. The first course is a hard-boiled egg. Do I wish any salt? *"S'il vous plait, oui."* Then there is cold roast beef and French bread. Followed by cheese and a plum or a peach.

"Do you have anything to drink?" I ask abstractly. Answer: yes; they have water. But it is not thereupon proffered, though you are left believing that a direct request would produce the plastic bottle. It isn't any lack of French hospitality, it is just that it would be such an awful *dérangement* if the observer along the way experienced an undeniable call of nature. Just the physical gyrations necessary to accomplish this bring to mind a Marx Brothers three-in-a-bed sequence. You pass.

What to do, as the pilot and copilot exchange rapid, technical French? I had arrived on the *Nautile* with two bulging plastic bags, causing the chief pilot, Georges, to frown and ask, Did I really need all that—*equipage*? Embarrassed, I had pulled out the larger of my three flashlights, and three of my six cassette tapes. But that did leave me with 1) two small flashlights; 2) a book (a thriller to distract me, during the long descent and the long ascent); 3) a little dictating machine (I might want to make notes, and there is hardly room for even the smallest laptop), which dictating machine serves also as a Walkman, for which, 4) I was left with three cassettes. The second parcel carried 5) a thick white sweater to augment protection from the 38-degree cold at ocean-floor level already provided by long winter underwear, regular sweater, and the fire-resistant coveralls provided by the French; 6) a little can of Right Guard, in case the chill exercised less than all its usual functions; and then 7) a set of kneepads furnished by Ralph

White, my new best friend, an American professional jack-of-all-trades, a genial member of the entrepreneur's team who knew more about diving, history, mechanics, ships, airplanes, and the sea than anyone I had ever met.

Why kneepads, for heaven's sake? You will see, Ralph said; and indeed I would see. When you are lying with your nose against the porthole you need to put your left knee somewhere, since there is no room to stretch out. So it ends up on the narrow knurled ice-cold titanium bottom strip between you and Georges. Try then bringing up your knee when it is protected only by underwear, pants, and fire suit for a half hour against the cold grid; and then give thanks to the Lord for Ralph. The kneepads plus gloves for hands that would become cold and, 8) perhaps most important, an inflatable rubber pillow, this to lay over the little metal bar that runs either under your chest while you are lying down, or else under your back when reclining during the vertical passages. There are moments when you wonder whether an extra million dollars might not have been dredged up to cushion that bisecting rod.

But the great moment is coming. We will reach bottom at 3,784 meters, and Georges will turn on the outside beams when we reach 3,550 meters. We are in place, standing guard by our portholes. The lights flash on. Nothing to see, though the water is startlingly clear, diaphanous to the extent of our light's beam, an apparent 25 to 30 feet ahead, never mind that it is pitch dark out there.

Then, gradually, it happens: We descend slowly to what looks like a yellow-white sandy beach, sprinkled with black rocklike objects. These, it transpires, are pieces of coal. There must be 100,000 of them in the area we survey, between the bow of the ship and the stern, a half mile back. On my left is a man's outdoor shoe. Left shoe. Made, I would say, of suede of some sort. I cannot quite tell whether it is laced up. And then, just off to the right a few feet, a snow-white teacup. Just sitting there, thank you, on the sand. I liken the sheer neatness of the tableau to a display that might have been prepared for a painting by Salvador Dalí. Will we, I ask Georges anxiously, pause to scoop up the shoe?

No. The expedition does not pick up articles of personal clothing.

What about the teacup?

Only if it is embroidered in blue. The distinction, I learn, is that the blue-bordered china is rarer than the plain white, which was used by the 712 steerage passengers. The 337 First Class passengers had the fancier, blue-bordered china. Enough of the former has been picked up in the twenty-six previous dives. Time is limited, and we will not use it up on redundancies.

On and on we float, our bottom resting sometimes six inches from the ocean floor, sometimes a meter or two. We are looking for targets of opportunity, which is why I am expected to keep looking hard to starboard, but also specifically for a piece of the command mechanism from the bridge (the signal handles brought back sharply by First Officer William Murdoch when he reversed engines, moments after the iceberg was sighted dead ahead). The control mechanism has been photographed lying on the ocean floor in the area we are now covering, and instructions are being radioed from above ("130 degrees, proceed for 60 meters") to direct us to our quarries. And then a portion of a leaded window, missing from a reconstruction of an ornamental vitrine window that had been a part of the luxuriant decorations in First Class. And a man's leather satchel, contents unknown.

We were below, searching and scooping, for six and one-half cold hours. Ralph said I would find it surprising how quickly the time passed. That was not exactly what I felt after two or three hours. But the sensation, in microcosm, was vivid, exhilarating, and uncomplicated by any philosophical misgivings about our mission. I did not feel any kinship to the voyeur; no more than when, a year earlier, I ogled the tombs in the Nile or, a dozen years ago, the catacombs in Lima beneath the great cathedral where the bones of thousands of Incas lie.

I was a passive part of an archaeological venture that was also an adventure—only about 150 men and women in the world have dived as deep in the water as I have now done. The excavation is singular because it is being conducted in a part of the planet heretofore thought totally inaccessible, let alone accessible to people who have in mind actually collecting an inventory of items that, for seventy-five years, have lain on the ocean floor, objects last seen by men and women two thirds of whom died a quite awful death, victims of the hubris of an assortment of thoughtless naval architects, cocky seamen, and mindless money men.

Finally the moment came to terminate our sortie, to begin our slow ascent. After a few minutes, permission was requested over the radio (permission granted) to jettison one of our two lead weight ballasts, permitting a sharp increase in our rate of ascent.

I tried to sit up, just to find something different to do with my bones. But I had to lean just slightly forward. Otherwise, I might lean just slightly back, in which case I might brush up against one of those hundred toggle switches behind me and, who knows, flip the one that would toss me out between the shoe and the teacup— the pressure out there was 6,000 pounds per square inch.

Time to use the Walkman? But to recover the satchel, dig out the relevant parts, and wire in my ears represented a series of exertions on the order of stopping to change one's socks while climbing to the top of Mount Everest.

So I half-froze, half-continued trying to read my stubbornly unprepossessing thriller with my flashlight between my teeth, my hands behind me supporting my arched back, and exchanged every now and then a drollery, in my kitchen French, with the pilots.

I looked for the one-hundredth time at the fast-changing depth meter. This time it joyfully told me that we had just about reached the surface. I knew we were within 50 meters when the little sub began to roll, reflecting surface turbulence. It seemed an age before the frogmen were there to secure us to the halyard coming down from the ship's crane. But eventually we were airborne into the mother ship's womb. The hatch was turned and I climbed out, a Superman grin on my face, I have to admit.

What began all this for me was that day in August when I saw that Senator Lowell P. Weicker of Connecticut had introduced a bill that would prohibit the import of any artifacts from the *Titanic* for commercial gain in the United States. To do any such thing, the senator inveighed, was to profane what ought to be an international maritime monument. Etc., etc. I dug out the Congressional Record thinking that maybe I'd find there a rationale for this legislation, and there I saw that Weicker, who is my senator, had said that "it is only a matter of time before the world is going to have to turn to these oceans for food and fuel."

So? Isn't that a reason for encouraging the ocean's exploration?

And, "When the Earth does turn to the oceans for its food and its fuel, do not forget it has to be a resource that lasts millions of years rather than just a decade or two to satisfy our most immediate desires." Which served only to remind me that my most immediate desire is another senator.

I ruminated, and wrote a column making two points, the first of them that you hardly consecrate the artifacts that went down on the *Titanic* by leaving them on the ocean floor. The second is a libertarian point. I do not understand where Congress got the idea that it has any business telling an adult American what he can and what he cannot purchase from a willing seller, if you're not talking drugs or machine guns. I mean, who told Congress it could come between me and the *Titanic,* which lies in international waters and is no one's property?

A couple of days later, a phone call—an invitation, of all things, to join the expedition and to dive down to the *Titanic.*

Well, why not?

I would do a little exploring of my own. We flew to St. Pierre, the little French island off Newfoundland where the *Abeille Supporter,* the French support ship on which I would spend the next ten nights, lay waiting to take us the thirty-six-hour ride out to the site where the diving was going on. We were a varied group, the central two members being John Joslyn of Los Angeles and Robert Chappaz of Paris. They brought with them a half-dozen friends, relatives, and investors (in some cases all three at the same time).

During the long and very stormy ride out to the site, I spent a little time trying to taxonomize this here operation, which for convenience I call Titanic-87. I swear, you would need Woodward, Bernstein, and *Deep Throat* to figure it out. This much I can report authoritatively, that involved in Titanic-87 are 1) the French Government (it directly subsidized the development of the *Nautile,* and indirectly subsidizes its rental); 2) the American Government (it pays most of the bills at Woods Hole and owns the exploratory vessel *Knorr,* the command vessel at the time the *Titanic* was discovered; 3) a French company which undertook to guarantee to the French Government that all the artifacts retrieved from the *Titanic* would be presented to museums (thus making the Weicker bill supererogatory anyway); 4) a semipublic French company that actually operates the *Nautile* and the *Nadir*; 5) an entirely private French company that operates the *Abeille Supporter*; 6) a California entertainment company (Westgate) that owns rights to the television show that will air October 28 on the doings of Titanic-87, and 7) individual investors whose return, if any, will come from ancillary activities that grow out of Titanic-87 (books, exhibits, T-shirts, for all I know).

The people I associated with during the ten days are, in my judgment, above all adventurers, pioneer types. Jennifer Carter, the amiable, attractive assistant producer, at once an academic dean, a diver, and a solicitous den mother, married to an Oscar-winning musician: she wanted above all to be the first American woman to have dived to that depth; she is. Al Briggs, Atlanta computer software, brother-in-law of George Tulloch, Greenwich BMW distributor and enthusiast, who fondles a theory about what it was that finally pushed the *Titanic* overboard that could revolutionize the *Titanic* story. Larry D'Addario, a young manager of a huge cement plant inherited when his father was killed in an airplane accident last year.

John Joslyn, perhaps uniquely experienced as a producer, had to come up, along with Tulloch's investor group, with the daily bill. Just the rental of the two French ships comes to $50,000 per day, as best I can figure it out, asking discreetly here and there: after all, the two ships require fifty-three people in crew, among them highly experienced scientists.

What is coming from it all? "Don't you understand?" a reader wrote me just before I left. "Senator Weicker and all those people just don't understand archaeology." It was this that set me to contemplating the question, When does the focus change? When do you put down the glasses that see only tales of distress and suffering and pick up the other set, which focuses on science and history, on surviving artifacts—the sort of things that bring us to museums for whatever reason? Because they are beautiful, or because they are unique; or because they are intimately associated with a great historic event.

What happened that night in April was certainly that. No one will deny it. Titanic-87 has been accused of "exploiting" the event. To say that is on the order of saying that Gauguin exploited Tahiti. Or, if you strain at that, that Quaker Oats exploits Iowa. The Titanic-87 people have refreshed a legend, are making possible scientific and historic discoveries, and have among other things consumed ten days of my time, willingly given, abundantly rewarded.

EIGHT

APPRECIATING

1

A Brief Exposure

One learns a lot about one's own culture by slipping on a banana peel every now and then.

Last Friday morning, at a hotel room in Detroit, I awoke in acute distress. Awoke, if that is what you call it, having slept for only twenty minutes, before which time I had been similarly awakened . . . and so on, back through the night, which was supposed to have begun when I turned off the lights at 1 A.M., having finished my homework and taken my routine medication to keep my always freeze-easy respiratory system lubricating away, the better to address the distinguished members of the Michigan State Bar at noon the next day on their fiftieth anniversary.

Meanwhile, I had a very concrete problem. A jab in the center of my chest had abruptly awakened me every twenty minutes over a seven-hour period, resulting in isolated pockets of sleep but zero repose. "What kind of pain, Mr. Buckley?" I was later asked, and had to remind myself that Harold Ross has taught us that "nothing is indescribable" before attempting to establish whether the pain in my chest was one tenth what you'd feel sticking your hand over a burning fire, two tenths the kind of pain you'd feel if somebody clamped a rubber band around your esophagus, three tenths what you feel when what's in your stomach tries to move up, instead of down, one tenth the feel of an icicle bullet fired through you from the resident Bulgarian. . . . It really isn't easy.

But everyone should know what I didn't, which is that when the hotel sends in the paramedics, they decide whether there is any reason to suppose your trouble might trace to the heart, and if the answer is yes, you find yourself on a gurney headed right through Times Square: at least four hundred people would have spotted you slithering out of the hotel into the ambulance. And since one hour and forty-five minutes later you were scheduled to address a press conference in advance of your post-luncheon speech, your nifty idea of sneaking off for a quickie test at the Cardiac Arrest Center in midtown Detroit and tiptoeing back to do your duty becomes a little surrealistic.

There they treat you as if you had had a heart attack—identical motions are indicated. And you learn for the first time (in my case) that doctors cannot rule out for twenty-four hours that what you had was a heart attack. They can, in the course of three or four hours, tell you they *think* it was something else, but scientific discipline forbids them to exclude "heart attack"—which is of course what everybody is quietly concluding.

And it is hard to begin to express one's appreciation as the unidirectional messages of goodwill (you are not allowed to get messages out) flood in. Wife and son materialized, and were permitted to mediate the traffic, requiring a little improvisation when quoting me, since I was at that point near torpor. I remember several messages with especially keen delight, primary among them that from an old friend who relayed that two of his closest associates had died within days of each other and he was even at that moment headed for a service to deliver a eulogy, and if things did not work out for me at the Harper–Grace Hospitals in Detroit, he could with very little work use the same eulogy, though if in my last moments I had any deathbed afterthoughts and joined the Democratic Party, that would make his burden easier. Another friend suggested that this was the proper moment at which to call in an exorcist.

A disruptive personal and public experience: The gentlemen of the bar did not get their speech; my friends (and critics) in the newspaper world did not get their column, though on that gurney they wheeled me out on there was no room for my toilet kit, I sneaked aboard my little Epson computer, hoping to catch breath enough to abort a national solecism before my noon deadline (by that point I was fast asleep).

The whole experience will quickly fade from the memory— such things do—but not the conviction that if you flirt with difficulties of the heart, head for Harper–Grace Hospitals, which are associated with Wayne State University. And if you are very lucky, Joshua Wynne, M.D., chief of the Division of Cardiology, will be there, and if you lie to him that you are pleased that Harvard is doing so well in football, he may give you an eyeshade, which is the only piece of equipment they don't have at that medical emporium of kind people.

What was it I did have? The docs didn't know. I suggested "premature stigmata," but I was not taken seriously.

2

Happy Birthday to Malcolm

AUGUST 24, 1989

Oh my goodness, what moral onanism is going on in connection with Malcolm Forbes's birthday party. Richard Cohen of *The Washington Post* tore into every aspect of the affair, gallantly excluding from criticism only the presence at it of his boss, Mrs. Katharine Graham. *The New York Times*'s editorialist showed some restraint, acknowledging that there have been more lavish parties than Mr. Forbes's ("There may never have been a more opulent party than the one for 450 given in 1971 by the Shah of Iran at Persepolis. Estimated cost: $100 million"), but even so concluded sadly that "the critics advance so many different reasons for their displeasures [as to] suggest they're expressing something deeper than reasons, something unlikely to be responsive to debate."

Yes, unresponsive to debate, though there will be debate. Representative Pete Stark, D-Calif., wishes to examine every aspect of any claim by Forbes Inc. to deduct the costs of the extravaganza. Sociologist Studs Terkel says that his horror over the entire thing is related to the fact that Mr. Forbes needs, in order to step onto his motor yacht, to "step over the bodies of the homeless." Michael Kinsley of *The New Republic* pretends to wonder whether Malcolm Forbes isn't provoking the public in the same way that Marie Antoinette did. And we all know what happened to her, do we not? Yawp.

In the turmoil, a struggle was made to distinguish between three separate questions. The first was: Is it "right" for someone to spend $2 million to celebrate his birthday in so extravagant a way? The second was: Is it in good taste—supposing that you have every right to spend your money that way—to spend it in that way? And the third: Should such an event qualify for a tax deduction?

Those who assailed the "right" of Mr. Forbes to fire off all those expensive Roman candles were not very conspicuous, and this is a credit to the creeping intelligence of a public that, however reluctantly, acknowledges that we have—all of us—the right to be our potty little selves, and if Richard Burton wants to buy the Hope diamond for Liz, there it is; and if a million people want to make pilgrimages to the grave of Elvis Presley, why, let a million people do what they want to do; and if Michael Jackson can make more money in one evening than Wolfgang Amadeus Mozart made in his lifetime, well, whoever said economic democracy and sound aesthetic judgments go hand in hand?

On the matter of taste, it amuses that some of the same people who insist that such modern art as puts crucifixes in bottles of urine must not be judged until artistic consensus settles in are so rapid in judging the social meaning of the Tangiers extravaganza.

Can we be so sure in passing judgment? Disparate challenges crowd the mind. Louis XIV, when he got the bill for his garden at Versailles, tore it up—lest any historian should discover the extraordinary expense of it. By contemporary standards, the poverty level of seventeenth-century France was, oh, 99 percent—but who is criticizing the gardens of Versailles? The nudie-porno *Oh, Calcutta!* stage show ran in New York for twenty years, earning its backers ten times the $2 million spent by Malcolm Forbes; but criticisms of it ran into a First Amendment fusillade inexplicably unrelated to current denunciations of any possibility that Forbes Inc. should be permitted to write off the seventieth birthday party as a deductible expense. It may take a while before the artistic consensus gets around to exalting "Piss Christ."

By contrast, nothing in the history of empirical verification, nothing since the explosion of Vesuvius, came more quickly than the knowledge that the canny seventy-year-old publisher had got, for his $2 million, publicity worth $20 million. If yesterday there was one magazine reader in America unaware of the existence of *Forbes,* Tangiers disposed of that problem.

So that we were left, really, with the question of taste, concerning which there is only this to say, which is that Malcolm Forbes is—Malcolm Forbes. It happens that a) I like him; and b) I admire him. This does not mean that I, any more than the six hundred others who were there, assuming we disposed of equivalent resources, would dispose of them in exactly that way to remark our seventieth birthdays.

But the thing about Malcolm Forbes is that he is the epitome of exuberance. He loves his motorcycles, his magazine, his balloons, his château, his sons, his yachts, his Fabergé collection, his toy soldiers, his country, with an exhibitionistic passion. He cannot bear for anyone not to know the measure of his elation over the trifles and substances that surround him. He wanted, in his Tangiers venture, to explode the biggest firecracker in the history of recent celebrations. That there were mistakes made, over which there is such gloating, is a part of the human experience: Compared to the Grenada invasion, Tangiers was relatively efficient. I was glad to have been there, even though I don't hesitate to acknowledge I was more uncomfortable physically than I have been at any time since I left basic training in the infantry.

Calm observers of the whole scene are left wondering only about the one crack in Malcolm Forbes's armor.

Why didn't he rope the whole thing off and charge the press admission? Would anybody question that he'd have collected, during his forty-eight hours, at least the same income that Mike Tyson gets for less than forty-eight minutes for his exclusively protected prizefighting? Maybe Forbes stockholders should look into this. On the other hand, all Forbes stockholders were there at Tangiers.

3

Theodore White, R.I.P.

MAY 22, 1986

I t is so with very few people who are discreetly hospitalized, but when Theodore H. White was struck down at his desk on Friday afternoon, by Sunday morning it seemed as if half of America knew of it, even though there had been no notice in the press. Friends, friends of friends, and friends of theirs relayed the news, because everyone cared so deeply who had read his books, and especially those who knew him. The sensation was on the order of hearing that fire threatened the library at Byzantium, storehouse of great deposits of national self-knowledge, a source of national pride.

But it was not long after hearing the first news that those made aware of his condition prayed he would not recover. The image of Teddy White sitting up, mute and mindless, was unbearable. Not Henry Mencken all over again! Because the stroke—word had got out—was of just that nature, deep, malevolent, voracious; a brain-eater. In White there was much brain to feed on. He had revolutionized the art of political reporting, the obituarists all agree. And in doing so he broadened the understanding, because his were the eyes of a journalist who could convey the inclinations of a small gathering of Americans who convened to hear a candidate by noting how much effort they put into wiping their own hands clean before accepting the politician's proffered hand. The voters spoke their intimate thoughts to him, his colleagues spoke theirs to him, presidents and presidential candidates sought him out. It was to him that Jackie Kennedy turned after Dallas.

Theodore H. White made one grave strategic mistake in his journalistic lifetime. Like so many disgusted with Chiang Kai-shek, he imputed to the opposition to Chiang thaumaturgical social and political powers. He overrated the revolutionists' ideals, and underrated their capacity for totalitarian sadism. Those who traveled with White to China in 1972, when first he revisited the desolation at the hands of the man for whom he had shown so great an enthusiasm, viewed the bitter confusion he felt. It was as if Mao had committed an act of personal disloyalty, a vice alien to White's nature. He saw in his own country a wildly successful, if aberrant and eccentric march toward general enlightenment; and he had seen in Yenan something that he thought would o'erleap the tenacious traditions of a China immersed in its anachronisms. He wrote *Thunder Out of China* in 1946, and twenty-six years later learned firsthand that the nature of the thunder that had hit China was not exuberant, rather it was convulsive. As was his custom, he integrated his new knowledge into his writing, and all his readers profited from the quality of revised insights.

When in 1965 he had completed the second of his magisterial series on the making of American presidents, this one on the contest between Lyndon Johnson and Barry Goldwater, he dared to say that Goldwater had galvanized dissatisfactions in America that would not be put down by the facile rhetoric and quick-fix social legislation of Lyndon Johnson. By daring to say this about the ideas of a man who had been devastated by a thunderous New Dealer, Theodore White was widely derided. Since then, only one Democratic president has sneaked into office, and two Democratic presidential contenders managed to lose forty-nine states. Teddy White had seen into the future, but his skills in reporting on the future made it very nearly, if never quite, palatable to some of the most disappointed ideologues.

He came to me late one morning in October of 1965. We had never met and he was writing a piece for *Life* magazine on the mayoralty contest in New York City, in which I was engaged as the candidate of the Conservative Party. In my little office he began to ask questions, and to take those copious notes of his, neat save for the cigarette ashes that spilt on them. I was feeling saucy and answered two or three of his questions with a levity not entirely appropriate to sober analytical interrogation. He would suppress a smile, even as his eyes would twinkle.

Finally, he put down his pencil and said: "Look, Mr. Buckley. I am doing business now. We will make friends later."

That was Theodore White's mode, and conjoined with his fine mind, his artist's talent, his prodigious curiosity, there was a transcendent wholesomeness, a genuine affection for the best in humankind. It is quite awful to know we will not see him again alive, altogether consoling for those who believe we will experience him again in a life to come.

4

The Perils of Baptism

APRIL 23, 1985

Toward the end of last week Lew Lehrman called a few friends appropriate to the message he had in mind to give them. He quietly communicated the most solemn decision any man can communicate: specifically, in the case of Lewis Lehrman, that on the following Sunday, at three in the afternoon, at St. Thomas More Church, he would be baptized into a different religious communion from that of his ancestors. Lew Lehrman, who in 1982 came within a few votes of becoming governor of the state of New York, and who campaigned unabashedly as a Jewish conservative, had decided to join the Catholic Church.

It is one thing for the private man to convert to Catholicism, or for that matter to Judaism. Another for the public man—in the case of Lehrman we deal with someone widely accepted as more, merely, than just any other office seeker. He is a magnetic field: brainy, wealthy, resourceful, determined. He has even been spoken of as a presidential candidate down the line.

All this may be dismissed as wild speculation. What can't be dismissed as political opportunism is his decision to become a Christian, indeed, a Catholic. For all the latitudinarianism of Vatican II, a Jew becoming a Catholic is on the order of a Christian becoming an Orthodox Jew.

The noisiest voice in town, following Lehrman's quiet conversion, was that of Jimmy Breslin. Never mind that Lehrman made no public announcement, nor reported his decision to anyone likely to turn his confidence into a news story. Breslin, in the *Daily News,* began a long, ornate account of the development by writing, "Lewis Lehrman, the politician, went out and changed his religion from Jewish to Roman Catholic and then announced it in all the political stories." Lehrman did no such thing, of course. When newspapermen called (dutifully) to check the rumor that he had poped, Lehrman confirmed that he had become a Catholic, and went on to say that such decisions are private, and please would the reporter ask him about the deficit, or about the takeover bid on CBS, or about the Mets?

Breslin went on with several long paragraphs about adolescent sex, the Catholic confessional, Breslin's autobiographical difficulties in growing up according to the Catholic code while all the time a sinner, etc., etc.—and well along the way the reader was reminded of the critic who wrote a few years back that, "Sometimes, on reading Goethe, one has a paralyzing suspicion that he thinks he is being funny." Breslin was as funny as the jokester who yuks about Jewish circumcisions or Baptists' immersions. But he intended political harm (Jimmy is an ardent Democrat), and so after all the boilerplate business of Breslin as a sixteen year-old who petted a girl and had apocalyptic thoughts about heaven and hell, he concluded his article:

"The outcry here [i.e., in Breslin's world], then, is not about Lehrman using a change of religion as if it is a change of voting addresses. . . . Politicians are allowed to do this sort of thing because most of them are either crazy or dishonest. My anger, however, is directed at the notion that a person can escape the anguish of being a young Catholic and then get all the benefits of being an old Catholic when, as a member of the true faith, you can get to heaven and these others can't."

That passage is as freighted with ignorance as any even Breslin could contrive. Suffice to say that it is not a Catholic position that heaven is only for Catholics (for preaching that doctrine, the Reverend Leonard Feeney of Boston was all but excommunicated in 1953), and the notion that a conservative Jew can multiply his votes by becoming a Christian is politically superficial. Lehrman's Jewish vote in 1982 was not large, and what there was of it came largely from conservative, Orthodox Jews, who would be most affronted—most hurt would be a better expression—by what they must deem apostasy. What saddens is the callousness of secular commentary, which supposes that any decision, if reached by a man of public affairs, is dictated by political considerations.

   Breslin, if he had been around, would have commented that in going to Mt. Sinai, Moses was after good ink; and that Paul, on the road to Damascus, figured he was safely past puberty. There can't be any higher price our public men pay than that of exposure to the cynics and the Philistines, who for reasons not readily explained cannot understand what it is that happens to people, even public people, when they believe they have heard the voice of God.

5

Sidney Hook, R.I.P.

JULY 21, 1989

Many years ago (I was twenty-six), on a balmy afternoon late in the spring, I rattled northward on a train to engage in a debate at Bennington College. I knew my adversary was a tough hombre, but I was simply unprepared for the ferocity with which he scorned me, my arguments, and even one or two of my friends. I did some counterpunching, but found myself unable to handle the sheer hot fire from the other end of the platform. At the reception later, the president of the college whispered to me, "You have to understand. A half hour before the debate, Sidney Hook learned that John Dewey had died. Sidney is his executor."

Those of us of who had gone through college without experiencing the least temptation to engage Karl Marx were ignorant of the library of technical material (*Towards the Understanding of Karl Marx, From Hegel to Marx,* etc.) that had made Professor Hook famous in his field of philosophy. But having disposed of the Marxist temptation, Hook went on, as indeed he went on until the week of his death, taking on other challenges. Within a few years of our first encounter at Bennington we were fighting in the same battle, though neither in the same war nor in the same trench.

Sidney Hook was a leader of the movement in the United States that held that Soviet communism was a totalitarian incubus that threatened the entire planet, and that here in America there were people one could properly call "fellow travelers" who by word and deed advanced the cause of the enemy and should be exposed and fought.

A tactical difference arose between Sidney Hook's circle of anti-communists and another circle which held that Senator Joseph McCarthy, though a whirlwind of imprecision, was making important points about the contamination of U.S. foreign policy, a circle that included such fellow veterans of the anti-communist wars as Max Eastman, James Burnham, and Eugene Lyons. And then, too, there was the distinguishing reason for going to war against communism. In Sidney Hook's case, it was exclusively because he chose freedom. In the case of some of the rest of us, it was because we chose freedom but also because we believe that communism is the enemy not only of man, but of God.

But Sidney Hook was, for everyone engaged in the battle, a profound and vigorous and eloquent companion-in-arms. His mind attacked a problem, or an enemy, as an acetylene torch would tackle dumb concrete. His memory was total (in his autobiography, published last year, he remembered episodes fifty years old as if they had taken place the day before Kennedy was shot); his polemical apparatus was formidable, and his knowledge was— with maybe an exception that comes to mind—encyclopedic.

Though he fancied himself the supreme rationalist, one happily records that he was a little less than that; in certain respects Sidney Hook was prideful. When he retired from New York University and went to the Hoover Institution as a fellow, his enemies felt they had got him at last. Got him? How?

By designating him a "conservative"! At such a charge, Hook would bridle. On my television program he insisted that he was still a socialist, but he agreed that dogmatic socialism was unappealing. On the other hand, if you take from socialism its dogma, you are left merely with this or that form of the welfare state, and by such standards Ronald Reagan is also a socialist. In respect of his longtime war against religion he did twenty-four-hour duty, and when a year or so ago I wrote for *The New York Times Magazine* a piece suggesting that the old relationship between doing right and doing what God commanded was missing nowadays, to the impoverishment of the world, he replied with Benningtonian fervor, insisting on the nonexistence of God—or, rather, on the insufficiency of the evidence of His existence.

Ten years ago a longtime friend of Sidney Hook confided to me the most wonderfully humanizing story of the lacuna in Hook's knowledge. They were lunching at his apartment by Washington Square and Hook asked his guest if they could walk together in the park after lunch. Hook sat down on a park bench and said to him: "Ralph, I want you to tell me something I don't know. What exactly do homosexuals do?" So, my friend told me through his laughter, "I told him. His glasses came down a bit on his nose, and then he said, 'That's disgusting!' "

I think back six years ago. He had had a stroke and was not expected to live. But he was making progress, and slowly recovering his voice. I was walking toward a lecture hall at Stanford and we met at a corner of the corridor. Instinctively I gave him a great hug. I think I greatly embarrassed him; but I'm so glad I did it.

6

Is Beethoven a "Monument"?

JANUARY 2, 1987

Conservatives raised on libertarian principles have long since remarked that any invasion of the sacred No Trespassing sign puts you on the slippery slope toward collectivist capitulation. People argue endlessly the question whether Ronald Reagan has restored conservative principles, and both positions can be taken with cogency. Yes, he has caused people to look government gift horses in the mouth; no, he has not reversed the great trends of the century that have given more and more responsibility to government, less and less to society. You will have noticed that recent talk about how to handle the financial crisis of college students goes forward almost exclusively in terms of how much more federal aid of one kind or another is needed. A generation ago there was no such thing as federal aid to a college student.

The great guidelines inherited from the political philosophy of Adam Smith called on government to look after the national defense, administer justice, and protect national monuments. Abraham Lincoln marched us a huge step forward (or, better, backward) when he suggested that government should also undertake anything the private sector could not undertake, or not undertake as well. And Catholic social policy gave us the principle of "subsidiarity," which states that nothing should be done by the public sector that can be done by the private sector, and nothing by a higher echelon of government that can be done by a lower echelon (subsidiarity is a position most Catholic bishops have either forgotten or wish that history would forget).

It is certainly true that we live in a mixed economy, and I find myself inquisitively exploring the mandate given by Adam Smith to preserve national monuments. The mind was propelled thataway when in an idle moment during a holiday I searched the wave band of a portable radio in quest of something to listen to.

There were between twenty and twenty-five options at that location, none of them relaying classical music. It required only a little Cartesian *Geländesprung* to alight at my conclusion: Isn't it the responsibility of the government to maintain monuments that are man-made, as well as those given us by nature? Nobody argues against the government's maintaining Yellowstone National Park. No one argues against the government's maintaining the Lincoln Memorial, and only about half of us argue against the government's maintaining Hyde Park.

Isn't it, by the same reasoning, a responsibility of government to maintain (to limit oneself to a single poet) Shakespeare? Happily, there isn't anything for the government to do to maintain Shakespeare, since we do not own Stratford-upon-Avon. And isn't it the responsibility of government to maintain (once again, to name only a single artist) Beethoven?

The cavil that Beethoven doesn't need looking after since his records sell by the trainload isn't at all satisfying to someone spelunking through the radio channels in search of Beethoven. Yes, you will find him in Chicago, and New York, and San Francisco, and several other oases. But you do not find him in many places, and you are entitled, it is my thesis, to ask whether the government is therefore doing its duty.

We remember that not so long ago, when the wavelength that became television's Channel 13 was available in the New York area, the Federal Communications Commission put great pressure on sellers and buyers to make it an outlet for educational television. Why not hold out one channel for classical music in every part of the world subject to U.S. airwave supervision?

One hesitates, in any exploration of political theory, to cite Switzerland because Switzerland is so heavily congested with paradoxes (e.g., everyone must have a firearm in his house and nobody ever gets shot), but in that very free society you can order for a buck a month or less a six-channel music box attached to your telephone, and lo! one of those channels gives you, eighteen hours a day, classical music, nonstop.

I doubt if anyone has gotten around to calculating whether the monthly dollar that comes in pays the expense of the six channels that reach out to you. But it is such a civilizing amenity, and so eminently defensible under the aegis of protecting the monuments, is it not? Who says that Mount Rushmore is In, but J. S. Bach is Out? Isn't Adam Smith a living instrument, like the Constitution? Do we need a Warren Court to ordain that it is a constitutional responsibility of the U.S. Government to make it possible for us to hear Beethoven on our vacations?

Had enough?

7

Olof Palme, R.I.P.

MARCH 8, 1986

There is something appealing about Olof Palme, even if he did his best during his long career to make Sweden uninhabitable. His dream of the beautiful socialist society totally interrupted any view of anything that stood in the way of his ideological dogma: If it is socialist, it has got to be good. If it is made in America, it is suspect; if it is made in the Soviet Union, one has to respect its presumptive goodwill.

There were no interruptions, no anomalies recognized by him, visible to the non-Swedish observer. His idealism was total. To be sure, there is a problem in totalist idealism, namely that it becomes so obsessive as to require one to enlist the powers of the state to advance it. So that the idealism of Olof Palme became the idealism of the Swedish Government, which meant that dissenters needed to go along. There was no choice.

After finishing at Kenyon College in Ohio, young Olof Palme visited thirty-four American states in search of poverty. There is no published Guide to Poverty in America, but it doesn't take long to find it, any more than it takes long to find congregations of sick people. From his recognition that there is poverty in the richest country in the world, Olof Palme drew his devotion to the socialism he nurtured in Sweden. When he studied in Czechoslovakia, his idealism brought him to marry a Czech girl purely for the sake of achieving her entry into Sweden. This effected, he promptly divorced her. One had the feeling about Olof Palme that if the law permitted it he'd have married all the women in the world who wanted to move elsewhere. As scholar James Burnham once remarked about Mrs. Roosevelt, she turned all the world into her personal slum project.

The great pity of it all was that, as so often happens to the ideologue, the vision is as busy excluding inconvenient data as it is incorporating congenial data. Olof Palme, friend of the common man, marching alongside the North Vietnamese ambassador to the Soviet Union to protest American armed colonialism in South Vietnam. Catch that one for irony, but don't tell it to the boat people, if you want them to mourn the tragedy of Olof Palme's death.

And then Olof Palme, the brilliant intellectual (straight A's at Kenyon), denouncing the carpet bombing of Hanoi, in which fewer than three hundred people were killed and which precipitated the peace, or rather hiatus, of 1972, denouncing the United States as on a par with the Nazis who were behind the bombing of Guernica in 1937. Olof Palme, the idealist, joins with Willy Brandt to form Socialist International, which within a few years becomes an organization for placating the Soviet Union; for denouncing any effort in Europe to defend itself against possible Soviet aggression by mounting a deterrent nuclear force, while uttering no significant criticism of the aggressive nuclear offensive inventory deployed by the Soviet Union.

One must suppose that Palme's point of view was significantly propelled by a knowledge of the Sweden drawn by Ingmar Bergman in his movie *Fanny and Alexander.* The hypocritical upper class in which Palme was born and reared. The cruelty to children by churchmen that is tolerated in that society. The prudery combined with rampant sexuality of the kind pictured in *The Other Victorians* by Steven Marcus. While he was education minister, before becoming prime minister, Olof Palme strengthened Marxist curricula, ignored any invigoration of Christian literature, and played a speaking part in the first hard-pornographic movie, *I Am Curious—Yellow.*

He left behind a Sweden in which it is estimated that as much as one third of all business is done in the underground economy in order to avoid the savage taxation with which Palme greeted any Swede who was so antisocial as to succeed in a commercial enterprise. In social legislation, he left behind a Sweden in which a father who spanks his son can be jailed, but who cannot be touched if he sleeps with his daughter.

The death that greeted him was in a way a testimonial to his idealism. Why would anyone want to kill Olof Palme, especially in Sweden? Only twelve hours earlier he had dismissed his body-guards. There are those who feel that if he had to depart this world suddenly, better he had died of radioactivity or by a submarine that, by navigational error, landed on the Swedish Parliament rather than in a Swedish fjord. But his death was a personal tragedy, and must be focused on discretely, even as his life was something of a public tragedy.

8

Paul Weiss, Eighty-five

JUNE 10, 1986

In recent months a book was published reciting the history of race prejudice at Yale University, with emphasis on the Excluded Jew. A few weeks ago, Paul Weiss celebrated his eighty-fifth birthday. It is remarkable to contemplate that when his name was proposed in the late forties for a professorship at Yale, there was active opposition to the idea of a tenured Jewish professor teaching undergraduates, the idea being that Jews simply didn't quite, er, fit in with Yale traditions. One should add that Yale was hardly alone in this ethnic provincialism. As much was true of most of the Ivy League colleges.

One Jewish scholar, graduating from the City College of New York in the mid-thirties, thought to go to the Far East to do his graduate work. Because he was interested in sinology? No, because New York universities of distinction made an exception: If you were an expert on China and were Jewish, OK, you could have tenure; not otherwise.

Paul Weiss ran into a second prejudice, not one, however, directed at Jews or Catholics or Zoroastrians. He reached the mandatory retirement age at Yale. That was in 1969. Paul Weiss was born the year Queen Victoria died. He accepted a chair of philosophy at Catholic University where he has been uproariously active, writing a dozen books (he has written twenty-four), teaching, coaching, wheedling, teasing: Some who have experienced him think of him as the supreme teacher.

At Yale he was the political liberal *à outrance,* but his orderly mind made it hard for him to defend some of liberalism's zanier forms. His exuberant wife quarreled with him only on the question of whom to vote for in 1948. She went for Henry Wallace, then the

choice of pro-communist and surrealistic liberals. She was the latter, and died tragically two years later.

Paul Weiss brought out his magnum opus, *Modes of Being,* a
classic in philosophical literature, while engaging in the usual liberal causes, foremost among them in the sixties being, of course,
civil rights. He engaged in a fascinating quarrel, never totally
healed, with his old protégé and colleague, the Reverend William
Sloane Coffin, who had been angered by a black doctor in New
Haven who failed to report for duty at a designated sit-in against
somebody. The doctor's point was that he had made it as a black
man, and sought now an integrated life as distinguished from a life
of political activism. Paul Weiss defended the doctor's decision, in
a dialogue worthy of Socrates.

At about that time, Professor Weiss had what I think of as his
Roman Spring. He took a sabbatical and went to live in bohemia
in New York City. There he took acting lessons, immersed himself
in the theater, learned the basic calisthenics of ballet, studied music, sculpting, poetry, playwrighting, and developed an addiction to
painting, which he continues to pursue in his search into the heart
of existence. Four books issued out of that experience.

It will strike some as strange that the first Jewish tenured professor in the Ivy League should find work at a Catholic university
so congruent to his interests. Paul Weiss would be amused at such
befuddlement because, you see, theology, to the extent that it is
based other than on revelation and its exegesis, is an inquiry into
the nature of man and into the nature of things, and metaphysics
is Weiss's bag. Nothing interests him more than the question of
what we are, what time is, what being and existence are. He
founded the *Review of Metaphysics* thirty-five years ago and served
as its editor for years.

The easy philosophical eclecticism of the Jewish professor in a
Catholic university reminds us of the ultimate appeal of universals.
No sense of strain is felt, in the higher circles, among men seeking
metaphysical truths. Paul Weiss's father was a tinsmith. Paul
worked his way through college by acting as a stenographer, went
then to Harvard for his Ph.D., where he became a protégé of
Alfred North Whitehead. He went on to the Sorbonne, to Radcliffe, to Bryn Mawr, to Yale. He is one of those stellar figures that

give pride to the republic and bring smiles to those who experienced him as a teacher.

I wish I could say that he had taught me a great deal, but I am not at home in metaphysics. As a human being he did teach me, and I remember most piquantly one of his aphorisms: "I am not as bright as my students. I have to think before I write." Paul Weiss rewrote his book *Reality* thirty-eight times in readying it for publication. In so doing, he edges S. J. Perelman up one point. Asked how many drafts he wrote, Perelman said thirty-seven. "Thirty-six would leave it too rough. Thirty-eight would leave it lapidary." Weiss's work is lapidary, but that's OK in his case.

9

Nixon's Penultimate Days

OCTOBER 31, 1989

T he reaction by Richard Nixon to the dramatization of *The Final Days* was one of massive retaliation: He changed his credit card from AT&T (the program's sponsor) to Sprint. He did this, by the way, without previewing the film, and indeed no one in his right mind would have expected him to reexperience the singular tortures of 1972–74. One can't imagine Sir Thomas More or Joan of Arc taking satisfaction from visiting again the events that led to their torture and execution. On the other hand, Leonard Garment, counsel to Mr. Nixon and a true cosmopolite, exploded in rage after seeing the film, denouncing all its implications in an Op-Ed piece for *The New York Times.*

Here is a view from someone unattached to the events of Watergate: In my judgment, the production was superb, and the characterization of Richard Nixon a masterpiece. If there is a prize out there for artistic impersonation, it should go to actor Lane Smith. The Richard Nixon of *The Final Days* is the portrait of a man who made a relatively trivial mistake in judgment but saw it magnified into a cosmic event that dominated the discourse of nations.

And the nobility of the outcome of it all is hard to deny. There is fleeting reference in the three-hour drama to the detection of Spiro Agnew as a petty thief, about whom nothing more was ever heard. But the obstinate loyalty inspired by Nixon could not have been effected by a lesser man, and is all the more striking given his obvious weaknesses. When he appears in the living room of the White House to inform his family that he has decided to resign, his son-in-law, lawyer Ed Cox, warns him: "They won't let you alone. They hate you with a passion." Nixon reacts by wondering out loud to his lawyer, Fred Buzhardt, "Will I be prosecuted?"

"Impossible to say."

"Well, if they want to put me in jail, let them. At least that will give me time to do some thinking. All the best writing is done from jail. Take Gandhi."

Buzhardt tries to console Nixon by telling him that if any other president had been subjected to similar scrutiny, almost certainly every one of them would have left office in similar circumstances.

So Leonard Garment tells us that words were put in Nixon's mouth he did not utter. Or, more accurately, not enough words were put in his mouth that he did utter. And Garment flatly denies the moving scene in which Nixon and Kissinger are said to have descended to their knees, under the prodding of Nixon, to seek divine help, a scene that ended with Nixon prostrate on the floor in tears. To which one can only say: Perhaps it didn't happen, but if it did, it adds to every inclination to esteem the man, Richard Nixon, the victim of the most lethal of all of Richard Nixon's enemies, Richard Nixon.

The salient dramatic point is that never in modern times has there been such a resurrection. Fifteen years after the most ignoble departure from the White House in history, Richard Nixon is in China, plying his international wares. Three years ago he received a standing ovation from the Washington press corps. He has written a half-dozen books, which have been seriously reviewed. He is widely respected by professional diplomats all over the world.

And, in their own way, the American people, viewing his weakness, recognize it as very nearly universal in character: that little mistake which began as a banana peel and ended as the last days of Pompeii. It is a universal theme, celebrated with great pith and wit by Tom Wolfe in his novel *Bonfire of the Vanities*. The drama can only serve to bring the American people closer to Richard Nixon, and that surely is what, above all things, he has wanted.

10

A Tribute to Herbert Hoover

SEPTEMBER 16, 1988

Remarks at the annual celebration of Herbert Hoover's birthday, at the Hoover Library in Iowa

I have always been intimidated by meticulous scholarship of the kind one associates with modern historians—their five thousand footnotes, and twenty-eight appendices. No wonder Arthur Schlesinger needs plenty of Rose's Lime Juice to get through the day! We pundits tend to speak in large and billowing terms, and my reaction, no doubt defensive, toward those who always get the arcane historical story exactly right brings to mind Goering's statement that anytime anyone mentions culture in his presence, he reaches for his Luger.

I was told by my hosts that it especially interests this audience for the speaker to recount his own experiences with the Chief. On this matter my memory was nicely jogged when George Nash was kind enough to send me, in addition to much other fascinating material, copies of my correspondence with Mr. Hoover during the last half dozen years of his life.

I went to him in 1954, as a relatively young man of twenty-nine. We had a friend in common. (I interrupt myself to remark that it is probably true that everyone in America had a friend in common with Herbert Hoover. Certainly anyone who was ever a member of the Boys' Club was, indirectly, a friend of Herbert Hoover, or for that matter any European who did not die of starvation during the early twenties.)

I told Mr. Hoover that, in my judgment, political discourse in the United States was suffering gravely from the absence of a conservative journal of opinion. In those days, I said to him—having only recently graduated from college—it was generally assumed, by what goes by the name of the thinking classes, that the conservative movement was a loose conspiracy of illiterate tycoons whose only interests were to maximize profits and burn books. I rattled on a little bit on the subject. He sat there at his desk, silent; looking just a little bit to one side as, I later came to know, was habitual. I was still going on when he cleared his throat for a minute and I stopped talking. "You need capital," he said simply. A clean knife, through all that butter. It flashed through my mind, though this was not the moment to recall it, that shortly before Herbert Hoover's inauguration as president, Calvin Coolidge is said to have remarked, while riding down in an elevator with a friend, "You know, there's going to be a hell of a depression." Mr. Hoover, as usual, had got to the point.

The file reveals that he gave me the names of four or five affluent friends in California, with all of whom I visited. It is historically interesting to recall that these gentlemen, most of them former associates of the Chief, and protégés, were so profoundly gloomy about the prospects for the American Republic that, for the most part, they acted as though to launch a magazine in an effort to do something about it was the equivalent of lying athwart History, yelling Stop!

Always he treated me with great courtesy. I note from the file I have just examined that he would write out in pencil his replies to letters, and the faithful Bunny Miller would take his phrases and complete them, supplying, so to speak, the surrounding boiler-plate.

The file to which I refer reminds me that I sent to Mr. Hoover a copy of the speech I gave that night at the Plaza Hotel, which included a tribute to him. Now, it was always widely rumored that Mr. Hoover had an insecure sense of humor. And I note that Mr. Glenn Campbell, when he was here giving this commemorative talk a few years ago, addressed that subject directly, making a distinction between what Mr. Hoover thought it appropriate to say and to enjoy when he was president, and when he was not president. But since at dinner one night with him (yes, twice he invited me and my wife to dine with him, on one occasion quite alone), he had said to me that—and I quote him exactly—"There was nothing wrong with Franklin Roosevelt that a major miracle couldn't cure," I felt he would not misunderstand the one paragraph in my speech which engaged in polemical levities.

My final extended experience with Mr. Hoover came after the

Supreme Court outlawed common prayer in the schools. The Chief expressed his indignation and surprise at this ruling, and word of this reached me. A few friends and I organized the Committee for Religious Liberty, and for a while it appeared that Mr. Hoover would be willing to serve as its Protestant co-chairman, with Lewis Strauss representing Jewish dissidents, and Robert Murphy, Catholic dissidents.

But fatigue was setting in. And I had from him, dated August 21, 1962, the longest letter he ever wrote to me. He gave ten reasons why he had finally decided not to serve. I quote a few of them:

"1. I am now eighty-eight, with the physical limitations that come from such years. Moreover, I have gone through severe physical ordeals in California and Iowa. You are a humane man, but even so, you may have forgotten an old college barber-shop chorus—'The old gray mare ain't what she used to be!'

"2. Every time I lend my name to some righteous movement, the public holds me responsible—even if my associates have guaranteed that I do not need to think about the organization again. And they load my days with letters about it. . . .

"5. I have two little books on the stove, jointly with Mr. Nichols [Bill Nichols of *This Week* magazine was an intimate of Mr. Hoover, and of my family], which I hope may add some cheer to the American home folks, and they require constant attention while cooking.

"6. For over thirty years I have been collecting the materials and preparing the publication of three volumes on certain phases of American foreign relations. I think they are of importance to the American people. At eighty-eight years, 'the night cometh.'

"7. There are probably twenty million males in the United States who have been to college. Is there not some one of them who can meet your needs?

"8. I greatly regret to refuse any request from such a valiant and self-sacrificing worker in the garden of common sense (which means the test of past experience before jumping off deep ends)."

And, finally, "10. I greatly value your piece about me. It spells friendship. Yours faithfully, Herbert Hoover."

. . .

The scale at which he worked defies common measurements. Oh yes, did I tell you that George Nash, in answering my original questions, told me that if I was missing any other piece of information, please not to hesitate to specify my needs, because he has access to sixteen million documents here at the Library. Sixteen million documents! Either written by Herbert Hoover or read by him. And he wrote thirty books. One of them was a translation from the Latin. Moreover, as Mr. Nash has documented, Herbert Hoover was the most important domestic political figure in the United States not just from 1928 to 1933, but from 1921 to 1933.

There is much learned research on his presidency, and on the measures he chose to combat the Depression. To the extent I am qualified to pass judgment on them, I am persuaded that the relevant knowledge, at that time, of fiscal and above all of monetary management was insufficient, resulting in Mr. Hoover's having made mistakes. Mistakes, however, which were not rectified by his successor, never mind the glamour with which FDR's terms of office are associated.

What did come, after Mr. Hoover left office, was a gradual reconstitution of the American idea of the reasonable division of responsibilities between the private and the public sector. On this point, be it noted, Mr. Hoover himself was always something of a pragmatist. It is widely conjectured that he might have got the Democratic nomination for president in 1920. And in 1928, he was nominated over the opposition of the Old Guard within the GOP.

Mencken is famous among other reasons for writing of the state that it is "the natural enemy of all well-disposed, decent, and industrious men." And it is certainly difficult to deny the near-cosmic damage done by the state during this century. The thirty million dead Russians and fifteen million dead Germans and forty-odd million dead Chinese were not slaughtered by the private sector. And, in America, $200 billion of welfare having been spent to document our concern for those who need help, we see a growing class of the perpetually demoralized: young men and women—boys and girls in many cases—whose professions, under state training, are childbearing, unemployment, and, in many cases, drugs and crime.

Herbert Hoover openly and explicitly acknowledged what he deemed to be the responsibility of the state to step forward and help those who needed help, and to worry about the formalities later. It was by feeding the people of Europe after the First World War that he solved the problem of starvation in Europe. By contrast, we attempt to attack the problem of starvation in Ethiopia these days by windy conferences having to do with questions of jurisdiction, and grain rots in Ethiopia sometimes within sight of those who simultaneously starve.

Mr. Hoover's pragmatism was informed by a series of general assumptions. One of them was that the social energy of American freemen was vital to the production of resourceful thought. For this reason he believed that success should be applauded, not discouraged by taxation and derogation. At the Democratic Convention in Atlanta, two weeks ago, the listener was invited to feel that any American whose entrepreneurial zeal translated into commercial success was carrying on the work of General Sherman marching through Georgia.

I do not know whether—after George Nash and the other scholars are quite through fixing Mr. Hoover's large place in history—they will have uncovered a political theorist.

I think I would be surprised if they did so. The most important rulers in the civilized world have not been primarily theorists. They have been men and women of character, intelligence, insight. In the case of Herbert Hoover, not only character, intelligence, and insight, but an ardent desire to help individual human beings—together with an ardent desire to preserve a society which, in his judgment, is unique. I am sure that many of you are familiar with his great paean to America, given here in 1948. Even so I quote these sentences from it:

> America means far more than a continent bounded by two oceans. It is more than pride of military power, glory in war, or in victory. It means more than a vast expanse of farms, of great factories or mines, magnificent cities, or millions of automobiles and radios. It is more even than the traditions of the great tide westward from Europe which pioneered the conquest of this continent. It is more than our literature, our music, our poetry. Other nations have these things also . . . [Here there is] that imbedded individualism, that self-reliance, that sense of service, and above all those moral and spiritual foundations . . . They [the Quakers I grew up with]

were but one atom of the mighty tide of many larger religious bodies where these qualities made up the intangibles in the word, *American.*

I do not venture to predict, as I have said, whether the scholars resident here are discovering a great political theorist. But there can hardly be any doubt that, every day, here in West Branch, these men and women are discovering a man who, every day, every year, looms larger and larger. A man fit to come from the loins of the America Herbert Hoover revered, the America he served so nobly.

11

Nancy and Ronald Reagan

JUNE 1985

You find yourself scrutinizing famous romances for the sudden slip that bares the brummagem nature of it all. Eliza Doolittle's little stumble over the hem of her evening gown, followed impulsively—irrepressibly—by the stream of cockney billingsgate. Fifteen years ago at the end of a long dinner party the Duke of Windsor, chatting earnestly to a fellow guest as they walked to the elevator, was about to push the lobby button when he noticed that his wife was not aboard. What issued from his mouth was on the order of civilized panic: "Wally! Wally! Have you forgotten—" From just around the corner the soothing reassurance came even before he finished. "I never forget you, David."

She materialized, smiling, always a little bit the coquette. And then his little sigh of relief, suppressed but audible.

Theirs was the real thing, and so is that of the ruling couple in the White House, self-evidently not in the least reluctant to say it to the world even as they say it to each other. There are a lot of wisecracks in circulation about the look on her face when she fastens it on him in public situations, which is most of the time. Affection, pride, uninhibited devotion, and just the redeemingly provocative touch of ginger (or I think I see it) of the kind that says, If you don't see what I see in him, you are blind.

When he was almost killed, the look on the one photograph that caught her full in the face en route to the hospital was the look on the face of the Pietà in St. Peter's, the same look one saw on the face of Jackie Kennedy when she stood in Air Force One while Lyndon Johnson took the oath of office, replacing as president the man whose corpse lay a few feet away.

The public impression is almost necessarily static: postage-stamp mutual devotion. And this hurts, because they are both trained in the theater and know the pitfalls of wooden productions. For that reason one is not surprised that, asked if they would dance together intimately for the camera, their answer was yes. I do not know whether that answer was preceded by much deliberation, but whether yes or no they were, finally, exuberantly delighted to proceed, as though they were Fred Astaire and Ginger Rogers, romancing and kicking up their heels. Not, if you reflect on it, an easy thing to do, never mind the authentic high temperature of mutual devotion: there is in the West a tradition against chiefs of state engaging in visible, let alone ostentatious, shows of biological informality. One need not question the mutual affection of the Queen of England and her duke to know that no *paparazzi* dressed in invisible ink would catch him while in the presence of a third person doing anything much more intimate than kissing her ring while she gave him another Order of the Garter. King Constantine of Greece fell desperately in love with Princess Anne-Marie when she was only seventeen, but there was none of *that* in any public situation. When Grace Kelly arrived in Monaco to become one with her prince, the kiss after the wedding was ever so chaste. Many many years went by before one had any intimation of their offstage closeness, and that came when the camera rested on the face of the widower during her funeral.

No, the tradition is against it. But the Reagans don't care. Oh, they observe the obvious protocols. But manifestly they think it altogether splendid to dance together in their own version of Camelot—which is theirs whenever, wherever they are together, just as surely as any aircraft becomes Air Force One if he is aboard.

She is not, one should perhaps know, by any means simply the silent female appendage some people so mistakenly suppose her to be. She has positions, stated and unstated, on most a) people, b) issues, and c) matters. These are ventilated or not, as she deems appropriate; with more or less firmness, as she deems prudent; and not all that rarely with less than subordinate inhibition, as when she will (in private) correct her husband on this point or that, concerning this or that issue; but always securely, because the planted axiom is that they are after the same thing: a better world, made so in part because of his leadership and idealism.

It is impossible to understand him without knowing how thoroughly spontaneous he can be, and how engaging this faculty is in nourishing a thirty-five-year-old romance. On a helicopter three years ago a friend leaned over and asked him whether the Secret Service was going to permit him to swim the following day (the occasion was a weekend in Barbados), and he answered, raising his voice as necessary to sound out over the helicopter blades, "Well. Nancy here tells me I'm the most powerful man in the world. Maybe that means I can go swimming?" The remark was uttered loudly enough for Nancy, across the way, to overhear, and she delighted in it, even if it flirted with full disclosure of the kind of thing exchanged in moments of utter privacy.

One has to be careful of her sensibilities. She does not like a bawdy joke, which, however, is different from suggesting that her attitude on hearing one is that of an affronted Victorian. It is, in one sense, a matter of compensation, or, if you like, overcompensation. You see, her mother, universally acclaimed as among the most entertaining women who ever graced a dinner table or a smoker, had a positive genius for a saucy story. Senator Barry Goldwater, on the telephone, once said to me, "Mrs. Davis has told me stories *I* wouldn't tell *you*!"

I remember a Thanksgiving evening in our house eight or ten years ago; he was carving the late-night turkey after a drive from the country, and four of us were seated around the kitchen table with wine, and cheese, whatever . . . He was on a roll. One story after another, some of them of an intricacy absolutely baroque— the kind of story which, if you wished to repeat it for the communicable joy of it, would require you to take time off to study it, as you would need to take time to memorize a Bach fugue or a canto of Pound. He was quite literally performing, the pleasuring of his audience being a professional pursuit in which he had over the years proved especially successful because in doing so he pleasures himself. Inevitably, carried on, he would recall the one about, oh, Lyndon Johnson and Elizabeth Taylor and Richard Burton in the Oval Office, and she would say, "Oh, Ron, no, no . . . ," but he would smile and give way to the theatrical imperative, and she would laugh along with the rest of us, because the jokes were funny, and she always retains perspective.

She yields, but so does he. "It's you," he tells her, "that they turn to when they're really in trouble." As so often is the case when the husband is most of the day on the public stage, it is left to the mother to be the disciplinarian, absorbing the potholes of life with adolescents, and now he tells her, in the presence of a third person, that notwithstanding her role as shock absorber her standing in the family remains supreme. She is not, this time, diverted, to indicate her satisfaction at his recognition of this, but you know that it has registered, fortifying what is never threatened by redundancy, her knowledge of his attributes as a husband who feels, who knows, who cares deeply, who appreciates her fully.

The last time I heard the legend of Philemon and Baucis adduced seriously was in the final paragraphs of Whittaker Chamber's book, *Witness*. Chambers was given to melodrama, but those who knew him and his wife, Esther, never doubted that it was so between them. It is always hard to think it might indeed be so when one thinks of public figures, where posturing is one of the professional obligations. But it is so also of them, as it proved to be so of Arthur and Cynthia Koestler. Chambers wrote of how the god Hermes in disguise had been treated hospitably by the poor, elderly couple who shared with him their board and hut. In the morning, Hermes asked them what was their most secret wish, and it transpired that it was for both the same, that they would leave life together, inasmuch as life apart would be unendurable.

"The god, now gleaming through his rags, raised his staff—the caduceus with the twined snakes, interlacing good and evil. Where Philemon and Baucis had stood, two trees rustled up whose branches met and touched when the wind blew." People curious to know how it is between the man and wife dancing together on the cover of *Vanity Fair* this month are going to have to put to one side their political feelings and recognize that that is the way they are.

12

Evelyn Waugh

JANUARY 19, 1992

Everybody knows who Evelyn Waugh was. Not so Diana
Cooper, to whom Waugh wrote about three hundred letters from 1932 until he died in 1966, twenty years before
her own death at a very advanced age. One way to begin
to situate her is to note the wedding presents she received in 1919 when, as the beautiful young daughter of the Duch-
ess of Rutland, she married the penniless, untitled Duff Cooper:
"The King and Queen gave a blue enamel and diamond brooch
bearing their own initials; Queen Alexandra a diamond-and-ruby
pendant; the French Ambassador a gold ewer for incense-burning;
the Princess of Monaco a diamond ring; Lord Wimborne a William and Mary gold dressing-case; King Manuel a gold sugar-
sifter; Lord Beaverbrook a motor car; Dame Nellie Melba a
writing-table." (The list of wedding gifts, as Philip Ziegler reports
in his biography *Diana Cooper,* occupied eighty-eight pages of a
large notebook.)

Lady Diana Cooper was, then, socially noticeable. By the time
Waugh met her, she had been a screen actress and also played on
the stage. In the late 1950s, she turned to writing, producing three
volumes of memoirs; Waugh wrote that he thought them "a single
work of art, one of the great autobiographies of the century."
Lady Diana's granddaughter, Artemis Cooper, provides samples
of these expressive skills in *The Letters of Evelyn Waugh and Diana
Cooper,* as when Lady Diana addressed Waugh severely (she often
did so) following Duff Cooper's death, just after the midnight that
brought in the new year, 1954:

> You have never, I think, known real Grief—panic, melan-
> cholia, madness, night-sweats, we've all known for most of

our lives—you and me particularly. I'm not sure you know
human love in the way I do. You have faith and mysticism—
intense inner interests—a diverting, virile mind—gusto for
vengeance and destruction if necessary, a fancy—a gospel.

What you can't imagine is a creature with a certain irides-
cent aura and nothing within but a beating frightened heart
built round and for Duff. . . . For two days I am quite alone
—in these empty rooms with one thought one prayer—'let it
end now'—an absurd feminine desire to die in the same way
exactly as Duff. [I have now a] fearlessness of death—so let it
come now before custom of living disinclines me for dying.

But such grief was not characteristic. Diana Cooper loved people and traveling and adventures and fun—and she loved Evelyn
Waugh, though one surmises that they were happier when planning to see each other than when in each other's company. The
dour Waugh ("I am an insensitive lout") was relentlessly adoring.
Among Lady Diana's attractions were her blue blood and her
tendency to move about "grand architecture"—bringing him "delight. . . . Still more the aesthetic joy of seeing you in your
proper setting of luxury and splendour. Still more, and incompara-
bly more, the happiness to know that you have kept a warm place
for me in your heart all through my ice age. I love you."

But she didn't *always* bring him delight. "Baby" (as he called
her) could irritate Waugh by what she said or by her occasional
bouts of silence or by misinterpreting his catechisms. "You know
perfectly well," she reassured him after one such misunderstanding, "you have no Baby as loyal as this Baby and that if you believe
anything else you are very foolish. I thought, if you want to know,
that you did it to irritate—or rather from Irritability's possession.
It's an unexorcisable demon. . . . O dear how sad it all is."

In the big 1980 volume of his letters edited by Mark Amory it
was made clear, as only Waugh could make things clear, that he
considered it the burden—the very function, the raison d'être—of
the correspondent *to inform and to entertain.* He was lavish in
discharge of this duty. Thus he tells Lady Diana of a visit to Hi-
laire Belloc: "Two civil and pretty grandsons received us. Sherry in
the hall. Then a long wait for Belloc. Shuffling and stumping.
Then an awful smell like the wolves at the zoo, then entry. A
tramp, covered in garbage. A sweet, wise, mad face. An awful

black growth like a truffle under one eye. First words: 'Old age is a curious thing. It leaves a man crawling like a beetle while his mind is as strong and young as ever.' Second words (rather disconcerting, because I have met him twenty times or more since you first introduced us . . .): 'It is a pleasure to make your acquaintance, sir.' "

Belloc was very nearly unique in eliciting something like awe. Mostly Waugh's world was populated by lesser creatures, such as those he came upon in his travels. During a cruise of the Mediterranean in the fall of 1933 he undertook, one by one, to describe his traveling companions. Miss Marjorie Glasgow was, for example, "a very rich young lady whom I had met before on account of her mother giving parties I used to go to before I became fastidious. She was the leader of the left-wing nudists. She was attended by three naked Counts, one Polish, one Belgian and one Italian, one carried her gramophone, another her backgammon board and the third her sunbathing mattress."

He was especially fine when transmitting hilarities in the matter-of-fact tones of the schoolteacher: "I wish you had come to Goa. It is really a very singular place. . . . At the moment it is full of pilgrims from all over India and Ceylon—the descendants of people Francis Xavier preached to without knowing their language. . . . Did you know that when F.X. went to Japan he asked the word for God and they told him the Japanese for [penis] so he spent weeks preaching phallic worship without knowing it."

Evelyn Waugh depended on his friends, especially when traveling—which was much of the time—for news of the kind he most wanted. "Please keep writing and tell me about the general election and who is sleeping with whom and so on." He spoke of vacations, but never seemed to let up. It isn't widely recognized how very much he worked, how copiously he produced. He proffered as the reason for writing the sheer need for the income to care for his wife and six children, athwart the predatory hands of a socialist government. "I cannot with the utmost economy live on less than £5,000 a year and I have to earn £62,000 to spend that and I am getting too old and downcast to earn it," he wrote in December 1951, surveying his crowded household. His children were all very well, but children were very simply "defective adults." He was "glad to possess" his own, but got "little pleasure from their use—like first editions." He found it comfortable to be comprehensive in his dislikes—"Hate everyone except you and Maimie"—even if he knew that was somehow wrong, and could make himself write: "I am full of regret for failures in gratitude and patience and service and that has made me think of my failures towards all I love. . . . Please . . . believe always in my love."

It is well known that Evelyn Waugh rejoiced in the upper class, in particular the titled nobility, however ironic his oblique references to this fixation ("After I left you I went to play dominoes with the poor"). Anyone wishing to document this affinity will lean heavily on the comprehensive footnotes appended to these letters by Artemis Cooper, the talented and industrious editor of this intricate volume. Here one runs into—or else that is the sensation—just about every titled person in Britain; somehow they all manage to figure in Waugh-Cooper colloquies. The footnote for Waugh's mother-in-law reads: "She was born the Hon. Mary Vesey, and married Aubrey Herbert M.P. (1880–1923) in 1910. Aubrey Herbert, who was twice offered the throne of Albania, was a half brother of the fifth Earl of Carnarvon (the patron of Howard Carter, who discovered the tomb of Tutankhamun)."

Lady Diana does not disappoint this appetite or conceal its mannerisms. "Will it be soon" that Waugh pays another visit? she wonders. "I fear the hols are over and you are happy at home. The house is warm and there are no guests for bed or board. You could do your [diet] here—no cook, no maître d'hotel, no one who can read or write. Pierro who puts 'CRI' for gruyère. Jacqueline—my life, my memory—is off with a garagiste to be knocked about by a frog husband, her place is taken by a Czech child—utterly unlearned. Antoinette, the Polish milker, is in command—she can't even make herself plain—but cooks with originality and charm. . . . Louise has had her lung out and is like a roebuck in spring. Phyllis, and my dearest sister Marjorie, to say nothing of Viola Tree and Clarissa's mother, might all have been saved most hideous deaths [from lung cancer]." There is nothing to do, nobody to go out with that one would care to go out with. "There is no sap in Nature—nor in me. Spiritless, not in pain or acute melancholy I languish chilly—not happily resigned."

It has long been my own reading of Waugh that his delight in the festoonery of the titled class was merely a perverse aspect of his resentful co-optation by a populist history-on-the-march that disregarded the forms he revered: in religion, the old Roman Catholic Church; in society, the standards of decorum and behavior that marked, if not so much the separation of classes, the acknowledgment of the idea of class. That the upper classes had long since lost any meritocratic credentials he seldom paused to notice. What Waugh bothered with was the loss of his privacy. "The only human relationships I abide are intimacy, formality and servility. What is horrible here [England] and in America is familiarity. That doesn't exist in Asia." And again, "I live in a world which seems to me to deteriorate daily before my eyes." But his problem, he knew, was also personal: "How right you are about not losing friends. . . . I lose mine fast. . . . You find something agreeable in almost everyone. I am put off by anything not wholly agreeable."

Diana Cooper was one exception. Not that she was always reliably agreeable. ("If only you could treat friends," he chided, "as something to be enjoyed in themselves not as companions in adventure.") But she was a lifelong source of joy for Waugh, the quality of which is transmitted by these letters to readers who knew neither of them, and presumably care little for their workaday concerns. Waugh wrote that "it ought always to be disappointing to meet an artist; if his work is not something otherwise invisible in him he can't have the real motive for work. Artists to be heard and not seen." But in his triumphantly readable letters Waugh tells us otherwise—though, granted, we experience him in the written word with the kind of safety that would not have protected us when experiencing him in person.

I have jocularly ventured for some years now that a dispositive proof of the existence of the Holy Spirit is that Evelyn Waugh died just after attending church on Easter Sunday in 1966, immediately after which the convention was introduced in the Catholic Mass of the sign of peace, a moment when worshipers are bid to shake hands with fellow worshipers to their right, to their left, in the pew ahead and in the pew behind. Such an exercise could not have coexisted with Evelyn Waugh, defender of the faith. Either he had to go, or else the ritual had to be postponed. The Holy Spirit made His choice. Waugh went, but not before having a certain satisfaction at the expense of the Cardinal most responsible for the "reforms" of the Second Vatican Council:

Combe Florey
7 February 1965

Darling
    . . . Nice to go to Rome. They are destroying all that was superficially attractive about my Church. It is a great sorrow to me and for once undeserved.
    If you see Cardinal Bea spit in his eye.

All love
Bo

To which Lady Diana replied:

10 Warwick Avenue
[postmarked March 7, 1965]

Can you imagine the luck—I went up in a tiny lift with Cardinal Bea in full canonicals preceded by two candles—so with a spluttered greeting I was able to spit in his eye for you. . . .

Pug

These letters are a great exotic flower in modern literature.

13

Malcolm Muggeridge, R.I.P.

NOVEMBER 22, 1990

T en years ago Malcolm Muggeridge and I shared the job of commentator for two programs based in the Sistine Chapel. Two weeks before we got to Rome he telephoned. "Do you know," he said, "I have met, I suppose, all the important men and women in my lifetime, and on the whole I think them an awful bore . . . but I want to meet the present pope. Could you arrange it?"

I laughed. One always—inevitably—laughed in his company, which is one reason why one so looked forward to it.

When Pope John Paul approached Muggeridge he looked over benevolently and said to him, "Ah. You are radio!" It is very difficult to answer that question coherently, so Muggeridge simply smiled a response. The pope turned to the next guest in line at the private audience and said to David Niven, "Ah, you were the great friend of my predecessor." David Niven mumbled something about having had great admiration for Pope Paul VI, whom he never knew and probably hadn't given five minutes' thought to. The poor, dear pope was confused about the composition of the audience he was giving.

After our blessing, Malcolm could not get over his amusement; but then, years later, visiting with him in his little country house, I saw neatly framed in a corner of his living room a photograph. Him and the pope.

When he died a week ago the commentators listed his affiliation with Christianity rather as though it had been the next post, after editor of *Punch*. They did not seem to know that he had become the foremost evangelist of Christianity in the English language.

On a television program in 1980, at his invitation. The hour was called, "Why I Am Not a Catholic." It was off to a wonderful start when he recounted his disillusion with a Catholic chaplain at the University of Edinburgh. Muggeridge had just been installed as chancellor (that is the habit in Great Britain: university chancellors are popularity contest winners of a sort), and the administration came out for giving the students free contraceptives; Chancellor Muggeridge objected; the Catholic chaplain denounced his objection as monstrous.

WFB: Excuse me, but why was it monstrous?

MUGGERIDGE: It was monstrous, according to him, because it accused the students of wanting to be promiscuous. But in a letter I wrote in answer to it, I said I wondered what the Reverend Father thought they wanted the contraceptives for. Was it to save up for their wedding day?

That was Muggeridge *vitale,* the mordant clairvoyance that taught him to see through communism in the early thirties and brought him as high a reputation as a journalist as has been achieved by anyone in this century. He was everywhere, doing everything, but his odyssey was not without purpose. He was moving toward Christianity.

"Why did this longing for faith assail me? Insofar as I can point to anything it has to do with this profession which both you and I have followed of observing what's going on in the world and attempting to report and comment thereon, because that particular occupation gives one a very heightened sense of the sheer fantasy of human affairs—the sheer fantasy of power and of the structures that men construct out of power—and therefore gives one an intense, overwhelming longing to be in contact with reality. And so you look for reality and ultimately you arrive at the conclusion that reality is a mystery."

Why did he relish the mystery?

"Because it leads you to God. . . . It's exactly like—Bill, it's exactly like falling in love. You see another human being and for some extraordinary reason you're in a state of joy and ecstasy over that person, but the driving force which enables you to express that and to bring it into your life is love. Without love, it's nothing; it passes. It's the same with seeking reality, and there's the driving force we call faith. It's a very difficult thing to define, actually."

He never did define grace, which is not definable, but in due course he and his wife joined the Catholic Church and he pursued his writing, and his lecturing, now as an explicit Christian, of the best kind, the kind whose second greatest pleasure in life is laughter. After his stroke three months ago his brother wrote to say that Malcolm still enjoyed hearing from his friends, but could on no account acknowledge his mail.

He yearned to die, and hoped only that his beloved Kitty would go first. She survives him, reinforcing his belief in what it is that teaches us most. "As an old man, Bill, looking back on one's life, it's one of the things that strikes you most forcibly—that the only thing that's taught one anything is suffering. Not success, not happiness, not anything like that. The only thing that really teaches one what life's about—the joy of understanding, the joy of coming in contact with what life really signifies—is suffering, affliction."

He suffered, even at the end. But throughout his lifetime he diminished the suffering of others, at first simply by his wit and intelligence; finally by his own serenity, which brought serene moments to those graced by his presence.

14

A Toast to William A. Rusher

AS DELIVERED DECEMBER 9, 1988

Ladies and gentlemen. I join with you all on this day, so unhappy in the sense that we are losing a beloved professional colleague, so happy in the sense that we have an opportunity to express our gratitude to him.

Clif White and Jack Casey and Tom Farmer have known him much longer than I have, although I dare say not so intimately. To know anyone intimately it requires that he have the authority to question your disposition to spend money. In this respect I am certain you will all be glad to know that the guest of honor is the quintessential Republican; at least, that could have been said of him before we reached the era of high-deficit Republicanism. I don't mean to say that he is tiresome about it, merely that he is thorough. And unrelenting. Even on Sundays. I remember the legend of Congressman Robert Rich of Pennsylvania, who was elected to the House of Representatives in 1930, and served there approximately twenty years. During the first nineteen of those years he uttered only a single declamation—the same declamation—on a dozen or more occasions, each year. The debate on a spending measure would take place and, after it became obvious that it would be approved, Congressman Rich would raise his hand and, recognized, would say, "Where are we going to get the money, gentlemen?" And sit down. It is recorded that in his declining years, following a debate that had gone on for three weeks and had kept his colleagues at their desks night after night, the moment finally came for a vote on the controversial measure, at which point, nearing midnight, Congressman Rich raised his hand. The entire chamber groaned. But under the rules the Speaker was powerless, and, grumpily, he recognized the member from Pennsylvania, who, struggling against his great age, rose to his feet, looked around at his colleagues, and said, "April Fool!"

Bill Rusher is not that versatile. But as publisher of a journal that holds out great promise of being the longest, most consistent money loser in American publishing history, he is at once badly cast and well cast. Badly cast in that it strikes anyone who for thirty years has viewed him coming jauntily to his office every morning not sooner than three minutes to ten, not later than two minutes to ten, that he could not be other than the president or vice president of a prosperous house of usury; well cast in that his serene and self-confident mien easily belies the probability that the first person he will encounter on entering his office is an irate creditor; the second, his secretary giving notice.

Our guest of honor is a man of most meticulous habits, and it is a miracle, of the kind that Providence less and less frequently vouchsafes us, that he should have endured for so long the disorderly habits of his colleagues. When so many years ago, in 1957, I asked him timidly whether he would consent to accept the responsibilities of publisher, he reached instinctively into his pocket and pulled out his notebook, presumably to see whether his notebook had any objections. Having passed that hurdle, *National Review* was subjected to a methodical probing over a period of three or four weeks. A few very close friends were directly consulted, and in due course the decision was reached. Our old friend Providence cooperated with us in keeping him away from the offices of *National Review* from which, had he examined them, he would no doubt have returned without faltering to the relative tranquility of the Senate Internal Security Subcommittee. But he was trapped; and began to impose order on our affairs.

To this end he began his famous graphs. We have graphs, at *National Review,* charting every quiver in the organization's metabolism. We have graphs that show us how we are doing in circulation, in promotion expenses, in political influence. We have graphs that chart the fidelity to conservative principles of most major, and all minor, public figures in America. We have a graph that will tell you at a glance whether Lauren Bacall is more or less conservative than Humphrey Bogart. For those who have the stomach for it, they will give you a synoptic understanding of the financial record of *National Review* over the last thirty-one years.

Bill's fastidious habits gave him an enormous advantage over the rest of us. There was never, for instance, any such phenomenon as an unanswered memorandum from William A. Rusher, and if his future associates in California think it works to say absentmindedly, "I never *got* that memorandum, Bill"—forget it, as I did, after trying it once thirty years ago, only to be reminded that I had received it in the presence of fourteen editors and three photographers. So much is our publisher the creature of habit that, he once confessed to me, on entering the washroom he reaches up to pull down the light-cord; and if it should happen that by mistake the previous patron of the washroom left the light on, why Mr. Rusher turns it off before he can control his reflex action, thus finding himself, as he does several times a year, in total darkness, and without practical recourse to his secretary. Occasionally his admirers show their envy of him, as when, while he was away on a lecture tour, we tiptoed into his office and exactly reversed every reversible physical accoutrement. Thus the picture of Lincoln now hung where the picture of Washington had hung for time immemorial; and the picture of Washington hung where the picture of Lincoln had hung. Thus when he depressed Button One, instead of the bookkeeper, his secretary answered; and when he depressed Button Two, the bookkeeper, not his secretary, answered. And when he turned over the leaves of his calendar, he found himself moving not toward the end of the month but toward the beginning of the month; and when he opened the drawer where his graphs were kept he found not his graphs but his pills; and so on. At which point, rising above it all, he got up to leave the room. We had tried hard to substitute the door leading out of his office for the door leading into his bathroom, but found the problem was metaphysically insoluble. So he left, returned to his apartment, telephoned his secretary on the outside line, issued a few crisp instructions, and retired to his club for the rest of the day, pending the restoration of order.

Such have been his tribulations at *National Review*. Yet it should not surprise that his colleagues rallied so enthusiastically to the idea of coming together to celebrate his achievements and his person on the eve of his retirement from *National Review*. The most exasperating people in the world are so often the most beloved, and he is no exception. Sometimes, at the fortnightly editorial conference, to which he descends with his notebook and his clippings, to pour vitriol on the ideologically feeble—sometimes he looks about him and, no doubt, feels as Congressman Rich felt surveying the expressions of those whom he would now summon to fiscal rectitude. But his performance at those meetings is one of the great running performances on the ideological stage. His scorn is not alone for those in public life whose activities during the week he finds contemptible, but also for those who lag a bit behind in exhibiting similar scorn. For them—especially if they are his colleagues—his scorn is especially withering. "I notice," he wrote me once after enduring an editorial conference during my absence and running hard into the opposition of some of our younger colleagues, "I notice the difficulty in planting my views against the opposition of Merrill Lynch Pierce Fenner and Smith sitting at the opposite end of the table. I find that Merrill seldom disagrees with Lynch, who seldom disagrees with Pierce, who always disagrees with me. Perhaps you will find an opportunity to suggest a good basic reading list to our younger members." But all is not lost; all is never lost; though there is in front of us the quite unendurable thought of next week's editorial conference without Bill Rusher, next month's financial crisis without Bill Rusher, 1990's election without Bill Rusher. But although it will be elsewhere, Bill will be marching on, gyroscopically certain, ever in command of himself, whether communicating his pleasure, or registering his doubts, or metronomically tut-tutting his disapproval. Always a presence, always a performance; and always—I speak for myself and for those who know him best—a friend to whom we are all grateful.

15

Clare Boothe Luce, R.I.P.

NOVEMBER 6, 1987

I first laid eyes on her in 1948. She was delivering the keynote address to the Republican Convention, and she said of Henry Wallace, who was running for president on the Progressive ticket, that he was "Joe Stalin's Mortimer Snerd." They all rocked with laughter, and the critics, of course, bit her again. I first met her at her quarters, on Fifth Avenue. She had telephoned and asked if I could come by to discuss the worsening crisis under President Diem in South Vietnam. I was there at four and she opened the door with paintbrushes in one hand. I told her by all means to finish what she was doing before we got down to the problems of Southeast Asia, and so she led me happily to her atelier, but instead of herself painting, she undertook to teach me there and then how to use acrylics, launching me in a mute inglorious career. Two months later there came in the mail at my office a big manuscript pulsating with scorn and indignation over the treatment of President Diem by Washington, with special focus on Diem's sister-in-law, Madame Nhu. She called it "The Lady's Not for Burning." I put the article on the cover of the next issue of *National Review* and had a startled call from the press editor of *Newsweek*. He wished to know how it came about that . . . Clare Boothe Luce . . . was writing for . . . *National Review*. I told him solemnly (I could manage a hidden smile, since we were speaking by telephone) that *tous les beaux esprits se rencontrent*— roughly translated, that beautiful spirits seek each other out. The following day, President Diem and his brother, the Dragon Lady's husband, were murdered. The only happy result of that Byzantine mess, for me, was that I was never again out of touch with Clare Boothe Luce, for whom, months ago, my wife and I scheduled a dinner—at her request—to be held here, in New York, on September 29, two weeks before she died.

I have thought a lot about her in the past few days and weeks. The last time we stayed with her in Honolulu we were met at the airport by her gardener, Tom. There were twelve of us for dinner. We were seated in her lanai, being served cocktails, while Tom was quietly lighting the outdoor gas lamps. Suddenly he fell. In minutes the ambulance arrived. Surrounded by Clare's anxious, silent guests, Tom was given artificial respiration. Clare gripped my hand and whispered to me, "Tom is going to die." There was dumb grief in her voice, and absolute finality. Two hours later, the hospital confirmed that Tom was dead. Clare said goodnight to her guests, and departed to keep the widow company.

Clare knew when an act was done. In so many respects, she was always a woman resigned.

I think back on her career . . . Look, you are a young, beautiful woman. Pearl Harbor was only yesterday, and you have spent several months poking about disconsolate Allied fronts in Asia and the Mideast. You have written a long analysis, cruelly objective, about Allied disorder, infinitely embarrassing to the Allies and correspondingly useful to the Axis powers. On the last leg of your journey, a sharp-eyed British customs officer in Trinidad insists on examining your papers. His eyes pass over your journal, he reads in it, snaps it shut, and calls in British security, which packs you off under house arrest. What do you do?

Well, if you are Clare Boothe Luce, you get in touch with the American consulate, and the American consulate gets a message through to your husband, Henry Luce. Mr. Luce calls General Donovan, the head of U.S. Intelligence. General Donovan arranges to appoint you *retroactively* an intelligence official of the United States Government. The British agree to let you fly to New York, and there they turn your report over to the British ambassador. He is so shaken by it that he instantly advises Winston Churchill of its contents. Churchill pauses from the war effort to cable back his regards to Clare, who meanwhile has been asked by the Joint Chiefs of Staff to brief them on her analyses, which, suitably bowdlerized, appear in successive issues of *Life* magazine and are a journalistic sensation.

Thus passeth a week in the life of the deceased.

The excitement and the glamour, the distinctions and the awards, a range of successes unequaled by any other American woman. But ten years later she was writing not about tanks and planes, but about the saints. She began coquettishly by quoting Ambrose Bierce, who had defined a saint as a "dead sinner, revised and edited." But quickly, Clare Luce's tone of voice altered. She wrote that perspectives are very changed now. "Augustine," she said, "came into a pagan world turning to Christianity, as we have come into a Christian world turning towards paganism."

St. Augustine fascinated her. She wrote that "he explored his interior sufferings with the same passionate zeal with which he had explored exterior pleasures, and he quailed to the depths of his being at the [projected] cost of reforming himself. 'These petty toys of toys,' "—she quoted him—" 'these vanities of vanities, my long-time fascinations, still held me. They plucked at the garment of my flesh, and murmured caressingly: Dost thou cast us off? From this moment shall this delight or that be no more lawful for thee forever?' Habit," Clare Luce commented, "whispered insistently in his ear: 'Dost thou think that thou canst live without these things?' And Augustine, haunted by Truth, hounded by Love, harried by Grace, 'had nothing at all to answer but those dull and dreary words: Anon, anon; or Presently, or, Leave me alone but a little while. . . .' "

Clare Luce knew that it was truly miserable to fail to enjoy some of life's pleasures. When asked which priest she wished to confess to on entering the Catholic Church, she had said, "Just bring me someone who has seen the rise and fall of empires." But some years later, told by someone how utterly admirable were the characters of Clare's play, *The Women*, she replied in writing, "The women who inspired this play deserved to be smacked across the head with a meat axe and that, I flatter myself, is exactly what I smacked them with. They are vulgar and dirty-minded and alien to grace, and I would not, if I could, which I hasten to say I cannot, cross their obscenities with a wit which is foreign to them and gild their futilities with the glamour which by birth and breeding and performance they do not possess." So much for the beautiful people.

"Stooping a dozen times a day quietly"—Clare Luce was writing now about another saint, St. Thérèse of Lisieux—"she picked up and carried the splinters of the cross that strewed her path as they strew ours. And when she had gathered them all up, she had the material of a cross of no inconsiderable weight. The 'little way of the Cross' is not 'the way of a little cross.' "

One of Clare's biographers, a friend since childhood, wrote five years ago about a trip with her, visiting first the Citadel in Charleston, and then Mepkin—"which used to be the Luces' southern retreat. . . . Here," Wilfrid Sheed wrote, "the welcome is very effusive, in the manner of priests in old movies . . . and it looks for an uneasy moment as if they are buttering up the patron.

"But Trappists are tricky. Being released from almost perpetual silence by guests, the talk bubbles out gratefully like fizz from a bottle. As this subsides, they turn out to be quite urbane and judicious talkers. . . . They genuinely seem to love Clare," and "she considered them her last family. I have never seen her more relaxed."

". . . After her daughter's death," Sheed continued, "Clare could no longer bear to go [to Mepkin] for pleasure, and [giving it away to a religious order] was an ingenious way of keeping it and letting it go at the same time. The expansionist abbot of Gethsemani, Kentucky, . . . was only too happy to take it, and I dimly remember the Luces' ironic discussion of this back in 1949 while the deal was being completed. They were onto the abbot's game but did not think less of a priest for being a shrewd businessman. And what better way to retire the place than Ann Brokaw had loved more than any other in the world?

"Clare immediately moved both her daughter's and her mother's remains to Mepkin, where they now share adjoining graves. And then, to everybody's surprise, it turned out sometime later that Presbyterian Harry had decided to join them, and he was buried in the middle, after a nervous ecumenical service. The cost-conscious abbot of the moment suggested a double tombstone with Clare's name on it too, cutting off, as she noted, all possibilities of future husbands or new religions"—at this point she must have given off that wonderful, wry nasal laugh.

Last Wednesday, in Washington, Clare's doctor confided to the White House that Clare would not live out the week, and that no doubt she would be pleased by a telephone call. The president called that night. Her attendant announced to her who it was who was calling. Clare Boothe Luce shook her head. You see, she would not speak to anyone she could not simultaneously entertain, and she could no longer do this. The call was diplomatically turned aside. The performer knew she had given her last performance, but at least she had never failed.

And then last Sunday, her tombstone at Mepkin no longer sat over an empty grave. She is there with Harry. Over the grave is— "a shady tree sculpted above the names, and to either side her mother, Ann Clare, and her daughter, Ann Clare, in a grove of oak and cypress and Spanish moss running down to the Cooper River."

When Bill Sheed wrote those lines, five years ago, he quoted Abbot Anthony telling him quietly as they walked away, "She's taking it pretty well this year. She's usually very disturbed by this."

Clare Luce, now at Mepkin finally, is no longer disturbed. It is only we who are disturbed, Hank Luce above all, and her friends —disconsolate, and sad, so sad without her, yet happy for her, embarked finally, after stooping so many times, to pick up so many splinters, on her way to the Cross.

16

William Shawn, R.I.P.

January 18, 1993

Mr. John O'Sullivan
National Review

Dear John:

You asked me to do an obit on William Shawn, and I replied that I could not write a formal piece about him because of the odd intimacy of my experiences with him. I speak of a man on whom I laid eyes twice in my life.

The day the newspapers carried the news of his death a letter from him arrived at the office. It was handwritten and had been mailed the day before he died. I quote it in full:

Dear Mr. Buckley:

Thank you for sending me copies of *WindFall* and *In Search of Anti-Semitism*. Since you are the author of both books, I am confident that I will not be disappointed. I have not yet read *Anti-Semitism,* but I've read enough of *WindFall* to see that I can read the rest with confidence. The Buckley style, thank goodness, is intact, and the humor is undiminished. I'll go on reading. Meanwhile, I send you warmest regards,

William Shawn

Obviously, he was "Mr. Shawn" to me, as he was Mr. Shawn even to authors older than I, who had much closer experiences with him than I. But from the beginning he was in his own way so very courteous to me that I took extravagant pains never to suggest that I was urging on him a familiarity he might have found uncomfortable. With almost anyone else with whom I have fairly extensive personal dealings, as you know, I'd have got around pretty early on, never mind how I addressed him/her, to signing off as "Bill." Never with Mr. Shawn. Always, "Wm. F. Buckley, Jr." I can't help believing that he knew what I was up to, and liked it.

I don't recall what it was that prompted me to send my manuscript *Cruising Speed* to him in 1970. The chances against *The New Yorker*'s running an intensely personal journal of a single week in the life of a youngish (I was forty-five) right-wing journalist were overwhelming. We all remember the usual things, the day Kennedy was killed, V-J Day; I remember the afternoon I reached Camden, South Carolina, to visit with my mother. Frances Bronson had left word to call her at the office. I did, of course, and she told me breathlessly that Mr. Shawn had *called her up* and told her that he very definitely wished to publish "Mr. Buckley's" book, which, he told her, was "beautifully written and witty" and that he would himself be editing the excerpts run by *The New Yorker*. No other professional experience in my lifetime has so buoyant a place in my memory.

He had assigned himself, I gather from reading about him and talking with a few *New Yorker* professionals, the job of personally editing one book manuscript every year, I think it was, and whether he selected me because, by lot, my manuscript came up at the time his turn had come to serve, or whether, for whatever reason, he selected mine as the book he wished to edit I don't know. But the experience was unique, a word he would frown upon unless it was used with great precision.

I use it with great precision. Others have written about it, but it is ever so hard to believe, even having lived through the experience, that the part of your book Mr. Shawn has elected to reproduce arrives one day in galley form. A single column, two inches wide, running down the middle of a long sheet of paper, clipped to the next galley. The appearance is identical to cutting out a column from *The New York Times* and pasting it on a long sheet of paper eight inches wide. There was no apparent reason at all for the extraordinary extravagance of the procedure: Why did it not come to you typewritten and double-spaced, cheaper to execute (these were the days of Linotype, when any alteration meant replacing an entire line of metal type), and easier to edit? One did not ask.

In the roomy spaces to the right and to the left appeared Mr. Shawn's handwritten "queries." He wondered whether this was the correct spelling of a name, whether, on reflection, one wished to say exactly this, worded exactly so, about that phenomenon, or that statement, by that man or woman. He questioned the use of a comma there, of a paragraph marking somewhere else. The author confronted also the queries of the "fact checker." No "fact" was ever taken for granted, if it could be independently verified. I remember that in one passage in my book I made a reference to the speech given by Tom Clark, with whom I was debating before the annual conference of the Chamber of Commerce. I had written that Clark's opening speech was "a half hour" long. On the side, a tiny note from the fact checker. "Listened to tape. He spoke for 22 minutes."

But this was the first of three drafts of the 30,000 words *The New Yorker* published in two installments. The second and the third drafts were completely reset at the printer, assimilating edited alterations, and they arrived with fresh queries and suggestions. But the great moment came when Frances told me that Mr. Shawn had called her to ask if I would lunch with him at the Plaza's Oak Room. He liked to talk to your secretary, much preferred doing this to talking to you; or in any event, that was so in my own case. For every conversation I had with him over the telephone, Frances had a half dozen. I acknowledge that this probably says something about Mr. Shawn, but conceivably says something about the relative advantages of talking to Frances Bronson instead of to me.

I went to the Plaza, of course, and we sat behind a small screen. I don't remember what he ate, but do remember that the waiter knew what to bring him, and I think I read somewhere that he pretty much always ate the same thing. He was genial only in the sense that his courtesy was absolute. There was only the barest amount of small talk. He wished to talk about the book he was editing, and to ask me a question or two concerning this point or the other. In particular I remember his telling me, in the most mild-mannered tones, that on reading the proofs I had returned— in most cases I had stuck by the punctuation I had originally used, rejecting the proffered alternatives—he had concluded that I was given to rather . . . eccentric uses of the comma. He said this by way of imparting information. It was not a reproach, or, rather, not exactly a reproach, but I could feel the tug of his great prestige, and so told him I would go back and look again at my footloose commas. The lunch ended fairly quickly and most agreeably, and a week or two later he called me, as he did four or five times before the manuscript finally appeared in print, to tell me, "Mr. Buckley, I really do not think that you know the correct use of the comma." I can't remember what it was that I replied, but do recall that I resolved not to fight *à outrance* over the remaining commas in the essay.

It is not everywhere known that, under Mr. Shawn, the author was given the final say as to what parts of his book would run, subject to the limitations of the space designated for that book. On some points Mr. Shawn would not give way—animadversions, for instance, which he thought for whatever reason unfair or unjustified. "Mr. Buckley, I do wish you would eliminate that paragraph about Mr. [Jones]. You see, we do not run a letters page and it isn't quite fair to leave him without an opportunity to defend himself. . . ." I don't know how other authors handled him, but in almost every case I yielded. His style was to cause the author to acquiesce in the change, rather than to dictate the change. With me this worked, though I remember a few cases in which, through an intermediary editor, I pleaded my case, and in all but one of these Mr. Shawn yielded.

Two years later, I sent him the first of my sailing books, *Airborne,* once again thinking the possibility remote that he would himself read it, let alone publish it. But he did, passing along, through Frances some nice words about my prose. A year or two later I wrote him to say that I had completed a book about the United Nations, but doubted he would wish to read it because United Nations life was intolerably boring. He replied instantly by mail asking to see it and one week later wrote to say he wished to publish my United Nations book. I made the dreadful mistake of declining, finally, to release it to *The New Yorker* because of its ruling that no book published in the magazine could appear in the trade press until six months had gone by. My publisher didn't want to let six months go by, and so I hurried out with it, only to discover that not more than sixteen people in the entire world are willing to read any book about the United Nations. I was pleased to hear from Mr. Shawn that I had written the only book about the United Nations that was both "literate and readable." I appreciated the compliment even though it was not hard to make, inasmuch as at the time there were no books about the United Nations, literate or illiterate, except an odd Brazilian memoir and a kind of coffee-table book by Conor Cruise O'Brien, designed to promote some artist.

A year or two later I wrote him to say that I had cruised again across the Atlantic, and did not suppose that he would wish to consider yet another book on yet another trans-Atlantic sail. Oh but he would; and he proceeded to publish *Atlantic High.* Five years later I told him that only out of courtesy was I mentioning to him my manuscript *Racing Through Paradise,* as it was inconceivable that *The New Yorker* would wish a third book by me with an ocean cruise as background. Inside of one week he advised me he wished to publish it. The last book of mine that he published was *Overdrive,* a sequel of sorts to *Cruising Speed,* in that it too was the journal of one week in my life. It was greeted as a most provocative, outrageous book, and was bitterly criticized by many reviewers. I winced at one reviewer, who wrote that perhaps Mr. Shawn's imminent departure from *The New Yorker* had something to do with the manifest deterioration of his literary judgment, as witness his publication of *Overdrive.* When a few months later I wrote the introduction to the soft-cover edition of the book, a long (glorious!) essay examining the criticisms of the book, I sent him a copy. He called me to say, in gentle accents but without running any risk of my misunderstanding him on the subject, that the critics of my book had had other things in mind than the quality of the book, which he was pleased to have sponsored.

I mentioned that he liked to speak to Frances. When a *New Yorker* check arrived for *Overdrive,* she called me in San Francisco to report jubilantly that the check was for $40,000. But later in the afternoon she called and said with some dismay that Mr. Shawn had telephoned her. "What he said was, 'Oh, Miss Bronson, our bookkeepers have made a most embarrassing mistake on the check for Mr. Buckley, and I would be grateful if you would simply mail it back to us, and we will mail the correct check tomorrow.' "

That could only mean, we both reasoned, that I had been over-paid. The following day a check arrived for $55,000. Mr. Shawn had his own way of twinkling at the world he treated so formally.

An interesting postscript. When he retired from *The New Yorker,* as you know there were great protests from his adamantly loyal staff. About nine months later I said to myself: Should I write and invite him to lunch with me? I'd never have done any such thing while he was still the editor of his magazine, with powers of life and death over you. Such an overture might have been thought a venture in self-ingratiation. So I put it very carefully in my little note to him, saying merely that it would give me great pleasure to lunch with him but I recognized that he didn't go out very much and that when he did he almost certainly had on his mind a professional objective. He called Frances a day or so later and said he would be most pleased to lunch, and a week or so later we met at the Carlyle, and talked together animatedly. He had read that week's issue of *National Review.* I can't believe that he (a hardy political liberal) read *NR* as a matter of habit, but could easily persuade myself that he had made it a point to read the current issue in order to prepare for our lunch. (He read, by the way, with the speed of light. Everything that appeared in *The New Yorker* he had himself read, some of it two and, as with my books, three or even four times.) The hour went quickly and pleasantly and there was a total absence of ambient pressure, I thought.

The difficult decision came one year later. What went through my mind was this, that if I did not invite him one more time to lunch, he might think that the first invitation was done out of a sense of duty to a retired editor who had acted generously to me, and that now that he was so far away from the scene, I had no further interest in him. I decided to invite him again to lunch. He replied to Frances that he would like very much to have lunch, and suggested that perhaps some time in the fall would be good. That was in 1991. In the fall, he called Frances to say that he still looked forward to our lunch but would rather not set a date for it right away; would this be agreeable? I wrote back that of course that would be agreeable; any time would do. I did not hear again from him until the letter I received the day he died.

He was a mythogenic character, a man totally taken by his muse and by his determination to hold to the standards he re-

spected. I hope someone, perhaps one of his talented sons, will one day produce if not exactly a "life" of William Shawn, a book about his priorities, his literary manners, his immense effect on our culture, and his enormous impact on his devoted admirers.
—Bill

17

Reginald Stoops, R.I.P.

OCTOBER 28, 1988

*The following eulogy by WFB was one of three delivered at Trinity
Episcopal Church in Newport, R.I., on September 16. Reg-
inald Stoops served informally as a scientific adviser to
National Review.*

"But how otherwise did you enjoy the evening, Mrs.
Lincoln?" has become gallows humor. Even so, it
was the line that came to mind on Wednesday
morning when my son, Christo, called me and gave
me the news. His second sentence—perhaps his
training as a journalist prompted it—was, "It happened at 11:22."
My eyes turned to a gaudy new chronometer sitting on my desk,
guaranteed not to lose more than seven tenths of one second in
one year. The exact time was 11:45.

Ten days ago I told Reggie that our navigational worries at sea
over the exact time were ended, that whenever we set out to cross
Long Island Sound—or Narragansett Bay—or the Atlantic Ocean
—we would never again have to worry about exactly what time it
was in Greenwich, England. He said that he longed to see the new
clock—our studied fantasy about the months and years we would
sail together after his freak illness never flagged in our thirty brief
conversations during the past two months. I commented that no
doubt he would insist on taking my chronometer apart and ridding
it of that seven tenths of one second annual problematic. I went
on to ask him what his weight was today, and he said 137 pounds,
which permitted me to say that we would have no further excuse
for singling out Danny Merritt to go up to the masthead; and he
laughed his gentle laugh, and said with that little hoarseness I was
becoming used to, "I guess you're right. On the other hand"—his
voice registered now a trace of curiosity—"they're giving me
something to make me fatter, so don't count on it." I didn't count
on it, because of course I knew; he by then knew it, and he knew
that I knew it, and so it goes.

I knew it even back on the eve of his marriage, in June, as a few others did, who managed more successfully than I to internalize that knowledge. But on Wednesday, thinking back to Mrs. Lincoln, I forced myself to think not about what had happened at 11:22 on that morning, but about what had happened during all the years I had known him. Was it one hundred nights or was it one thousand and one nights that we shared, in fine and awful circumstances, the cockpit of a boat, and I experienced the soft delights of his understated company? Oh yes, he could drive grown men to tears with the deliberateness of his reactions. Rehearsing an emergency drill, the second night of our Pacific crossing, Dick Clurman asked him where the life preservers were stored. He reacted as if he had been asked to give a brief definition of the Fourth Dimension. The pause, the slight clearing of the throat, the innocent look of a man accosted by an angular question, but followed by the exhilarating frankness of his innocent reply ("I'm not quite sure at this point"). In the book from which that passage comes, I quoted from Christopher's journal. He had written, a few days before we landed in New Guinea, "You find out on a trip like this who you can *absolutely* depend on. And really, the answer is, Pup and I agreed, that the person who is absolutely dependable in every situation is Reggie."

"We didn't mean"—I added in my book—"that anyone on board had ever broken the inflexible rule of interpersonal courtesy, merely that Reg is a critical mass of intelligence, good nature, and composure. He has never complained about anything." A year later, at a reunion of the crew, he presented us all with T-shirts on which the entire paragraph I have quoted was reproduced in DRINK COCA-COLA-sized type.

"He has never complained about anything," I reminded myself on Wednesday, thinking back first on the pleasures he had got from life, and then of the pleasure he had given to everyone who experienced him.

But the climax was ahead of him, when those words were written, coinciding—Providence can be that way: Providence has its elfin ways—coinciding with the beginning of the last stages of his illness. Given the human predicament, one can only with dumb hesitation rail against the God who, at one and the same time, took his life, but also gave him the supreme gift, the woman he married, who did more than all of science's opiates to make those three months endurable; to make that, paradoxically, a period of unparalleled happiness.

When finally I brought myself to visit him other than on the telephone, face to face, it was just before midnight Monday, and we embraced, after his very best friend, my son, Christopher, had kissed him on the forehead. He pronounced my name and managed a smile. I looked at his fine face and thought back this time to another moment of great strain. It was mid-March in 1957. The little dinghy in which we had set out to retrieve a duck blind a mile in front of my house on Long Island Sound had upset, and we realized, suddenly, that our lives hung on our ability to swim, in our heavy winter clothing, in freezing water, to a promontory a half mile away. For a full minute we could not judge whether we were making headway against the northerly wind, but we were. Gradually, painfully, we made progress. Fifty yards from land he looked at me and said, "Go ahead. I can't make it." I could not help him with my frozen hands, but I sang raucously to him, and I prayed with unfeigned imperiousness, ordering him to continue to beat his arms, however limply, against the waves. In five more minutes we were there, crawling on our stomachs to shelter.

What brought this to mind was the infinite dignity on his frozen countenance that afternoon, thirty-one years ago, which I saw again on Monday night, on his pallid, skeletal face: struggling to live almost as a matter of good manners, but resigned to die; determined only that he would never complain, never let go that fierce dignity which he carried in good times and bad times, drunk or sober, exhausted or animated, in sickness and in health.

I had a bouncy friend who once managed a witticism. "When I get to St. Peter," he said, "I'm going to ask him to take me to the man who invented the dry martini. Because I just want to say, 'Thanks.'"

I am a Christian who, believing that our Redeemer lives, knows that one day I'll be once again in his company, on that endless journey in the peace he now enjoys. When that time comes for me, as for others here, I shan't forget to say, as in my prayers I have said so often during the last days, Thanks. Thanks for the long play that came before that fatal bullet struck him down. Thanks, everlastingly, for the memory, everlasting.

18

Christopher Columbus

APRIL 5, 1992

So what was it like for Columbus when he set sail? What makes that question so sempiternally alluring is this: *We'll never know.* One prominent historian shrewdly remarked that the quintessence of the heroism of Columbus wasn't the prospect of endless days and nights at sea, the struggle with mutinous sentiments aboard or with wild savages on land. It lay in his simple act of weighing anchor in Gomera on that sixth day of September 1492.

The passage (Spain to the Canaries) was not a big deal in 1492 —the islands had been discovered at the turn of the century and were now being colonized. The dramatic moment came when Columbus pulled up his anchor and headed for the unknown.

It is hard to imagine that he felt about that apocalyptic event as prosaically as he wrote about it. What he set down in his journal was: "Shortly before noon I sailed from the harbor at Gomera and set my course to the west . . . I sailed all day and night with very little wind; by morning I find myself between Gomera and Tenerife." Those simple, declarative phrases hardly come in with the thunder and lightning one thinks of as appropriate to a launch that would discover a new world. Indeed, the New World.

What was it like?

A few friends and I who have sailed together in the past resolved to explore the point, with rigorous determination not to delude ourselves into presuming that we were undertaking anything like a re-creation of the historic crossing of the Admiral of the Ocean Seas, as Ferdinand and Isabella agreed Columbus should be titled upon completion of his mission (in the unlikely event that he did complete it).

On that November morning in 1990 setting out from Lisbon we were aboard a 71-foot ketch called *Sealestial,* chartered for this occasion as twice before we had chartered it to cross the Pacific, and to cross the Atlantic (eastward). There were six of us who did the sailing and the navigating, four who did the maintenance.

By contrast, Columbus had three well-founded boats . . . eighty to ninety feet long (they were called caravels), each one carrying forty to fifty sailor-soldiers and provisions for three months at sea, with plenty of mirrors and beads for the natives. No charts, no radio, no loan, no GPS, no sextant (by modern standards), no chronometer.

Our vessel had everything on board designed to cope with every situation imaginable, except those situations we actually ran into (the sails and much of the rigging came apart, the electronics didn't work, the water all but ran out); yet, by modern standards, ours was a routine passage, about as remarkable as a scenic bus ride, San Francisco to Los Angeles.

What made it otherwise special was the sensation that came to us inescapably within minutes of setting out. It was this, that although our vessel and its facilities were very different from the Santa María commanded by Christopher Columbus, all else was the same. *That* is authentic re-creation.

Nothing has happened in five hundred years that seriously affects the winds or the seas or the clouds or the stars that soothe and torment the sailor making his way across the Atlantic Ocean, following the trade winds. The speeds at which we traveled were comparable to his, except that when there were calms, we had the option to turn on a motor. Columbus could only sit. Patiently?

Don't you see, in those days the nervous metabolism was very different. If today what we see on a television channel for fifty-six seconds bores us, we flick over to another channel, and after that to a third or fourth or fifth. Columbus didn't know whether this afternoon's calm would last for one hour, for one day or for four days. He and his crew sat, or paced the deck. For distraction, they ate and they chatted and they plotted and they prayed and they gambled.

We? We turned on the motor, activated the autopilot, and we moved along, playing chess and writing in our journals, reading books, watching movies, eating gourmet meals, and rat-tat-tatting occasional messages home with our "Comsat" units, stitching together torn sails, and listening to the BBC.

All of this so different—and yet we came away from it all with some idea of what it had been like for Columbus.

There were, for instance, the storms—we both had them. But also there were the prevailing westerly trade winds, on which Columbus successfully (and we, following his example) counted. He was exploring a route that would become the great superhighway of all ships heading from Europe to the Americas for the next three hundred years.

To follow the route you needed to travel about seven hundred miles to the Canaries, and from there three thousand miles south southwest to the easternmost islands of the Caribbean, and then another thousand miles to Florida. Between the Canaries and the Caribbean lies—nothing. We chose to put in at the closest spot of land, the island of Barbados. Columbus passed north of it, hitting one of three Bahamian islands (the question of exactly which one is hotly disputed) in the neighborhood of Salvador.

He arrived thirty-six days after leaving Gomera, and it is seriously surmised that if he had taken as much as one day more, he'd have lost his command to the mutineers. If we had been one day later, I'd have been thrown overboard, together with my sextants, my almanac, my tables, and my plotting sheets.

There isn't any sense in which by undertaking such a passage you are playacting the vanity that you are a true son of Christopher Columbus.

Contrast the men and women who a generation ago set out aboard a raft of sorts called *Kon Tiki,* attempting more or less exactly to duplicate what they imagined to be the route and the circumstances of the aboriginals who traveled from South America to the Asian islands. Theirs was an exact effort at re-creating; their purpose, validate a (shaky) thesis, namely that the historical movement of human beings into Polynesia was counterclockwise, from Mainland Asia up to Alaska, down the North American continent to Peru or thereabouts, and then westward.

A sailing journey in a modern craft with up-to-date instruments from Europe to the Caribbean can be done without any sense of a shared adventure with the man who did it first, even as you don't have to think about Lewis and Clark to take a trailer trip from St. Louis across the Continental Divide to the Pacific Ocean.

On the other hand, if you undertake a trans-Atlantic sail along Columbus's route you will be tempted to say to yourself from time to time—looking out over the resolute blue-green seas, up at the playful clouds, flirtatious today, menacing tomorrow; plunging through nights sometimes so dark you could bump into a new continent without any warning, sometimes ambered by the moon, like sailing over a lit-up baseball stadium—you will say to yourself, "So it was for Columbus and his men. Just like this."

In a word, you get some sense of the highs—and some of the lows—experienced by the men who did it for the first time. The good news is that, as with most human experiences, what sticks in the memory is the highs.

Here is how Columbus's biographer described the good days experienced by Columbus. Samuel Eliot Morison was a professor at Harvard, an admiral in the Navy, the historian of our naval adventures in the Second World War, and a yachtsman who traced in his own vessel the voyage of Columbus shortly before the war, to write the book that would win a Pulitzer Prize, *Admiral of the Ocean Sea.* Thus he could write:

> This leg [when he hit the trade winds] of the voyage must have been a most pure delight to the Admiral and his men. The fleet sped along, making an average day's run of 183 miles. In the trades, vessels always roll a good deal, but the steady and favorable wind singing in the rigging, the sapphire white-capped sea, the rush of great waters alongside, and the endless succession of fat, puffy trade-wind clouds, lift up a seaman's spirits and make him want to shout and sing. For days on end the sheets and braces needed no attention. On moonless nights the sails stand out black against the star-studded firmament; and as the ship makes her southing, every night new stars and constellations appear. Most of his men were new to southern waters, and one can imagine them, as in Hérédia's sonnet, leaning entranced over the bulwarks of the white caravel and seeing in the phosphorescent sea an augury of the gold of the Indies.

We would have all those sensations, and one has to suppose
that the skies today, and the seas, are as they were then; and, of
course, the stars, those fixed coordinates of a restless world. We
had all that, and we had also a storm which after thirty-six hours
left us limp with misery, lost, exhausted, wet, demoralized; but
then, at sea, when this happens you experience also the balm that
comes after, as the sun shines, the wind rights itself, the gear is
repaired, the stars relocate you, and soon the pleasures on board
are full-throated.

It is a fine adventure, such a crossing under sail, even if it is
not to be confused with the original. You must travel with people
who a) know how to sail (at least four of them); b) how to navigate
(at least two); c) how to cope with emergencies (one or two); and
d) how to cope with each other (everyone).

Years ago the physicist Oppenheimer described the nuclear
age, with America and the Soviet Union glaring at each other, as
"two scorpions in a bottle." It is common lore in the seafaring
community of ocean racers that any latent disharmony tends to
fester aboard a small boat, when one person's innocent affectation
can evolve as an affront at the end of the second week, an armed
assault at the end of the third. Choose your companions with
much attention to dispositional harmony, in good times and bad.

Bear in mind that it is more than modern man can easily do to
learn to go from the rap-tempos of modern nonstop distractions to
the unsubornable tempos of the sea and the tides and winds who
know not the hysterical volatilities of contemporary life and can
no more be manipulated to suit your fancy than grass can be got to
grow more or less quickly, to indulge madame's inclinations.

So . . . make an effort. Bring along a VCR—hardly an extravagance in a venture as extravagant to begin with as chartering
a sailboat to take you across the Atlantic Ocean. And though
you'll find that all of you are busier than ever you thought you'd be
(sailboats require a lot of attention, for all that they gave the
impression of autonomous passivity), subtly inquire whether your
companions can also be happy reading a book.

Above all, know that you are setting out with men and women
—it doesn't matter how young (well, no, I'd say sixteen is minimum) or how old (well, not too old: burials at sea are inconvenient). But no one aboard should be so jaded as to be dulled to

the feel of the seas, the smell of the wind, the divine festoonery of the clouds and the stars, because for most amateurs the experience is once in a lifetime. Columbus did it four times. But you see, Columbus is what we were quietly celebrating, never presuming to imitate him.

19

Gratitude

The ending of remarks, at a testimonial dinner, on receipt of the "Julius Award" from the School of Public Administration, UCLA, March 21, 1990

I know that you expect from me a reflection or two on the matter of giving; indeed, on the matter of gratitude, which, really, is the theme of the evening. I am happy to take five more minutes of your time because I have long believed that we need to cultivate the faculty for gratitude.

When I was thirteen years old I was chaperoned here and there, along with two sisters of about the same age, about the greater environs of London. My music teacher, whom I loved and still do, was by my side when I went to the counter of a little souvenir shop in Stratford-upon-Avon and paid out three or four shillings for Shakespearean sundries I had picked out. An elderly lady behind the counter took my money, returned me some change, and then suddenly withdrew from the display case a tiny one-square-inch edition of *Romeo and Juliet* and, smiling, gave it to me. A gift. I took the sixpence she had just before given me in change, and deposited it in her hand: a reciprocal gift. Once outside, I received a resonant rebuke. My teacher told me I had done an offensive thing; she informed me that a gift is a gift. I must learn, she went on, to accept gifts. They are profaned by any attempt at automatic reciprocity. I cannot give you all tonight a Julius award.

Many years later I read in a biography of Abraham Lincoln about an episode that had briefly convulsed the receiving line at the White House. A lady in that line, after taking the president's hand in formal greeting, thrust forward with her left hand a huge bundle of long-stemmed roses, depositing them, in effect, all over Mr. Lincoln. The president—and the receiving line—were immobilized. Abraham Lincoln smiled. And said after the briefest pause, "Are these really for me?"

"Yes," his guest replied, beaming.

"In that case," the president said, "I can think of nothing that would give me more pleasure than to present them to you."

The flowers were returned; there were smiles all around, the lady took back her roses, and the line moved on. That is an unusual, perhaps a singular exception to my music teacher's injunction against the social sin of reciprocal gifts. Few people in public life or private have managed such extemporaneous grace.

Many years went by. And then, just last summer, I received on my trusty electronic MCI a message from a friend, a computer expert. He said that the retrieval system I had been yearning for, one which would permit me to locate individual book titles in my library via my computer, had been completed: he had worked on it in the interstices of his busy schedule for over a month. "It is yours," his message read on the screen, "as a belated Christmas present." I flashed back on my own computer screen that I insisted he send me a bill for professional services. One minute later, my mind traveled back and I was again a little boy at a souvenir store at Stratford, embarrassing a kindly woman who had attempted an act of generosity. There and then I shed the grown-up equivalent of tears at my awkwardness.

But, as I reflect on it, there is a distinction. The gift automatically repaid in roughly equivalent tender is corrupted. It ceases to be a gift, and the philanthropic impulse is traduced. The unrequited gift, in Burke's phrase, is one of the unbought graces of life: any effort to repay vulgarizes the offering, and one risks repaying a kindness with an act of aggression. We do not expect from those who will benefit from the scholarships you make available tonight a return to you of their scholarship gifts.

But a country—a civilization—that gives us gifts we dispose of cannot be repaid in kind. There is no way in which we can give to the United States a present of a bill of rights in exchange for its having given us a Bill of Rights.

Our offense—the near universal offense, remarked by Ortega y Gasset as the fingerprint of the masses in revolt—is that of the Westerner—rich or poor, learned or ignorant—who accepts without any thought of any debt incurred the patrimony we all enjoy, those of us who live in the free world. The numbing, benumbing thought that we owe nothing to Plato and Aristotle, nothing to the prophets who wrote the Bible, nothing to the generations who fought for freedoms activated in the Bill of Rights; we are basket cases of ingratitude, so many of us. We cannot hope to repay in kind what Socrates gave us, but to live lives without any sense of obligation—to those who made possible lives as tolerable as ours, within the frame of the human predicament God imposed on us, to our parents who suffered to raise us, to our teachers who labored to teach us, to the scientists who prolonged the lives of our children when disease struck them down—is spiritually atrophying.

We cannot repay the gift of the Beatitudes, with their eternal, searing meaning—*Blessed are the poor in spirit for theirs is the kingdom of heaven.* But our ongoing failure to recognize that we owe a huge debt that can be requited only by gratitude, defined here as appreciation however rendered of the best that we have, and a determined effort to protect and cherish it—any failure here marks us as the masses in revolt: against our benefactors, our civilization, against God himself.

To fail to experience gratitude when walking through the corridors of the Metropolitan Museum of Art, when listening to the music of Bach and Beethoven, when exercising our freedoms to speak, or, as will happen in California and elsewhere next November, to give, or to withhold, our assent, is more than to profane spontaneous generosity. It is to decline to express, however clumsily, to feel, however coarsely, our gratitude for the fruits of genius, for generosity, human and divine, for the great wellsprings of human talent and concern that gave us Shakespeare, Abraham Lincoln, Mark Twain, our parents, our friends and, yes, the old lady in Stratford. We need a rebirth of gratitude for those who have cared for us, living and, mostly, dead; the high moments of our way of life are their gifts to us. We must remember them in our thoughts and in our prayers, and in our deeds. Remember them as you are doing tonight, in this act of gratitude to your School of Public Administration.

NINE

CELEBRATING

1

Happy Birthday to J. S. Bach

MARCH 23, 1985

Three hundred years ago on March 21 Johann Sebastian Bach was born. The event is as though God had decided to clear his throat to remind the world of his existence. That existence had been greatly dishonored by the terrible Thirty Years' War that had ended only a generation before Bach's birth, a war whose reverberations we still experience, even as the ayatollah continues to dishonor the Muslim creed he misunderstands himself to incarnate.

Bach has the impact of a testimonial to God's providence not because he wrote the most searingly beautiful church music ever heard (about "The Passion According to St. Matthew" one can say only that it does credit to the Gospel according to St. Matthew), but because he wrote the most beautiful music ever written. If one were to throw away the three hundred cantatas, the hundred-odd chorale preludes, the three oratorios, the passions, and the Mass (which would be the equivalent of destroying half of Shakespeare), still the other half would sustain Bach as a creature whose afflatus is inexplicable, for some of us, in the absence of a belief in God.

If it is true, as the poet says, that one can't look out upon a sunset without feeling divinity, then it is also true that one can't close the door on that sunset and, entering the darkened chapel, listen to the organist play one of Bach's toccatas and fugues without sensing divinity.

It is not necessary to believe in God in order to revel in Bach. It is not necessary, for that matter, to love one's country in order to fight for it, nor even to love one's family in order to protect it. And there is no need to make heavy weather over the point, though there is a need for such human modesty as Einstein expressed when he said that the universe was not explicable except by the acknowledgment of an unknown mover. The music of Bach disturbs human complacency because one can't readily understand finiteness in its presence.

Carl Sagan, who sometimes sounds like the village atheist, reports that the biologist Lewis Thomas of the Sloan-Kettering Institute answered, when asked what message he thought we should send to other civilizations in space in that rocket we fired up there a few years ago with earthly jewels packed in its cone, "I would send the complete works of Johann Sebastian Bach." Then he paused, and said, "But that would be boasting." There are those who believe it is not merely to boast, but to be vainglorious to suggest that the movements of Bach's pen could have been animated by less than divine impulse.

There are sobering lessons to contemplate on Bach's birthday. One of them is that when he lived he was almost entirely unnoticed. True, he was renowned as a virtuoso at the harpsichord and the organ. When he died, one of his biographers notes, there were something on the order of ninety obituaries written, only three of which, however, mentioned him as a composer. This is tantamount to remembering Shakespeare as a great actor.

The thought reminds us of what it is that we almost let slip through our fingers—and reminds us, even more darkly, of what it is that we have irreversibly let slip through our fingers. We are reluctant to believe that anyone else ever existed of such artistic eminence as JSB; but we can never know, can we? Nor can we ever understand how it was that so musically minded a culture as that of what we now know as East Germany could have greeted so indifferently a genius so overpowering.

And it reminds us, too, that there are among us men and women who will not drink from this most precious vessel of our cultural patrimony. To some he does not speak. If we understand that, then we understand, surely, what the problems are in Geneva, where grown men are actually talking to each other as if it were a challenge to formulate arrangements by which the world should desist from the temptation to destroy itself. If a human being exists who is unmoved by the B minor Mass it should not surprise that human beings exist who are unmoved by democracy, or freedom, or peace. They have eyes but they do not see, ears but they do not hear. Well, Bach tended to end his manuscripts with the initials "S.D.G."—*Soli Deo Gloria,* To God alone the glory. But God shares that glory, and did so three hundred years ago when Johann Sebastian was born.

2

Fernando Valenti and the "Goldberg Variations"

S ome years ago, as the word was getting around that he would soon die from leukemia, Dinu Lipatti played a concert in France that was rumored would be his last, as indeed it proved to be. It was recorded, and it is not merely the act of a morbid imagination that causes one, listening to the Bach and the Chopin, to detect in it a strain of poignant yet somehow exultant fatalism.

When, in the fall of 1980, the harpsichordist Fernando Valenti surmised from what his doctors said that he would not survive the cancer detected in his throat, he was practicing to record Bach's "Goldberg Variations." He had played them before, as a very young man: then he buried them, devoting the thirty-five years after his graduation from college to giving recitals and making recordings (over eighty records)—of Bach, to be sure, but his specialty has always been Scarlatti (in rendering Scarlatti he has no peer). But the itch to do the "Goldberg" came, and would not go. And now it appeared that if he made the recording, it would be his valedictory.

It happened that the season was full of "Goldbergs." A generation ago if one wanted to hear the "Goldberg Variations," one needed to buy the recording of Wanda Landowska, and then, a little later, Rosalyn Tureck's on the piano, and Ralph Kirkpatrick's on the harpsichord. Then, of course, Glenn Gould came along, and his convulsive rendition swept the attention of the musical world. The critics were carried away by the sheer effrontery of his conception, so that whether one thought it a musical epiphany or sheer travesty, his interpretation was for twenty years the center of attention of what is arguably the supreme achievement of the baroque keyboard. In 1982 two events coincided ironically: Glenn Gould, age fifty, died, and Fernando Valenti, age fifty-four, did not die. And, at about the same time, they had recorded the "Goldberg," Gould again to an uproarious reception.

A casualty was Fernando Valenti's "Goldberg Variations" (sine qua non), scarcely noticed when it was first released. He had repaired to a studio in New Jersey, and there, in three days, he did the "Aria and Thirty Variations," written in 1742 at the behest of Count Kayserling for his friend Goldberg.

Although Bach stipulated that all the variations should be repeated, Valenti repeats none of them, and inevitably—for those who knew he was uncertain whether he would survive the season —there is something of the sense of his rushing forward to arrive at the final Variation before the grim reaper cut him off. But that said, one finds in the performance an absolutely secure sense of tempo. One very quickly discerns, on hearing Valenti, that he is technically capable of taking any of the movements at the speed of Glenn Gould or Andras Schiff but generally elects not to, and the result is that sense of ultimate composure that perfect music, perfectly executed, brings. After Variation 30, before the last reiteration of the Aria, there is a pause of (by Valenti's standards) melodramatic length: it lasts perhaps five, six seconds. And then the Aria proceeds, stately as a winged chariot, until, six bars before the end, there is, in the slight rubato, just a hint of that reluctance to conclude anything so nearly divine: the artist expressing his reluctance to conclude life itself, and in so doing, giving life so noble a sound.

3

A Storm: Afterthoughts

OCTOBER 3, 1985

A careful reading of after-storm sentiment reveals that many people were disappointed over the modest level of damage done to other people. Everyone was geared up to seeing that night's television give us gruesome details on the devastation visited on the Eastern seaboard by Gloria. It seemed only fair, after all, that Providence should distribute its displeasures with some sense of equality. The Northwest has its volcanoes, the West its earthquakes, the Midwest its tornadoes, the South and East, hurricanes.

We (my wife and I) arrived at our home just after noon on Friday, and then came the throat-catching first view of the property. The lordly weeping willow tree, planted at my direction only twelve years ago and already a bower of serene delight, contributing what seemed almost 45 degrees of the leafy profile of a leafy lawn: down, as unambiguously as though it had been winched down, its private parts torn up from the earth, exposed to the air. Alongside it a large maple, also gone. And then by the terrace, a Japanese cherry tree that seemed small and tough and sinewy enough to withstand anything, but it was gone. The beach was relatively calm, the beneficiary of a low tide.

And suddenly the sun, brilliant; the wind, dead, as suddenly as though a great switch had been thrown. "We are," I said to my wife, "in the eye of the hurricane, and you can expect the worst to begin in about ten minutes." The barometer in my study read 28.8. What then happened was: nothing. Suddenly the glass was at 31.00. Oh, the winds blew, but nothing you'd have noticed if the radio hadn't been on telling you nonstop about the hurricane churning by. For some reason not explained, the tail end of the hurricane simply gave up, the full force husbanded by the leading edge. It was over.

Except that we had no electricity, a condition that began at ten that morning and lasted until five the following morning. Nineteen hours without power; translated, in our case, to nineteen hours of powerlessness.

Among my infrequent nightmares is that I should one day find myself the Connecticut Yankee at King Arthur's court. You will perhaps remember the charming book by Mark Twain in which a time warp captures the Connecticut Yankee and transports him to the court of King Arthur. There, surveying the primitive charm, he introduces, well, the technology of the day of Mark Twain, which included electricity, motors, engines, and an almanac's knowledge of natural phenomena like the date and time of a total eclipse.

My nightmare concentrates on my utter mechanical uselessness. My memory is rusty, but I am fairly certain that King Arthur, unlike the Incas who came along a thousand years later, had the wheel. I am very sorry about that because I could have taught King Arthur about the wheel. But what else? I could give him the idea for a screwdriver, but would not know how to cast one, if that is the correct word. If King Arthur had some peanuts, I could teach him to make peanut butter, but I confess I am getting close to the old saw about how if you had some ham we could have a ham sandwich, if I had some bread.

And so I reflected on the huge, continuing debt we owe for our creature comforts to the men of science, and to the engineers. Meanwhile, having no light to read by, we went to a movie. The most awful bore I can remember since last I heard a speech in the United Nations. I will give any reader who sends me twenty-five cents the name of that movie so that he can avoid it; or else I will not do so if the director whose last name rhymes with Borghese will send me a million dollars and the promise to let me see his next script sometime before the next hurricane.

Meanwhile, it is over, and it is strangely refreshing to suffer blows less than mortal, and to be reminded of how much there is to be grateful for. There is a quickening of the spirit, and we are reminded of a few sentences of Cardinal Newman: "Spring passes into summer and through summer and autumn into winter. Only the more surely, by its more ultimate return, to triumph over that grave toward which it resolutely hastens from its first hour. We mourn over the blossoms of May because they are to wither. But we know withal that May is one day to have its revenge upon November, by the revolution of the solemn circle that never stops. Which teaches us in our height of hopes ever to be sober. And in our depths of desolation, never to despair."

4

A Quiet American

November 5, 1985

PORTLAND, Ore.—At exactly 6 A.M., Joe materialized in the lobby of the hotel. The night before, when he said he would drive me to the airport to catch the 6:50 A.M. flight, I demurred—too early in the morning, I said. No no no, no sweat; he even handed me his business card, writing out his home telephone number on the back of it. Shortly after the alarm woke me, at 5:40, I couldn't resist the temptation to dial the number. Just in case . . . Joe answered the phone. Told me he was on the way out the door; I mustn't worry.

He was driving a white Mercedes sports car, so I needed to put several of my bags into his back seat. In a matter of seconds we were off, his headlights illuminating the way. He drove with the natural skill of the American who learns to drive when he is about thirteen. And Joe drove according to protocol: speed limit, plus 10 percent.

I repeated I was sorry he had had to rise so early. No problem, no problem, he said. "I always get up early. Five o'clock, as a rule." Of course I asked why, and he replied that he jogged. "Every morning?" "Pretty much every morning." He paused, and then said that he was going to try out for the Hawaiian marathon next summer. I said I had heard that it was awfully tough, awfully competitive; didn't it go for twenty-five miles or something like that? Yes, he said—twenty-six miles, actually. "But I figure at forty-two I'd better try now, or else I'm not going to do it ever."

He went on: "I came back from the Army in 1967. Vietnam. I was a platoon leader in the infantry there. When I got back here to Portland, I took a job as a carpenter."

Had he known the trade—carpentry—before the war?

No. He was sort of handy at fixing things, he said, because he had grown up on a farm, with his twelve brothers and sisters. "I figured it this way, when I got out of the Army, that I was worth twenty dollars an hour. But all they paid me at the construction company where I went to work was two-fifty per hour. So I figured I would have to earn the equivalent of seventeen-fifty per hour more by picking things up. I got to work early, left late, studied the blueprints, figured out how blueprints corresponded with the work done, and after about a year I started my own construction company. It was tough, but after Vietnam, where I got shot at just about every day, everything was . . ."

"Absorbable?"

"Yes. Absorbable."

After a few years, he said, he was doing well. Very, very well. But, he said, he thought he saw it coming. High interest rates discouraged house builders. "So I figured I'd sell my business, and I did, that was in 1978. Sold it just about in time."

Well, what did he do then? "I figured I had a lot to learn about America, so I took a year or so and drove around the country. Learned a lot. A whole lot. And then one day somebody asked me to play volleyball, and I swear, I just fell in love with the game."

Volleyball courts, he explained, require the right kind of insulation, so that the balls will bounce as they should. He pondered existing procedures for building those walls and figured they were pretty old-fashioned. So he sat down and figured out a way to piece together little squares or diamonds or whatever that, at far lower cost, bring about the desired effect. "It's great. So now I manufacture the insides of volleyball courts. As a matter of fact, most of my work is in some way exercise-oriented these days. I guess that's where I got the idea of jogging, and keeping fit."

"You must feel wonderful, doing all that physical work. How many hours a day do you run?" Two hours. Did he use a Walkman? He smiled, true pleasure on his face brightened by the headlights coming the other way. "I certainly do. It keeps my mind occupied."

I asked if the airport was as frequently socked in by early morning fog as I had heard, and he said yes, but if it was that bad that morning, he would simply drive me on to Seattle for my connection. "Nothing to it, a hundred and fifty miles, that's all. What are your favorite books?" he asked me. I told him I liked this and that.

"You know who I like to read?" he said. "I like to read Emerson. Ralph Waldo Emerson. I read him every six months."

Ralph Waldo Emerson would be pleased if he knew Joe Hollman was reading him. We arrived at the airport, and I felt like Antaeus. I had just touched earth, and it's a fine feeling.

5

Dedicating a Competitor for the America's Cup

OCTOBER 1986

About seventeen years ago I attended with my wife a state dinner at the White House, in fact for us the first. I was not intimidated by the presence there of our host, the President of the United States, whom I had met here and there, when he was engaged in climbing the grimier rungs that lead to that high office. But the prospect of being presented to him by the Chief of Protocol was positively unnerving. Getting dressed a half hour earlier, across the street at the Hay Adams, I said to my wife, "You do realize that the Chief of Protocol is Bus Mosbacher, who won the America's Cup?" To which she replied, "You evidently don't realize that you have told me that five times in the last five days."

That night it was with great awe that I took the hand of Bus Mosbacher, staring at him as I suppose I'd have stared at Christopher Columbus, or Galileo. You see, in those days I used to do ocean racing quite regularly, and hard though we tried, we never managed, somehow, to come in with the winners. I remember, after my fifth Bermuda Race, being asked by a reporter what was my ambition during these races, disconsolately replying, "My ambition is to beat at least one boat."

I managed, in the receiving line, to shake the awesome hand that guided the tiller that in 1962 had defeated the Australian challenger; and then to greet the president; and then to greet the guest of honor, who, by ironic masterstroke, was the Prime Minister of Australia, Mr. John Gorton. I remember thinking that surely President Nixon should have presented the Prime Minister to Mr. Mosbacher, rather than the other way around.

It was I think thirty years ago that I became a member of the

New York Yacht Club and my sponsor, pointing to the Cup at 44th Street, said to me, "Do you know, more money has been spent attempting to win that Cup than was spent on the Spanish Armada?" Well, no, I hadn't known this, nor did I know what was the anticipated reply to such an observation.

I remember groaning, at Cape Canaveral in July of 1969, when one of those awful people who wrote editorials said that for the cost of Apollo II, which was going up the following day to land on the moon, we could build 4,082 lower-middle-income dwelling units.

But one cannot parse life's enterprises in any common coin. If Vladimir Horowitz had exercised his fingers on a sewing machine instead of on a keyboard, stroke for stroke, he might have stitched a blanket that would keep 82,000 Eskimos plus Mary McGrory warm on a cold winter's night.

The sailing sport is an appanage of a class of enthusiasts who are aristocratically concerned with excellence at sea. For them no sacrifice is implausible. I think it's a sign of great spiritual health that even as men risk their lives to ascend a mountain peak, others devote a part of their lives and the produce of a part of their lives to designing, and manning, the fastest vessel of its size in the world.

We will have the Cup back, but we will do this without severing diplomatic bonds with that young, robust, alluring country whose Prime Minister our sometime Chief of Protocol took such splendid care of back in 1969.

It happened that seated next to me at the White House banquet was a young Australian diplomat on the staff of the Prime Minister who served as his speechwriter. This he confided to me after a few bottles of wine, White House protocol having neglected only to remember to make draft beer available to that evening's guests. And so, as Prime Minister Gorton waxed into a robust and affectionate speech about U.S.–Australian relations, his speechwriter's face was caught in contortions of bliss as he heard pronounced, one after another, the words he had written. And toward the end of the toast he dug his elbow quietly into my side and whispered, "Listen! Listen! Listen now . . ." Whereupon the Prime Minister, reaching for his glass to conclude his toast, declaimed to his distinguished audience, "Continue as you

are, my American friends, friends of liberty, and friends of progress, and we"—my Australian speechwriter closed his eyes now
in transport, in anticipation of the rhetorical coda—"we will go
waltzing, Matilda, with you."

Well now, the sentiment was lovely; the cultural embrace between the two peoples, enduring.

But on one point, there remains the need for a little clarifica-
tion.

The America's Cup belongs back here, because we are very
lonely without it. Indeed I myself have pledged that until we have
it back, I shan't waltz at all, let alone with kangaroos.

So that, one day in February of 1987, at about four in the
afternoon, in the waters off Perth, the Australians must know what
it was that Cinderella experienced. It is a pity that such a rein-
troduction into realism must be done to Australia by so large a
company of spirited people, above all the crews of our many contenders, but also their backers, among others the man who served
as Chief of Protocol when the Australian Prime Minister was with
us. But you see, the protocols of the America's Cup are that it
belongs in America: so that we are, after all, here engaged in
nothing less, and nothing more, than a venture in repatriation.

Here's to the American challenger. May she bring us back
what we have come to regard as an American birthright, so that
my wife and I can waltz again, under the Milky Way, when all is
right again with our Cup, come home.

6

The Tribute to Jack Kemp

DECEMBER 2, 1988

At the big affair for Jack Kemp in Washington on Thursday, former Education Secretary William Bennett told a charming story that might be called "The Essence of Kemp." It was the day in New Orleans when George Bush tapped Dan Quayle as his successor. Bennett was scheduled to dine with Kemp and did not look forward to a forlorn evening with a disappointed candidate for the vice presidency. He picked him up at the designated bar where, as Bennett put it, Kemp was "downing a double cherry Coke." But he found it difficult to engage his attention because Kemp was spiritedly conversing with the bartender, stressing the wonderful opportunities in America, bartending being one of them: After all, hadn't Abraham Lincoln tended bar?

Bennett waited until supply-side economics and growth had been fully visited on the man who gave Kemp his cherry Coke, and then could they begin dinner? No. Jack Kemp had to go backstage to the kitchen, shake hands, and deliver to the hungry, unseen pilgrims his sermon about America, and jobs, and opportunity. "What comes after a Saturday night speech by Hubert Humphrey?" Walter Mondale once quipped. Answer: "Sunday." Jack Kemp will never give up.

The White House advance people were going mad, stark, staring mad. The president had to be back at the White House at 7:48. You'd have thought that at 7:49 the Cold War would officially end —how can you be late for that? But a hundred-odd guests who had paid a special surcharge were in the side room for their bonus: a picture taken with President Reagan. Two people per shot, one at either side, never mind if the two had never met. And then the dais needed to be introduced as its members filed in to be applauded by the crowd of 1,000, who had paid $1,000 each to be at the dinner.

Then entered Vice President Bush and his wife. Then Ronald Reagan without his wife. Then—the one legacy of the Dukakis campaign—the requisite Pledge of Allegiance. For that crowd to recite the Pledge of Allegiance was as necessary as requesting of the cheerleaders of the Notre Dame football team an oath of loyalty before the game. And then "God Bless America." And then introductory remarks by the toastmaster. And then Caspar Weinberger—he had flown in from London just in time for the occasion. And then remarks by Secretary of State-designate James Baker—and then!

Time for the guest of honor to introduce the president. There cannot have been such a spectacle since Julius Caesar bade farewell to his legions. More than 100 names of guests were read out breathlessly, Kemp demanding that they rise and stay standing. Politicians, writers, journalists, athletic stars—an eclectic list, bound together by enthusiasm for Jack Kemp and for voodoo economics ("déjà voodoo," Bush would tease himself later in the evening). Tears welled in the eyes of the most concentrated bundle of energy in political America as Jack Kemp, paying due respect to Winston Churchill, stripped him of the title of Lion of the Twentieth Century and awarded it to Ronald Reagan.

At that point the White House people would have settled for less, since the show was running eighteen minutes behind time. But Reagan, ever genial, generous and stern in reiterating his beliefs, read out the whole of his twenty-minute speech, was awarded a football by Kemp at the closing, tossed it a grand distance of three yards, and went out in a flourish.

American politics at its exuberant best, and not without meaning. The guest of honor had competed for the presidency against George Bush, present to pay his compliments. George Bush had competed against Ronald Reagan in 1980, and they lavished praise upon one another. The guest of honor had relinquished his seat in Congress ("like Niagara losing Niagara Falls," the toastmaster commented), raising the question: Was the crowd paradoxically here to celebrate the retirement of Jack Kemp?

And yet it had not been billed as a farewell dinner, and Kemp hardly was there to deliver an apopemptic address. The three principal figures on the dais—Kemp, Bush, Reagan—had conspired to beat one another in enterprises of various kinds and for very big stakes. And tonight they were there to declare each other indispensable. An evening's tribute to the man defeated by George Bush, whose political ascendancy was made possible by that defeat: there to praise as the principal political architect of Reaganomics the candidate he had flattened, first in New Hampshire, then in the South.

A tribute to the essential cohesion of American politics, true. But, in its own way, distinctive. In Kemp there is a magnetism that attaches only to the innocent, to the true believer. No doubt when he got home on Thursday night he had a triple cherry Coke and talked to Joanne about the wonders of supply side.

7

On the Thirtieth Anniversary of National Review

DECEMBER 5, 1985

Jonathan Schell shocked the moral literary world two or three years ago when he counted up and advised us that the explosive energy of the combined nuclear resources of the superpowers amounts to eight hundred million times the power of the bomb that went off over Hiroshima forty years ago. I remember that when I read that figure it conjured to my mind not so much the awful destructive potential of man as the infinity by which we measure the value of what we have, over against what it is that, otherwise, we would not have. The president, speaking at a great graveyard in Germany last May, reminded us forcefully of the terminal consequences of engaging, whether willingly or by conscription, in massive, ugly efforts to take from others their lives, their fortunes, and their sacred honor.

A year before *National Review* was founded, I spent an evening with Whittaker Chambers, and he asked me, half provocatively, half seriously, what exactly it was that my prospective journal would seek to save. I trotted out a few platitudes, of the sort one might expect from a twenty-seven-year-old fogy, about the virtues of a free society. He wrestled with me by obtruding the dark historicism for which he became renowned. *Don't you see,* he said, *the West is doomed, so that any effort to save it is correspondingly doomed to failure?* I drop this ink stain on the bridal whiteness of this fleeted evening only to acknowledge soberly that we are still a long way from establishing, for sure, that Whittaker Chambers was wrong. But that night, challenged by his pessimism, I said to him that if it was so, that Providence had rung up our license on liberty, stamping it as expired, the Republic deserved a journal that would argue the historical and moral case that we *ought* to have survived: that, weighing the alternative, the culture of liberty deserves to survive. So that even if the worst were to happen, the journal in which I hoped he would collaborate might serve, so to speak, as the diaries of Anne Frank had served, as absolute, dispositive proof that *she* should have survived, in place of her tormentors—who ultimately perished. In due course that argument prevailed, and Chambers joined the staff.

To do what, exactly? The current issue of *National Review* discusses of course the Summit conference, the war in Afghanistan, Sandinista involvement in Colombia; but speaks, also, of the attrition of order and discipline in so many of our public schools, of the constitutional improvisations of Mr. Rostenkowski, of the shortcomings of the movies *Eleni* and *Macaroni,* of the imperatives of common courtesy, of the relevance of Malthus, of prayer and the unthinkable, of the underrated legacy of Herman Kahn. Some of these subjects are greatly attenuated from the principal concerns of *National Review.* Attenuated yes, but not disconnected: because freedom anticipates, and contingently welcomes and profits from, what happens following the calisthenics of the free mind, always supposing that that freedom does not lead the mind to question the very value of freedom, or the authority of civil and moral virtues so to designate themselves. There are enough practitioners in this room to know that a journal concerned at once to discharge a mission and to serve its readers needs to be comprehensively concerned with the flora and fauna of cultural and political life. We have done this in *National Review,* and because we have done this, you are here—our tactical allies, most of you; our strategic allies, all of you.

How is our cause being handled by our guest of honor? Two or three years ago I was asked by the Philadelphia Society to speak on the theme, "Is President Reagan doing all that can be done?" It was a coincidence that my wife, Pat, and I had spent the weekend before with the President and Mrs. Reagan in Barbados, where he spoke to me of some intractable problems.

I digress to recall that during one of our swims I said to him, "Mr. President, would you like to earn the *National Review* Medal of Freedom?" He confessed to being curious as to how he would qualify to do this, and I said, "Well, I will proceed to almost drown, and you will rescue me." We went through the motions, and I have conferred that medal on him, *in pectore.*

I told the Philadelphia Society that the most powerful man in the Free World is not powerful enough to do everything that needs to be done. But I speculated on what I continue to believe is the conclusive factor in the matter of American security against ultimate Soviet aggression, which is the character of the occupant of the White House, the character of Ronald Reagan. The reason this is so, I argued, is that the Soviet Union, for all that from time to time it miscalculates, has never miscalculated in respect of matters apocalyptic in dimension. And the Soviet Union knows that the ambiguists with whom it so dearly loves to deal are not in power at this time. So that if ever the Soviet Union were tempted to such suicidal foolishness as to launch a strike against us, suicidal is exactly what it would prove to be. The primary obstacle to the ultimate act of Soviet imperialism is the resolute determination—to repeat my own formulation—to value what we have, over against what they do not have, sufficiently to defend it with all our resources.

Ronald Reagan, in my own judgment, animates his foreign policy by his occasional diplomatic indiscretions: because, of course, it *was* a diplomatic indiscretion to label the Soviet Union an "evil empire." *Ce n'est que la vérité qui blesse*: It is only the truth that wounds. And he correctly switches gear, as required, when wearing diplomatic top hat and tails. He did not talk the language of John Wayne—or of Thomas Aquinas—while in Geneva. But how reassuring it is for us all, every now and then, to vibrate to the music of the very heartstrings of the leader of the Free World, who, to qualify as such, has, after all, to feel a substantial commitment to a free world. When the president ventures out to exercise conviviality with the leader of the Soviet Union, the scene is by its nature wonderful, piquant. It brings to mind the Russian who, on discovering that his pet parrot is missing, rushes out to the KGB office to report that the parrot's political opinions are entirely unrelated to his own.

Mr. President, fifteen years ago I was interviewed by *Playboy* magazine. Toward the end of the very long session I was asked the question, Had I, in middle age, discovered any novel sensual sensation? I replied that, as a matter of fact, a few months earlier I had traveled to Saigon and, on returning, had been summoned by President Nixon to the Oval Office to report my impressions. "My novel sensual sensation," I told *Playboy,* "is to have the President of the United States take notes while you are speaking to him."

You need take no notes tonight, Mr. President. What at *National Review* we labor to keep fresh, alive, deep, you are intuitively drawn to. As an individual you incarnate American ideals at many levels. As the final responsible authority, in any hour of great challenge, we depend on you. I was twenty years old when the bomb exploded over Hiroshima. Last week I became sixty. During the interval I have lived as a free man, in a free and sovereign country. I pray that my son, when he is sixty, and your son, when he is sixty, and the sons and daughters of our guests tonight will one day live in a world over which that awful shadow has finally dissipated. Then they will be grateful that, at the threatened nightfall, the blood of their fathers ran strong.

Index